Dinner for Everyone

Dinner for Everyone

100 iconic dishes made 3 ways— easy, vegan, or perfect for company

Mark Bittman

PHOTOGRAPHS BY AYA BRACKETT

Clarkson Potter/Publishers
New York

Published in the United States by Clarkson Potter/Publishers,
an imprint of the Crown Publishing Group, a division of
Penguin Random House LLC, New York.
crownpublishing.com
clarksonpotter.com

CLARKSON POTTER is a trademark and POTTER with colophon
is a registered trademark of Penguin Random House LLC.

Library of Congress Cataloging-in-Publication Data
Names: Bittman, Mark, author.
Title: Dinner for everyone : 100 iconic dishes made 3 ways—easy,
     vegan, or perfect for company / Mark Bittman.
Description: First edition. | New York : Clarkson Potter/
     Publishers, [2019] | Includes index.
Identifiers: LCCN 2018003810| ISBN 9780385344760 | ISBN
     9780385344777 (ebook)
Subjects: LCSH: Vegetarian cooking. | LCGFT: Cookbooks.
Classification: LCC TX837 .B5279 2019 | DDC 641.5/636—dc23
LC record available at https://lccn.loc.gov/2018003810

ISBN 978-0-385-34476-0
Ebook ISBN 978-0-385-34477-7

Printed in China

Book and cover design by Jan Derevjanik
Photographs by Aya Brackett

10 9 8 7 6 5 4 3 2 1

First Edition

To Holden,
and all of the
dinners
in his future

Introduction

"What's for dinner?" is a daily, inevitable question. Depending on the rhythms of your life, you may either embrace the response as an invitation to cook, dodge it and head to the nearest restaurant, or pick up the phone or go online for delivery. Even though we know that preparing the evening meal is one of the most rewarding and nurturing of all the human rituals, deciding what to eat and how to pull it together remains a modern-day challenge.

I want cooking dinner at home to make you happy. For encouragement and inspiration on even the toughest days, here are foolproof recipes that let you choose from Easy, Vegan, and All Out—"perfect for company"—versions of all your favorite dishes.

Experienced cooks can dig right in and explore the all-new ways to interpret old standbys. Those of you who are new to the dinner game might try cooking one or two Easy and Vegan recipes a week and build from there. Your skills will improve, you'll learn about new ingredients and seasonings, and the process of shopping and preparation will become more streamlined; actually, making dinner will help you feel comfortable in the kitchen way faster than could any television show, and—sooner than you might think—you'll be making yourself and those around you happy almost every night.

I'd suggest that you start by expanding your definition of "dinner." You can certainly build the evening meal around a large portion of well-sauced animal protein, then surround it with multiple starches and vegetables. Or not! These days, it makes way more sense to define dinner in terms of your cravings and situations, even if that means soup, or a simple bowl of noodles, or breakfast food, or a pot of beans and some bread; there should also be room at the table for all-vegetable entrees and hearty salads. You can always make something ahead of time and pull it from the freezer when you need a break. Whether your desires on any given night run to simply cooked stir-fries or burgers, or you're ready to commit to projects like big-deal

roasts, and enchiladas or fresh pasta, there are many ways we can rethink how we prepare and eat them. That's why I'm offering a spectrum of options here.

I also take advantage—you should too—of the wide range of cuisines, techniques, and ingredients now available everywhere. Our appetites are more diverse than ever before; once-unfamiliar foods have become commonplace. These recipes capture the excitement of eating and cooking today by updating these 100 Dinners in ways that are both fresh and familiar.

Each Dinner category offers three different recipes: Easy dishes that can be executed on rushed weekdays; Vegan meals for your good health and that of the planet (which are, for the most part, also on the quick-and-easy side); and ambitious All Out kitchen projects for leisurely weekends or special occasions. *Dinner for Everyone* answers nearly every craving, mood, and constraint. With gorgeous photographs for each meal and a simple and intuitive organization, you'll find just the right recipe—even if it wasn't the thing you had in mind when you started turning the pages.

Using the Book

To choose the 100 Dinners that made the cut, I turned to classics screaming for an update (the Italian hunter's stew known as Cacciatore or the 1960s favorite skillet meal, Beef Stroganoff), popular dishes from around the world (Ma Po Tofu and Moussaka), and specialty techniques (like jerk or *en papillote*—dubbed The Big Reveal). Some are broad archetypes (Pasta with Vegetables, Chowder) and many are American standards (Casseroles, Caesar Salad, Macaroni and Cheese). You'll recognize all of them—either by photo or name—with many recipes that still closely follow the classic. And since each bundle offers three unique interpretations, along the way you're in for lots of pleasant surprises.

THE EASY RECIPES

I've heard the same concerns from home cooks everywhere, and forever: "Cooking during the week has got to be easy or I just won't do it." And my rallying cry has always remained the same: Cook as often as you can, make dinner as simple as you need to, and don't try to mimic restaurant food, since your meals are going to be better than most of what you end up eating out anyway.

The Easy recipes are always the first to appear in each group and are exponentially simpler than the touchstones they celebrate. Many take 30 minutes or less to cook. But since that parameter runs the risk of limiting your options to stir-fries and broiling, I've included many hands-off simmering or roasting recipes that may require a little longer to cook, but free you to do something else while the heat does its thing, like make sides, help the kids with homework, or watch TV. Those are "easy" in a different way.

There are shortcuts here to be sure—that's the only way you could ever hope to enjoy the taste of homemade tamales, beef stew, or pot pie on a weeknight—but you'll always be cooking from scratch. These recipes also minimize cleanup with as few bowls, pans, and utensils as possible, streamlined ingredients to minimize prep and waste, and the most expedient techniques imaginable.

THE VEGAN RECIPES

Diet and nutrition are not as complicated as they're made out to be: We know that eating more fruits and vegetables and less junk food and animal products is the way toward optimal health, and eating vegan on a part-time basis—a concept I've been advancing for more than a decade—accomplishes all of this. Once part-time veganism was a radical notion; now it's everywhere. And despite the trendiness, fruits and vegetables will always be healthy. So why not cook vegan food more often?

Interpreting nonvegan dishes poses interesting challenges, because there's usually more to a superior vegan dish than exchanging a slab of meat for a slab of tofu or simply removing the cheese. To replace the meat and dairy *and* feel satisfied, you often need a mix of grains, vegetables, and beans—foods that require trimming, chopping, complex seasoning, or simmering, and which may also require a bit more time. But you can speed things up by working ahead: making big batches of grains and beans on the weekends, for example, so they're always ready to go. The recipes reveal dozens of tricks that will help ease you both into vegan cooking and into fast-cooking strategies.

Though the connection between the vegan recipe and the dish that inspired it (Chicken Salad or Chop House, for example) might not be immediately obvious, the flavor essence and satisfying elements of the original hide in plain sight. Sometimes I capture the same technique, sometimes the seasonings, sometimes a key ingredient, often a combination of all of these. In any case, I hope you agree these are among the most creative, dependable, and accessible vegan recipes anywhere, without a slice of fake meat or soy cheese in sight.

Dinner can be downright blissful when you have time, inspiration, and excellent ingredients. While weeknight cooking can sometimes seem like a race for survival, what I call All Out cooking is for pleasure, which often means preparing food to share with others. And in the name of celebration, you can show off a bit and serve something impressive.

These are you've-got-to-try-at-least-once versions of fantastic, even mind-blowing dishes; often they're the archetype. Going through the steps might remind you of the person who taught you to cook, lovingly and with care. Sometimes—as with Duck Confit—the process is quite simple and only requires patience. Occasionally—for, say, the Thanksgiving turkey, your elaborate whole-bird, stuffing-and-gravy affair or a traditional French Bistro Cassoulet—making the components is complicated, but the meal is totally relatable. In all cases, it's comforting to know that the "ultimate" version is also the original, a throwback to when we had more time to transform simple ingredients into something special.

This level of cooking is both educational (you'll learn new techniques) and aspirational ("I always wanted to make that"). See what sounds good based on season, event, and—most important—your mood and desires. Maybe you want to challenge yourself and start on a path that builds the confidence to push more and get even more proficient. Perhaps a friend made a request for a celebration. Or you want a meal that's perfect for company. Sometimes you'll simply respond to a craving and set aside time for a project. These recipes are for all those occasions.

Good Cooking, the Bittman Way

I'm not fussy or dogmatic but I hold true to a small set of kitchen beliefs:

- You need oil, butter, or other animal fats to make food and seasonings taste better. (And fat is part of a healthy diet.) The best and most versatile are extra virgin olive oil (just "olive oil" throughout the book), and good-quality, relatively neutral-tasting vegetable oil (like safflower, sunflower, or grapeseed); preferably choose cold-pressed for both—that is, not chemically extracted. Other fats in these recipes include butter (always unsalted), dark sesame oil (made from toasted seeds), and the occasional rendered pork or poultry fat.

- With good ingredients, salt and pepper are often all you need to make food taste good. "Salt" in this book means (preferably) the coarse, noniodized kosher kind and pepper comes (preferably) from a grinder filled with black peppercorns. The quantities are almost always up to you. Likewise, "Taste and adjust the seasoning" is intentionally vague to encourage you to do just that. I do use a wide range of herbs and spices in these recipes, but if you don't have something, you can either experiment with what you've got or add nothing more than salt and pepper. Tasting is the crux of becoming an intuitive home cook.

- My approach to equipment is also simple and flexible. In most cases—and definitely for all the Easy recipes—all you need are a couple of standard large rimmed baking sheets, one large (6-quart or so) pot, and one large (12-inch) skillet. All pots and pans should have ovenproof handles and lids, but you can also cover pots and pans in foil. No recipe will require more than two pots at a time, and never two pots of the same size at the same time. But extra pots and pans can be handy: medium (10-inch) and small (8-inch) stainless steel or nonstick skillets, cast-iron grill pans or skillets, a heavy Dutch oven, a super-big heavy-bottomed stockpot, a 9 by 13-inch baking dish and roasting pan. These are the sorts of things you'll acquire the more you cook.

- A few of these recipes assume you have a food processor. You can manage without—or (often) use a blender instead—but I recommend getting one if you can swing it; it'll make your cooking easier and, generally, faster. Some of the weekend recipes involve the use of special tools or equipment, like a pasta machine or a sausage stuffer, and you'll find that clearly indicated where necessary (and often alternatives listed).

That's it. Now let's figure out what you're cooking for dinner first.

The Dinners

● Easy ● Vegan ● All Out

Caesar Salad 17
- ● Chicken Caesar
- ● Grilled Vegetable Caesar
- ● Tableside Salad with Marinated Sardines

Hearty Salad 20
- ● Classic Ham Salad, Only Better
- ● Tofu Larb
- ● Posole Salad

Chicken Salad 25
- ● Chicken Salad with Corn and Miso Dressing
- ● Everything-but-the-Chicken Salad
- ● Seared Duck Salad with Hot, Sweet, and Sour Dressing

Seafood Salad 29
- ● Sardine Niçoise
- ● Seaweed Salad
- ● Grilled Octopus Salad, Greek Style

Noodle Salad 32
- ● Peanut Bun
- ● Gingery Noodle Salad with Snow Peas
- ● Vietnamese Bean Thread Salad with Shrimp and Chicken

Pho 37
- ● Fast Pho with Tea Broth
- ● Mixed Mushroom Pho
- ● Pho with Fresh Noodles

Chicken Noodle Soup 40
- ● Hot and Sour Chicken Noodle Soup with Cracklings
- ● Chickpea Noodle Soup
- ● Chicken Soup with Egg Noodles
- + *Chicken Stock*

Onion Soup 45
- ● Charred Onion Soup over Torn Bread
- ● Mostly Onion Soup with Cannellini Crostini
- ● Hearty French Onion Soup
- + *Beef Stock*

Gumbo 48
- ● Sausage Gumbo
- ● Okra Gumbo
- ● Full-On Gumbo with Cayenne Hush Puppies

Seafood Soup 53
- ● Shrimp and Egg Drop Soup with Wonton Ribbons
- ● Watercress and Seaweed Soup with Yuba
- ● Perihuela

Chowder 57
- ● Corn-and-Cheddar Chowder
- ● Offbeat Vegetable Chowder
- ● North American Clam Chowder

Vegetable Soup 60
- ● Senegalese Peanut Soup
- ● Hearty Minestrone
- ● Borscht with Beef

Bean Soup 65
- ● Fagioli e Pasta
- ● Smoky Three-Bean Soup with Tomatillo Salsa
- ● Chickpea Soup with Colorful Garnishes

Chili 68
- ● Santa Fe–Style Green Chile Stir-Fry
- ● Tempeh-Peanut Chili
- ● Texas Red with Tamale Dumplings

Dal with Flatbread 73
- ● Garlicky Dal with Buttery Flatbread
- ● Sprouted Lentils with Winter Squash and Whole Wheat Flatbread
- ● Mung Beans with Ginger and Homemade Chapati

Cassoulet 76
- ● Sausage Cassoulet
- ● Lentil Cassoulet with Lots of Vegetables
- ● Pork Cassoulet with Seared Duck Breast

Rice and Beans 81
- ● Sweet and Salty Coconut Rice with Lima Beans
- ● Red Beans and Rice with Tangy Zucchini
- ● Sticky Rice and Adzuki Beans in Lotus Leaves
- + *Basic Beans*

Pilaf 85
- ● The Best Green Rice
- ● Brown Rice and Brussels Sprout Pilaf with Shiitake Bacon
- ● Stuck Pot Chicken and Rice
- + *Vegetable Stock*

Risotto 89
- ● Baked Rice and Peas
- ● Barley Risotto with Beets and Greens
- ● Vanilla-Scented Lobster Risotto

Sushi 92
- ● Spicy Tuna Rice Bowl
- ● Quinoa Nori Rolls
- ● Hand-Cut Nigiri and Sashimi with Pickled Ginger

Paella 97
- ● Shrimp Paella, Under the Broiler
- ● Vegetable Paella
- ● Mixed Paella with Mussels

Fried Rice 100
- ● Beef Fried Rice with Frozen Vegetables
- ● Cauliflower Fried Rice with Fresh Chiles
- ● Bibimbap
- + *Brown or White Basmati Rice (or Other Long-Grain Rice)*

Rice Noodles 105
- ● Seared Beef with Rice Vermicelli
- ● Wide Noodles with Tempeh and Warm Kimchi
- ● Pad Thai with Crisp and Spicy Soft-Shell Crab

● Grilled Vegetable
Caesar, page 18

Caesar Salad

A salad that's definitely all about the dressing, which is capable of making grass clippings taste good. To keep things relatively conventional, I let creamy, rich, and slightly salty Caesar dressing turn romaine lettuce into three different mains. The shortcut recipe starts with premade mayo—either your own from an earlier moment of foresight (see page 216) or bottled. I make the flavorful egg-free dressing for Grilled Vegetable Caesar frequently, whether I'm eating vegan or not. (Hint: Capers contribute brininess.) Or bring back a little pomp and try Tableside Salad with Marinated Sardines, featuring a milder-tasting, heartier fish than the traditional anchovies.

● CHICKEN CAESAR

makes: 4 servings
time: 25 minutes

¾ cup mayonnaise (see page 216)

2 teaspoons fresh lemon juice

3 anchovy fillets, minced, plus a little of their oil

Dash Worcestershire sauce

Salt and pepper

¾ cup grated Pecorino or Parmesan cheese (about 3 ounces)

8 ounces romaine lettuce (about 2 hearts or 1 medium head), rinsed, dried, and chopped

2 large boneless, skinless chicken breasts (about 1½ pounds), cut into 1-inch chunks

8 ounces bread, cut into bite-sized chunks

2 tablespoons olive oil

1 tablespoon minced garlic

1. Heat the oven to 400°F. Put the mayonnaise, lemon juice, anchovies, Worcestershire sauce, and 2 tablespoons water in a large bowl. Whisk with a fork to combine, smashing the anchovies as you stir. Taste and add some salt if you'd like and lots of black pepper. Taste and adjust the seasoning again. Transfer about two-thirds of the dressing to a salad bowl and stir in ½ cup cheese. Put the romaine on top of the dressing but don't toss yet and chill the bowl if there's space in the fridge.

2. Toss the chicken with the remaining one-third mayonnaise mixture and spread in a single layer on a rimmed baking sheet or in a large ovenproof skillet. Put the bread on a separate rimmed baking sheet; drizzle with the oil, sprinkle with the garlic and salt and pepper, and toss to coat. Put both pans in the oven and cook, tossing everything with a spatula every 5 minutes or so, until the chicken is cooked through and both the chicken and croutons are lightly browned, 10 to 20 minutes.

3. When the croutons are ready, shake the pan to make sure they're coated with the seasonings, add them to the salad bowl along with the chicken, and toss to coat. Sprinkle with the remaining ¼ cup cheese and serve right away.

● GRILLED VEGETABLE CAESAR

makes: 4 servings
time: 25 minutes

8 ounces (about ½ loaf) rustic whole-grain bread, torn into 1-inch pieces

8 tablespoons olive oil

Salt and pepper

1 tablespoon nutritional yeast

2 medium zucchini, sliced into ½-inch coins

1 pound asparagus, trimmed of woody ends

1 large garlic clove, halved

1 tablespoon drained capers

¼ cup vegan mayonnaise (see page 218)

2 tablespoons red wine vinegar

1 teaspoon soy sauce

2 hearts romaine lettuce, or 1 small head, rinsed, dried, and chopped

1 small red onion, halved and sliced

1. Heat the oven to 400°F. Prepare a charcoal or gas grill for direct cooking. (Or turn on the broiler and position the rack about 4 inches below the heat after you've made the croutons.) Put the bread on a rimmed baking sheet, drizzle with 2 tablespoons oil, and sprinkle with salt and pepper; toss to coat. Cook, stirring every 5 minutes, until the croutons are golden and crisp, 10 to 15 minutes. When the croutons are done, toss them with the nutritional yeast.

2. Put the zucchini and asparagus on a rimmed baking sheet and drizzle with 2 tablespoons oil and sprinkle with salt and pepper; toss to coat. When the fire (or broiler) is ready, grill or broil the vegetables until they are tender and charred, turning them as necessary to prevent burning, 6 to 12 minutes for the asparagus and 10 to 15 minutes for the zucchini. Rub a large bowl with the garlic. Cut the vegetables into bite-sized pieces and transfer to the bowl.

3. Put the capers in a small bowl and mash them with a fork. Add the vegan mayonnaise, the vinegar, and soy sauce and sprinkle with salt and lots of black pepper. Whisk to combine, then whisk continuously while you slowly pour in the remaining 4 tablespoons oil. Taste and adjust the seasoning. To serve, add the lettuce and onion to the grilled vegetables, drizzle with half the dressing or more to taste, and scatter some croutons on top. Toss, adding more dressing or croutons if you like, and serve. Pass the remaining dressing and croutons at the table.

● TABLESIDE SALAD
with marinated sardines

makes: 4 to 8 servings
time: at least 1 day, largely unattended

1 cup and 6 tablespoons olive oil, or more
    as needed

8 small sardines, each about 4 inches long
    (about 1 pound), cleaned

Salt and pepper

¾ cup sherry vinegar

6 tablespoons fresh lemon juice

2 bay leaves

1 fresh thyme sprig

8 ounces (about ½ loaf) crusty Italian bread

1 tablespoon minced garlic and 1 clove, halved

3 hearts romaine lettuce

2 eggs

2 oil-packed anchovies

Dash Worcestershire sauce, or to taste

One 4-ounce piece Parmesan cheese

1. Heat the oven to 450°F. Spread 1 tablespoon oil on a rimmed baking sheet. Add the sardines, sprinkle them with salt and pepper, then drizzle with another tablespoon oil. Roast the sardines, turning halfway through, until they flake easily with a fork, 7 to 12 minutes total.

2. When the fish are cool enough to handle, gently remove the fillets. Put one fish on a cutting board and cut through the fillet to the spine just below the gills; turn the knife to carefully cut the fillet from the bone in once piece, working toward the tail. Transfer the fillet to a plate. Turn the fish and repeat with the other side. Do the same for all the sardines.

3. Put ¾ cup oil in a 9 by 13–inch glass dish (or similar shallow vessel). Add the vinegar, 4 tablespoons lemon juice, the bay leaves, and thyme and sprinkle with salt. Whisk with a fork to combine. Nestle the fillets into the marinade. Cover and refrigerate for at least 8 hours or up to 3 days, carefully turning them now and then.

4. Put 2 tablespoons oil in a large skillet over medium heat. Tear the bread into bite-sized pieces. When the oil is hot, add the bread pieces and minced garlic, and sprinkle with salt and pepper. Cook, stirring occasionally, until the bread is golden and crisp, 3 to 5 minutes. Transfer to a bowl.

5. When you're ready to serve, rinse and dry the lettuce; separate each heart into individual leaves, leaving the leaves whole. Remove the sardines from the marinade, keeping them as intact as possible. Bring them and the remaining ingredients to the table to assemble the salad: Rub the inside of the serving bowl with the halved garlic clove, then discard. Add the eggs to the bowl and beat them with a fork. Gradually drizzle in the remaining 2 tablespoons lemon juice and then the remaining 6 tablespoons oil, beating all the while, to make an emulsified sauce. Stir in the anchovies and Worcestershire sauce, using the fork to mash the anchovies and incorporate them into the dressing; add a tablespoon or so more oil if you'd like the dressing a little thinner.

6. Add the lettuce and toss to coat. Taste a piece, then sprinkle with salt, lots of pepper, and a little more Worcestershire sauce if you like; toss again. Add the croutons and toss one last time. Use a vegetable peeler to shave some ribbons of Parmesan over all and serve right away topped with sardine fillets.

Hearty Salad

I draw from three great cuisines for a bundle of salads as hearty as they are unexpected. From Laos and parts of Thailand comes a sweet, spicy, crisp, and refreshing larb—where tofu replaces the usual seared chopped meat. Posole is a rich Mexican stew usually based on pork and always including hominy; here are all the same flavors and textures without the broth, tossed in a lime dressing and served chilled or warm. And it's probably been a while since you've enjoyed an all-American ham salad—no doubt with good reason—so I've spiked the recipe with crunchy kohlrabi and tangy pickles to bring it into this century.

● CLASSIC HAM SALAD, ONLY BETTER

makes: 4 to 6 servings
time: 5 minutes

½ cup mayonnaise (see page 216)

1 tablespoon Dijon mustard, or to taste

1 tablespoon cider vinegar, or to taste

Salt and pepper

1 pound boneless ham steaks, chopped

1 small red onion, halved and sliced

¾ cup bread-and-butter pickles, drained
   and chopped

1 pound kohlrabi or celery root, peeled
   and chopped

1. Combine the mayonnaise, mustard, and vinegar in a large bowl and season with salt and pepper. Whisk to combine, taste, and adjust the seasoning.

2. Add the ham, onion, pickles, and kohlrabi to the bowl and toss to combine. Taste and adjust the seasoning, adding more mustard and vinegar if you'd like, and serve.

Posole Salad,
page 23

● TOFU LARB

makes: 4 to 8 servings
time: 30 minutes

2 tablespoons sticky (glutinous) rice kernels

1 pound pressed or extra-firm tofu

2 garlic cloves

¼ cup good-quality vegetable oil

Salt and pepper

1 teaspoon turbinado sugar

2 cups loosely packed mixed fresh herbs (like cilantro, basil, mint, or Thai basil), chopped

2 shallots, peeled and sliced

4 fresh red chiles (like Thai bird or Fresno), seeded if you like and chopped

2 tablespoons soy sauce, or more to taste

4 limes, quartered

16 to 20 leaves Bibb or iceberg lettuce

1. Put the rice in a large skillet over medium heat and cook, stirring often, until deeply golden and fragrant, 3 to 5 minutes. Transfer to a spice grinder (or use a mortar and pestle) and grind to a powder.

2. Pulse the tofu and garlic in a food processor until crumbly. Heat the oil in a large skillet over medium-high heat. When it's hot, add the tofu mixture. Sprinkle with salt, pepper, and the sugar, and cook, stirring occasionally, until the mixture has browned in places, 8 to 12 minutes.

3. Transfer the tofu mixture to a large bowl and add the herbs, shallots, chiles, and soy sauce. Squeeze in the juice from 2 limes and toss to combine. Taste and adjust the seasoning.

4. Put the lettuce on a platter with the tofu mixture and remaining lime wedges. To eat, spoon some tofu-herb salad into a lettuce cup, sprinkle with the ground toasted rice, and squeeze over additional juice from the remaining 2 limes.

● POSOLE SALAD

makes: 4 servings
time: about 3 hours

1 cup dried white hominy

Salt

1 bay leaf

2 teaspoons cumin seeds

2 teaspoons coriander seeds

1 ancho or other mild dried chile

1 pound boneless pork shoulder, cut into
    1-inch chunks

1 large onion, quartered

3 garlic cloves, lightly crushed

Pepper

1 12-ounce bottle Mexican lager

Good-quality vegetable oil as needed

½ cup fresh lime juice, or to taste

2 jalapeños, seeded and chopped

2 cups shredded green cabbage

4 ounces radishes, trimmed and chopped

4 scallions, chopped

1 cup fresh cilantro sprigs, tough stems removed

¼ cup toasted pumpkin seeds

1. Combine the hominy with a large pinch of salt and enough water to cover by at least 2 inches in a medium saucepan. Bring to a boil, then adjust the heat so the mixture bubbles gently. Cook, stirring occasionally, until the hominy is tender and tastes done to you. Start checking after 30 minutes; it could take up to 2 hours, depending on how old and dry your hominy is. Drain and leave the hominy in the colander to cool.

2. Meanwhile, wrap the bay leaf, cumin, coriander, and chile in cheesecloth and secure tightly. Put it in a large pot with the pork, onion, and garlic and sprinkle with salt and pepper. Add the beer and water as needed to cover by 1 inch. Turn the heat to high, bring to a boil, and skim any foam that comes to the surface. Partially cover and adjust the heat so the mixture bubbles steadily. Cook until the meat can be easily pierced with a fork, 1 to 1½ hours.

3. Remove the cheesecloth bundle with a slotted spoon and discard. Right in the pot, break the meat into bite-sized pieces with a spoon and cook uncovered until all the liquid has evaporated. Continue to cook the meat in the remaining fat, keeping your eye on the meat the entire time and adjusting the heat as necessary to prevent the meat from burning, until it's crisped and browned; add a little oil if it sticks or becomes dry. Cooking off the liquid and browning the meat could take up to 1 hour.

4. Transfer the pork to a large bowl and turn the heat under the pot to medium. Add the lime juice and jalapeños to the pot and cook, stirring, until all the browned parts on the bottom of the pan have come loose. Season with salt and pepper, then pour over the still warm meat. Toss to coat, then taste and adjust the seasoning, adding more lime juice if you'd like. Add the hominy, the cabbage, radishes, scallions, and cilantro, and toss to combine. Taste and adjust the seasoning again and serve. Top with the pumpkin seeds.

Everything-But-the-
Chicken Salad,
page 26

● Chicken Salad with
Corn and Miso Dressing,
page 26

Chicken Salad

The world has enough recipes for the deli-style chicken salad—chopped or shredded chicken with mayonnaise, aromatics, and fruit—so I've taken the elements you crave into brand-new spins. Only the Easy version actually uses chicken, and the star ingredient is miso, to boost the flavor of simply cooked breast meat while bringing out the sweetness of the corn. The Vegan salad is another shocker: grated jicama bound in a mustardy mayonnaise dressing with grapes and the classic tarragon. And the All Out recipe calls on duck to turn the ordinary into something special yet obviously familiar.

CHICKEN SALAD
with corn and miso dressing

makes: 4 to 6 servings
time: 20 minutes

2 boneless, skinless chicken breasts (about 1½ pounds)

5 tablespoons good-quality vegetable oil

Salt and pepper

1 cup frozen corn

¼ cup rice vinegar

3 tablespoons white or yellow miso

1 tablespoon dark sesame oil

One 1-inch piece fresh ginger, peeled and chopped

4 scallions, whites and greens separated and chopped

1. Turn the broiler to high and position the rack 4 inches below it. Cut each chicken breast in half horizontally to make 2 thin cutlets and press down on each with the heel of your hand to flatten. Put the chicken on a rimmed baking sheet, rub all over with 1 tablespoon vegetable oil, and sprinkle with salt and pepper.

2. Broil the chicken, turning once, until lightly browned on both sides and white or just barely pink inside, 2 to 5 minutes per side. Put the corn in a colander and run under cold water just to thaw, a minute or 2.

3. Put the vinegar, miso, sesame oil, ginger, and remaining 4 tablespoons vegetable oil into a blender and blend until smooth. Cut the chicken into bite-sized pieces; dry the corn with a towel.

4. Combine the chicken, corn, the scallion whites, and the dressing in a large bowl and toss to coat. Garnish with the scallion greens and serve at room temperature.

EVERYTHING-BUT-THE-CHICKEN SALAD

makes: 4 servings
time: 25 minutes

OTHER VEGETABLES THAT WORK If you don't have jicama, try kohlrabi, parsnips, celery root, even turnips if you like that extra cabbage-y flavor.

1 pound jicama, peeled

Salt

½ cup raw sunflower seeds

½ cup vegan mayonnaise (see page 218)

1 tablespoon Dijon mustard

1 tablespoon white wine vinegar

2 tablespoons olive oil

3 teaspoons chopped fresh tarragon

Pepper

1 cup seedless red grapes, halved

3 celery stalks, chopped

½ small red onion, chopped

8 large, sturdy romaine leaves

1. Use the shredding attachment on a food processor or the largest holes on a box grater to grate the jicama. Mix the vegetable with a generous pinch of salt, then let it sit in a colander in the sink or over a bowl for 20 to 30 minutes. Rinse the jicama, then wring it as dry as you can manage in a towel. Transfer to a large bowl.

2. Put the sunflower seeds in a medium skillet over medium heat. Cook, shaking the pan occasionally, until they are slightly darker and fragrant, 3 to 5 minutes. Transfer to the bowl with the jicama. Put the mayonnaise, mustard, vinegar, oil, and 1 teaspoon tarragon in a small bowl and sprinkle with salt and pepper. Whisk to combine, then taste and adjust the seasoning.

3. Put the grapes, celery, onion, and remaining 2 teaspoons tarragon in the large bowl and drizzle on some of the dressing. Toss gently to coat, then taste and adjust the seasoning, adding more dressing if you like. To serve, put the lettuce leaves on a serving platter or in individual bowls and top with a heaping spoonful of salad.

● SEARED DUCK SALAD
with hot, sweet, and sour dressing

makes: 4 to 6 servings
time: at least 8 hours, largely unattended

BUYING AND COOKING THE DUCK Duck breasts can sometimes be labeled in confusing ways, so let the total weight be your cue and aim for each breast to be about 1 pound. And if you'd prefer the meat more well done, wait until the thermometer reads about 140°F; more than that and they'll become dry and rubbery. Still, don't be afraid to go hard on the searing in Step 3. Duck skin needs at least the full 8 minutes to get golden brown and crisp, and to render enough fat.

2 boneless duck breasts, skin on
     (12 to 16 ounces each)

Salt

1 cup pitted fresh or frozen sweet cherries
     (no need to thaw)

1 small shallot, chopped

1 small hot red chile (like Thai or Fresno),
     thinly sliced

¼ cup sherry vinegar

Pepper

¼ cup good-quality vegetable oil

2 tablespoons dark sesame oil

½ large head savoy cabbage or other hardy green
     cabbage, chopped (about 6 cups)

2 tablespoons chopped fresh chives, for garnish

1. Fit a rimmed baking sheet with a wire rack. Use a sharp thin-bladed knife to score the skin of the duck breasts in a crosshatch pattern about ¾ inch wide; be careful to cut only through the skin, not the flesh. Sprinkle the skin generously with salt and rub it in. Put the duck on the prepared rack and refrigerate, uncovered, for 8 to 12 hours. Combine the cherries, shallot, chile, and vinegar in a small bowl and sprinkle with salt and pepper. Refrigerate for at least 8 or up to 24 hours.

2. Transfer the cherry mixture to a blender and add the oils. Run the machine until an emulsion forms, about 30 seconds. Taste and adjust the seasoning.

3. Heat the oven to 400°F. If the duck looks wet, blot it dry with paper towels. Put a large, dry, ovenproof skillet over medium-high heat. When it's hot, add the duck breasts skin side down and cook until they're very well browned, have rendered a lot of fat, the crosshatch pattern starts to open up a bit, and they release easily from the pan, 8 to 12 minutes. Turn the breasts skin side up and transfer the skillet to the oven. Roast, undisturbed, until the duck is rare, 3 to 5 minutes. (An instant-read thermometer inserted into the meat should read about 125°F.) Transfer the duck to a cutting board and let it rest for 5 to 10 minutes.

4. Pour off all but 2 tablespoons of the duck fat (save it in the refrigerator or freeze it for another use) and put the skillet over medium-high heat. Add the cabbage and toss to coat in the fat and just barely wilt it, a minute or 2. Mix the cabbage and some of the cherry dressing and divide among serving plates. Thinly slice the duck breast crosswise at a slight angle, skin and all, and put the slices on top of the dressed cabbage. Drizzle with more dressing, garnish with the chives, and serve.

Grilled Octopus Salad,
Greek Style, page 31

Seafood Salad

The oceans are filled with so much more than potential shrimp cocktails and crab Louis. My new favorite seafood salads are made with the less common, sustainable species. The results are a richer, easier Niçoise (don't be daunted by the number of steps), a seaweed two-for-one deal (crisp salad now and hot soup later), and a restaurant-style grilled octopus and vegetable presentation.

● SARDINE NIÇOISE

makes: 4 servings
time: 40 minutes

1 pound small red potatoes

Salt

8 ounces green beans, trimmed

4 eggs

6 tablespoons olive oil

1 tablespoon chopped garlic

4 thick slices rustic bread

1 cup pitted Kalamata olives, chopped

4 tablespoons red wine vinegar

1 tablespoon chopped fresh thyme, or
    1 teaspoon dried

Pepper

2 cans sardines, packed in olive oil

2 romaine lettuce hearts, trimmed

1 pint cherry tomatoes

1 cucumber, peeled and chopped

1. Put the potatoes in a large pot with enough water to cover by 2 inches and a large pinch of salt and bring to a boil. Adjust the heat so the water bubbles steadily and cook, stirring once or twice, until they can just be pierced with a fork, 15 to 20 minutes. When they're ready, add the beans and cook until bright green, 2 to 3 minutes. Drain the vegetables and rinse with cold water.

2. At the same time, bring a medium pot of water to a boil over medium-high heat. Adjust the heat so the water bubbles gently. Lower the eggs into the water with a spoon and onto the bottom of the pan so they don't break. Adjust the heat so the water bubbles gently and cook the eggs for 9 minutes. Remove the pan from the heat, pour out the water, then fill the pan with cold water and ice and let sit until the eggs are cool enough to handle.

3. Turn on the broiler and position the rack 4 inches below the heat source. Mix the oil and garlic in a bowl with a fork to mash a bit. Put the bread on a rimmed baking sheet and spread a little of the oil and garlic mixture on top; let sit. Mix the remaining oil mixture with the olives, vinegar, and thyme, and sprinkle with salt and pepper. Whisk until combined, taste and adjust the seasoning.

4. When the potatoes are ready, toast the bread under the broiler, turning once, until as brown and crisp as you like, 3 to 5 minutes total. Top each piece of toast with one-fourth of the sardines and halve the toasts.

5. Tear the romaine into bite-sized pieces and put in a large bowl. Quarter the eggs and halve the potatoes, and add to the bowl along with the beans, the tomatoes, and cucumber. Drizzle the salad with the dressing and toss to coat; taste and adjust the seasoning and serve with the sardine toasts.

● SEAWEED SALAD

makes: 4 servings
time: about 2 hours, including time to marinate

½ ounce dried kombu

½ ounce dried arame

½ ounce dried wakame

One 2-inch piece fresh ginger, peeled

3 cups cooked adzuki beans (see page 82; or two 15-ounce cans), drained

2 carrots, julienned

4 ounces daikon radish, peeled and julienned

½ cup chopped fresh cilantro

1 hot red chile (like Thai or Fresno), seeded if you like and sliced

¼ cup soy sauce

3 tablespoons rice vinegar

3 tablespoons mirin (see page 290)

1 tablespoon dark sesame oil, or to taste

Salt

2 tablespoons sesame seeds

1. Bring 2 quarts water to a boil in a large pot. Add the kombu and arame and immediately remove the pot from the heat and cover. Steep until the kombu is tender, 5 to 10 minutes. Transfer just the seaweed to a colander, run under cold water, and return the pot to a boil. Repeat with the wakame, adjusting the steeping time to just a minute or 2.

2. Squeeze the drained seaweed to remove excess water and pick out any hard bits. Chop any big pieces and put in a large bowl. (You can cool the broth and store in the refrigerator for a few days or the freezer for up to 2 months.)

3. Use a microplane or the smallest holes on a box grater to grate the ginger into a pulp. Add to the seaweed along with the beans, carrots, radish, cilantro, chile, soy sauce, vinegar, mirin, and sesame oil. Toss to coat, then taste and adjust the seasoning, adding salt if necessary.

4. Let the salad marinate for at least 1 hour and up to 4. Just before serving, put the sesame seeds in a medium skillet over medium heat. Toast, shaking the pan occasionally, until they are golden and fragrant, 3 to 5 minutes. Sprinkle the toasted seeds over the salad and serve.

● GRILLED OCTOPUS SALAD, GREEK STYLE

makes: 6 to 8 servings
time: 1½ hours

One whole octopus (2 to 3 pounds), cleaned and rinsed

2 garlic cloves, lightly crushed

2 fresh oregano sprigs and 1 tablespoon chopped

Salt

¾ cup olive oil

3 tablespoons red wine vinegar, or more as needed

Pepper

1 small shallot, chopped

¼ cup crumbled feta cheese

1 small fennel bulb

2 oranges

2 tablespoons fresh lemon juice

1 cup Kalamata olives, pitted and chopped

1. Put the octopus in a large pot with the garlic, oregano sprigs, and enough water to cover; add a large pinch of salt. Bring to a boil, then adjust the heat so the water bubbles gently and cook for 45 minutes. At this point, start checking every 10 minutes to see if the octopus is nearly tender: poke it with a sharp thin-bladed knife; when the knife enters fairly easily, the octopus is ready (it should take another 15 to 35 minutes). Be careful; it can go from underdone to mushy very fast. Look for the texture of imitation crabmeat (sorry). Drain in a colander.

2. Combine ½ cup oil and the vinegar in a blender and season with salt and pepper. Run the machine until a creamy emulsion forms, about 30 seconds. Taste and add more vinegar a teaspoon or so at a time until the balance tastes right to you. Add the shallot, the tablespoon chopped oregano, and the feta and turn the machine on and off a few times until the shallot is minced. Taste and adjust the seasoning again.

3. Heat a charcoal or gas grill for direct cooking until quite hot and put the rack as close to the heat source as possible. Or heat a large grill pan over 2 burners until smoking hot. Trim the stems from the fennel and chop ¼ cup of the fronds for garnish. Cut the fennel in half lengthwise, then slice crosswise as thin as you can manage. Slice off about ¼ inch from both ends of the oranges so you can stand them on the cutting board. Use a very sharp knife to cut as close to the flesh as possible, removing the skin and bitter white pith in long pieces; you'll lose some flesh, but try not to cut off too much. Cut the oranges crosswise into "wheels."

4. Cut the octopus into large pieces; they don't have to be the same size, but it helps them cook evenly if each piece has relatively uniform thickness. Whisk together the remaining ¼ cup oil and the lemon juice. Brush the octopus pieces with this mixture and grill them quickly on all sides until crisp, 8 to 10 minutes total. Put the fennel, oranges, the olives, and grilled octopus in a large bowl and drizzle with the dressing. Toss to combine, then serve, garnished with the chopped fennel fronds.

Noodle Salad

Give me vegetable-driven noodles served cool or at room temperature any night, especially in summer. Bean sprouts and rice vermicelli (or sticks) tossed effortlessly in a peanutty dressing deliver an unbeatable crisp-and-chewy combination; the eggs make it a one-bowl meal, so don't skip them. Or combine hearty whole wheat angel hair with slivered vegetables and watch in amazement as they twirl together on your fork. With a tad more prep time, you can cook chicken, shrimp, and clear noodles in seasoned water to infuse everything with incredible flavor, then sip the delicious broth alongside or save it for a future soup base.

● PEANUT BUN

makes: 2 to 4 servings
time: 15 minutes

Salt

About 8 ounces rice noodles
   (vermicelli or sticks, as you like)

8 ounces bean sprouts

4 eggs

½ cup peanut butter

1 teaspoon sugar

3 tablespoons fish sauce, or to taste

2 small hot red chiles (like Thai bird or Fresno),
   seeded if you like and chopped

1 tablespoon fresh lime juice, or to taste

½ cup chopped scallions

¼ cup chopped roasted peanuts

Lime wedges

1. Bring a large pot of water to a boil and salt it. Put the noodles in a large bowl. When the water boils, add enough water to the bowl to cover, stir, then let the noodles soak until they are soft and pliable. Start checking after 3 minutes; thicker noodles could take up to 15. When the noodles are nearly tender, add the sprouts to soak for a minute or 2. Reserve ½ cup of the soaking liquid, then transfer everything to a colander, run under cold water for 1 minute, and shake off any excess water. Meanwhile, bring the remaining water back to a boil, carefully add the eggs, cover, and turn off the heat. Steep the eggs for 9 minutes, then drain and run under cold water until cool.

2. Whisk together the peanut butter, sugar, fish sauce, 1 teaspoon of the chiles, and the lime juice in a small bowl. Add ¼ cup of the reserved liquid and continue to whisk. The dressing should easily coat the back of a spoon. If it's too thick, whisk in more hot water 1 tablespoon at a time. Taste and adjust the seasoning, adding more lime juice, chiles, and salt if you'd like.

3. Combine the noodles and sprouts with half the dressing in a large bowl and toss gently with 2 forks. Peel the eggs and halve lengthwise. Garnish the noodles with the eggs, scallions, and peanuts and serve at room temperature, passing the lime wedges and the remaining dressing and chiles at the table.

GINGERY NOODLE SALAD
with snow peas

makes: 4 servings
time: 20 minutes

Salt

2 tablespoons sesame seeds

One 2-inch piece fresh ginger, peeled

6 scallions, whites and greens separated and
    chopped

¼ cup soy sauce

2 tablespoons fresh lemon juice

2 tablespoons dark sesame oil

2 tablespoons good-quality vegetable oil

Pepper

1 pound snow peas, trimmed

8 ounces whole wheat angel hair pasta,
    broken in half

1. Bring a large pot of water to a boil and salt it. Put the sesame seeds in a medium skillet over medium heat and toast, shaking the pan occasionally, until they are golden and fragrant, 3 to 5 minutes. Transfer to a bowl.

2. Use a microplane or the smallest holes on a box grater to grate the ginger into a large bowl. Add the scallion whites, soy sauce, lemon juice, and oils and sprinkle with salt and pepper. Taste and adjust the seasoning.

3. Stack the snow peas a few at a time and slice them lengthwise into 3 or 4 thin strips. It's okay if some peas pop out or split; just save them all together. Cut all the remaining pods.

4. When the water boils, add the pasta and stir. Cook, stirring occasionally, until it's tender but not mushy; start checking after 5 minutes. When the pasta is ready, stir the snow peas into the pot and immediately drain, shaking off as much excess water as possible (but don't rinse). Add to the bowl with the dressing and toss gently to coat. Garnish with the scallion greens and sesame seeds, and serve warm or let sit for up to 1 hour and serve at room temperature.

VIETNAMESE BEAN THREAD SALAD
with shrimp and chicken

makes: 4 servings
time: 1 hour

One 2-inch piece fresh ginger, unpeeled,
   cut into several coins

2 star anise

1 tablespoon salt, or more as needed

2 bone-in chicken breasts (about 1½ pounds)

1 pound medium or large shrimp, unpeeled

½ cup good-quality vegetable oil

½ cup fresh lime juice, or more as needed

1 carrot, grated

1 shallot, minced

¼ cup fish sauce

2 tablespoons sugar

Pepper

8 ounces bean thread noodles

1 large cucumber, peeled, seeded, and sliced into
   thin crescents

⅔ cup chopped fresh mint

⅔ cup chopped fresh cilantro

⅔ cup chopped fresh Thai basil

2 or 3 fresh hot red chiles (preferably Thai),
   thinly sliced

1. Fill a large pot with 6 cups water and add the ginger, star anise, and 1 tablespoon salt; bring to a boil. Add the chicken and bring the water back to a boil. Adjust the heat so the liquid bubbles gently but steadily, cover, and cook for 20 minutes. Remove the pot from the heat and then let the chicken sit until it's no longer pink inside, another 8 to 12 minutes; it's done when an instant-read thermometer inserted into the thickest part reads 155 to 165°F. Remove the chicken from the poaching liquid and cool to room temperature.

2. Bring the poaching liquid to a boil and add the shrimp. When it returns to a boil, remove from the heat and cover. Let the shrimp sit until uniformly pink, 3 to 5 minutes. Remove the shrimp with a slotted spoon and cool to room temperature.

3. Put the vegetable oil, lime juice, carrot, shallot, fish sauce, sugar, and lots of pepper into a large bowl and whisk to combine. Taste and adjust the seasoning.

4. Once again return the poaching liquid to a boil and then remove from the heat. Add the noodles and soak until transparent and just tender, at least 5 and up to 15 minutes. Drain into a strainer, reserving the broth; discard the star anise. Cut the noodles with kitchen scissors in a few places until the strands are manageable. Toss the noodles in the bowl with the dressing. (It will look overdressed but don't worry.)

5. Remove the skin and bones from the chicken breasts and shred the meat with your fingers. Peel and chop the shrimp. Add the chicken and shrimp to the noodles along with the cucumber, herbs, and as much chile as you like. Toss gently to coat and taste and adjust the seasoning. Serve at room temperature, or refrigerate for up to 30 minutes and serve slightly chilled.

Mixed Mushroom Pho,
page 38

Pho

With a spoon in one hand and chopsticks in the other, you engage all the senses to eat this touchstone of Vietnamese cooking. Turning water into pho in 30 minutes takes liberties—and some black tea. Will it be authentic? Not at all. So look past that and focus on what you can achieve: fresh, raw garnishes; thin-sliced beef and onions; and tender, slightly chewy noodles. Mushrooms and seaweed provide the solution for the invigorating meatless broth, while at the other end of the spectrum a carefully constructed beef stock lays the foundation for a fairly traditional bowl that takes a little more effort.

● FAST PHO
with tea broth

makes: 4 servings
time: 30 minutes

INGREDIENT SUBSTITUTION Instead of a sweet onion, try scallions, red onions, shallots, or the white part of a leek.

2 tablespoons good-quality vegetable oil

1 pound boneless sirloin, flank, or rib-eye steak

Salt and pepper

1 tablespoon Chinese five-spice powder, or more to taste

3 black tea bags

One 2-inch piece fresh ginger, sliced

⅓ cup soy sauce or fish sauce, or more as needed

10 ounces dried rice vermicelli noodles

1 sweet onion (like Vidalia), halved and sliced

2 cups fresh herb sprigs (like cilantro, mint, or basil)

2 cups bean sprouts

2 fresh hot red or green chiles, sliced

Lime wedges

1. Put the oil in a large pot over medium-high heat. When it's hot, add the steak, sprinkle with salt and pepper, and cook, turning as necessary, until well browned on all sides but still rare in the middle, 5 to 8 minutes total. Transfer the steak to a plate to rest.

2. Add the five-spice powder to the pot and cook until fragrant, less than 1 minute. Add 10 cups of water and bring to a boil, scraping up any browned bits from the bottom. When the mixture boils, add the tea bags and ginger. Turn off the heat and let steep for 5 to 7 minutes. Remove and discard the tea and ginger. Add the soy sauce and sprinkle with salt and pepper. Taste and adjust the seasoning.

3. Return the stock to a gentle boil. Add the noodles and cook, stirring occasionally, until almost tender, 2 to 3 minutes. Slice the steak against the grain as thinly as you can manage. Add the sliced steak, any accumulated juices, and onion to the stock and turn off the heat.

4. Taste and adjust the seasoning of the stock again, adding more soy sauce or spices if you like. Divide the noodles, steak, and broth evenly among 4 bowls and serve right away, passing the herbs, bean sprouts, chiles, and limes at the table.

MIXED MUSHROOM PHO

makes: 4 servings
time: 45 minutes

Salt

1 large piece kombu

1 ounce dried shiitake mushrooms

2 pounds assorted fresh mushrooms (like king, shiitake, oyster, and button), rinsed

12 ounces carrots, cut into chunks

1 onion, cut into chunks

One 2-inch piece fresh ginger, sliced

4 bay leaves

¼ cup soy sauce

2 teaspoons Chinese five-spice powder

¼ cup good-quality vegetable oil

Pepper

1 pound thin, flat white or brown rice noodles

3 tablespoons fresh lime juice, or to taste

2 scallions, chopped

1 small bunch watercress, rinsed and trimmed

1 fresh hot chile (like Thai or Fresno), sliced, or to taste

1. Bring a large pot of water to boil and salt it. Put the kombu and dried shiitakes in a bowl and cover with 2 cups boiling water from the pot.

2. Trim any tough stems from the fresh mushrooms and reserve them; slice the caps and tender stems. In another pot, combine 6 cups water, the mushroom stems, carrots, onion, ginger, bay leaves, soy sauce, and five-spice powder and bring to a boil. Adjust the heat so the mixture bubbles steadily and let it simmer while you prepare the remaining ingredients, at least 20 minutes or up to 1 hour.

3. Put the oil in a large skillet over medium-high heat. When it's hot, add the sliced mushrooms and sprinkle with salt and pepper. Cook, stirring frequently, until they release their liquid and the pan is dry, 3 to 5 minutes. Lower the heat to medium and cook, stirring once in a while, until the mushrooms shrink and crisp, another 10 to 15 minutes. Turn the heat to low.

4. While the mushrooms crisp, add the noodles to the boiling water and cook, stirring occasionally, for 5 minutes, then start tasting. The noodles are done when they are just tender but a little firmer than you ultimately want them (watch brown rice noodles closely; they go from firm to mushy in a flash). Drain the noodles in a colander, rinse them under cold tap water until cool, and then put them in a bowl covered with cold water until you're ready to assemble the soup.

5. Strain the kombu and mushroom-soaking liquid into the large pot used to cook the noodles. Discard the kombu. Chop the rehydrated shiitake mushrooms, add to the skillet with the sautéed mushrooms, and stir.

6. Strain the stock into the pot with the mushroom-soaking liquid and discard the solids; turn the heat to medium-high. Add a splash of stock to the skillet and scrape up any browned bits from the bottom of the pan, then add the mushroom mixture to the stock along with the lime juice. Bring the mixture to a boil, then turn off the heat. Taste and adjust the seasoning.

7. Drain the noodles, run them under hot tap water, and drain them again. Divide the noodles, scallions, and watercress evenly among 4 bowls and ladle the broth over. Serve right away, passing the chile at the table for garnish.

● PHO
with fresh noodles

makes: 4 servings
time: about 3 hours

8 star anise

4 black peppercorns

4 whole cloves

3 bay leaves, preferably fresh

One 3-inch cinnamon stick

4 garlic cloves, smashed

1 onion, cut into chunks

One 3-inch piece fresh ginger, sliced

4 pounds oxtail or beef bones

3 tablespoons fish sauce

1 tablespoon sugar

Salt

1 pound beef tenderloin

Pepper

1 pound flat, narrow, fresh rice noodles

8 ounces fresh sugar snap peas, sliced

1 large shallot, thinly sliced and separated
into rings

1 bunch fresh cilantro, tough stems removed

1 bunch fresh basil (preferably Thai), tough
stems removed

1 cup fresh mint

2 to 4 fresh hot red or green chiles, sliced

Lime wedges

1. Put the star anise, peppercorns, cloves, bay leaves, and cinnamon stick in a large pot over medium heat. Cook, stirring constantly until toasted and fragrant, 3 to 5 minutes, then remove. Add the garlic, onion, and ginger and cook, stirring rarely and only to prevent scorching, until charred in places but not burned, 3 to 5 minutes. Add the oxtail or bones, toasted spices, and 12 cups water.

2. Bring the mixture to a boil, then adjust the heat so it bubbles gently. Cook, stirring every once in a while and skimming any foam off the top, until the broth is rich and fragrant and reduced by almost half, 2 to 3 hours. Strain through a mesh sieve into another pot, pressing on the solids to extract as much juice as possible. Discard the solids. Add the fish sauce and sugar, and taste and adjust the seasoning. Use the stock right away, or cool and refrigerate for up to 3 days. Either way, skim the fat that rises to the top before proceeding.

3. When you're ready to make the pho, heat the oven to 450°F and bring a large pot of water to a boil and salt it. Pat the tenderloin dry and season very generously with salt and pepper. Put the beef on a rimmed baking sheet and roast until the internal temperature (for rare) is 125°F, 15 to 20 minutes. Transfer the beef to a cutting board to rest. Use a splash of water to deglaze the baking sheet and scrape up any browned bits; add the liquid to the stock.

4. Add the noodles to the boiling water and remove the pot from the heat. Stir to make sure the noodles don't clump, and let steep for 1 minute, then start tasting; they're done when just slightly silky. Drain the noodles into a colander, rinse them under cold tap water until cool, and then put them in a bowl covered with cold water.

5. Return the stock to a boil and slice the tenderloin crosswise against the grain as thin as you can manage. Rewarm the noodles under hot running water, shake off the excess water, then divide evenly among 4 bowls. Ladle boiling stock over the noodles, then top with the sliced beef. Serve right away, passing the peas, shallot, herbs, chiles, and lime at the table for garnish.

Chicken Noodle Soup

When you want chicken, noodles, and broth, you need it. Capture the nostalgia and satisfaction of the ultimate homemade soup with legit shortcuts for Easy, a vegan broth based on chickpeas and vegetables, or a full-on project that includes rich chicken stock and hand-rolled noodles. There's no excuse not to have a bowl on the table tonight.

● HOT AND SOUR CHICKEN NOODLE SOUP
with cracklings

makes: 4 servings
time: 30 minutes

2 tablespoons good-quality vegetable oil

1½ pounds bone-in chicken thighs, drumsticks, or a mixture

Salt and pepper

4 scallions, whites and greens separated and chopped

2 celery stalks, chopped

1 tablespoon chopped garlic

1 tablespoon chopped fresh ginger

5 tablespoons rice vinegar

¼ cup soy sauce

8 ounces dried ramen noodles (3 packages) or any long wheat noodles

1 tablespoon dark sesame oil

1. Heat the oven to 400°F. Put the vegetable oil in a large pot over medium-high heat. Sprinkle the chicken on the skin side with salt and pepper. When the oil is hot, add the chicken, seasoned side down, in a single layer; it's okay if the pot is crowded. Cook, undisturbed, until the chicken is browned in places and the pieces release easily from the pan, 5 to 10 minutes.

2. Transfer the chicken to a plate and put the scallion whites, celery, garlic, and ginger in the hot fat; cook, stirring constantly, until fragrant, less than a minute. Carefully peel off the crisp chicken skin, chop it into bite-sized pieces, and put it in a cast-iron skillet. Transfer to the oven to bake while you finish the soup, checking occasionally to make sure it doesn't burn, until it's as crisp as you like; remove it with a slotted spoon and transfer to a paper towel–lined plate to drain.

3. Add the vinegar, soy sauce, 8 cups water, and lots of pepper to the pot and stir to scrape up any browned bits. Return the chicken to the pot and bring the mixture to a boil, then adjust the heat so it bubbles gently. Cover and cook, undisturbed until the meat is no longer pink, and begins to come off the bones, 15 to 20 minutes.

4. When the chicken is ready, bring the soup to a steady boil and add the noodles. Cook, stirring occasionally, for 3 minutes, then start tasting. When the noodles are tender but still have some bite, turn off the heat. Add the sesame oil and taste and adjust the seasoning. Serve hot, garnished with the scallion greens and chicken skin.

Chicken Soup with
Egg Noodles, page 42

CHICKPEA NOODLE SOUP

makes: 4 servings
time: 2 to 4 hours

1 cup dried chickpeas, washed and picked over

2 garlic cloves, smashed

1 or 2 fresh sage sprigs and 1 tablespoon chopped

4 bay leaves

Salt and pepper

4 tablespoons olive oil, plus more for serving

1 onion, chopped

2 carrots, chopped

4 celery stalks, chopped

1 cup small-cut pasta or broken spaghetti

¼ cup chopped fresh parsley, for garnish

1. Put the chickpeas, garlic, sage, and bay leaves in a large pot and add 10 cups cold water. Bring the water to a boil, then adjust the heat so the water barely bubbles, and cover. Start checking the chickpeas after 30 minutes, and every 15 minutes or so after that. When they can be broken but aren't yet fully tender, add a large pinch of salt and several grinds of black pepper. Depending on the chickpeas, they may take over 4 hours. Continue cooking and checking until the beans are done the way you like them. Taste and adjust the seasoning, then drain, reserving the cooking liquid; discard the bay leaves and sage.

2. Rinse the pot, add the oil, and turn the heat to medium. When it's hot, add the onion, carrots, and celery and sprinkle with salt and pepper. Cook, stirring occasionally, until the vegetables are soft, 5 to 10 minutes.

3. Turn off the heat and add the chickpeas and 8 cups of the cooking water (or all the cooking water plus enough tap water to equal 8 cups). Use a potato masher right in the pot to break up enough of the chickpeas to thicken the liquid, but leave most of them whole.

4. Return the soup to a boil. Add the pasta and cook, stirring occasionally, for 5 minutes, then start tasting. Cook until the pasta is tender but still has some bite. Taste and adjust the seasoning, then serve hot, garnished with the parsley and a drizzle of olive oil.

CHICKEN SOUP
with egg noodles

makes: 4 to 6 servings
time: about 4 hours

1 whole chicken (3 to 4 pounds)

6 tablespoons unsalted butter

Salt and pepper

1 pound chicken wings

2 onions, 1 cut in half and 1 chopped

1 head garlic, cloves separated (don't bother to peel)

4 large celery stalks, 2 whole and 2 chopped, leaves reserved for garnish

3 large carrots, 1 whole and 2 chopped

2 bay leaves

6 fresh parsley sprigs

½ cup dry white wine or water

2 cups flour, or more as needed

2 whole eggs, plus 3 egg yolks

2 tablespoons chopped fresh chives, for garnish

1. Heat the oven to 400°F with a rack in the lower third. Put a large ovenproof skillet on the rack. While it heats, rub the outside of the chicken with 3 tablespoons butter and lots of salt and pepper. When the pan is scorching hot, 10 or 15 minutes later, carefully put the chicken in breast side up. Roast, undisturbed, until an instant-read thermometer inserted in the thickest part of the thigh reads at least 155°F or you cut into a thigh down to the bone and the juices run clear, 40 to 60 minutes, depending on the size of the bird.

2. Remove the pan from the oven; lift the bird to let any accumulated juices inside spill into the pan, then transfer the chicken to a cutting board. Let it rest until it's cool enough to handle. (Now is a good time to prepare the vegetables.) Break apart the carcass and remove as much meat as you can from the bones, leaving the wings intact, reserving the bones, and discarding the skin. Shred or chop the meat into bite-sized pieces, and refrigerate until ready to finish the soup.

3. Put the bones, wings, halved onion, garlic cloves, whole celery, whole carrot, bay leaves, and parsley sprigs in a large pot with 10 cups water. Sprinkle with salt and pepper and bring to a boil. Put the skillet you used for roasting over medium heat and add the wine. Cook, stirring up the browned bits from the bottom of the pan, and pour the mixture into the large pot.

4. Reduce the heat so the liquid bubbles steadily and cook, stirring occasionally, until the liquid reduces by an inch or so and the stock is fragrant, at least 1 hour. Strain into a heatproof bowl, pressing on the vegetables to extract as much liquid as possible; discard the solids. Skim some fat from the top if you'd like and taste and adjust the seasoning. (At this point you can cool the stock and refrigerate for up to 5 days or freeze for several months.)

5. Make the egg noodles: Combine 2 cups flour and 1 teaspoon salt on a counter or large board. Make a well in the middle. Put the eggs and yolks into this well. Beat the eggs with a fork, slowly and gradually incorporating the flour, a little at a time. When it becomes too hard to stir with the fork, use your hands. When all the flour has been incorporated, knead the dough, pushing it against the board and folding it repeatedly, until it is not at all sticky and has become quite stiff. A pastry blade or spatula is handy for scraping up bits of dough as you work; add only small amounts of flour during kneading if you absolutely need it to prevent sticking.

6. Sprinkle the dough with a little flour and cover with plastic or a cloth; let it rest for 30 minutes. (At this point, you may tightly wrap the dough in plastic and refrigerate it for up to 24 hours.)

7. Sprinkle your work surface lightly with flour. Cut off about one-third of the dough; wrap the rest in plastic or cloth while you work. Roll the dough lightly in the flour and use your hands to flatten it into a rectangle. Use a rolling pin to roll the dough out to $\frac{1}{8}$-inch thickness, turning it as you work and sprinkling with flour only as necessary to prevent the dough from sticking. Cover the pasta with a towel and repeat the process with the remaining dough. Trim any rough edges off the sheets, and cut into noodles roughly $\frac{1}{2}$ inch wide and about 2 inches long. Sprinkle with a little additional flour and cover.

8. Put the remaining 3 tablespoons butter in the large pot over medium heat. When it foams, add the chopped onion and sprinkle with salt and pepper. Cook, stirring occasionally, until the onion is soft and starts to turn golden, 5 to 8 minutes. Add the stock and chicken, and bring it just to a boil, then lower the heat so that the liquid bubbles steadily. Add the chopped celery and carrots and cook, stirring occasionally, until the vegetables are as crisp or tender as you like them, anywhere from 10 to 30 minutes.

9. When you are ready to serve, add the noodles to the bubbling stock and cook until as tender or as chewy as you like, 2 to 5 minutes. Remove the pot from the heat, taste, and adjust the seasoning. Garnish with the chives and celery leaves if you like, and serve.

CHICKEN STOCK

The directions for stock in the recipe above does double duty. Follow Steps 1 through 4 to get about 2 quarts of warming, deeply amber chicken stock and at least 4 servings of perfectly cooked meat for salad, sandwiches, or bowls. Or maybe you just want a head start on this chicken soup; the stock will keep in the refrigerator for several days or freeze it for up to 3 months.

Hearty French
Onion Soup,
page 46

Onion Soup

A crock of mediocre bouillon topped with too much cheese used to be the gateway to so-called fancy French cooking. Thankfully, times have changed. For Charred Onion Soup over Torn Bread, I mimic Old Bay seasoning to get lots of flavor in little time. One way to make an interesting soup without a meat-based stock is to combine deeply browned vegetables with a flavorful liquid, like apple cider. Real-deal French onion soup starts with an intense homemade beef broth. Don't even think about using the boxed kind here; you're better off making the Easy or Vegan options.

● CHARRED ONION SOUP
over torn bread

makes: 4 servings
time: about 1 hour, largely unattended

QUICK STALE BREAD Fresh bread is great here, but if you'd like something more like croutons, try the oven-drying technique on page 223.

⅓ cup ketchup

3 tablespoons Dijon mustard

4 bay leaves

1½ teaspoons celery seeds

1½ teaspoons paprika

¾ teaspoon ground ginger

¾ teaspoon ground nutmeg, allspice, or cloves

Salt

One 6-ounce piece Parmesan cheese, with the rind

4 onions, halved and sliced (about 6 cups)

2 tablespoons soy sauce

Pepper

1 cup white wine

1 baguette or other crusty bread, torn into bite-sized pieces

1. Turn on the broiler and position the rack 4 inches below the heat source. Put the ketchup, mustard, bay leaves, celery seeds, paprika, ginger, and nutmeg in a large pot with 8 cups water and a large pinch of salt. Bring to a boil. Grate ¼ cup Parmesan for garnish and put the remaining piece—rind and all—into the pot with the spices. Adjust the heat so the stock bubbles steadily. Let it simmer while you cook the onions, stirring occasionally to keep the cheese from sticking to the bottom of the pot.

2. Put the onions on a rimmed baking sheet with the soy sauce and sprinkle with salt and pepper; toss to coat. Broil, stirring once, until the onions are just soft and charred in places, 12 to 15 minutes. Add the onions to the pot with the stock. Pour the wine onto the hot baking sheet and scrape up any browned bits; add to the pot. Cook, stirring once in a while, until the stock darkens and the onions become silky, about 30 minutes (or up to 45 minutes if you have the time).

3. Discard the bay leaves. Remove the cheese and chop it up, including as much of the rind as you'd like, and return it to the pot; run a potato masher through the pot to break up the onions and thicken the broth. Taste and adjust the seasoning. To serve, put some bread in the bottom of each bowl, ladle in the soup, and garnish with the grated cheese.

MOSTLY ONION SOUP
with cannellini crostini

makes: 4 servings
time: 1 hour

4 large onions, halved and sliced (about 6 cups)

1 leek, sliced and rinsed well

1 fennel bulb, trimmed, halved, and sliced

1 parsnip, peeled and chopped

¼ cup and 2 tablespoons olive oil

Salt and pepper

1 quart apple cider

1 bay leaf

2 fresh thyme sprigs

1 whole-grain baguette or other whole-grain loaf

1½ cups cooked navy or cannellini beans
　　(see page 82; or one 15-ounce can, drained),
　　liquid reserved

1 teaspoon minced garlic

1 tablespoon nutritional yeast

1 tablespoon chopped fresh rosemary

1. Put the onions, leek, fennel, and parsnip in a large pot over medium-high heat. Cook, stirring frequently, until the vegetables are browned in places and sticking to the pan but not burning, about 10 minutes. Add ¼ cup oil and a large pinch of salt and pepper, and continue to cook and stir until the vegetables soften, 3 to 5 minutes more.

2. Pour in half the cider and scrape any browned bits off the bottom of the pan; then add the rest along with 2 cups water, the bay leaf, and thyme. Bring to a boil, then adjust the heat so the mixture bubbles gently. Cover and cook, stirring occasionally, until the soup is flavorful and the vegetables are super soft, at least 20 minutes. Remove the bay leaf and taste and adjust the seasoning.

3. Heat the oven to 400°F. Slice the bread in ½-inch-thick slices, put it on a rimmed baking sheet, and toast, turning as needed, until the slices are lightly browned on both sides, about 10 minutes.

4. Put the beans, garlic, nutritional yeast, rosemary, and the remaining 2 tablespoons oil in a blender or food processor and sprinkle with salt and pepper. Turn the machine on and very slowly add as much of the reserved bean liquid or water as you need to make a smooth but not watery puree. Taste and adjust the seasoning.

5. Spread the bean puree on the toast, and return to the oven until warmed through, 2 to 3 minutes. Serve the soup with the bean toast on top.

HEARTY FRENCH ONION SOUP

makes: 4 servings
time: 3½ hours

3 pounds beef marrow bones or a mixture of
　　marrow and other beef bones

About 1 pound boneless chuck steak,
　　cut into chunks

4 carrots, cut into chunks

4 celery stalks, cut into chunks

2 leeks, cut into chunks and rinsed well

2 bay leaves

1 bunch fresh parsley

2 tablespoons black peppercorns

3 whole cloves

Salt

1 cup red wine

4 tablespoons unsalted butter

4 large onions, halved and sliced

½ baguette or other crusty bread, cut into
　　½-inch slices

2 tablespoons chopped fresh thyme

2 tablespoons cognac or other brandy

½ cup grated Parmesan cheese (about 2 ounces)

1 cup grated Gruyère cheese (about 4 ounces)

Pepper

1. Heat the oven to 400°F. Put the bones, beef, carrots, celery, and leeks in a large roasting pan. Put in the oven and roast until everything is well browned, about 1 hour; shake the pan occasionally and add a little water if necessary to prevent the mixture from burning.

2. Transfer the roasted meat and vegetables to a large stockpot along with 1 bay leaf, about two-thirds of the parsley, and the peppercorns and cloves; sprinkle with 2 teaspoons salt. Add 3 quarts of water. Bring nearly to a boil, then partially cover and adjust the heat so the mixture just barely bubbles. Meanwhile put the roasting pan on 2 burners over medium heat. Add the wine and cook until it bubbles, scraping off the browned bits from the bottom. Transfer the liquid to the stock-pot. Cook the stock, skimming off any foam that rises to the top, until the meat falls from the bones, 1 to 2 hours. Chop the remaining parsley.

3. Fish the bones out of the stock. When cool enough to handle, scrape any meat and marrow from inside and out, and reserve. Strain the stock through a mesh sieve, pressing on the solids to extract as much liquid as possible. Discard the solids and skim the fat off the top. (The stock can be made to this point and refrigerated for several days or frozen for 3 months. This makes about 2 quarts and you'll need 6 cups for the soup.)

4. Put the butter in a large pot over medium heat. When it melts, add the onions and sprinkle with salt and pepper. Cook, stirring occasionally, until they're soft and beginning to brown, 10 to 15 minutes. Reduce the heat and continue cooking, stirring occasionally, until they turn jammy. This can take up to 1 hour total; don't rush. Add the reserved meat and marrow from making the stock.

5. Reheat the oven to 400°F. Put the bread slices on a rimmed baking sheet and bake, turning half-way through, until crisp and lightly golden.

6. Meanwhile, add 6 cups stock to the onion mixture and bring to a boil. Reduce the heat so the soup bubbles very gently. Add the thyme, the remaining bay leaf, most of the remaining parsley, and the cognac, and season with salt and pepper. Cook for 15 minutes, then remove the bay leaf. (At this point, you may refrigerate the soup, covered, for up to 2 days; reheat before proceeding.)

7. Ladle the soup into 4 ovenproof bowls, and top each with a few croutons, then sprinkle with the cheese. Put the bowls in a roasting pan or on a sturdy baking sheet and bake just long enough to melt the cheese, 5 to 10 minutes. Serve right away, sprinkled with some reserved parsley.

BEEF STOCK

I see no point in making beef stock unless you include at least some marrow bones in the mix. For the richest stock imaginable—or to make a major component of Hearty French Onion Soup ahead of time—follow the directions through Step 3. In fact, this stock is so good, you may as well double the recipe. Then use what you need for the soup and freeze the rest for up to 3 months.

Gumbo

What distinguishes gumbo from other soups and stews is how it's thickened: either the flour-and-fat thickening agent known as a *roux,* or by harnessing the less appealing qualities of okra. For huge timesaving, you can toast the flour for the roux in a dry skillet while you cook the sausage. This takes some attention, but you'll end up with the classic flavor and color. The Vegan recipe takes the other, lighter traditional path to thicken the stew, then keeps the fresh theme going with herbs and ripe summer produce. The rich Full-On Gumbo with Cayenne Hush Puppies is loaded with chicken, seafood, and a special Louisiana-style hamlike product called tasso.

● SAUSAGE GUMBO

makes: 4 servings
time: 30 minutes

⅓ cup flour

1½ pounds andouille or Italian sausages, cut into bite-sized pieces

1 red onion, chopped

2 tablespoons olive oil

1 green bell pepper, cored and chopped

4 celery stalks, chopped

Salt and pepper

2 tablespoons tomato paste

2 teaspoons dried oregano

¼ teaspoon cayenne, or more to taste

1. Put the flour in a medium skillet over medium-low heat. Cook, stirring frequently with a spatula and adjusting the heat to prevent scorching, until the mixture turns golden brown and no white remains, 5 to 10 minutes. Taste the flour carefully, it will be very hot: it should be pleasantly nutty and not at all like raw flour.

2. Meanwhile, put the sausage and onion in a large pot over medium-high heat. Cook, stirring occasionally, until the onion is soft and the sausage is browned in spots, 5 to 10 minutes.

3. Scrape the toasted flour into the pot with the sausage mixture. Add the olive oil, bell pepper, and celery and sprinkle with salt and pepper. Cook, stirring occasionally, until the vegetables soften, 3 to 5 minutes. Add the tomato paste, oregano, and cayenne and cook, stirring constantly, until the mixture darkens, 2 to 3 minutes.

4. Add 4 cups water and bring to a boil. Adjust the heat so the mixture bubbles steadily and cook until the soup is slightly thickened, 10 to 15 minutes. Taste, adjust the seasoning, and serve hot.

● Okra Gumbo, page 50,
  pictured with
● Cayenne Hush Puppies,
  page 50

OKRA GUMBO

makes: 4 servings
time: about 1 hour

¼ cup olive oil, or more as needed

1½ pounds okra, left whole but with tops trimmed

Salt and pepper

1 large onion, chopped

1 red bell pepper, cored and chopped

1 celery stalk, chopped

2 tablespoons chopped garlic

1 or 2 small hot red chiles (like Thai or serrano), seeded if you like and chopped

About 2 pounds ripe tomatoes, chopped (or one 28-ounce can diced, with the juice)

2 bay leaves

1 tablespoon chopped fresh oregano

1 tablespoon chopped fresh thyme

Chopped fresh parsley, for garnish

1. Put the oil in a large pot over medium-high heat. When it's hot, add the okra and sprinkle with salt and pepper. Cook, stirring once in a while, until browned and crisp in places, 3 to 5 minutes. Remove with a slotted spoon and lower the heat to medium.

2. Add the onion, bell pepper, celery, garlic, and as much chile as you'd like. Sprinkle with salt and pepper and cook, stirring occasionally, until the vegetables soften and turn golden, 5 to 8 minutes. Add the tomatoes and herbs to the pot along with 2 cups water.

3. Bring the mixture to a boil, then lower the heat so it bubbles gently. Cook, stirring occasionally, until the tomatoes start to break down, about 10 minutes. Add the okra and continue to cook, stirring less frequently, until the okra is very tender and the stew has thickened, another 10 to 20 minutes. Taste, adjust the seasoning, remove the bay leaves, and serve hot, garnished with parsley.

FULL-ON GUMBO
with cayenne hush puppies

makes: 6 to 8 servings
time: about 2 hours

6 tablespoons good-quality vegetable oil, plus more for deep-frying

4 bone-in chicken thighs (about 1½ pounds)

Salt and pepper

1 pound medium shrimp, unpeeled

3 bay leaves

4 ounces tasso, thinly sliced

1 cup flour

1 large onion, chopped

1 green bell pepper, cored and chopped

2 celery stalks, chopped

2 tablespoons chopped garlic

2 tablespoons chopped fresh oregano

1½ cups cornmeal

1 tablespoon baking powder

½ teaspoon cayenne, or to taste

1 cup milk

3 scallions, chopped

1 egg

24 oysters, shucked, liquor reserved

8 ounces lump crabmeat, picked over

1. Put 2 tablespoons oil in a large pot over medium heat. When it's hot, sprinkle the chicken with salt and pepper and put it skin side down in the pot. Cook undisturbed until the pieces are browned and release easily, 5 to 10 minutes. Turn and cook until the meat is firm but still a little pink at the bone, another 5 to 10 minutes. Transfer it to a plate and remove the pot from the heat but don't clean it out.

2. While the chicken cooks, peel the shrimp. Put the shrimp in a bowl and refrigerate; put the shells in a large saucepan. Add 4 cups water and the bay leaves, sprinkle with salt and pepper, and bring to a boil. When the chicken is cool enough to handle, remove the meat and put in a bowl; add the skin and bones to the pan with the shrimp shells. Adjust the heat so the stock bubbles steadily and cook, stirring occasionally until the gumbo is ready to assemble, up to 30 minutes.

3. Add the remaining 4 tablespoons oil to the fat in the large pot and set over medium heat. When it's hot, add the tasso and cook, stirring frequently to scrape up any browned bits, until it darkens and releases some fat. Transfer to the bowl with the chicken. Add ½ cup flour and stir until smooth; the mixture (a roux) should coat the back of a spoon; if not, add more oil 1 tablespoon at a time. Adjust the heat so the roux sizzles but doesn't burn and cook, stirring frequently, until it's darkened to the color of iced tea and smells nutty, 10 to 20 minutes.

4. When the roux is ready, add the onion, bell pepper, celery, garlic, and oregano. Sprinkle with salt and pepper, and cook, stirring frequently, until the vegetables are soft, 5 to 10 minutes. Carefully strain the stock into the roux and stir until smooth. Add the chicken and tasso to the pot and adjust the heat so the mixture bubbles steadily. Cover and cook, stirring occasionally, until the liquid thickens, about 5 minutes. Keep warm. (Or cool and refrigerate the gumbo for up to 2 days; gently reheat before proceeding.)

5. When you're ready to eat, make the hush puppy batter: Mix the cornmeal, remaining ½ cup flour, the baking powder, cayenne, and a large pinch of salt together in a bowl. Beat the milk, scallions, and egg and pour the mixture into the dry ingredients, stirring just to combine (do not beat).

6. Heat the oven to 200°F. Put a wire rack on a rimmed baking sheet. Put 2 to 3 inches oil in a large pot and bring to 375°F over medium heat. When the oil is hot, drop in some of the batter by the tablespoonful, taking care not to crowd them. Keep the oil bubbling gently and fry the hush puppies, turning until browned and crisp all over, about 2 minutes total. Transfer to the wire rack with a slotted spoon and put in the oven to keep warm. Repeat with the remaining batter.

7. Uncover the gumbo and add the shrimp, oysters, and crabmeat; raise the heat to a gentle boil and cook, stirring now and then, until the seafood is opaque but not overcooked, 3 to 5 minutes. Taste and adjust the seasoning, and serve right away. Pass the hush puppies at the table.

● Perihuela, page 55

Seafood Soup

These are spiced, brothy, briny soups from around the world. If you haven't had it, Perihuela is similar to the Bouillabaisse on page 250, but the different flavorings and accompaniments—and pedigree—make them unique eating experiences. The Watercress and Seaweed Soup with Yuba is equally interesting. This is one of a couple vegan recipes in the book that calls for chewy and mild tofu skin, known as yuba, one of my all-time favorite foods. Since making shrimp or stock is neither fast nor easy for weeknights, the secret way to crank up flavor in a hurry is to simmer anchovies, soy sauce, and lemon juice in water along with peeled shrimp. Egg drops and fresh wonton "noodles" make the Easy soup a meal.

SHRIMP AND EGG DROP SOUP with wonton ribbons

makes: 4 servings
time: 20 minutes

2 tablespoons good-quality vegetable oil

4 scallions, white and green parts separated and chopped

1 tablespoon chopped garlic

1 tablespoon chopped fresh ginger

Salt and pepper

2 anchovy fillets, or to taste

¼ cup fresh lemon juice, or to taste

1½ pounds peeled medium shrimp

16 wonton skins, cut into wide ribbons

4 eggs

1. Put the oil in a large pot over medium heat. When it's hot, add the scallion whites, garlic, and ginger and sprinkle with salt and pepper. Cook, stirring frequently, until the aromatics are soft and beginning to color, 3 to 5 minutes. Add the anchovies and cook, mashing with a spoon until they've dissolved.

2. Add the lemon juice and scrape up any browned bits off the bottom. Add the shrimp and 7 cups water and bring the mixture to a boil. Continue cooking until the shrimp just begin to turn opaque, a minute or 2.

3. Add the wonton skins and adjust the heat so the broth bubbles gently. Put the eggs into a bowl and beat with a fork. Pour the eggs into the pot in a slow stream, stirring constantly. You want them to scramble softly and form ribbons, so it's essential to keep stirring until the eggs are cooked, 1 to 2 minutes. Remove from the heat, taste, and adjust the seasoning. Serve right away, garnished with the scallion greens.

WATERCRESS AND SEAWEED SOUP with yuba

makes: 4 servings
time: 45 minutes

About 6 ounces tofu skins (see page 254)

1 piece kombu, 4 to 6 inches long

One 2-inch piece fresh ginger, peeled and sliced

½ cup dried seaweed (like wakame or hijiki, or a combination), about ½ ounce

4 cups watercress, rinsed, trimmed, and chopped

3 tablespoons soy sauce

1 tablespoon rice vinegar

1 teaspoon mirin (see page 290)

Pinch cayenne (optional)

Salt and pepper

2 scallions, chopped

Dark sesame oil, for drizzling

1. Put the tofu skins in a bowl, cover with warm water, and soak until pliable and easy to separate, about 10 minutes. Drain and pat dry with paper towels, then slice into ribbons.

2. Put the kombu, ginger, and 8 cups water in a medium saucepan over medium heat. As soon as it begins to steam, turn off the heat and let steep until the kombu is tender and the broth flavorful, 10 to 15 minutes; do not allow the mixture to boil. Remove the kombu and chop into bite-sized pieces; discard the ginger. (The dashi can be cooled and refrigerated for up to 2 days; reheat before proceeding.)

3. Put the dried seaweed in the hot stock. Soak until tender, 2 to 3 minutes. Add the chopped kombu, tofu skins, the watercress, soy sauce, rice vinegar, mirin, and cayenne if using and season with salt and pepper. Put over medium heat so that it's steaming but never bubbling and cook until the tofu skins are warmed through and tender, 3 to 5 minutes. Taste and adjust the seasoning. Ladle the steaming soup into 4 bowls, garnish with the scallions and a drizzle of sesame oil, and serve hot.

● PERIHUELA

makes: 4 servings
time: 1 hour

ABOUT THE CHILES Ají panca is a fruity chile that gives Peruvian cooking its unique flavor. It's sold in South American grocery stores and online in several forms—dried, ground, or paste. Ground pasillas or smoky dried ground chipotles are fine substitutes. Whatever you find will work, just be sure to taste as you go since the potency varies.

8 ounces unpeeled large shrimp, rinsed

1 pound bones and/or cleaned heads from any firm, white fish

2 onions, 1 cut into chunks (don't bother to peel) and 1 chopped

2 fresh cilantro sprigs and ¼ cup chopped fresh, for garnish

1 garlic clove, smashed, and 1 tablespoon chopped

1 cup dry white wine

2 bay leaves

2 tablespoons good-quality vegetable oil, plus more for frying

4 ounces purple potatoes, scrubbed

Salt

1 tablespoon chopped fresh ginger

Pepper

1 tablespoon chopped fresh oregano, or 1 teaspoon dried

1 teaspoon ground cumin

1 teaspoon ají panca powder or paste, or ground pasilla chile

1 pound boneless, flaky white fish (like cod or sea bass), cut into 2-inch pieces

8 ounces lump crabmeat

20 littleneck clams, scrubbed

Lime wedges

1. Peel the shrimp and put the shells in a large pot with the fish bones, unpeeled onion, cilantro sprigs, smashed garlic clove, ½ cup wine, and 1 bay leaf. Add 6 cups water and bring just about to a boil, then adjust the heat so the mixture bubbles gently. Cook until very fragrant, 50 to 55 minutes. Cool slightly, then strain, pressing the solids to extract as much liquid as possible. (Use immediately or refrigerate for up to 3 days or freeze for up to a few weeks.)

2. Put 2 to 3 inches oil in a large pot over medium heat and bring to 350°F. Put a wire rack on a rimmed baking sheet. Use a mandoline or sharp knife to slice the potatoes as thin as you can manage, no more than ⅛ inch thick. When the oil is ready, fry the potatoes in batches until golden and crisp, 3 to 5 minutes. Remove the chips to the wire rack with a slotted spoon or strainer. Sprinkle with salt.

3. Heat 2 tablespoons oil in a large skillet over medium heat. When it's hot, add the chopped onion, chopped garlic, and ginger and sprinkle with salt and pepper. Cook, stirring occasionally, until the onion is soft and golden, 5 to 8 minutes. Add the oregano, cumin, and ají panca and cook until the spices are fragrant and have darkened, about 1 minute.

4. Pour in the remaining ½ cup white wine and cook, scraping any browned bits off the bottom of the pan, until the wine has mostly evaporated. Add the remaining bay leaf and the stock and bring the mixture to a boil.

5. Adjust the heat so the soup bubbles gently. Carefully lower the fish, shrimp, crab, and clams into the pan and cook without stirring until the fish is opaque and the clams have opened, 8 to 10 minutes. Taste and adjust the seasoning. Divide the soup among 4 bowls, top with the fried potatoes and cilantro, and serve right away, passing the lime wedges at the table.

Chowder

Always hearty and filling, chowder usually starts with a béchamel-like combination of flour, fat, and milk. Since you'll be chopping a lot for the Corn-and-Cheddar Chowder, take a shortcut, skip the roux, and use the thickening power of potatoes for the same effect in a fraction of the time. The Vegan chowder also makes good use of surprise ingredients—like edamame, jicama, and horseradish. Obviously a clam chowder in this book is mandatory. But instead of bacon, crisped fresh Mexican-style chorizo provides smokiness, which is closer to the earliest New England stews made with the Portuguese linguiça sausage.

● CORN-AND-CHEDDAR CHOWDER

makes: 4 servings
time: 30 minutes

12 ounces russet or Yukon Gold potatoes, peeled and cut into 1-inch chunks

1 tablespoon chopped garlic

6 cups milk, or more as needed

Salt and pepper

2 bay leaves

3 tablespoons unsalted butter

4 cups frozen corn kernels (or shuck 4 ears fresh corn)

2 celery stalks, chopped

3 tablespoons flour

6 ounces grated white or yellow cheddar cheese (about 1½ cups), plus more for garnish

2 tablespoons chopped fresh chives, for garnish

1. Put the potatoes and garlic in a large pot with the milk over medium heat; sprinkle with salt and pepper. When the liquid begins to boil, adjust the heat so the liquid bubbles gently and add the bay leaves. Cover and cook, stirring occasionally to prevent the milk from scalding, until the potatoes are tender but not yet breaking apart, 10 to 15 minutes.

2. Melt the butter in a medium skillet over medium heat. Add the corn and celery and sprinkle generously with salt and pepper. Cook, stirring occasionally, until the celery softens and the corn is heated through, 5 to 8 minutes. Add the flour and cook, stirring constantly, until the mixture darkens slightly and smells toasted, another 3 to 5 minutes.

3. Add the corn mixture to the potatoes along with the cheese. Cook, stirring frequently, until the soup is steaming and has thickened a bit, 5 to 10 minutes. Taste and adjust the seasoning, remove the bay leaves, then garnish with more black pepper, cheese, and the chives, and serve.

OFFBEAT VEGETABLE CHOWDER

makes: 4 servings
time: 30 minutes

CHIVE TALKING My favorite way to use the leftover chive oil (which keeps in the fridge for about a week) is to make mayonnaise (see page 216) or stir some into simply cooked grains or beans.

½ cup and 2 tablespoons olive oil

1 large leek, green and white parts separated and chopped

Salt and pepper

2 tablespoons flour

8 ounces jicama, peeled and chopped

8 ounces kohlrabi, peeled and chopped

8 ounces celery root, peeled and chopped

4 cups unsweetened nut milk (like almond or cashew)

½ cup fresh chives, cut into chunks

2 cups frozen edamame

¼ cup jarred horseradish, or to taste

1. Heat 2 tablespoons oil in a large pot over medium heat. When it's hot, add the leek and sprinkle with salt and pepper. Cook, stirring occasionally, until the leek softens, 3 to 5 minutes, then add the flour and cook, stirring often, until it's golden, another 3 to 5 minutes.

2. Add the jicama, kohlrabi, celery root, nut milk, and enough water to just submerge the vegetables if necessary. Bring the mixture to a boil, then adjust the heat so it bubbles gently. Cover and cook, stirring once in a while until the vegetables are tender but not yet falling apart, 10 to 15 minutes. Remove about 1½ cups of the soup from the pot and mash it in a small bowl with a fork or a potato masher. (Or carefully puree it in a blender or food processor.) Return the puree to the soup, cover, and keep warm.

3. Put the chives and remaining ½ cup oil in a blender and blend until smooth. Let the mixture infuse while you finish the soup.

4. Uncover the soup and add the edamame and horseradish. Cook until the beans are heated through and the soup has thickened a bit, 3 to 5 minutes. Taste and adjust the seasoning, mindful that the horseradish heat will build. Strain the chive oil through a fine-mesh sieve and drizzle some over the soup as a garnish.

● NORTH AMERICAN CLAM CHOWDER

makes: 4 servings
time: 1 hour

3 tablespoons olive oil

1 onion, chopped

2 garlic cloves, sliced, and 1 teaspoon minced

1½ cups white wine

About 4 pounds large clams (like quahog or little necks), scrubbed well

6 ounces fresh chorizo

1 large shallot, chopped

1 fennel bulb, trimmed and chopped

2 large Yukon Gold potatoes (about 1 pound), peeled and cut into ½-inch chunks

Salt

2 cups heavy cream

Pepper

2 tablespoons chopped fresh cilantro

2 teaspoons grated lemon zest

1 teaspoon grated lime zest

1 tablespoon fresh lime juice, or to taste

1. Put 2 tablespoons oil in a large pot over medium heat. When it's hot, add the onion and sliced garlic and cook, stirring occasionally, until they begin to soften, 3 to 5 minutes. Add the wine and nestle in the clams; bring to a boil, and cover. Cook, shaking the pot occasionally, until the clams open, 5 to 15 minutes, depending on how big they are.

2. When they're cool enough to handle, remove the clams from their shells (discard any that didn't open), chop the meat, and transfer to a bowl. Strain the cooking mixture through a fine-mesh sieve, reserving the liquid. Wipe out the pot.

3. Return the pot to medium heat and squeeze the chorizo from its casings into the pot. Cook until crisp, stirring frequently to break the sausage into pieces, 5 to 10 minutes. Remove with a slotted spoon and cook the shallot, fennel, and potatoes in the chorizo fat until the vegetables soften, 5 to 10 minutes. Add 2 cups of the clam cooking liquid (or the cooking liquid plus enough water to total 2 cups), sprinkle with salt, and bring to a boil. Cook, stirring occasionally, until the potatoes can just be pierced with a fork, 10 to 15 minutes. (At this point, you can refrigerate the soup and its components, covered, for up to several hours; reheat before proceeding.)

4. Add the cream, clams, and chorizo to the pot; sprinkle with salt and pepper. Adjust the heat so the soup barely bubbles without coming to a full boil, and cook, stirring frequently until thickened and heated through, 3 to 5 minutes. Taste and adjust the seasoning and keep warm.

5. Combine the remaining tablespoon oil, the minced garlic, cilantro, lemon and lime zests, and lime juice in a small bowl. Taste and adjust the seasoning. Divide the soup among 4 bowls, garnish with the herb mixture, and serve hot.

Vegetable Soup

Any of these hearty, mixed vegetable soups will make a satisfying dinner. The Senegalese Peanut Soup is a welcome addition to the everyday rotation, especially if you use the same work-around as many home cooks in Senegal and substitute fish sauce for the traditional (and harder to find) fermented seasoning. The Vegan recipe is a full-blown minestrone, with greens, beans, and pasta as flexible components. And think of Borscht with Beef as a uniquely extravagant beet soup, with all sorts of great, meaty flavors and finishing textures.

● SENEGALESE PEANUT SOUP

makes: 4 servings
time: 35 minutes

2 tablespoons good-quality vegetable oil

1 onion, chopped

2 tablespoons chopped fresh ginger

½ cup roasted peanuts, chopped

¼ teaspoon cayenne, or to taste

Salt and pepper

Two 10- to 12-ounce bags frozen butternut squash

One 16-ounce bag frozen collard greens or kale

One 14-ounce can diced tomatoes, with their juice

½ cup peanut butter, chunky or smooth, or to taste

3 tablespoons fish sauce, or to taste

Lime wedges

1. Put the oil in a large pot over medium heat. When it's hot, add the onion and ginger and cook, stirring occasionally, until the onion is soft, 3 to 5 minutes. Add the roasted peanuts and the cayenne and sprinkle with salt and pepper. Cook until fragrant, just a minute or 2.

2. Add the squash, greens, and tomatoes and 5 cups water. Bring to a boil, then adjust the heat so the soup bubbles gently. Cook, stirring occasionally and breaking up the tomatoes, until the vegetables are cooked through, 15 to 20 minutes.

3. Add the peanut butter and fish sauce and stir until they're fully incorporated. Taste and adjust seasoning, adding more peanut butter or fish sauce if you like. Serve hot, passing the limes at the table.

Hearty Minestrone,
page 62

● HEARTY MINESTRONE

makes: 4 servings
time: about 1 hour

½ ounce dried porcini mushrooms

2 cups boiling water

¼ cup olive oil, plus more for drizzling

1 onion, chopped

1 carrot, chopped

1 celery stalk, chopped

1 tablespoon chopped garlic

Salt and pepper

One 28-ounce can diced tomatoes

1 pound sturdy, leafy greens (like kale or escarole), chopped

2 cups cooked kidney beans, chickpeas, or cannellini beans (see page 82; or one 15-ounce can), drained

8 ounces small-cut whole wheat pasta (like macaroni, orzo, or ditalini)

1. Put the dried mushrooms in a medium bowl and add the boiling water. Soak until soft and pliable, 5 to 30 minutes, depending on the thickness. Lift the mushrooms from the liquid with a slotted spoon or your fingers, leaving any sediment in the bowl and reserve the soaking water. Chop the mushrooms.

2. Put the oil in a large pot over medium heat. When it's hot, add the onion, carrot, celery, garlic, and chopped mushrooms and sprinkle with salt and pepper. Cook, stirring frequently, until the vegetables are soft and golden, 15 to 25 minutes.

3. Pour in the mushroom soaking liquid, leaving the sediment behind, and add 3 cups water; stir to scrape up any browned bits from the bottom of the pot. Add the tomatoes, greens, and beans, and bring the mixture to a boil; adjust the heat so the soup bubbles steadily. Cover and cook, stirring occasionally, until the tomatoes break down and the greens are almost tender, 5 to 20 minutes, depending on the green. (At this point, you can cool the soup and refrigerate for up to 3 days.)

4. Add the pasta and raise the heat if necessary to keep the mixture bubbling. Cook, stirring occasionally, until the noodles are tender but still have some bite; start checking after 5 minutes. Taste, adjust the seasoning, and serve drizzled with more olive oil.

● **BORSCHT** with beef

makes: 4 to 6 servings
time: 3 hours, largely unattended

2 tablespoons good-quality vegetable oil

2 pounds bone-in beef chuck roast

Salt and pepper

1 onion, chopped

1 celery stalk, chopped

1 carrot, chopped

2 bay leaves

8 cups beef stock (see page 47)

4 tablespoons unsalted butter

2 cups shredded green or savoy cabbage

2 tablespoons chopped garlic

1 Granny Smith or other tart apple, peeled, cored, and chopped

¼ cup red wine vinegar

1 pound waxy fingerling potatoes, chopped

1½ pounds beets, peeled and grated

Sour cream, for serving

¼ cup chopped fresh dill, for garnish

1. Put the oil in a large pot over medium-high heat. When it's hot, add the beef, and sprinkle with salt and pepper. Cook, turning once, until browned on both sides, 8 to 12 minutes total. Transfer to a plate.

2. Pour off all but 3 tablespoons fat. Add the onion, celery, and carrot to the pot and sprinkle with salt and pepper. Cook, stirring often, until soft, 3 to 5 minutes. Return the beef to the pot and add the bay leaves and stock. Bring to a boil, then adjust the heat so the mixture bubbles gently. Cover and cook, stirring occasionally and skimming any foam that rises to the top, until the beef is very tender and nearly falling off the bone, 1½ to 2 hours.

3. Remove the beef, and when cool enough to handle, shred the meat and discard the bones. Remove and discard the bay leaves. (At this point, you can cool the soup and meat and refrigerate separately for up to 3 days.)

4. Melt the butter in a large skillet over medium-high heat. Add the cabbage and garlic, sprinkle with salt and pepper, and cook, stirring occasionally, until the cabbage is tender, 10 to 15 minutes. Add the apple and cook, stirring, until it starts to soften, 3 to 5 minutes. Turn off the heat and stir in the vinegar, scraping up any browned bits from the bottom of the pan.

5. Bring the stock to a boil and add the cabbage mixture, the potatoes, and beets and adjust the heat so the mixture bubbles gently. Cook until the potatoes are tender, 15 to 20 minutes. Return the beef to the pot, and taste and adjust the seasoning. Serve the soup hot, garnished with sour cream and dill.

Smoky Three-Bean Soup with Tomatillo Salsa, page 66

Bean Soup

Three versions of a winter workhorse keep things interesting without getting too heavy. Only the Chickpea Soup with Colorful Garnishes requires cooking the beans from scratch; it's the backbone of the broth. (Skip the bean-peeling step if it's a deal-breaker.) The designated Vegan recipe takes all that you love about classic three-bean salad, puts it in a pot, and then adds a fresh and creamy tomatillo salsa. Fagioli e Pasta—where the Italian macaroni-and-beans tradition is skewed toward the legumes—is flexible enough for ease since the new proportions can become a template for all sorts of combinations of components.

● FAGIOLI E PASTA

makes: 4 servings
time: 30 minutes

3 tablespoons olive oil, plus more for serving

2 tablespoons chopped garlic

Salt and pepper

1 tablespoon chopped fresh rosemary

One 14-ounce can tomato puree

3 cups cooked pinto beans (see page 82; or two 15-ounce cans), drained

½ cup small-cut pasta (like macaroni or small shells)

1 cup grated Parmesan cheese (about 4 ounces)

1. Put 3 tablespoons olive oil in a large pot over medium-high heat. When it's hot, add the garlic and sprinkle with salt and pepper. Cook, stirring occasionally, until it softens, 3 to 5 minutes. Add the rosemary and stir until fragrant, less than a minute.

2. Add the tomatoes, and cook, scraping any browned bits off the bottom of the pot. Add 6 cups water and raise the heat to high. When the mixture boils, stir in the beans and pasta. Adjust the heat so it bubbles steadily. Cook, stirring occasionally, for 5 minutes, then start tasting the pasta; it should be tender but still have some bite. If the soup starts to look dry, add water a little at a time.

3. When the pasta is ready, stir in half the cheese and turn off the heat. Taste, adjust the seasoning, and serve, garnished with the remaining cheese and a drizzle of olive oil.

● SMOKY THREE-BEAN SOUP
with tomatillo salsa

makes: 4 servings
time: 45 minutes

5 tablespoons olive oil

1 onion, chopped

1 tablespoon chopped garlic and 1 clove, peeled

Salt and pepper

1 teaspoon smoked paprika

1 teaspoon ground cumin

2 canned chipotle chiles, chopped, with adobo
    sauce to taste

1½ cups cooked kidney beans (see page 82;
    or one 15-ounce can), drained

1½ cups cooked chickpeas (see page 82;
    or one 15-ounce can), drained

2 cups husked and chopped tomatillos

3 scallions, finely chopped

1 ripe avocado, pitted, peeled, and cut into chunks

¼ cup chopped fresh cilantro leaves

3 tablespoons fresh lime juice, or to taste

8 ounces green beans, trimmed and cut into
    bite-sized pieces

4 cups tortilla chips (optional)

1. Put 3 tablespoons oil in a large pot over medium heat. When it's hot, add the onion and chopped garlic and sprinkle with salt and pepper. Cook, stirring occasionally, until the onion is silky and golden, 8 to 10 minutes. Add the paprika, cumin, chiles, and adobo sauce and cook until fragrant and slightly darkened, 2 to 3 minutes.

2. Add the kidney beans, chickpeas, and 6 cups water. Bring the soup to a boil, then adjust the heat so it bubbles gently. Cook, stirring once in a while, until the beans are breaking apart and the flavors have had a chance to blend, 15 to 20 minutes.

3. Put the tomatillos, scallions, avocado, cilantro, remaining garlic clove, and the lime juice in a blender and sprinkle with salt and pepper. Puree until smooth. Taste and adjust the seasoning.

4. When the soup is ready, add the green beans and return the liquid to a gentle bubble. Cover and cook until they're tender, 5 to 10 minutes. Taste and adjust the seasoning, adding more adobo sauce if desired. Serve the soup garnished with a spoonful of the tomatillo salsa, and with chips if you'd like.

CHICKPEA SOUP
with colorful garnishes

makes: 4 servings
time: 1½ to 3 hours

1 lemon

½ cup olive oil

2 cups dried chickpeas, washed and picked over

¼ cup tahini, with 1 tablespoon of the oil

Salt and pepper

¼ cup fresh cilantro

½ cup pomegranate seeds

1. Peel the lemon in long strips and remove any remaining white pith with a knife. Juice the lemon and reserve 3 tablespoons. Use a rolling pin to pound the lemon zest and release the oils. Put the strips in a small saucepan with the olive oil over medium heat. Let the mixture bubble gently for 15 minutes, then remove from the heat. When cooled to room temperature, transfer the pot to the refrigerator to continue steeping for up to 8 hours. Remove the lemon zest and store the infused oil in a sealed container in the refrigerator for up to 3 days.

2. Put the chickpeas in a large pot with enough water to cover by at least 3 inches and turn the heat to medium-high. Bring to a boil, then adjust the heat so the water bubbles gently. Cover and cook, stirring occasionally, until the chickpeas are very tender, anywhere from 45 minutes to 3 hours, depending on the beans.

3. Drain the chickpeas and reserve the cooking liquid. When they're cool enough to handle, pinch off the outer skin from each bean; it's fine if the beans don't stay intact. Discard the skins.

4. Puree the chickpeas until smooth in a food processor (add a little of the cooking liquid if necessary to help the machine do its work). Clean out the pot and add the puree and the reserved cooking liquid. Bring to a simmer, then adjust the heat so that the soup bubbles gently. Add the tahini and reserved lemon juice and whisk until smooth. Continue cooking, stirring occasionally and adding a splash of water if the soup is too thick, until thick and smooth, 3 to 5 minutes. Sprinkle with salt and pepper. Taste, and adjust the seasoning. To serve, divide among 4 bowls, drizzle with the lemon oil and garnish with the cilantro and pomegranate seeds.

Chili

You can't hope to please everyone with only three interpretations, so I had to make some choices: I nod to New Mexico with an Easy chili stir-fry; the bean- and tomato-free All Out number courts the Lone Star state; and I help vegans rise above the fray with Tempeh-Peanut Chili, the least traditional of the three.

● SANTA FE–STYLE GREEN CHILE STIR-FRY

makes: 4 servings
time: 30 minutes

2 tablespoons good-quality vegetable oil, or more as needed

1½ pounds boneless chicken thighs, cut into bite-sized pieces

Salt and pepper

1 tablespoon ground cumin

2 large mild green chiles (like Hatch or poblano), seeded and sliced

1 onion, halved and sliced

4 garlic cloves, sliced

1 jalapeño, seeded and chopped

¼ cup chopped fresh cilantro, for garnish

1. Put 2 tablespoons oil in a large skillet over medium-high heat. When the oil is hot, add the chicken pieces all at once, sprinkle with salt and pepper, and cook, stirring occasionally, until they release their liquid, just a couple minutes.

2. Continue to cook, stirring more frequently, until the chicken browns and crisps in places, 15 to 20 minutes. Add the cumin and stir until fragrant, less than a minute. Transfer the chicken to a plate.

3. If the pan isn't glistening, swirl in another tablespoon or so of oil. Add the chiles, onion, garlic, and jalapeño and sprinkle with salt and pepper. Cook, stirring occasionally, until the vegetables soften, 3 to 5 minutes. Pour in 1 cup water and scrape up any browned bits from the bottom of the pan; cook and stir once in a while until the vegetables are soft and silky, another 3 to 5 minutes.

4. Return the chicken to the skillet. Cook until the sauce is thick and glossy, another 2 to 3 minutes. Taste, adjust the seasoning, and serve, garnished with cilantro.

● Texas Red with Tamale
Dumplings, page 71

● TEMPEH-PEANUT CHILI

makes: 4 to 6 servings
time: 1 hour

SPICE SUBSTITUTE Omit the first three ingredients and Step 1 and use 2 tablespoons good-quality chili powder, if you like.

½ ounce dried chiles (like ancho, chipotle, or pasilla)

1 teaspoon cumin seeds

½ teaspoon coriander seeds

3 tablespoons good-quality vegetable oil

8 ounces tempeh

2 large carrots, chopped

1 celery stalk, chopped

1 onion, chopped

1 green bell pepper, cored and chopped

Salt and pepper

1 tablespoon chopped garlic

2 tablespoons tomato paste

1 tablespoon chopped fresh oregano, or 1 teaspoon dried

One 28-ounce can whole tomatoes

½ cup peanut butter

1 cup chopped fresh cilantro

Juice of 2 limes, or more as needed

1 cup roasted, unsalted peanuts

1. Toast the chiles in a dry medium skillet until browned in spots and fragrant, 2 to 3 minutes. Add the cumin and coriander seeds, and continue to cook, shaking the skillet to prevent scorching, until fragrant, about 1 minute. Remove the stems and core from the chiles; if you prefer your chili spicy leave some of the seeds, and grind the chiles to a powder with the toasted spices using a spice grinder or mortar and pestle.

2. Put the oil in a large pot over medium-high heat. When it's hot, crumble in the tempeh and cook, stirring occasionally to break it up more, until the bits are well browned, about 10 minutes. Add the carrots, celery, onion, and bell pepper and sprinkle with salt and pepper. Cook, stirring occasionally, until the vegetables are soft and golden, 5 to 8 minutes.

3. Add the garlic, tomato paste, oregano, and ground spice mixture and stir until the tomato paste has darkened a shade or so and the mixture becomes fragrant, 1 to 2 minutes. Stir in the tomatoes, peanut butter, and 4 cups water. Bring to a boil and make sure the peanut butter is fully incorporated, then adjust the heat so the mixture bubbles gently.

4. Cook, stirring once in a while until the vegetables become very soft and the tomatoes break into pieces, 30 to 40 minutes. (You can make the chili to this point up to 2 days ahead of time and refrigerate and gently reheat before proceeding.) Add the cilantro, lime juice, and peanuts and stir; taste and adjust the seasoning, add more lime if you'd like, and serve.

● **TEXAS RED** with tamale dumplings

makes: 4 to 6 servings
time: 2½ hours

2 ounces dried chiles (like guajillo or pasilla)

3 cups boiling water

2 pounds bone-in beef chuck roast (including blade or arm roast), or 1½ pounds boneless with a separate small beef bone

2 garlic cloves, lightly smashed

1 teaspoon ground cumin

Salt and pepper

5 tablespoons good-quality vegetable oil

2 onions, chopped

¾ cup and 1 tablespoon masa harina

1 cup strong black coffee

¾ teaspoon baking powder

4 tablespoons cold unsalted butter or lard, cut into pieces

1 egg

¼ cup buttermilk, or more as needed

4 ounces queso fresco cheese, crumbled

Chopped fresh cilantro, for garnish

1. Heat the oven to 250°F. Toast the chiles in a dry skillet over medium heat for a minute or 2 on each side, then soak in the boiling water until soft, 15 to 30 minutes, depending on the chile. While the chiles soak, trim the beef of excess fat and cut the meat off the bone into 2-inch cubes. Reserve the bone.

2. Drain the chiles, saving the soaking liquid, and remove and discard the seeds and veins (for a hotter paste, save some of the seeds). Put the chiles and any seeds you're using in a blender or food processor with the garlic, cumin, and a pinch of salt and pepper. Puree until smooth, adding the soaking water a little at a time to help the machine do its work. You want the paste fairly smooth, but not thin.

3. Put 2 tablespoons oil in a skillet over medium-high heat. Add the chile-garlic paste and cook, stirring, until dark, about 2 minutes. Remove from the heat and taste and adjust the seasoning.

4. Put the remaining 3 tablespoons oil in a large oven-proof pot over medium-high heat. When it's hot, add the bone and beef a few pieces at a time to avoid crowding and sprinkle with salt and pepper. Brown well on all sides, 5 to 10 minutes total. As the meat becomes brown, transfer it to a plate and add more to the pot until all the pieces are deeply browned.

5. Remove all but about 4 tablespoons fat from the pot and lower the heat to medium. Add the onions and cook, stirring occasionally until soft and golden, 8 to 10 minutes. Add 1 tablespoon masa harina and cook, stirring, until lightly browned, 1 to 2 minutes. Add the beef bone, chile-garlic paste, chile soaking liquid and enough water to total 4 cups, and the coffee and bring to a boil. Return the meat to the pot, and cover. Transfer the pot to the oven and cook for 60 minutes, then stir, and add a little water if the bottom is scorching. Cover and return to the oven, cooking until the meat is very tender, another 30 to 60 minutes.

6. To make the dumplings, combine the remaining ¾ cup masa harina, baking powder, and a pinch of salt in the food processor. Pulse a few times to mix, then add the butter and pulse until the mixture has the consistency of cornmeal. Add the egg and pulse 2 or 3 times more. With the machine running, slowly pour in ¼ cup buttermilk until the dough just comes together; if your dough hasn't come together, add more buttermilk 1 tablespoon at a time. Gently shape into 1-inch balls and put them on a greased plate; the dough will be sticky, so you can use 2 spoons to do this. Drape with a towel and refrigerate for at least 30 minutes and up to 2 hours.

7. When the meat is tender, discard the bone, and stir in a little water if the chili looks too thick. Carefully put the dumplings on top of the chili and cover again. Return the pot to the oven and cook until the dumplings are springy to the touch and cooked through (a toothpick inserted should come out clean; for fluffiness don't undercook), 25 to 30 minutes. To serve, scoop spoonfuls of the chili and dumplings into shallow bowls, and garnish with the queso fresco and cilantro.

Dal with Flatbread

The family of Indian bean dishes known as dals—which are often served as side dishes—easily become a favorite dinner of mine with flatbread on the side. The Easy recipe takes ingredients most of us have around and builds in quick-cooking red lentils; give a little special attention to the tortillas and they're a remarkable stand-in for paratha. Garam masala is the unifying blend for Sprouted Lentils with Winter Squash. Homemade bread and a crunchy topping takes the whole thing over the moon. When you have some time to cook, simmering dried mung beans until they burst maximizes their nutty flavor and unusual color to make a gorgeous All Out dal inspired by my friend Julie Sahni. The bread alongside is my own hybrid of chapati and roti.

● GARLICKY DAL
with buttery flatbread

makes: 4 servings
time: 40 minutes

4 tablespoons unsalted butter

1 onion, chopped

2 tablespoons chopped garlic

2 to 3 dried chiles (like de árbol), or to taste

1 tablespoon curry powder (see page 299)

1½ cups dried red lentils, rinsed and picked over

2 carrots, chopped

Pepper

Four 10-inch flour tortillas

1 lemon or lime, halved

1 cup yogurt

Salt

1. Put 2 tablespoons butter in a large pot over medium-high heat. When it melts, add the onion, garlic, and chiles and cook, stirring occasionally, until the onion starts to soften, 3 to 5 minutes. Add the curry powder and cook until fragrant, about 30 seconds.

2. Add the lentils, carrots, lots of pepper, and enough water to cover by 1 inch. Bring to a boil, then adjust the heat so the mixture bubbles gently. Cover and cook, stirring occasionally and adding small amounts of water as necessary, until the lentils are tender, 25 to 30 minutes. The dal should be creamy, not soupy.

3. While the lentils cook, melt about a teaspoon of the remaining butter in a large skillet over medium-high heat. Line a plate with a clean cloth or a piece of foil. When the butter melts, add 1 tortilla, swirl to coat in butter, then immediately turn it over. Cook until it's pliable then fold it in half, press down, and toast on both sides; the whole process should take about a minute. Repeat with the other tortillas, adding more butter to the pan for each, and wrapping them as they finish to keep warm.

4. Squeeze the citrus juice into the yogurt and stir to combine. Uncover the dal and raise the heat to cook off any excess water. Sprinkle with salt, taste, and adjust the seasoning. Serve hot topped with a spoonful of yogurt and the flatbread on the side.

● SPROUTED LENTILS
with winter squash and whole wheat flatbread

makes: 4 servings
time: about 1 hour

PLAN B If you can't find—or don't like—sprouted lentils, use red lentils and cook them for 25 to 30 minutes in Step 3.

1 cup whole wheat flour

Salt and pepper

1 small kabocha or other winter squash (about 1 pound), peeled and seeded

2 tablespoons good-quality vegetable oil, plus more for the pan

1 cup dried sprouted lentils, rinsed and picked over

1 jalapeño, seeded and chopped

2 tablespoons chopped fresh ginger

1 tablespoon chopped garlic

1 tablespoon garam masala

4 cardamom pods

¼ cup chopped pistachios

¼ cup unsweetened shredded coconut

1 tablespoon brown or black mustard seeds

1. Heat the oven to 450°F. Put the flour in a bowl with 1½ cups water, sprinkle with salt and pepper, and whisk until smooth. Let the mixture rest for 10 to 30 minutes. Use the grating attachment on a food processor or the largest holes on a box grater to grate the squash. You should have about 5 cups.

2. Pour enough oil into a large ovenproof skillet to cover the bottom. Put the skillet in the oven until the oil is heated and fragrant. Whisk the batter if it has separated, carefully pull out the skillet, and pour in the batter. Bake until the bread releases easily from the pan and is crisp and golden on the bottom, 30 to 40 minutes.

3. Meanwhile, put the squash, 2 tablespoons oil, the lentils, jalapeño, ginger, garlic, garam masala, and cardamom in a saucepan and sprinkle with lots of pepper. Add 3 cups water and bring to a boil, then adjust the heat so the mixture bubbles gently. Cook, partially covered, stirring occasionally and adding water if necessary, until the lentils are tender, 20 to 30 minutes. The dal should be creamy, not soupy. Raise the heat to cook off any excess water. Fish out the cardamom, sprinkle with salt, taste, and adjust the seasoning.

4. Put the pistachios, coconut, and mustard seeds in a medium skillet over medium heat. Cook, shaking the pan occasionally, until toasted and fragrant, 3 to 5 minutes. Cut the flatbread into wedges. Divide the dal among 4 bowls, top with the pistachio mixture, and serve hot, with the bread on the side.

● MUNG BEANS
with ginger and homemade chapati

makes: 4 servings
time: about 2 hours

1⅓ cups mung beans, rinsed and picked over

1 teaspoon salt, plus more as needed

1½ cups all-purpose flour, plus more for dusting

1½ cups whole wheat flour

3 tablespoons good-quality vegetable oil,
   plus more for frying

1 onion, chopped

¼ cup chopped fresh ginger

1 cup diced canned tomatoes

1 teaspoon ground turmeric

1 bay leaf

Pepper

6 tablespoons unsalted butter

2 teaspoons mustard seeds

1 teaspoon cumin seeds

1 teaspoon coriander seeds

½ teaspoon fenugreek seeds

1 or 2 dried chiles (like de árbol), crumbled

¼ cup chopped fresh cilantro, for garnish

1. Put the beans in a large pot with enough water to cover by about 4 inches. Bring the water to a boil, then adjust the heat so the water barely bubbles, and cover. The beans are done when slightly firmer than you usually like them and still intact. Start checking after 30 minutes, and every 15 minutes or so after that. Depending on the age of the beans, they may take up to 2 hours. Generously salt the water and let them sit off the heat, covered, for 30 minutes.

2. Put the flours and 1 teaspoon salt in the food processor. With the machine running, slowly pour in 1½ cups warm water to form a barely sticky dough ball. Add 1 tablespoon water and pulse a few times if the dough is dry and grainy; if the dough sticks to the side of the bowl, add 1 tablespoon flour and pulse. Put the dough on a floured surface, cover, and let rest for at least 30 minutes and up to 2 hours.

3. Lightly flour your work surface and divide the dough into 8 equal pieces. Gently press each into a 4-inch disk. Dust each with flour to prevent sticking, cover with parchment, and stack.

4. Drain the beans and reserve the cooking liquid. Put 3 tablespoons vegetable oil in a large pot over medium-high heat. When it's hot, add the onion and cook, stirring occasionally, until soft, 5 to 8 minutes. Add the ginger and cook until starting to turn golden around the edges, 2 to 3 minutes.

5. Add the drained beans, the tomatoes, turmeric, and bay leaf to the pot and sprinkle with lots of black pepper. Add enough bean cooking liquid to cover by about 1 inch. Bring to a boil, then adjust the heat so the mixture bubbles gently. Cover and cook, stirring occasionally and adding water if necessary, until the beans are tender and the tomatoes start to break down, 10 to 15 minutes. The dal should be creamy, not soupy. Uncover the pot and raise the heat to cook off any excess water. Sprinkle with salt, taste, and adjust the seasoning. Remove the bay leaf.

6. While the dal is cooking, roll out one disk of dough to a ⅛-inch-thick round. Put a thin film of oil in a large skillet over medium heat. When it's hot, pat off any excess flour from the chapati and put it in the skillet. Cook for 15 seconds, then turn. Cook until the bottom starts to blister, char, and puff, about 1 minute (enough time to roll out the next disk). Turn again and cook the first side again until charred, about 1 minute. Transfer to a platter or bowl and cover with a towel. Repeat with the remaining dough, adding oil to the skillet as necessary.

7. Melt the butter in a small saucepan over medium-high heat. Add the mustard seeds, cumin seeds, coriander seeds, and fenugreek seeds and cook until fragrant, about 30 seconds. Add the chiles and turn off the heat. Divide the dal among 4 bowls, drizzle with the spice mixture, garnish with the cilantro, and serve with the chapati.

Cassoulet

One of my favorite bean dishes, which I make a million ways. Flageolets—slightly green imma-ture kidney beans— are just as fabulous as traditional Tarbes in the fairly traditional All Out recipe. For the simple Sausage Cassoulet, use whatever you have handy in a can or the freezer. For the vegetable-forward Vegan interpretation, lentils, a completely untraditional choice, work perfectly. For all, the goal is to let the beans cook until they start to break apart, which helps thicken the stew. And don't skimp on the fat.

● SAUSAGE CASSOULET

makes: 4 servings
time: 40 minutes

2 tablespoons olive oil, plus more for drizzling

1½ pounds mild Italian sausage, cut into chunks

1 red onion, chopped

2 tablespoons chopped garlic

2 tablespoons chopped fresh thyme,
    or 2 teaspoons dried

Salt

⅛ teaspoon cayenne, or to taste

1 cup white wine or water (or bean-cooking liquid,
    if you've got it), plus more as needed

One 28-ounce can diced tomatoes

3 cups cooked white beans (see page 82;
    or two 15-ounce cans, rinsed and drained)

4 thick bread slices, any kind

1. Turn the broiler to high and position the rack 4 inches below it. Put the oil in a large pot over medium heat. When the oil is hot, add the sausage. Cook, stirring occasionally and breaking up the pieces until they're no longer pink, 5 to 10 minutes. Raise the heat to medium-high and add the onion and garlic, and cook, stirring often, until the sausage sizzles and browns and the vegetables soften and become golden, 3 to 5 minutes.

2. Add the thyme, a pinch of salt, and the cayenne. Stir once or twice, then add the wine. Cook, scrap-ing up any browned bits from the bottom of the pot, until the liquid reduces by about half, just a couple minutes. Add the tomatoes and half the beans and bring to a boil. Reduce the heat so the mixture bubbles steadily, and cook uncovered, stirring once in a while, until the stew thickens and darkens, 10 to 15 minutes.

3. Tear the bread into bite-sized pieces onto a rimmed baking sheet and transfer to the broiler. Watch and shake the pan as necessary until the pieces brown in places. Remove and let cool.

4. Add the remaining beans to the pot and add more wine or water, ¼ cup at a time, if the stew looks too thick. Stir until heated through, just a couple minutes. Taste, adjust the seasoning, and serve, topped with the bread and a drizzle of olive oil.

● Pork Cassoulet with
Seared Duck Breast,
page 78

LENTIL CASSOULET
with lots of vegetables

makes: 4 servings
time: 50 minutes

8 ounces Le Puy lentils, rinsed and picked over

¼ ounce dried porcini mushrooms

1 cup boiling water

¼ cup olive oil

1 leek, trimmed, well rinsed, and chopped

1 carrot, chopped

1 small celery root, peeled and chopped

2 tablespoons chopped garlic

Salt and pepper

¼ cup dry red wine or water

One 14-ounce can diced tomatoes

½ small head green cabbage (about 8 ounces),
    quartered, cored, and cut into thin ribbons

2 tablespoons chopped fresh parsley

2 tablespoons chopped fresh thyme,
    or 2 teaspoons dried

1 bay leaf

⅛ teaspoon cayenne, or to taste

1. Put the lentils in a large pot with enough water to cover by about 1 inch and bring to a boil. Once the water boils, cover and turn off the heat; let the lentils sit.

2. Put the dried mushrooms in a small heatproof bowl and cover with the boiling water. The mushrooms will take anywhere from 15 to 30 minutes to soften. When they're ready, lift them from the soaking liquid carefully to leave any grit behind; chop the mushrooms and reserve the liquid.

3. Heat the oil in a large skillet over medium heat, add the leek, carrot, celery root, mushrooms, and garlic; sprinkle with salt and pepper. Cook, stirring occasionally until the vegetables soften, 5 to 10 minutes. Add the wine, and cook, stirring and scraping up any browned bits from the bottom of the pan.

4. Add the vegetable mixture to the lentils along with the tomatoes, cabbage, and the herbs. Carefully pour in the mushroom soaking liquid, leaving behind the grit in the bottom of the bowl. Stir to combine and bring to a boil. Reduce the heat so the mixture bubbles steadily, and cook, stirring occasionally and adding a splash of water if the mixture starts to look dry, until the vegetables are silky and the lentils start to break down and thicken the stew, 25 to 35 minutes. Stir in the cayenne. Remove the bay leaf. Taste, adjust the seasoning, and serve.

PORK CASSOULET
with seared duck breast

makes: 8 to 12 servings
time: at least 5 hours

4 cups dried Tarbes, flageolet, Great Northern,
    or cannellini beans, rinsed and picked over

Small bunch fresh parsley, leaves and stems
    separated

1 small bunch fresh thyme

2 bay leaves

1 tablespoon allspice berries

Salt and pepper

8 ounces mildly smoky slab bacon

1 pound boneless pork shoulder, cut into 1-inch
    cubes

4 tablespoons olive oil

2 onions, halved and sliced

1 head garlic, cloves separated and peeled

3 to 4 cups chicken stock (see page 43), or more
    as needed

1½ pounds ripe Roma (plum) tomatoes, cored,
    peeled if you like (see page 189), and chopped

¼ teaspoon cayenne, or to taste

1 pound fresh pork sausage (like chipolata or
    breakfast-style; not Italian)

2 cups fresh breadcrumbs (see page 173)

2 boneless duck breasts (about 1 pound each)

1. Put the beans in your largest ovenproof pot with enough water to cover by 2 inches and bring to a boil. Wrap the parsley stems, thyme, bay leaves, and allspice in a piece of cheesecloth and tie it into a bundle with string to make a bouquet garni.

2. Once the water boils, add the herb bundle and lower the heat so the water bubbles gently. Cover and cook, stirring every now and then, until the beans are tender and just starting to burst, anywhere from 45 to 90 minutes depending on their type and age. As they cook, add water only as needed to keep them submerged by no more than an inch. When they're ready, add a large pinch of salt, fish out the herbs, and remove the pot from the heat to sit, covered.

3. While the beans cook, cut the bacon into bite-sized chunks and put it in a small saucepan with enough water to cover; turn the heat to medium, and when the water boils, lower the heat to a gentle bubble. Cook until soft, stirring once or twice, 20 to 30 minutes. Transfer the bacon to the pot of beans with a slotted spoon and discard the cooking liquid.

4. Sprinkle the pork cubes with salt and pepper. Put 2 tablespoons oil in another large pot over medium-high heat. When it's hot, add the pork and cook, turning as necessary, until well browned, 5 to 10 minutes. Add the onions and garlic and cook, stirring occasionally until soft, 3 to 5 minutes. Add 2 cups stock and stir to scrape up any browned bits from the bottom of the pan, then add the tomatoes and cayenne. Bring to a boil, then reduce the heat so the mixture bubbles gently. Cover and cook, stirring occasionally, until the pork is fork-tender, 1 to 1½ hours. Taste and adjust the seasoning.

5. Heat the remaining 2 tablespoons oil in a medium skillet over medium-high heat. Add the sausage and cook, turning once or twice until well browned. Transfer the sausage to a cutting board and slice into 1-inch rounds (don't bother to wash the pan; you will use it later to cook the duck breasts). Heat the oven to 400°F. Chop the parsley leaves. Stir the sausage and the pork mixture into the pot of beans. If the cassoulet seems too dry, add 1 cup or so more stock. Cover the top with the breadcrumbs and half the chopped parsley leaves and bake, uncovered, until bubbly and crisp around the top and edges, 20 to 30 minutes.

6. When the cassoulet is ready, turn off the oven but leave the pot inside. Score the skin of the duck breasts with a sharp knife in a crosshatch pattern, being careful not to cut into the flesh, and rub all over with lots of salt. Put the skillet over medium-high heat. When it's hot, add the breasts skin side down. Cook, undisturbed, until the breasts release easily from the pan and are deeply golden, 8 to 12 minutes. Turn, lower the heat so the fat sizzles, and cook until the centers are medium-rare (an instant-read thermometer inserted into the meat should read about 125°F), 3 to 5 more minutes. Transfer the duck to a cutting board and let sit for 5 to 10 minutes.

7. Remove the cassoulet from the oven. Slice the duck breasts on the diagonal and tuck them into the breadcrumbs; pour the drippings from the pan over the top, and serve, garnished with the remaining parsley.

Rice and Beans

Just when you thought you'd seen every possible version of this economical, nutritious, and ubiquitous food pairing, here are three more. Sweet and Salty Coconut Rice with Lima Beans is a tropical paradise disguised as a mound of rice and beans, and also happens to be meatless. Just trust me and try this. And the official Vegan one's also a doozy: Cooking the red beans and rice together like a casserole, and then topping it with tangy zucchini, takes the Louisiana classic into a different—vegetable forward—direction; you'll still want to finish the entire pot. The next one tops 'em all: The rice and beans come together in packages to demonstrate what might happen with a Pan-Asian point of view.

● SWEET AND SALTY COCONUT RICE
with lima beans

makes: 4 servings
time: 30 minutes

¼ cup unsweetened shredded coconut

2 tablespoons coconut oil or good-quality vegetable oil

2 tablespoons chopped fresh ginger

4 scallions, whites and greens separated and chopped

1½ cups white rice (preferably long-grain)

One 14-ounce can coconut milk

1 tablespoon sugar

1 teaspoon salt, or more to taste

1 pound frozen lima beans

1. Put the shredded coconut in a large dry skillet over medium heat. Cook, stirring constantly, until the coconut is fragrant and golden, 3 to 5 minutes. Transfer to a bowl.

2. Put the oil in the pan and return to medium heat. When it's hot, add the ginger and scallion whites. Cook, stirring, until tender, 3 to 5 minutes. Add the rice and cook, stirring constantly, until glossy, about 1 minute. Add the coconut milk, sugar, salt, and 1½ cups water and bring to a boil. Lower the heat to a gentle bubble and cover. Cook for 10 minutes; don't stir, but use a spoon to check the bottom once or twice to make sure the mixture isn't sticking or burning—add a splash of water and reduce the heat if it is.

3. Add the lima beans, and stir once, then continue cooking until the rice is tender, 4 to 6 minutes. If liquid evaporates before the rice is done, stir in water, about ¼ cup at a time. Remove from the heat, taste, and adjust the seasoning. Fluff the rice with a fork, then cover, and let sit for at least 5 minutes and up to 15. Serve warm, garnished with the scallion greens and toasted coconut.

● RED BEANS AND RICE with tangy zucchini

makes: 4 servings
time: about 2 hours

5 tablespoons olive oil

1 onion, chopped

1 green bell pepper, cored and chopped

1 celery stalk, chopped

1 tablespoon chopped garlic

½ teaspoon dried thyme

½ teaspoon sweet paprika

¼ teaspoon pepper, or more as needed

¼ teaspoon cayenne

¾ cup dried red beans, rinsed, picked over, and soaked if time allows

1 bay leaf

1½ cups long-grain brown rice (preferably basmati)

1 cup chopped tomato (canned are fine; no need to drain)

Salt

1 pound zucchini (preferably small), trimmed

2 tablespoons red wine vinegar

Pepper

Southern-style hot sauce

1. Put 3 tablespoons oil in a large ovenproof pot over medium heat. When it's hot, add the onion, bell pepper, celery, and garlic and cook, stirring occasionally, until the onion is soft, 3 to 5 minutes. Add the thyme, paprika, pepper, and cayenne and cook, stirring constantly, until fragrant, about 1 minute.

2. Add the beans and bay leaf and cover with water by 2 inches. Bring to a boil, then adjust the heat so that the mixture bubbles very gently. Partially cover and cook, stirring occasionally and adding water if the pan looks dry or the mixture threatens to burn, until the beans are about three-quarters of the way done; start checking after 45 minutes. The beans should be tender on the outside but still firm in the middle, 60 to 90 minutes total. Remove the bay leaf.

3. Heat the oven to 450°F and put a rimmed baking sheet on the middle rack. Use an immersion blender or potato masher to puree about half the beans right in the pot. Add the rice, tomato, and a good pinch of salt and enough water so the mixture is soupy, and covered by about ½ inch of liquid. Bring the mixture to a boil, then reduce the heat so it bubbles gently. Cover and cook, stirring occasionally to prevent burning and adding more water as necessary, until the rice and beans are tender, 15 to 20 minutes. Taste, adjust the seasoning, and keep warm.

4. Halve or quarter the zucchini and cut them into sticks about 3 inches long. Put them in a large bowl and toss with the remaining 2 tablespoons oil and the vinegar. Sprinkle with salt and pepper. Carefully put them on the heated baking sheet in the oven. Cook, turning halfway through, until the zucchini is browned and tender, 10 to 15 minutes. Serve the rice and beans in shallow bowls, topped with the zucchini, and pass the hot sauce at the table.

BASIC BEANS

Rinse 1 pound dried beans (any type) in a strainer under running water, picking out anything that doesn't belong. Put the beans in a large pot with enough cold water to cover by about 3 inches. Bring to a boil, then reduce the heat so the water barely bubbles. Cover and cook, undisturbed, for 30 minutes. Try a bean. If it's at all tender, add a large pinch of salt and enough water to cover the beans by 1 inch, if necessary. If the beans are still hard, don't add the salt yet and make sure they're covered by about 2 inches water. Check for doneness every 5 to 15 minutes and add water to keep the beans just submerged. Small beans will take as little as 5 minutes more; older or larger beans can take up to 1 hour or more. If you haven't added salt yet, do so as soon as the beans are tender. Stop cooking when the beans are as firm or creamy as you like them. Taste and adjust the seasoning. Makes 8 servings in 1 to 4 hours, depending on the age and type of the beans.

● STICKY RICE AND ADZUKI BEANS
in lotus leaves

makes: 8 servings
time: about 1 day, largely unattended

THE RIGHT WHITE RICE Sticky rice can also be sold as glutinous rice, sweet rice, or waxy rice, but not all glutinous or sweet rice is sticky rice. Look for Thai sweet or sticky rice and you'll be fine.

1½ cups sticky rice

8 large lotus leaves

⅔ cup adzuki beans, rinsed and picked over

3 tablespoons good-quality vegetable oil

1 pound boneless pork shoulder, excess fat removed, cut into chunks

¼ cup soy sauce

¼ cup mirin (see page 290)

1 tablespoon rice vinegar

1 tablespoon chopped garlic

1 tablespoon chopped fresh ginger

2 scallions, sliced

1 fresh hot red chile (like Thai or cayenne), seeded and chopped

Salt and pepper

1. Put the rice in a fine-mesh sieve and rinse under cold running water until the water runs clear. Transfer the rice to a bowl and cover with water. Put the lotus leaves in a separate bowl and cover with water, and repeat with the beans in another. Soak everything for 8 to 12 hours.

2. Put the oil in a large pot over medium-high heat. When it's hot, add the pork, taking care not to crowd the pan and working in batches if necessary, until the pork is browned on all sides, 10 to 15 minutes total. Transfer to a plate.

3. Add the soy sauce, mirin, vinegar, garlic, ginger, scallions, and chile to the pot and sprinkle with salt and pepper. Cook, stirring constantly and scraping up any browned bits from the bottom of the pan, until the aromatics are soft, 3 to 5 minutes.

4. Drain the beans and add them to the pot along with the pork and enough water to cover by 1 inch. Bring the mixture to a boil, then adjust the heat so it bubbles very gently. Cover and cook, stirring occasionally, until the pork and beans are tender, 45 to 60 minutes, adding water as needed to keep the beans just submerged. Taste and adjust the seasoning.

5. Cut eight 12-inch pieces of string. Trim the lotus leaves so that you have eight 8 by 10-inch rectangles, with the grain of the leaves running the long way; reserve the scraps. Rig a steamer over simmering water.

6. Drain the rice. Line the steamer with some of the lotus trimmings, then with cheesecloth, and top with the rice. Steam until tender, 25 to 30 minutes. It's almost impossible to overcook sticky rice, so you can keep it warm over low heat for an hour longer or even more. Make sure the pot doesn't boil dry and keep the steamer setup ready (remove the cheesecloth when you remove the rice).

7. Spoon an eighth of the rice onto the center of one of the lotus leaves, then top with an eighth of the pork mixture. Fold 1 long end over, then the other, and finally the 2 shorter ends. Tie around the middle with string. Repeat with the remaining leaves and filling.

8. Add more water to the steamer if necessary and return to a boil. Put the rice packages in the steamer and cook until warmed through, 10 to 15 minutes. Untie the lotus bundles, partially open them, and serve hot.

Brown Rice and Brussels
Sprout Pilaf with Shiitake
Bacon, page 86

Pilaf

It doesn't take much to toast rice, cook it fluffy, and turn it into a main dish. Lamb makes the
Best Green Rice so much more than herb-flecked pilaf. Lamb not your thing? Then go ahead
and try ground chicken, pork, beef, buffalo, or even turkey (if you must). The mushroom shards
scattered atop Brown Rice and Brussels Sprout Pilaf with Shiitake Bacon are chewy, smoky,
and meaty (it's a cliché to say that about mushrooms, but it's true). Making Stuck Pot Chicken
and Rice—with its distinctive bottom crust called *tahdig*—is an act of faith that will bring you to
your knees.

Stuck Pot Chicken and Rice,
page 87

THE BEST GREEN RICE

makes: 4 servings
time: 45 minutes, largely unattended

5 tablespoons olive oil

1 pound ground lamb or beef

Salt and pepper

3 scallions, chopped

2 garlic cloves, peeled

1 cup fresh cilantro, tough stems removed

1 jalapeño, seeded and cut into chunks, or to taste

1½ cups rice (preferably basmati)

Lemon wedges

1. Put 1 tablespoon olive oil in a large skillet with the lamb over medium heat. Sprinkle with salt and pepper and cook, stirring occasionally to break up and turn the lamb, until it's brown and crisp, 8 to 10 minutes.

2. While the lamb cooks, put the scallions, garlic, cilantro, jalapeño, and remaining 4 tablespoons olive oil in a blender or food processor and season with salt and pepper; puree the seasoning until smooth.

3. Add the rice to the browned meat and stir until the rice is glossy and fragrant, 3 to 5 minutes. Add the seasoning paste and cook, stirring often, until fragrant and slightly darker, 2 to 3 minutes. Season well with salt and pepper, then turn the heat down to low and add 2½ cups water. Stir once, then cover.

4. Cook until most of the liquid is absorbed, 10 to 15 minutes. Turn the heat to the absolute minimum (if you have an electric stove, turn the heat off and let the pan sit on the burner) and let rest for another 15 to 30 minutes. Fluff with a fork, taste and adjust the seasoning, and fluff again. Serve with the lemon.

BROWN RICE AND BRUSSELS SPROUT PILAF
with shiitake bacon

makes: 4 servings
time: about 1 hour

6 tablespoons olive oil

8 ounces shiitake mushrooms

½ teaspoon smoked paprika

Salt and pepper

12 ounces Brussels sprouts, trimmed

1 small onion, chopped

2 tablespoons chopped garlic

1½ cups long-grain brown rice (preferably basmati)

½ cup apple cider, white wine, or water

2½ cups vegetable stock (opposite) or water

¼ cup chopped fresh dill

1. Heat the oven to 400°F and position 2 racks toward the center with a few inches in between them. Line 2 rimmed baking sheets with foil and smear each with 1 tablespoon oil. Remove the stems from the mushrooms and save them for another use (like stock, opposite). Slice the caps crosswise as thin as you can manage.

2. Spread the mushroom slices on the prepared pans in a single layer (it's okay if they overlap a bit) and sprinkle with the paprika, salt, and pepper. Transfer the pans to the oven and bake, switching racks and rotating the pans halfway through, until the mushrooms release their water and the pan is almost dry again, 20 to 30 minutes. Lower the heat to 325°F and continue to cook the slices, rotating again to ensure even browning, until they dry and shrivel a bit, and release easily from the pan, another 5 to 10 minutes. Transfer to a wire rack to cool completely.

3. Meanwhile, use the slicing blade on a food processor or a knife to thinly slice the Brussels sprouts.

4. Put 2 tablespoons oil in a large skillet over medium-high heat. When it's hot, add the onion and garlic. Cook, stirring often, until the onion softens, 3 to 5 minutes. Add the rice, lower the heat to medium, and stir until the rice is glossy, completely coated with oil, and starting to toast, 3 to 5 minutes. Sprinkle generously with salt and pepper, then add the apple cider. Cook, scraping any browned bits from the bottom of the pan, until the cider has mostly evaporated, just a minute or 2. Turn the heat down to low and add the stock and Brussels sprouts. Bring to boil, lower the heat to a steady, gentle bubble, stir once or twice, then cover.

5. From this point, the rice will take about 40 minutes to become tender; check after 30 minutes to make sure there's enough liquid and, if not, add about ¼ cup more. When the rice is tender, turn the heat to the absolute minimum (if you have an electric stove, turn the heat off and let the pan sit on the burner), and let rest, covered, for another 15 to 30 minutes. Add the remaining 2 tablespoons oil and the dill and fluff with a fork. Taste and adjust the seasoning, fluff again, garnish with the mushroom bits, and serve.

VEGETABLE STOCK

Cut into chunks: 4 carrots, 2 onions (don't bother to peel), 2 all-purpose potatoes, and 2 celery stalks. Put them in a pot with 5 or 6 garlic cloves, a good-sized bunch of parsley, 3 quarts water, and some salt and pepper. (Add tomatoes or fresh or dried mushrooms if you'd like.) Bring to a boil, then adjust the heat so the mixture bubbles gently. Cook until the vegetables are tender, about 30 minutes. Strain the stock through a fine-mesh sieve, pressing on the vegetables to extract as much liquid as possible. Discard the solids. Cool to room temperature, then refrigerate for up to 1 week or freeze for up to 6 months. Makes 2 quarts stock in 1 hour.

● STUCK POT CHICKEN AND RICE

makes: 4 servings
time: about 2 hours

1 tablespoon olive oil

4 bone-in chicken thighs (about 2 pounds)

Salt and pepper

1 small onion, halved and sliced

4 teaspoons minced garlic

1 teaspoon ground cinnamon

½ teaspoon ground cardamom

½ teaspoon turmeric

1 cup chicken stock (see page 43) or water

1 cup dates, pitted and halved

1 cup dried apricots, halved

1 large or 2 small waxy potatoes (like red or other thin-skinned variety)

1½ cups white basmati rice

4 tablespoons unsalted butter

Large pinch saffron

1 cup whole-milk yogurt

3 tablespoons chopped fresh mint

2 tablespoons chopped fresh parsley

1 teaspoon grated lime zest

1. Put the oil in a large pot over medium-high heat. When it's hot, add the chicken, skin side down, sprinkle with salt and pepper, and cook undisturbed until it releases easily from the pan, 3 to 5 minutes. Repeat seasoning and browning the chicken on the other side, another 3 to 5 minutes. Remove the chicken and pour off all but 2 tablespoons of fat.

2. Add the onion, sprinkle with salt, and cook over medium heat, stirring occasionally, until softened and golden, 10 to 15 minutes, scraping up any browned bits from the bottom of the pot as they loosen. Add 3 teaspoons garlic and the cinnamon, cardamom, turmeric, and lots of black pepper and

(recipe continues)

stir until fragrant, about 30 seconds. Add the stock, and stir again. Return the chicken to the pot, adjust the heat to a steady, gentle bubble, and cover.

3. Cook for 10 minutes, turn the chicken, and add the dates and apricots, and more liquid if necessary to keep the chicken partially submerged. Continue to cook, turning occasionally and checking the liquid, until the thighs are tender enough to pierce easily with a fork and the meat is nearly falling from the bone, 30 to 40 minutes. (At this point, you can refrigerate them in the braising liquid for a day or so and then reheat.) Remove the chicken from the pot, and when cool enough to handle, remove the skin and shred the meat. Strain the braising liquid. Put the meat in a bowl and add just enough of the cooking liquid to keep the fruit mixture moist without pooling. Rinse and dry the pot.

4. Peel the potato(es) and cut crosswise into thin slices. Fill the pot with water and a big pinch of salt and bring to a boil. Stir in the rice and return to a boil, then lower the heat so the water bubbles steadily. Cook undisturbed, until the rice is partially done but still retains some bite; start checking after 5 minutes. Drain the rice and let sit; wipe out the pot.

5. Melt the butter in the same pot over low heat, stir in the saffron, remove from the heat and let the spice steep in the fat for about 5 minutes. Add ¼ cup water to the pot, then carefully arrange the potato slices in the bottom of the pot in a single layer (it's okay if they overlap). Add half the rice, then the chicken, and top with the remaining rice. Wrap a clean kitchen towel around the lid of the pot so that the corners are tied together on top and don't fall anywhere near the flame; cover the pot.

Turn the heat to medium-high. When you hear the water spattering—about 5 minutes—turn the heat down to very low. Cook, completely undisturbed, until the potatoes start to smell toasty—you will know—but not burned, 40 to 50 minutes. If you don't smell anything after 1 hour, turn the heat up to high until you do, no more than 3 minutes; keep your nose and ear to the pot. Remove from the heat and let sit, covered, for another 5 minutes.

6. While the pilaf cooks, whisk together the yogurt, remaining teaspoon garlic, the mint, parsley, and lime zest and sprinkle with salt and pepper. Taste and adjust the seasoning. Warm the braising liquid on the stovetop, skimming any fat off the top.

7. Uncover the pilaf, cover the top with a large shallow bowl, and invert the pot to release the rice. If the potatoes don't come out intact, use a spatula to scrape the pieces out of the pan and put the pieces on top of the rice. Serve hot, passing the minty yogurt and braising liquid at the table.

Risotto

Everyone needs a little attention now and then, but risotto isn't as high maintenance as its reputation. Especially if you cheat. No way is the Baked Rice and Peas a true risotto, but it's got all the creaminess without babysitting the pot. When you make Barley Risotto with Beets and Greens, go for heartiness and satisfaction and choose the whole-grain barley, even though it takes longer to cook. Vanilla-Scented Lobster Risotto is a contemporary, somewhat surprising combination that seems a tad contrived. Until you try it.

● BAKED RICE AND PEAS

makes: 4 servings
time: 30 minutes

4 tablespoons unsalted butter

1 small onion, chopped

1½ cups long-grain rice (preferably basmati)

Salt and pepper

1½ cups frozen peas

1½ cups grated Parmesan cheese (about 6 ounces)

2 tablespoons chopped fresh chives, mint, or parsley, for garnish

1. Heat the oven to 350°F. Melt 2 tablespoons butter in a large ovenproof pot over medium heat. Add the onion and cook, stirring often, until soft, 3 to 5 minutes. Add the rice and sprinkle with salt and pepper. Cook, stirring constantly, until the rice is glossy, about a minute.

2. Add 2½ cups water, bring to a boil, then cover the pot and put in the oven. Bake for 10 minutes undisturbed, then add the peas, cheese, remaining 2 tablespoons butter, and another ½ cup water (for a firmer mixture) or ¾ cup water (if you like it a little soupier) and gently stir into the rice with a fork. Cover again and return to the oven until the rice is as tender as you like, another 5 to 10 minutes. Taste, adjust the seasoning, garnish, and serve.

● BARLEY RISOTTO
with beets and greens

makes: 4 servings
time: about 1 hour

1½ cups whole-grain ("hulled") barley

½ cup chopped walnuts

4 to 5 cups vegetable stock (see page 87) or water

4 tablespoons olive oil, or more as needed

1 onion, chopped

Salt and pepper

½ cup dry white wine or water

12 ounces beets, peeled and grated

2 cups arugula, or chopped beet greens if they came with the beets

1. Put the barley in a large dry skillet over medium heat. Cook, shaking the pan often, until the barley is golden and fragrant, 3 to 5 minutes. Transfer to a bowl. Put the walnuts in the skillet and repeat the process to toast them the same way. Warm the stock or water in a medium saucepan.

2. Put the olive oil in the skillet over medium heat. When it's hot, add the onion and cook, stirring occasionally, until soft, 3 to 5 minutes. Add the barley and cook, stirring often, until it is glossy and

(recipe continues)

Barley Risotto with
Beets and Greens,
page 89

coated with oil, 2 to 3 minutes. Sprinkle with salt and pepper, then add the white wine. Cook, scraping up any browned bits from the bottom of the pan, until the liquid bubbles away.

3. Use a ladle to add the warm stock, 1 cup or so at a time, stirring after each addition. When the stock has just about evaporated, add another ladleful. The mixture should be neither soupy nor dry. Adjust the heat so the mixture bubbles and stir frequently.

4. After 20 minutes, add the beets. Continue cooking the same way, tasting the grains regularly—you want it to be tender but still with a tiny bit of crunch—it could take as long as 40 minutes to reach this stage, depending on the barley. When the barley is as tender as you like, add the arugula or beet greens a handful at a time, stirring until each addition is wilted. Taste and adjust the seasoning. Garnish with the walnuts, and serve hot.

● VANILLA-SCENTED LOBSTER RISOTTO

makes: 4 servings
time: 2 hours

Salt

2 lobsters (1½ pounds each)

½ vanilla bean

1 large fennel bulb, cut into chunks, fronds reserved for garnish

4 tablespoons unsalted butter

1 large shallot, chopped

1½ cups Arborio or other short-grain rice

Pepper

½ cup dry white wine

¼ cup mascarpone cheese

1. Put 6 cups water in a large pot and bring to a boil, then salt it. Use tongs to put the lobsters in the pot one at a time. Let the water return to a boil, then cook for 8 minutes for each lobster's

first pound and an additional 3 minutes per pound thereafter. Insert an instant-read thermometer into the tail meat between the body and the tail joint; lobster is done at 140°F. Use tongs to transfer the lobsters to a colander and let cool. Reserve the liquid in the pot.

2. To shell the lobsters, twist the claws to remove them and use a nutcracker to split them and a pick to pull out the meat. As you work, put the pieces of shell in the large pot with the cooking water and the meat in a bowl. Twist the lobster in half to separate the tail from the body. Cut through the soft side of the tail and crack it open to remove the tail meat. Cut through the underside of the front part of the body and crack open the claws and remove all the meat; cut it into bite-sized pieces, then break them up gently with your hands.

3. Halve the vanilla bean lengthwise and scrape out the seeds with a paring knife; reserve the seeds. Add the pod and fennel to the pot with the shells and cooking water and bring to a boil, then adjust the heat so the broth bubbles gently. Cook for 30 minutes. Strain the stock through a fine-mesh sieve, gently pressing on the shells to extract as much liquid as possible, and discard the solids. Taste, adjust the seasoning, and keep warm.

4. Melt the butter in a large skillet over medium heat. Add the shallot and cook, stirring occasionally, until soft and translucent, 3 to 5 minutes. Add the rice and cook, stirring often, until coated with butter and glossy, 2 to 3 minutes. Add the vanilla seeds and sprinkle with salt and pepper, then add the wine. Stir, scraping up any browned bits from the bottom of the pan, and let the liquid bubble away.

5. Begin adding the hot lobster stock, ½ cup or so at a time, stirring and waiting until the liquid has just about evaporated before adding more. The mixture should be neither soupy nor dry. Adjust the heat so the risotto bubbles; stir frequently. Cook for 20 minutes, then start tasting the rice; you want it to be tender but with some texture in the center; it could take as long as 30 minutes.

6. When the rice is ready, stir in the mascarpone and then the lobster meat. Taste, adjust the seasoning, and serve, garnished with the fennel fronds.

Sushi

The translation of *sushi* is "rice," not "fish." So that's the focus of all three recipes. *Chirashi*—the Japanese name for sushi bowls—are already quicker than rolls and pieces, while my easy rice technique delivers legit sweet-sour taste and stickiness. The Vegan recipe strays further, deliciously. Go against all your instincts and overcook the quinoa to make rolling in the nori a snap. Buying sustainable seafood for your own nigiri and sashimi is less daunting with the help of a good fishmonger and the Monterey Bay Aquarium Seafood Watch Guide; the directions in the recipe take the pressure off the cutting and assembling so you can wow your friends and family.

● SPICY TUNA RICE BOWL

makes: 4 servings
time: 25 minutes

1½ cups short-grain white rice

¼ cup rice vinegar

2 tablespoons sugar

Salt

Two 6-ounce cans tuna (preferably packed in oil), drained

¼ cup mayonnaise (see page 216)

3 tablespoons soy sauce

2 tablespoons fresh lemon juice

3 scallions, whites and greens separated and chopped

1 celery stalk, chopped

½ teaspoon wasabi powder (or mustard powder), or to taste

Pepper

1 ripe avocado, peeled, pitted, and sliced

2 tablespoons sesame seeds

1. Put the rice in a small saucepan with 3 cups water, the rice vinegar, sugar, and a large pinch of salt. Bring to a boil, then adjust the heat so the mixture bubbles steadily and enthusiastically without boiling over. Cook undisturbed for 5 minutes, then stir, cover, and cook, checking every few minutes, until craters appear on the surface of the rice and no water is visible when you tip the pan, another 5 to 10 minutes. Stir again, cover, and remove from the heat; let the rice sit.

2. While the rice is cooking, mix the tuna, mayonnaise, soy sauce, lemon juice, scallion whites, celery, and wasabi powder in a bowl and sprinkle with pepper. Taste and adjust the seasoning, adding salt if you like.

3. To serve, stir the rice with a flat wooden spoon or a rubber spatula, using a fast, scooping-and-folding motion and pressing down gently until the rice is sticky and cooled a little, just a minute or 2; taste and add salt if necessary. Divide the warm rice among 4 bowls, top with the tuna mixture and sliced avocado, and garnish with the sesame seeds and scallion greens.

● Hand-Cut Nigiri
and Sashimi with
Pickled Ginger,
page 95

● QUINOA NORI ROLLS

makes: 4 servings
time: 1 hour

1½ cups white quinoa

Salt

7 tablespoons rice vinegar

2 tablespoons and 1 teaspoon sugar

2 tablespoons dark sesame oil

8 ounces fresh spinach

Pepper

8 ounces daikon, peeled and grated

¼ cup white or yellow miso

1 cup walnuts

1 tablespoon chopped fresh ginger

1 teaspoon soy sauce

8 sheets toasted nori

6 ounces pressed or smoked tofu, julienned

1. Rinse and drain the quinoa in a strainer. Put it in a medium saucepan with 3½ cups water and a large pinch of salt and bring to a boil. Lower the heat so it bubbles gently, cover, and cook, adding water ¼ cup at a time if the quinoa starts to stick to the pan, until the grains are very tender and bursting, and the pan is dry, 25 to 30 minutes.

2. Meanwhile, combine 4 tablespoons vinegar, 2 tablespoons sugar, and 1 teaspoon salt in a small saucepan over medium heat. Cook, stirring constantly, until the sugar dissolves. Transfer the seasoning mixture to a bowl and put in the freezer to cool the mixture. Mix 1 cup water with 2 table-spoons vinegar in another bowl.

3. When the quinoa is ready, transfer to a very large bowl. Mix the hot quinoa with a flat wooden spoon or a rubber spatula, using a fast, scooping-and-folding motion and pressing down. While you're mixing, sprinkle the quinoa with the cooled seasoning mixture. If the spoon becomes encrusted with quinoa, dip it in the vinegar-water mixture, then shake off the excess and continue. The grains will cool as they absorb the vinegar. Use right away, or cover with a damp cloth and let sit for up to 1 hour.

4. Put the sesame oil in a large skillet over medium heat. When it's hot, add the spinach a handful at a time and stir until soft; continue adding spinach until it is all incorporated and wilted, 3 to 5 minutes. Sprinkle with salt and pepper, taste, and adjust the seasoning. When the spinach is cool enough to handle, squeeze any excess moisture from the spinach and chop it.

5. Put the daikon, the remaining teaspoon sugar, and remaining tablespoon vinegar in a bowl and sprinkle with salt and pepper. Toss to combine, then taste and adjust the seasoning.

6. Put the miso, walnuts, ginger, and soy sauce in a blender and blend until smooth, stopping the machine and scraping down the sides and adding water 1 tablespoon at a time until the mixture is just barely pourable. (You can refrigerate the sauce, covered, for up to 3 days.)

7. Put a nori sheet on a bamboo mat or piece of plastic wrap. Using your hands, spread it evenly with a ½-inch layer of seasoned quinoa, leaving a 1-inch border on every side; dip your hands in the vinegar-water mixture as needed to keep them clean.

8. Put a thin strip of julienned tofu along the edge closest to you, next to a ½-inch-thick layer of spin-ach, and ½-inch-thick layer of daikon. Use the mat to roll the nori tightly around the quinoa, forming it into a log; you can unroll and readjust if you're having trouble. Repeat with the remaining nori sheets and fillings. Slice the rolls into 1-inch pieces and serve with the miso sauce.

● HAND-CUT NIGIRI AND SASHIMI with pickled ginger

makes: 4 servings
time: at least 1 day, largely unattended

One 4-inch piece fresh ginger, peeled

Salt

10 tablespoons rice vinegar

3 tablespoons sugar, or as needed

1 lemon

1½ cups short-grain white rice (preferably sushi rice)

1 tablespoon wasabi powder

12 ounces trimmed sushi-grade fish (like Arctic char or Alaskan salmon; see the headnote, page 92)

Soy sauce

1. Slice the ginger as thin as you can manage, using a mandoline or the slicing blade of a food processor. Mix with 1½ teaspoons salt and let stand for an hour. Rinse thoroughly, drain, and put in an airtight nonreactive container.

2. Put 4 tablespoons rice vinegar, 4 tablespoons water, and 1 tablespoon sugar in a small saucepan over medium heat. Cook, stirring to dissolve the sugar, just until steaming. Taste and add more sugar if you like. Cool slightly and combine with the ginger. Use a vegetable peeler to make 2 large pieces of lemon zest (save the lemon for another use) and add to the ginger. Cover and refrigerate for at least 1 day and up to 2 weeks.

3. Put the rice in a large saucepan with 2¾ cups water and a pinch of salt. Bring to a boil, then adjust the heat so the mixture bubbles gently. When small craters appear on the surface of the rice and all visible moisture disappears, turn off the heat, 10 to 15 minutes total. Remove from the heat and let sit, still covered, until the rice can be fluffed with a fork, at least 15 minutes.

4. While the rice is cooking, combine another 4 tablespoons vinegar, the remaining 2 tablespoons sugar, and 1 teaspoon salt in a small saucepan over medium heat and cook, stirring constantly, until the sugar dissolves. Put the saucepan in a large bowl filled with ice and stir the vinegar mixture until cool.

5. When the rice is ready, transfer to a very large bowl. Mix the hot rice with a flat wooden spoon or a rubber spatula, using a fast scooping-and-folding motion and pressing down. While you're mixing, sprinkle the rice with the vinegar mixture. If the paddle becomes encrusted with rice, dip it in water, then shake off the excess and continue. You want the rice to cool as it absorbs the vinegar. If you need to, cover with a damp towel for up to 2 hours.

6. Put the wasabi powder in a small bowl and add 2 tablespoons water. Whisk until smooth, then add more water ¼ teaspoon at a time until it is your preferred consistency.

7. Hold a very sharp, clean, narrow-bladed or boning knife at a 45° angle and trim about a 1-inch triangle from one corner of the block of fish (you can chop this up and serve it as tartare) so you have a diagonal face to begin making slices. Starting with that angled side, slice the fish without sawing as thin as you can manage into diagonal strips. Continue cutting slices until you get about 1 inch from the end, when the slices become too short. If the fish sticks to the knife, rinse and dry the knife. Keep the slices covered with plastic so they don't dry out.

8. Mix 1 cup water with the remaining 2 tablespoons vinegar in a small bowl (for the "hand water"). Dip your hands into the mixture; take about 3 tablespoons rice and gently shape it into a ball; the rice should hold together easily. Put the ball of rice in your cupped hand and press down with 2 fingers from your other hand to make a mold. Squeeze and rotate until you have an oblong rice ball that keeps its shape.

9. Smear a little wasabi on the bottom of a slice of fish and drape it over the rice. Repeat with the remaining rice and fish. (If you have more fish than rice, put the remaining fish slices on a serving platter with the sushi.) Serve immediately with more wasabi, the pickled ginger, and soy sauce for dipping.

Vegetable Paella,
page 98

Paella

Like sushi, the national dish of Spain is also supposed to be about rice, though what goes on top is going to flavor the kernels mightily. Shrimp Paella, Under the Broiler is a trip to the Mediterranean via Shortcut City with an impressive impact. I love the short-grain brown rice in the Vegetable Paella: nice bite and deep nutty taste, soaks up the juices in the pan like a sponge, then separates into individual grains during the resting time. And if you decide to go for Mixed Paella with Mussels, you'll be treated to the real deal.

● SHRIMP PAELLA,
under the broiler

makes: 4 to 6 servings
time: 30 minutes

THAT CRUST Since you mostly cook this paella on the stove, you start the characteristic bottom crust known as *soccarat* on the bottom before a fast pass under the broiler, rather than at the end of the cooking process. If your skillet is too large to fit under the heat, transfer the rice to a rimmed baking sheet (bring all the crusty bits along for the ride) and then top with the shrimp in Step 4.

7 tablespoons olive oil

1½ pounds unpeeled medium shrimp, thawed

1 tablespoon chopped garlic

2 teaspoons smoked paprika

Salt and pepper

1 onion, chopped

1½ cups long-grain rice (preferably basmati or jasmine)

2 tablespoons tomato paste

1½ cups peas (frozen are fine)

¼ cup chopped fresh parsley, for garnish

Lemon wedges

1. Turn on the broiler and position the rack 4 inches below the heat source. Put 4 tablespoons olive oil, the shrimp, garlic, and paprika in a bowl and sprinkle with salt and pepper; stir to combine. Marinate the shrimp while you cook the rice.

2. Put the remaining 3 tablespoons oil in a large skillet over medium-high heat. When it's hot, add the onion, sprinkle with salt and pepper, and cook, stirring occasionally, until it softens, 3 to 5 minutes. Add the rice and cook, stirring occasionally, until it's shiny, another minute or 2. Add the tomato paste and cook, still stirring, until it darkens, 2 to 3 minutes.

3. Add the peas and 3 cups water and stir. Bring to a boil, then adjust the heat so the mixture boils steadily but gently. Cover and cook, undisturbed, until small craters appear on the surface, 10 to 15 minutes. Then raise the heat and cook without stirring until the rice smells toasty; use a spoon to move the rice to the side and peek at the bottom of the pan once in a while to make sure it's not burning. Remove from the heat.

4. Scatter the shrimp over the rice and press gently; drizzle the juices from the bowl over the surface. Broil, watching carefully, until the shrimp are pink and cooked through, 2 to 3 minutes. Serve directly from the pan, garnished with the parsley, passing the lemon wedges at the table.

● VEGETABLE PAELLA

makes: 4 servings
time: 45 minutes

Salt

8 ounces ripe tomatoes, chopped

Pepper

4 tablespoons olive oil, or more as needed

1½ cups short-grain brown rice

1 onion, chopped

1 tablespoon chopped garlic

8 ounces green beans, cut into 1-inch pieces

1 red bell pepper, cored and sliced

1 small eggplant, chopped

1 tablespoon tomato paste

2 teaspoons paprika

Large pinch saffron threads

2 to 3 cups vegetable stock (see page 87) or water

¼ cup chopped fresh parsley, for garnish

1. Heat the oven to 450°F. Bring a medium saucepan of water to a boil and salt it. Put the tomatoes in a medium bowl, sprinkle with salt and pepper, and drizzle them with 1 tablespoon olive oil; toss gently to coat.

2. When the water boils, stir in the rice and adjust the heat so that the water bubbles steadily. Cook, stirring once or twice, for 12 minutes, then drain thoroughly.

3. Put the remaining 3 tablespoons oil in a large skillet over medium-high heat. Add the onion and garlic, sprinkle with salt and pepper, and cook, stirring occasionally, until the onion softens, 3 to 5 minutes. Transfer to a bowl with a slotted spoon. Add the green beans, bell pepper, and eggplant to the skillet, sprinkle with salt and pepper, and cook, stirring once in a while, until browned in spots but still crisp, 5 to 10 minutes; add more oil if the mixture looks too dry. Transfer to the bowl and toss to combine; taste and adjust the seasoning.

4. Add the rice to the pan and stir until shiny and toasted, about 1 minute. Add the tomato paste, paprika, and saffron and stir until fragrant, about 1 minute more. Add 2 cups stock; stir gently to combine. The rice should be submerged by ½ inch; if not, add a little more liquid.

5. Scatter the browned vegetables on top, followed by the tomatoes; drizzle with any accumulated juices. Put the pan in the oven and cook, undisturbed, for 15 minutes. Check to see if the rice is dry and just tender. If not, return the pan to the oven for another 5 minutes. If the rice looks too dry at this point, but still isn't quite done, add a small amount of stock or water. When the rice is ready, turn off the oven and let it sit for at least 5 and up to 15 minutes. Garnish with the parsley and serve.

MIXED PAELLA
with mussels

makes: 4 to 6 servings
time: 2 hours

2 onions, 1 unpeeled, cut into chunks, and 1 peeled and chopped

1 carrot, cut into chunks

1 celery stalk, cut into chunks

1 ripe tomato, chopped (canned is fine)

1 garlic clove, smashed, and 1 tablespoon minced

½ cup dry white wine

1 pound bones and/or cleaned heads from any white-fleshed fish

1 bay leaf

2 fresh parsley sprigs

Salt and pepper

2 tablespoons olive oil

8 ounces semi-cured Spanish chorizo, casings removed

2 cups short-grain Spanish rice (like Bomba) or Arborio rice

Large pinch saffron threads

½ cup chopped pitted olives

1 lemon, halved

2 pounds mussels, scrubbed

2 tablespoons chopped fresh chives, for garnish

1. Combine the unpeeled onion, carrot, celery, tomato, smashed garlic, wine, fish bones, bay leaf, and parsley sprigs in a large pot and add 4 cups water. Sprinkle with salt and pepper. Bring to a low boil, then adjust the heat so the mixture barely bubbles and cook, stirring once or twice until full-flavored, 25 to 30 minutes. Cool slightly, then strain, pressing on the vegetables and fish to extract as much stock as possible. Use immediately or refrigerate for up to 3 days or freeze for up to a few weeks.

2. Heat the oven to 450°F. Warm the stock in a small saucepan if it isn't already. Put the oil in a large skillet over medium heat. When it's hot, crumble in the chorizo and cook, stirring occasionally, until browned and crisp, 5 to 10 minutes. Add the chopped onion and minced garlic, and cook, stirring occasionally, until it softens, 3 to 5 minutes.

3. Add the rice and saffron and cook, stirring occasionally, until it's coated with oil, another minute or 2. Carefully add the stock and stir until just combined. Put the olives and lemon halves on the rice and put the pan in the oven. Bake, undisturbed, for 10 minutes.

4. Nestle the mussels in the rice and cook for another 5 minutes. Check to see if the rice is dry and tender. If not, return the pan to the oven for 5 minutes, adding a little more stock or water if the rice looks too dry. When the rice is ready, turn off the oven and let the paella sit in the oven for at least 5 and up to 15 minutes.

5. Put the pan over high heat and cook undisturbed until you can smell the bottom toasting (but not burning), 2 to 3 minutes. Carefully squeeze the hot lemon halves over the paella, garnish with the chives, and serve from the pan.

● Cauliflower Fried Rice
with Fresh Chiles,
page 103

Fried Rice

Please don't tell me you only eat fried rice in restaurants. Even the most complicated rendition is nothing more than a glorified stir-fry. For the Easy recipe, observe the directives "use frozen vegetables and a very hot pan" (they'll remain vibrant and crisp). Cauliflower Fried Rice with Fresh Chiles hardly takes any longer if you've got cooked brown rice handy. The All Out dish—a familiar Korean Bibimbap—is essentially deconstructed fried rice you mix together at the table. Just don't skimp on the variety of toppings and let everyone play with his or her own bowls, adding plenty of the sweet, spicy sauce.

● Beef Fried Rice
with Frozen
Vegetables,
page 102

BEEF FRIED RICE
with frozen vegetables

makes: 4 servings
time: 20 minutes

12 ounces boneless sirloin steak

5 tablespoons good-quality vegetable oil

2 cups frozen vegetables (like peas, edamame, corn, green beans, or carrots, alone or in combination; do not thaw)

Salt and pepper

1 tablespoon chopped garlic

1 tablespoon chopped fresh ginger

3 cups cooked long-grain rice (see below), chilled

2 eggs

¼ cup rice wine, beef stock (see page 47), or water

2 tablespoons soy sauce

1 tablespoon dark sesame oil

1. Cut the beef into ½-inch cubes. Put a large skillet over high heat. When it's hot, add 1 tablespoon oil, swirl to coat the bottom, and add half the vegetables; sprinkle lightly with salt and pepper. Cook, undisturbed, until they thaw and release from the pan, but are still crisp, 2 to 3 minutes. Adjust the heat if the mixture threatens to burn. Use a spatula to transfer them to a platter. Let the pan heat up again and repeat with the remaining vegetables.

2. Put 1 tablespoon oil in the pan, swirl again, and when it's hot, add the steak. Again season lightly with salt and pepper and cook, undisturbed, to let the bottom brown and crisp, about 30 seconds. Then cook, stirring occasionally, until the beef is no longer pink, 2 to 3 minutes total. Transfer to the platter with the vegetables.

3. Put the remaining 2 tablespoons oil in the skillet, followed by the garlic and ginger. When they're fragrant, about 15 seconds later, begin to add the rice, a bit at a time, breaking up any clumps with your fingers and stirring it into the oil. When all the rice is added, let it cook, undisturbed, until it starts to sizzle and brown, adding a little water if necessary to prevent burning, then push it to the sides so that the pan is exposed at the center; break in the eggs, scramble with a fork until set, then incorporate them into the rice.

4. Return the meat and vegetables to the pan and stir with the spatula to combine. Add the rice wine and cook, stirring, for about a minute. Add the soy sauce and sesame oil, taste, adjust the seasoning, and serve.

BROWN OR WHITE BASMATI RICE (OR OTHER LONG-GRAIN RICE)

Put 1½ cups any brown or white long-grain rice in a medium saucepan with 3 cups water and a large pinch of salt. Bring to a boil, then adjust the heat so the mixture bubbles steadily but not violently. Cover and cook, undisturbed, for about 10 minutes for white rice or for 20 minutes for brown. Then start checking every few minutes for small craters to appear; you should be able to tip without seeing any pooling water. (This takes about 5 minutes more for white rice or 15 minutes for brown.) Remove from the heat and let sit—still covered—for at least 5 or up to 15 minutes. Taste and adjust the seasoning and fluff with a fork. Makes 4 servings in 15 to 45 minutes, depending on the type of rice.

CAULIFLOWER FRIED RICE
with fresh chiles

makes: 4 servings
time: 45 minutes

1 small head cauliflower

One 2-inch piece fresh ginger, peeled and cut into chunks

3 garlic cloves, peeled

2 small fresh chiles (like cayenne or Thai bird), seeded and cut into chunks, or to taste

5 tablespoons good-quality vegetable oil

Salt and pepper

1½ pounds silken tofu, drained

4 scallions, greens and whites separated and chopped

2 cups cooked long-grain brown rice (see opposite), chilled

¼ cup rice wine, dry white wine, or water

2 tablespoons dark sesame oil

2 lemons, quartered

1. Cut just the florets (without much stem) off the cauliflower and chop into bite-sized pieces. Cut the stems into chunks. Put the ginger, garlic, and chiles in a food processor and pulse a few times, then add the cauliflower stems (not the florets) to the food processor and pulse until the pieces are chopped but not pureed. Taste and adjust the seasoning, adding more chile if you like.

2. Put 1 tablespoon vegetable oil in a large skillet over medium-high heat. When it's hot, add the chopped cauliflower florets, sprinkle with salt and pepper, and cook, stirring occasionally, until brown and crisp, 2 to 3 minutes. Lower the heat if the mixture threatens to scorch. Transfer to a platter. Repeat with 1 more tablespoon oil and the chopped stem mixture, and add it to the platter.

3. Add another 2 tablespoons oil to the pan. Crumble in the tofu with your hands and season generously with salt and pepper. Cook, stirring occasionally, until the liquid cooks off and the tofu is golden and dry, about 10 to 15 minutes. Transfer the tofu to the platter with the vegetables.

4. Put the remaining tablespoon oil in the skillet and add the white parts of the scallions. Cook until fragrant, about 1 minute. Add the rice and cook, stirring often and breaking up any clumps, until starting to brown, 2 to 3 minutes. Return all the cauliflower and tofu to the pan and stir with a spatula to mix. Add the rice wine and cook, stirring, for about a minute. Add the sesame oil, then taste and adjust the seasoning if necessary. Turn off the heat, mix in the scallion greens, and serve with the lemons.

● BIBIMBAP

makes: 4 servings
time: 1 hour

8 tablespoons soy sauce

1 small Asian pear, cored, peeled, and cut into chunks

2 garlic cloves, peeled

One 1-inch piece fresh ginger, peeled and cut into chunks

3 tablespoons turbinado sugar

1 pound boneless rib-eye steak, thinly sliced

2 scallions, white and green parts separated and sliced

3 tablespoons gochujang, or more to taste

6 tablespoons dark sesame oil

6 tablespoons good-quality vegetable oil, or as needed

4 cups cooked short-grain white rice (see page 92)

2 cups bean sprouts

1 teaspoon Korean red chile flakes, or pinch cayenne

Salt and pepper

3 tablespoons rice vinegar

10 ounces spinach leaves

4 eggs

2 carrots, peeled and cut into matchsticks

1. Put 6 tablespoons soy sauce, the Asian pear, garlic, ginger, and 2 tablespoons sugar into a food processor or blender and process until pureed. Mix with the sliced beef and white parts of the scallions and marinate at room temperature while you prepare the rest of the dish, or up to 8 hours in the refrigerator.

2. Make the sauce: Put the remaining 2 tablespoons soy sauce, remaining tablespoon sugar, 3 tablespoons gochujang, and 4 tablespoons sesame oil in a small bowl and whisk until combined.

3. Put 3 tablespoons vegetable oil in a skillet over high heat. When it's hot, add the rice, and press into an even layer. Cook, undisturbed, until the rice smells toasted—you will know—but not burned, 10 to 15 minutes. Remove from the heat.

4. Heat 2 tablespoons vegetable oil in another large skillet over medium-high heat. When it's hot, add the bean sprouts and toss a few times to coat. Cook, undisturbed, until they begin to sputter, just a couple minutes; then stir them around a bit. Sprinkle with the chile flakes and salt and pepper and stir again, adding a few drops of water if they're starting to stick to the pan. Stir once or twice more. The bean sprouts are ready when barely tender and the chile is fragrant, a couple minutes total. Transfer to a bowl and mix with the vinegar and scallion greens. The mixture will pickle slightly while it sits.

5. Add the spinach to the skillet a handful at a time, stirring as you go, and cook until tender, less than a minute. Add the remaining 2 tablespoons sesame oil and cook until the spinach is soft and the pan is dry, another minute or 2. Transfer to a bowl, taste, and adjust the seasoning.

6. Lift about half the beef from the marinade, letting any excess liquid drip off, and add it to the skillet. Turn the heat to high, and cook, stirring a few times, until it's lightly browned but still pink inside, 1 to 2 minutes. Transfer to a bowl and repeat with the remaining beef, adding more oil as necessary. Taste and add a little salt if you'd like and lots of pepper.

7. Add the remaining tablespoon vegetable oil to the skillet. When it's hot, crack in the eggs. As soon as the whites turn opaque—in about a minute—turn the heat to low and sprinkle with salt and pepper. Cook the fried eggs until the whites are completely firm with the yolks as runny as you prefer, 3 to 5 minutes. Carefully transfer them to a plate.

8. To serve, break the rice into chunks and divide among 4 bowls. Add the components in individual mounds of beef, spinach, pickled bean sprouts, and fresh carrots; finally, top each serving with a fried egg. Serve immediately, passing the gochujang sauce at the table.

Rice Noodles

Nothing is quite as much fun as starting with a blank slate—like rice noodles—and seasoning them assertively. The strategy for Seared Beef with Rice Vermicelli is simple: When you get home from work, set a pot to boil and pop the beef in the freezer. Crisped, slightly sour tempeh and shortcut kimchi pack a double order of zing in the Vegan recipe; you don't need much else besides the noodles. The brief soft-shell crab season in spring is what makes the Pad Thai with Crisp and Spicy Soft-Shell Crab special, but I've got an alternative so you can eat it year-round.

● SEARED BEEF
with rice vermicelli

makes: 4 servings
time: 30 minutes

Salt

1 pound boneless sirloin, flank, or rib-eye steak

6 tablespoons good-quality vegetable oil

12 ounces dried thin rice vermicelli

One 3-inch stalk lemongrass, peeled, trimmed, and chopped; or 1 tablespoon grated lime zest

⅓ cup fish sauce or soy sauce

2 tablespoons sugar

2 tablespoons chopped garlic

1 fresh red chile (like Thai bird), seeded if you like and chopped

1 teaspoon pepper

1 cucumber, thinly sliced

¼ cup fresh mint leaves

¼ cup fresh lime juice, or as needed

1. Bring a pot of water to a boil and salt it. Wrap the steak and put it in the freezer to chill for up to 30 minutes (this makes slicing easier).

2. When ready, slice the steak against the grain as thin as you can manage. Put 2 tablespoons oil in a large skillet over medium-high heat. When it's hot, add half the beef and cook, undisturbed, until the bottom is browned, 2 to 3 minutes. Turn the beef and brown the other side, another 2 to 3 minutes, then use a slotted spoon to transfer to a large shallow bowl. Repeat with the remaining beef.

3. Add the noodles to the boiling water and stir. Turn the heat off and let soak until the noodles are tender but still have some bite, 3 to 5 minutes; check them frequently. Drain the noodles and immediately transfer them to the bowl with the beef mixture.

4. Return the skillet to medium-high heat and add the remaining 2 tablespoons oil, the lemongrass, fish sauce, sugar, garlic, chile, and pepper. Stir to combine, scraping up any browned bits from the bottom of the pan and making sure the sugar has dissolved. Pour the mixture over the beef and noodles. Add the cucumber, mint, and lime juice, toss to coat, taste, and adjust the seasoning, adding more lime juice if you like. Serve warm or at room temperature.

● Pad Thai with Crisp and
Spicy Soft-Shell Crab,
page 108

WIDE NOODLES
with tempeh and warm kimchi

makes: 4 servings
time: 45 minutes

Salt

8 ounces brown rice fettuccini

4 tablespoons good-quality vegetable oil

8 ounces tempeh

Pepper

2 tablespoons chopped fresh ginger

2 tablespoons chopped garlic

4 cups sliced napa cabbage

3 scallions, green and white parts separated
    and sliced

1 fresh red chile (like Thai or Fresno), seeded
    if you like and chopped

1 teaspoon sugar

2 tablespoons rice vinegar

¼ cup chopped fresh cilantro, for garnish

1. Bring a pot of water to a boil and salt it. Add the noodles to the boiling water and stir. Cook for 5 minutes, then start checking. When the noodles are tender but still have some bite, drain. Reserve about 1 cup cooking liquid and shake off any excess water from the noodles. Keep the pot handy.

2. Meanwhile, put 2 tablespoons oil in a large skillet over medium-high heat. When it's hot, crumble in the tempeh. Cook, stirring frequently, until the bits are deeply colored and crisp on all sides, 5 to 7 minutes. Use a slotted spoon to transfer the tempeh to a plate. Sprinkle with salt and pepper.

3. Wipe out the pan, add the remaining 2 tablespoons oil, and put over medium-high heat. When it's hot, add the ginger and garlic. Cook, stirring often, until fragrant, about a minute. Add the cabbage, scallion whites, chile, and sugar and sprinkle with salt and pepper. Cook, stirring occasionally, until the cabbage has softened but still has some crunch, 5 to 8 minutes. Add the vinegar, taste, and adjust the seasoning.

4. Put the noodles in the large pot with the mixture from the skillet; toss to coat, adding some of the reserved noodle cooking liquid to loosen the mixture. Taste and adjust the seasoning again. Serve hot or warm, garnished with the tempeh, scallion greens, and cilantro.

● PAD THAI
with crisp and spicy soft-shell crab

makes: 4 servings
time: about 1 hour

4 live soft-shell crabs (or 1½ pounds cleaned colossal shell-on shrimp)

Salt

12 ounces dried flat rice noodles

5 tablespoons good-quality vegetable oil

3 eggs, lightly beaten

4 lime leaves

2 hot Thai chiles, green or red, sliced, or to taste

2 tablespoons chopped garlic

4 scallions, cut into 1-inch pieces

2 cups bean sprouts

¼ cup fish sauce

4 teaspoons tamarind paste

4 teaspoons sugar

1 cucumber, peeled, seeded, and julienned

¼ cup chopped peanuts, for garnish

Lime wedges

1. To prepare live crabs, use sharp kitchen scissors to cut off the eyes and mouth, and the gills (under the shell on either side). Turn the crab over and remove the flap that looks like a "T" on males and a bell on females (called the "apron"). Cut into quarters.

2. Bring a pot of water to a boil and salt it. Add the noodles to the boiling water and stir. Turn the heat off and let soak until the noodles are tender, anywhere from 5 to 30 minutes, depending on the noodles. Drain and shake off any excess water.

3. Put 2 tablespoons oil in a large skillet over medium heat. When it's hot, add the eggs. For the first minute or 2, stir quickly with a fork held flat against the bottom of the pan, so you make a thin "crepe" with very small curds. Cook just until set then transfer to a cutting board. Cut into ¼-inch strips. Cut the lime leaves into strips (use scissors if you like) as thin as you can manage.

4. Raise the heat to high and add the remaining 3 tablespoons oil to the skillet. When it's hot, add the crab (or shrimp), chiles, garlic, scallions, and half the bean sprouts to the pan and cook, stirring often, until the crab is cooked through and crisp, 3 to 5 minutes (a little less for shrimp).

5. Add the drained noodles, egg strips, the fish sauce, tamarind, and sugar to the pan and cook, stirring constantly, until the noodles are heated through. Toss once or twice, taste and adjust the seasoning, and transfer to a platter. Top with the cucumber, lime leaves, peanuts, and remaining bean sprouts. Serve right away, passing the lime wedges at the table.

Udon Noodles

The thick, wonderfully chewy wheat noodles of Japan are sold dried and increasingly fresh or frozen. You can make them yourself—the amazingly effective kneading method involves using your body weight and feet!—and top them with tender braised short ribs. For less ambitious nights, Yaki Udon with Chicken is a straightforward Japanese restaurant staple that, when made at home, relies mostly on pantry items and long-storing vegetables. The noodles in the Vegan recipe are a convenient excuse to eat caramelized carrots and the rich miso dressing.

● YAKI UDON with chicken

makes: 4 servings
time: 30 minutes

Salt

3 tablespoons good-quality vegetable oil

1 pound boneless, skinless chicken thighs, cut into bite-sized pieces

1 small head napa or savoy cabbage, chopped (about 4 cups)

4 scallions, green and white parts separated and chopped

2 carrots, peeled and grated

2 tablespoons chopped fresh ginger

2 tablespoons ketchup

¼ cup soy sauce

¼ cup Worcestershire sauce or soy sauce

2 tablespoons mirin (see page 290)

Hot sauce, to taste

8 ounces dried udon noodles, or 12 ounces fresh

1. Bring a pot of water to a boil and salt it. Put the vegetable oil in a large skillet over medium-high heat. When it's hot, add the chicken and cook, stirring once or twice, until it's no longer pink inside and is starting to brown in spots, 5 to 10 minutes. Transfer to a plate with a slotted spoon and return the skillet to medium-high heat.

2. Add the cabbage, scallion whites, carrots, and ginger to the skillet and sprinkle with salt. Cook, stirring occasionally, until the vegetables soften, adding a bit of water as needed to keep them from sticking, 3 to 5 minutes. Combine the ketchup, soy sauce, Worcestershire sauce, mirin, and a few dashes of hot sauce in a small bowl and whisk. Taste and adjust the seasoning.

3. Add the noodles to the boiling water and stir. Cook until just barely tender; start checking after about 3 minutes for dried, about 1 minute for fresh. Reserve about 1 cup cooking water and drain the noodles, running briefly under cold water. Return the noodles to the pot.

4. When the vegetables are soft, transfer them to the pot with the noodles; add the chicken and sauce and set over medium heat. Add ¼ cup reserved noodle cooking water to the skillet, scrape up any browned bits, and add them to the pot. Toss the noodles and vegetables together and cook until the mixture is steaming, adding more cooking water as necessary to coat everything in sauce. Taste, adjust the seasoning, and serve hot or warm, garnished with the chopped scallion greens.

● Homemade Udon
with Glazed Short Ribs

● UDON
with ginger-roasted carrots and miso sauce

makes: 4 servings
time: 45 minutes

1 pound carrots, peeled

4 tablespoons good-quality vegetable oil

Salt and pepper

2 tablespoons minced fresh ginger

6 tablespoons white or yellow miso

¼ cup rice wine or sherry

2 tablespoons dark sesame oil

1 teaspoon Japanese red chile blend
(*shichimi togarashi*), or to taste

¼ cup raw sunflower seeds

12 ounces fresh udon noodles, or 8 ounces dried

8 ounces snow peas, trimmed and sliced

2 tablespoons chopped fresh chives, for garnish

1. Heat the oven to 425°F. Cut the carrots into 2-inch-long matchsticks, put them on a rimmed baking sheet, drizzle with 2 tablespoons vegetable oil, and sprinkle with salt and pepper. Toss to combine and roast, shaking the pan, a few times, until they're soft and browned in spots, 5 to 10 minutes. Mix the roasted carrots with the ginger, stir, and continue roasting until the carrots are tender and caramelized, 10 to 15 minutes.

2. Bring a pot of water to a boil and salt it. Whisk together the miso, rice wine, remaining 2 tablespoons vegetable oil, the sesame oil, ¼ cup water, and the chile blend. Taste and adjust the seasoning. Put the sunflower seeds in a small dry skillet over medium heat. Toast, shaking the pan occasionally, until golden and fragrant, 3 to 5 minutes. Transfer to a bowl.

3. When the water boils, add the noodles and stir. Cook until they're tender but still have some bite; start checking after about 1 minute for fresh, about 3 minutes for dried. Drain, rinse with cold water, and return the noodles to the pot.

4. When the carrots are done, add them to the pot with the noodles along with the snow peas and some of the sauce. Taste and adjust the seasoning, adding more sauce if you like. Serve hot or at room temperature, garnished with the chives and toasted sunflower seeds.

● HOMEMADE UDON
with glazed short ribs

makes: 4 servings
time: at least 5 hours

1¼ cups warm tap water

4½ teaspoons salt, plus more as needed

3¼ cups flour, or more as needed

2 tablespoons good-quality vegetable oil

2 pounds bone-in beef short ribs

Pepper

¾ cup soy sauce

¼ cup cider vinegar

½ cup brown sugar

2 canned chipotle chiles with some of the adobo sauce, or to taste

2 tablespoons chopped garlic

2 tablespoons chopped fresh ginger

2 tablespoons sesame seeds

2 hot green chiles (like Thai or serrano), sliced

3 scallions, chopped

1. Mix the water and 4½ teaspoons salt until the salt has completely dissolved.

2. Put 1 cup salted water and the flour in a large bowl and mix with one hand until the dough comes together in a ball, adding the remaining water 1 tablespoon at a time, if necessary. Or put the salted water and flour in the bowl of a stand mixer and mix with a dough hook at medium speed about 5 minutes. The dough should be very dry but not

(recipe continues)

grainy; add a few drops of water if the dough is dry and gritty; add a sprinkle of flour if it's at all sticky. Turn out onto a floured surface and knead until smooth and elastic, about 5 minutes, sprinkling with flour as necessary to prevent sticking. Wrap the dough in plastic and refrigerate for at least 3 hours or up to overnight.

3. Heat the oven to 325°F. Put the oil in a large pot over medium-high heat. When it's hot, add only enough of the short ribs to cook in a single layer without crowding (you'll have to work in batches). Sprinkle with salt and pepper and cook, adjusting the heat so they sizzle without burning, until the ribs are well browned on all sides, 15 to 20 minutes total. Transfer them to a plate as you finish and repeat with the remaining ribs.

4. Pour off all but 2 tablespoons of the fat, and lower the heat to medium. Add 1 cup water, the soy sauce, vinegar, brown sugar, chipotles and adobo, garlic, and ginger and cook, stirring constantly and scraping any browned bits off the bottom, until the mixture comes to a boil and the sugar has dissolved.

5. Return the ribs to the pot, cover, and transfer to the oven. Cook, stirring occasionally and adding a splash of water if the mixture seems dry, until the meat is very tender and almost falling off the bone, 1½ to 2 hours. Use a slotted spoon to transfer the meat to a plate and let the cooking liquid cool.

6. Take the dough from the refrigerator and let it come to room temperature, about 1 hour. Lightly flour your work surface, unwrap the dough and knead for a couple of minutes until it's smooth and elastic. Cover and let it rest for 20 minutes.

7. Put the dough in a strong 1-gallon freezer bag, and press out all of the air. This is the fun part: put the bag of dough on the floor (you can put it on a towel and cover it with another towel) and step on the bag to knead the dough with your feet until it spreads out, filling the bag. Take the dough out and fold in half, then in half again, into a smaller square. Repeat this kneading and folding 2 more times. With your hands, shape the dough into a ball, cover it with a towel, and let it rest 20 minutes.

8. Put the sesame seeds in a dry medium skillet over medium heat. Toast the seeds, shaking the pan occasionally, until they're golden and fragrant, 3 to 5 minutes. Transfer them to a bowl.

9. Sprinkle your work surface with flour, turn out the dough, and sprinkle it with a little flour. Roll out with a rolling pin, adding flour and rotating and turning the dough as needed until the dough is a ⅛-inch-thick square. Fold the square in thirds, and use a sharp knife to slice the dough crosswise into noodles about ⅛ inch wide. Toss the noodles with a little flour to prevent sticking. (At this point you can freeze the noodles in an airtight container for up to 2 weeks.)

10. Bring a pot of water to a boil. Skim the fat from the short rib cooking liquid. Taste, and if the sauce is too intense, add water ¼ cup at a time; keep the mixture hot. Add the noodles to the boiling water and stir. Cook, stirring often, until the noodles are tender but still have some bite; start checking after 1 minute. Drain the noodles and shake off any excess water. Return the noodles to the cooking pot and toss with as much of the braising liquid as you'd like. Serve with a short rib on top, garnished with toasted sesame seeds, chiles, and scallions.

Chinese-Style Noodles

Making Chinese-style noodles is neither difficult nor time consuming. So take a weekend afternoon and give the Homemade Egg Noodles with Fermented Black Beans and Clams a whirl. For a more time-sensitive option, try pan-frying squiggly dried Cantonese soup noodles in the Beef Stir-Fry recipe and take them in a whole new direction. For Vegans, eggless dried lo mein noodles are available almost everywhere now. The thickish strands deliver classic heft and wheaty flavor that stand up to a quick-braised vegetable medley with lotus root and water spinach. After this tantalizing sampling from a seemingly endless variety of possibilities, I hope you're inspired to explore more of your own ingredient combinations.

● BEEF STIR-FRY
over crisp wonton noodles

makes: 4 servings
time: 30 minutes

Salt

12 ounces boneless beef sirloin or rib-eye steak

12 ounces chow mein or other thin egg noodles

4 tablespoons good-quality vegetable oil, or as needed

1 tablespoon chopped garlic

Pepper

12 ounces snow peas, trimmed

3 tablespoons soy sauce

2 tablespoons oyster sauce

1 teaspoon sugar

1. Bring a large pot of water to a boil and salt it. Put the beef in the freezer. When the water boils, add the noodles and cook, stirring frequently, until they just begin to soften, about 2 minutes. Scoop out about 1 cup cooking water and drain the noodles, shaking to remove as much water as possible.

2. Put 3 tablespoons oil in a large skillet over medium-high heat. When it's hot, add half the noodles; let them sit until the water cooks off and they start to sizzle, brown, and release from the pan, 2 to 3 minutes. Stir with a spatula to turn the noodles in bunches and repeat a couple more times until they're tender and crisp in places, being careful not to break them up too much, another 6 to 8 minutes total. Spread them in a large shallow bowl or on a platter. Repeat with the remaining noodles, adding more oil if necessary.

3. Return the pan to medium-high heat (no need to wipe it out) and add the remaining tablespoon oil. Slice the partially frozen beef as thin as you can manage. When it's hot, add the beef and garlic and sprinkle with salt and pepper. Cook, stirring once or twice, just until it is no longer pink, about 3 minutes.

4. Raise the heat to high and add the snow peas, soy sauce, oyster sauce, sugar, and ¼ cup of the reserved cooking water. Cook, stirring constantly until the peas turn bright green and are crisp tender and the sauce is thick, 1 to 2 minutes. If the sauce needs to reduce, cook for another minute or 2 (you want about ¼ cup sauce). Taste and adjust the seasoning, spoon the stir-fry over the noodles, and serve right away.

● LO MEIN with greens and lotus root

makes: 4 servings
time: 30 minutes

Salt

8 ounces lotus root, peeled (or Yukon Gold
　　potatoes or jicama)

8 ounces dried eggless lo mein noodles

14 ounces smoked or pressed tofu, drained
　　and patted dry

3 tablespoons good-quality vegetable oil,
　　or more as needed

Pepper

1 red onion, halved and sliced

2 tablespoons chopped garlic

2 tablespoons chopped fresh ginger

1 pound water spinach, choy sum, or other tender
　　Chinese green, rinsed and chopped

3 tablespoons soy sauce, or to taste

1 tablespoon dark sesame oil

¼ teaspoon red chile flakes, or to taste

¼ cup chopped roasted cashews, for garnish

1. Bring 2 pots of water—1 large and 1 medium—to a boil and salt them. Halve the lotus root lengthwise and slice crosswise into half-moons about ¼ inch thick. When the smaller pot boils, add the lotus and cook, stirring occasionally until it's tender, 4 to 6 minutes. Drain, rinse under running water, and drain again.

2. When the large pot boils, add the noodles and cook, stirring occasionally, for 5 minutes, then start tasting. (If using fresh, check after a minute.) When the noodles are tender but still have some bite, scoop out about 1 cup cooking water, then drain the noodles; run the noodles under cold water and drain again.

3. Cut the tofu crosswise into about 12 slices; stack the slices and cut them into thin ribbons no more than ½ inch wide.

4. Return the large pot to medium heat. When it's dry and hot, add the vegetable oil, swirl, then scatter in the tofu and sprinkle with salt and pepper. Cook, undisturbed, until the pieces have browned on one side and release easily, 5 to 10 minutes. Transfer the tofu to a plate, leaving as much oil in the pot as possible.

5. Add a little more oil to the pot if it looks dry and turn the heat to medium-high heat. Add the onion, garlic, and ginger and cook, stirring, for about 1 minute. Add the greens and sprinkle with salt and pepper. Cook, stirring occasionally, until the vegetables soften, 3 to 5 minutes, depending on the type; add reserved cooking water as necessary to keep them from sticking. Add the soy sauce, sesame oil, and red chile flakes.

6. Add the tofu and lotus to the pan and stir to combine. Add the noodles and toss with tongs, adding more reserved cooking water to make a smooth sauce. Taste and adjust the seasoning. Serve garnished with the cashews.

HOMEMADE EGG NOODLES
with fermented black beans and clams

makes: 4 to 6 servings
time: at least 90 minutes

2 cups flour, or more as needed

1 teaspoon salt, or more as needed

1 egg

1 tablespoon Szechuan peppercorns

6 star anise

10 whole cloves

One 3-inch stick cinnamon

2 tablespoons fennel seeds

½ cup fermented black beans

2 tablespoons Chinese black vinegar or
    sherry vinegar

¼ cup good-quality vegetable oil

4 scallions, white and green parts separated
    and chopped

½ cup rice wine or dry sherry

3 pounds littleneck or other small hard-shell
    clams, scrubbed

¼ cup chopped fresh cilantro, for garnish

1. Put the flour and salt in a large bowl. Beat the egg with ⅓ cup cold water and gradually stir it into the flour mixture until the dough comes together in a ball. The dough should be quite dry but hold together when pinched; if it doesn't, add another tablespoon or so of water. Lightly dust a work surface with flour and turn out the dough. Knead until it's a smooth and elastic ball, 4 to 5 minutes, sprinkling with flour as necessary to prevent sticking. (Or use a food processor: Put the flour and salt in the container and add the egg and water mixture gradually while the machine is running; the dough should be dry but form a shaggy ball. Let the machine run for about 15 seconds, then finish the kneading by hand, using as much flour as necessary to keep it from sticking to the work surface.)

2. Shape the dough into a ball, dust with flour, and cover with plastic wrap or a damp towel. Let it rest for at least 20 minutes or up to 2 hours. (The dough may be made up to a day ahead to this point and refrigerated, tightly wrapped; bring to room temperature before proceeding.)

3. Put the peppercorns, star anise, cloves, cinnamon stick, and fennel seeds in a spice or coffee grinder and grind to a fine powder. (Reserve 2 tablespoons and store the rest in an airtight container for up to 6 months.) Combine the fermented black beans and vinegar in a small bowl and let soak for 20 to 30 minutes.

4. Knead the rested dough for a minute, then cut the ball into quarters. (If you're making noodles by hand, see opposite.) Roll one portion of dough lightly in the flour and use your hands to flatten it into a rectangle about the width of the rolling machine. Set the machine to its thickest setting and crank the dough through the rollers. If it sticks, dust it with a little more flour. Repeat. Set the machine to its next-thinnest setting and repeat twice, sprinkling with a little more flour any time it starts to stick. Continue to work your way down (or up, as the case may be—each machine is numbered differently) through the numbers, passing the dough through twice at each setting, until you get to the second-thinnest setting. If at any point the dough tears, bunch it together and start again. Use only as much flour as you need to keep the machine running smoothly.

5. Cut each dough sheet into rectangles roughly 16 inches long; trim the ends to make them neat. At this point the dough is ready to cut. By hand, fold each rectangle into quarters, so you have roughly a 4-inch square, and cut vertically to make noodles about ⅛ inch wide. To cut the dough by machine, pass one rectangle at a time through the spaghetti cutter. Cook right away or hang the strands over clean hangers, chopsticks, dowels, or even a sheet-draped chair to dry for up to a couple of hours.

6. Bring a large pot of water to a boil and salt it. Heat the oil in a large skillet over medium heat. When it's hot, add the white parts of the scallions and the fermented beans. Cook, stirring often, until the scallions begin to soften, 3 to 5 minutes. Add the reserved 2 tablespoons spice mixture and cook until fragrant, about 30 seconds. Then add the rice wine and bring to a boil, scraping any browned bits off the bottom, and using a wooden spoon to mash some of the beans.

7. Add the clams to the pan and cook, stirring occasionally, until the first few of them open, 3 to 5 minutes. Cover for a minute or 2, then uncover and continue to cook, stirring occasionally, until almost all the clams are open (any that are not open at this point should be discarded), 2 to 3 minutes. Turn off the heat and leave the pan covered.

8. Cook the noodles in boiling water just until tender, about 3 minutes. Reserve at least 1 cup cooking water, then drain the noodles, rinse, and drain again. Immediately add the noodles and a splash of the cooking water to the bean mixture, and turn the heat to medium. Toss to coat, adding a little more cooking water if necessary to create a sauce. Taste and adjust the seasoning, then garnish with the scallion greens and cilantro, and serve.

FRESH PASTA OR NOODLES BY HAND

If you're going to make fresh pasta at least occasionally, then you should invest in a food processor and a rolling machine—either a simple but good-quality hand-cranker or something that attaches to your upright mixer. But you can always make and roll pasta by hand:

To make the pasta dough by hand if you don't have a food processor: Combine the dry ingredients directly on a work surface. Make a well in the middle and add the liquid (eggs, water, pureed vegetables, etc.), making sure they stay in the well. Beat the liquids with a fork, slowly and gradually incorporating the flour. When it becomes too hard to stir with the fork, use your hand. When all the flour has been mixed in, knead the dough, pushing it against the counter and folding it repeatedly, until it is not at all sticky and has become quite stiff. Add a small amount of flour during kneading only if you absolutely need it.

To shape pasta by hand if you don't have a pasta machine: Roll one portion of dough lightly in flour and press with your hands to flatten it into a rectangle about 1 inch thick. Work from the center of the dough outward with a rolling pin, adding flour and rotating and turning the piece as needed until the dough is a square about ⅛ inch thick. Fold the square in thirds, and use a sharp knife to slice the dough perpendicularly into noodles about ⅛ inch wide. Toss the noodles with a little flour to prevent sticking. (At this point you can freeze the noodles in an airtight container for up to 2 weeks.) Repeat with the remaining pieces.

Soba Noodles

These Japanese buckwheat noodles are less starchy than pasta and so they're good served at room temperature or even slightly chilled. For noodles that come together in a flash, the cook-and-assemble method in Soba with Sesame Chicken and Broccoli is unbeatable. Almost-Raw Vegetables with Soba and Sesame Sauce has lots of chopped "coddled" ingredients everyone will love. And since fresh soba is truly made by hand—with relative ease, in fact, compared to other pastas, the noodles in the All Out dish deliver rustic, thick, chewy strands with a coarse texture that attracts the dipping sauce like a magnet.

● SOBA
with sesame chicken and broccoli

makes: 4 servings
time: 30 minutes

Salt

6 boneless, skinless chicken thighs
  (about 1 pound)

2 tablespoons good-quality vegetable oil

Pepper

2 tablespoons sesame seeds

12 ounces dried soba noodles

1 pound broccoli, stems and florets chopped into
  bite-sized pieces

2 scallions, chopped

3 tablespoons soy sauce, or more to taste

2 tablespoons dark sesame oil

1. Bring a pot of water to a boil and salt it. Turn on the broiler and position the rack 4 inches below the heat. Spread the chicken pieces on a rimmed baking sheet in a single layer and coat with the vegetable oil; sprinkle with salt and pepper. Sprinkle on both sides with the sesame seeds. Broil, turning the thighs once or twice to prevent the seeds from burning, until the chicken is cooked through and golden in places and the pan is almost dry, 10 to 15 minutes total.

2. Add the noodles to the boiling water, cook for 3 minutes, stirring occasionally, then start tasting; when the noodles are pliable but not quite ready, add the broccoli and cook until it turns bright green, another minute or 2. Drain the noodles and broccoli, rinse with cold running water to stop the cooking, then shake the colander and drain again.

3. Slice the chicken into narrow strips and put in a large serving bowl with any pan juices and the scallions, soy sauce, and sesame oil. Toss to coat, add the noodle mixture and toss again. Taste, adjust the seasoning, and serve warm or at room temperature.

● ALMOST-RAW VEGETABLES
with soba and sesame sauce

makes: 4 servings
time: 30 minutes

Salt

Two 1-inch pieces fresh ginger, peeled

½ cup tahini

¼ cup white miso

4 teaspoons soy sauce, or to taste

2 teaspoons Dijon mustard

3 tablespoons good-quality vegetable oil

1 tablespoon dark sesame oil

1 tablespoon minced garlic

12 ounces dried soba noodles

1½ cups frozen edamame (no need to defrost)

3 cups mizuna or arugula, rinsed

1 cup chopped radishes

2 carrots, peeled and grated

Lemon juice, if desired

¼ cup chopped fresh cilantro, for garnish

Lemon wedges

1. Bring a pot of water to a boil and salt it. Grate 1 piece of ginger into a bowl, then put in a small fine-meshed strainer and press out the juice; you should have about 1 teaspoon. Discard the solids. Combine the ginger juice with the tahini, miso, 1 teaspoon soy sauce, the mustard, and ½ cup water in a small bowl and whisk until smooth. Add a little more water or soy sauce until the mixture is pourable. (The sauce can be refrigerated for up to 3 days. Let it return to room temperature before proceeding.)

2. Put the vegetable oil and sesame oil in a medium skillet over medium-low heat. Chop the remaining piece of ginger. When the oil is hot, add the ginger and garlic and cook, stirring often, until golden and fragrant, 2 to 3 minutes. Remove from the heat.

3. Add the noodles and edamame to the boiling water, and cook, stirring occasionally, for 3 minutes, then start tasting. When the noodles are tender but still have some bite, drain them and the edamame, but don't rinse.

4. Put the hot noodles and beans in a large bowl with the oil mixture, then add the mizuna, radishes, carrots, remaining 3 teaspoons soy sauce, and two-thirds of the tahini sauce. Toss to coat, then taste and adjust the seasoning, adding more soy sauce, lemon juice, or tahini sauce to taste. Garnish with the cilantro and serve at room temperature, passing the lemon wedges at the table.

HANDMADE SOBA
with shiso ponzu

makes: 4 servings
time: at least 10 hours, largely unattended

2 cups buckwheat flour

1 cup all-purpose flour, or more as needed

Tapioca flour, for dusting

Salt

2 tablespoons roasted, unsalted pistachios

1 teaspoon chopped garlic

2 teaspoons chopped fresh ginger

1 loosely packed cup fresh shiso leaves, rinsed
   and dried (or ½ cup parsley and ½ cup mint),
   plus 4 shiso leaves for garnish, sliced

1 cup soy sauce

⅔ cup yuzu juice (or ⅓ cup lemon juice mixed with
   ⅓ cup lime juice)

⅓ cup mirin (see page 290)

1 tablespoon sugar

1 tablespoon crumbled Japanese dried chile
   (*wagiri togarashi*), or to taste

1. Put the buckwheat and all-purpose flours in
a bowl and whisk to combine. Slowly add ¾ cup
lukewarm water, stirring constantly, until a ball forms
(you might not need all of the water). Add a few
drops of water if the dough is dry and grainy; add a
tablespoon of all-purpose flour if the dough sticks
to the side of the bowl. Transfer the dough to the
counter and knead until it's smooth and soft, about
5 minutes.

2. Shape the dough ball into a 6 by 3-inch rectangle and sprinkle both the top and bottom lightly
with tapioca flour. Using a rolling pin and even,
back-and-forth motions, roll out the dough into a
rectangle as thin as you can manage, no more than
¼ inch thick. Sprinkle the dough with tapioca flour
only as necessary as you work.

3. Fold the rectangle into thirds like a letter; sprinkle
the top with more tapioca flour. Using a very sharp
knife, slice the dough crosswise into noodles about
¼ inch thick. Toss the noodles with more tapioca
flour to prevent clumping. Put the noodles on a
parchment-lined baking sheet and refrigerate, covered with plastic, until ready to use, for up to 3 days.

4. Bring a large pot of water to a boil and salt it. Put
the pistachios, garlic, and ginger in a food processor
and pulse until finely chopped. Transfer to a bowl.
Put the shiso leaves in the food processor with the
soy sauce, yuzu juice, mirin, sugar, and ⅓ cup water
and pulse until the leaves are finely chopped; transfer to the bowl with the pistachio mixture. Add the
chile and mix, then taste and adjust the seasoning.

5. Add the noodles to the boiling water, and cook,
stirring occasionally, for 1 minute, then start tasting.
When the noodles are tender but still have some
texture, drain. Rinse the noodles under cold tap
water until they are cool. Shake off any excess water.
Divide the noodles among 4 bowls and serve cool,
with individual bowls of sauce for dipping.

Dumplings

Almost every cuisine features stuffed dumplings. The fillings and dipping sauces are what make them taste wildly different. The process doesn't get any easier than Pork Pan Stickers. After quick assembly, you'll get the best of pot stickers—their crisp bottoms and juicy stuffing—in my oven-baked method. On the other hand, simply boiled dumplings are underrated, especially when the dough is spiked with festive poppy seeds, as in the all-vegetable Potato and Sauerkraut Pierogi. And to impress friends and family with homemade dim sum, try the open-topped Seafood Siu Mai with Hot Chile Oil. All of these dumplings are so rich that you'll only need a side of simply steamed greens.

● PORK PAN STICKERS

makes: 6 to 8 servings
time: 50 minutes

12 ounces ground pork

4 scallions, chopped

½ cup soy sauce

2 tablespoons dark sesame oil

Salt and pepper

30 or more round dumpling skins (about 8 ounces)

4 tablespoons good-quality vegetable oil, plus more for greasing

2 tablespoons distilled white vinegar or rice vinegar

1 teaspoon sugar

Pinch red chile flakes (optional)

1. Heat the oven to 425°F and move the rack as low as it will go. Put the pork and scallions in a bowl with ¼ cup soy sauce and the sesame oil; sprinkle with salt and pepper, and stir gently with your hands to combine without overmixing. Fill a small bowl with hot tap water. Put another ½ cup hot tap water in the bottom of a large rimmed baking sheet and drizzle the vegetable oil over it.

2. Put 1 tablespoon pork mixture in the center of a dumpling skin, then dip your finger in the bowl of water and moisten the edge of the wrapper. Fold in half and press tightly to seal; try to make sure there is no air trapped between the filling and wrapper. Continue with remaining skins and pork mixture. Put the dumplings on the prepared baking sheet, close together without touching.

3. Grease the dull side of a large piece of foil with some oil. Cover the baking sheet with oiled side down and seal the edges tightly without pressing down on the dumplings. Transfer the pan to the oven and put it on the lowest rack. Bake, undisturbed, until you see steam escaping or the foil moving, 8 to 12 minutes. Remove the foil, and continue baking until the wonton skins are crisp and sizzling on the bottom and release easily from the pan, 3 to 5 minutes more.

4. Mix the remaining ¼ cup soy sauce, the vinegar, sugar, and red chile flakes, if using, in a small bowl with ¼ cup water. Serve the dumplings hot, passing the sauce at the table.

● POTATO AND SAUERKRAUT PIEROGI

makes: 6 to 8 servings
time: 90 minutes

¾ cup all-purpose flour, or more as needed

¾ cup rye or whole wheat flour

2 tablespoons poppy seeds

¾ teaspoon salt, or more as needed

1 onion, halved and sliced

6 tablespoons olive oil

12 ounces all-purpose potatoes (like Yukon Gold), scrubbed and cut into 1-inch chunks

1½ cups sauerkraut, rinsed, drained, and squeezed dry

Pepper

½ cup grainy mustard

¼ cup chopped fresh dill

2 tablespoons sweet white wine (like Riesling)

1. Put the flours, poppy seeds, and ¾ teaspoon salt in a large mixing bowl. Gradually stir in up to ⅓ cup cold water; you want the dough to come together into a ball but remain fairly dry. If some loose flour remains, add water 1 tablespoon at a time. Lightly dust a clean work surface with flour and turn out the dough; knead until smooth and elastic, 3 to 5 minutes, sprinkling as necessary with only enough flour to prevent sticking.

2. Shape the dough into a ball, lightly dust with flour, and cover tightly with plastic wrap. Let it rest for at least 20 minutes or up to 2 hours. (You can make the dough up to a few days in advance; wrap it tightly and refrigerate.)

3. Put the onion in a large skillet over medium heat. Cover and cook, stirring every 5 minutes or so, until dry and beginning to stick to the pan, 15 to 20 minutes. Add 2 tablespoons oil and a large pinch of salt and turn the heat down to medium-low. Continue cooking, stirring occasionally, until the onion is as golden as you like, another 5 to 20 minutes.

4. Meanwhile, put the potatoes in a large pot, sprinkle generously with salt, and cover with at least 2 inches of water. Bring to a boil, then reduce the heat so the water bubbles gently but steadily and cook, stirring once in a while, until the potatoes are tender, 15 to 20 minutes. Drain the potatoes, transfer to a large bowl, and mash roughly; the mixture should still have small chunks and be fairly stiff. Add the onion, sauerkraut, and 2 tablespoons oil and stir just to combine, then taste and season with salt and pepper.

5. Rinse out the pot, fill it two-thirds full of water, and bring to a boil. Add a large pinch of salt. Whisk together the mustard, dill, and wine and sprinkle with salt and pepper; taste and adjust the seasoning.

6. Knead the dough a few times, then divide it in half. On a lightly floured surface, use your palms to roll each piece into a 1-inch-thick log, then cut into 1-inch pieces. Roll each piece into a ball between your hands and cover with a damp towel. Working with one at a time and using a rolling pin, roll the balls out from the center in two directions to make a 4-inch round, dusting with flour as necessary. (To make ahead of time, stack them, dusting with flour between each, wrap tightly, and refrigerate for a few days or freeze for up to 2 weeks.)

7. Fill a small bowl with warm water. Pour the remaining 2 tablespoons oil in a shallow bowl or platter. Lay a dough round on a lightly floured work surface, then put a heaping tablespoon stuffing in the center; brush or dab the edge of the wrapper with water. Fold the circle in half and press the edges tightly to seal, making sure there is no air trapped between the stuffing and wrapper.

8. When the water comes to a boil, add some dumplings to the pot, working in batches and adjusting the heat to maintain a steady but gentle bubble. Cook, stirring only to keep the dumplings from sticking to the bottom, until they're tender, puffy, and float easily but are not breaking apart, 1 to 3 minutes. Transfer them with a slotted spoon to the prepared platter and toss gently to coat in oil. Repeat with the remaining dumplings. Serve the pierogi warm with the mustard sauce on the side.

● SEAFOOD SIU MAI with hot chile oil

makes: 4 to 6 servings
time: 2 hours

1 cup all-purpose flour, plus more for dusting

⅓ cup rice flour, plus more for dusting

½ teaspoon salt, or more as needed

¾ cup and 1 tablespoon good-quality vegetable oil

¼ cup boiling water

3 tablespoons red chile flakes

1 tablespoon Szechuan peppercorns

2 star anise

1 cinnamon stick

8 ounces cleaned squid, chopped

8 ounces peeled shrimp, chopped

One 2-inch piece peeled fresh ginger, cut into coins

20 fresh chives, chopped

2 tablespoons soy sauce

1 tablespoon rice vinegar

2 teaspoons dark sesame oil

Several large napa or savoy cabbage leaves

1. Put the flours and ½ teaspoon salt in a large mixing bowl with 1 tablespoon oil. Add the boiling water and stir quickly until the dough starts to come together. It should be quite dry but hold together when pinched; if it doesn't, add another tablespoon or 2 or of water. Knead it in the bowl until smooth and elastic. Roll it into a ball, cover with plastic, and let sit for at least 30 minutes or up to 1 hour.

2. Put the remaining ¾ cup oil, the red chile flakes, Szechuan peppercorns, star anise, cinnamon, and a pinch of salt in a small saucepan over low heat. Cook, stirring once in a while and adjusting the heat so the spices toast but don't burn, until the mixture is fragrant, 10 to 15 minutes. Let the oil steep until you're ready to cook the dumplings.

3. Knead the dough ball a few times, then cut into 4 pieces. To make the extra-thin wrappers:

With a pasta machine: Start on the widest setting, and gradually run each dough ball through to the thinnest setting you can manage without tearing the dough; you want it to be nearly translucent. Dust the dough as necessary with rice flour as you work. Cut the sheets into 3-inch circles.

By hand: On a lightly floured surface, roll each piece into a 1-inch-thick log, then cut into ½-inch pieces and roll each one out from the center to form a 3-inch round, dusting with a bit more rice flour as necessary.

Dust the wrappers lightly with rice flour, stack them, and cover with plastic wrap to rest. (You can refrigerate them for up to a couple hours before filling.)

4. Line a colander with cheesecloth and add the squid and shrimp. Twist the cheesecloth to squeeze out any excess liquid. Put the ginger, chives, soy sauce, vinegar, and sesame oil in a food processor and run the machine until smooth. Transfer to a medium bowl. Add the seafood to the food processor and pulse until chopped, then transfer to the bowl and stir to combine.

5. Set up a steamer in a large pot and fill with water to just below where the dumplings will sit. Line the basket with the cabbage leaves. Bring the water to a boil. Strain the chile oil into a serving bowl.

6. To make the dumplings, gently roll the seafood mixture into 1-inch balls and put them on a sheet of wax paper. With clean wet hands, open a wrapper over one palm and put a ball in the center. Make a loose fist to bring up the sides, leaving the very top of the ball exposed. Pleat the edges with the other hand making sure the wrapper is sealed all the way around. Continue to fill and pleat dumplings until you have enough to fill the steamer basket.

7. Put the dumplings in the steamer, open side up, close but not touching. Make sure there's enough water in the pot and that it's bubbling steadily. Cover and steam the dumplings until the filling is cooked through and the dough is translucent, 7 to 10 minutes. Repeat with the remaining dumplings. Serve with the chile oil.

Gnocchi Gratin,
page 129

Gnocchi

As gnocchi are known to be ornery, the key to getting pillowy lightness with these Italian dumplings is to add only enough flour to bring the dough together. Don't worry; the recipes include all my best tips. The first thing you'll notice in the Gnocchi Gratin is probably the rich dairy sauce, then you'll bite into the sublime dumplings. On weeknights, when you're less apt to fuss, cut out the potatoes in favor of a biscuitlike concoction spiked with Parmesan cheese; drop spoonfuls into a bright tomato sauce to simmer for about 10 minutes. The Butternut Squash Gnocchi and Warm Pecan Gremolata provides an opportunity to expand your Vegan options.

● PARMESAN DUMPLINGS
in tomato sauce

makes: 4 servings
time: 30 minutes

3 tablespoons olive oil

2 tablespoons chopped garlic

One 28-ounce can crushed tomatoes

Salt and pepper

1½ cups flour

¾ cup grated Parmesan cheese (about 3 ounces), plus more for serving

1 tablespoon baking powder

2 tablespoons cold unsalted butter, cut into chunks

½ cup milk, or more as needed

1 teaspoon grated lemon zest

½ teaspoon red chile flakes, or to taste

1. Put the oil in a large skillet over medium heat. When it's hot, add the garlic and cook, stirring frequently, until fragrant and golden, 2 to 3 minutes. Add the tomatoes and 1 cup water and sprinkle with salt and pepper. Bring the mixture to a boil, then adjust the heat so it bubbles steadily. Cover and cook for at least 15 minutes and up to 30, stirring occasionally, while you make the dumplings.

2. Put the flour, cheese, baking powder, and 1 teaspoon salt in a large bowl and mix with a fork. Add the butter and cut it in with a fork or two until the mixture has the texture of cornmeal. Slowly pour in the milk (you might not need all of it) and stir just until the mixture forms a ball.

3. Uncover the tomato sauce, stir in the lemon zest and red chile flakes, taste, and adjust the seasoning. If the sauce is too thick, add a splash of water to loosen a bit. You're looking for the consistency of a thick pureed soup because the dumplings will absorb water as they cook. Drop the dough into the sauce by heaping tablespoons, cover the pan, and cook for 10 minutes, undisturbed. When done, the dumplings should be light and cooked all the way through; a toothpick or fork inserted should come out clean. If not, cover and cook for another 3 to 5 minutes. When the dumplings are ready, stir gently to coat in the sauce, taste and adjust the seasoning, and serve hot, topped with more grated cheese.

BUTTERNUT SQUASH GNOCCHI
and warm pecan gremolata

makes: 4 servings
time: 1½ hours

1½ pounds butternut squash

6 tablespoons olive oil, or more as needed

Salt and pepper

½ to ¾ cup flour, or more as needed

1 cup chopped pecans

2 tablespoons chopped garlic

½ cup chopped fresh parsley

1. Heat the oven to 425°F. Peel and halve the squash, scoop out the seeds, and cut it into 2-inch chunks. You should have about 6 cups. Put the squash on a rimmed baking sheet, drizzle with 2 tablespoons oil, sprinkle with salt and pepper, and toss to coat. Spread the chunks in a single layer and roast, undisturbed, for 20 minutes. Check the squash and if the pieces release easily from the pan, toss with a spatula; if not, check again in another 5 minutes. After tossing, roast until the squash is dry, smells toasted, and is easily pierced with a fork, 5 to 10 minutes more.

2. Bring a large pot of water to a boil and salt it. Puree the squash in a food processor until smooth (or pass it through a ricer or food mill) and season to taste. Sprinkle about half the flour on a clean counter or cutting board, and gently knead it into the squash, sprinkling in more flour a little at a time, until the dough just comes together. Do not over-work the dough; it's better to have too little flour than too much at this point. Pinch off a piece of dough, and drop it in the boiling water. If it holds its shape, you've added enough flour. If it disintegrates in the water, knead in a bit more flour, and try again; the gnocchi won't be perfectly smooth and will float to the top when ready. Repeat with as many test dumplings as necessary.

3. Roll the dough into one or several ropes about ½ inch thick, then cut into ½-inch pieces. Make grooves in each gnocchi by gently rolling it along the back tines of a fork; as each piece is ready, put it on a baking sheet lined with parchment or wax paper; do not let the gnocchi touch.

4. Put the remaining 4 tablespoons oil in a skillet over medium heat. When it's hot, add the pecans and garlic and cook, stirring, until fragrant, 2 to 3 minutes. Add the parsley and continue cooking until the garlic and pecans are golden, another minute or 2. Turn the heat to low to keep the mixture warm but prevent burning.

5. Add a few of the gnocchi to the boiling water and stir gently. Cook, adjusting the heat so the mixture doesn't boil too vigorously, until they float to the top. Wait a few seconds, then remove them with a slotted spoon or mesh strainer and add to the skillet with the sauce. Continue cooking the gnocchi in small batches. When all the gnocchi are cooked, turn the heat under the sauce to medium and cook, stirring gently and adding a splash of cooking water if necessary, to make a slightly creamy sauce. Taste and adjust the seasoning. Top the gnocchi with the sauce and serve right away.

● GNOCCHI GRATIN

makes: 4 servings
time: about 2 hours

1½ pounds starchy potatoes (like russets), scrubbed

Salt and pepper

½ to ¾ cup flour, or more as needed

8 tablespoons (1 stick) unsalted butter

16 or more small whole sage leaves

½ cup grated Parmesan cheese (about 2 ounces)

½ cup grated or chopped high-quality melting cheese (like Taleggio or Gruyère), about 2 ounces

1. Heat the oven to 400°F. Put the potatoes on a rimmed baking sheet and bake until the skin hardens into a shell but the potato is tender when pierced at the center, about 1 hour. Immediately split them open to let the steam escape. Carefully scoop out the flesh and discard the skins.

2. Bring a large pot of water to a boil and salt it. Working in batches, pass the potato flesh through a ricer or food mill. (You could also use a potato masher, but not a food processor, which will make the potatoes gummy.) Sprinkle with salt and pepper, then taste and adjust the seasoning. Sprinkle about half the flour on a clean counter or cutting board, and gently knead it into the potatoes, sprinkling in more flour a little at a time, until the dough just comes together. Don't overwork the dough; it's better to have too little flour than too much at this point. Pinch off a piece of dough, and drop it in the boiling water. If it holds its shape, you've added enough flour. If it disintegrates in the water, knead in a bit more flour, and try again; the gnocchi won't be perfectly smooth and will float to the top when ready. Repeat with as many test dumplings as necessary.

3. Roll the dough into one or several ropes about ½ inch thick, then cut into ½-inch pieces. Make grooves in each gnocchi by gently rolling it along the back tines of a fork. As each piece is ready, put it on a baking sheet lined with parchment or wax paper; do not allow the gnocchi to touch one another.

4. Adjust the heat so the water barely bubbles. Add a few gnocchi and stir gently. Cook, adjusting the heat so the water doesn't boil too vigorously, until they float to the top. Wait a few seconds, then remove them with a slotted spoon or mesh strainer to a wide, shallow oven-safe baking dish. Cook the remaining gnocchi in the same manner.

5. Heat the oven to 425°F. Line a small plate with paper towels. Put the butter in a small saucepan over medium heat and cook, stirring occasionally, until the butter is golden brown and smells nutty. Remove from the heat immediately and add the sage leaves. Stir; when you can smell the sage and the leaves start to crisp around the edges, transfer them with a slotted spoon to the towels and drizzle the butter onto the gnocchi.

6. Sprinkle the cheese over the gnocchi and bake until the cheese is melted and browned in spots, 10 to 12 minutes. Garnish with the crisped sage leaves and serve right away.

Couscous

The teeny pasta from North Africa is a versatile delight. So remember Couscous and Chicken with Tunisian Spices when you don't feel like cooking—or think there's nothing in the house. The ingredients are almost entirely pantry staples and may require no more advance thought than taking chicken out of the freezer or picking up some on the way home from work. Whole Wheat Couscous with Charred Eggplant requires a little more time to prepare the vegetables—but not much. For Perfect Couscous with Braised Lamb, look for a coarse, preferably hand-rolled dried couscous for this classic technique from the Mediterranean food expert Paula Wolfert. But the supermarket kind works fine too.

● COUSCOUS AND CHICKEN
with tunisian spices

makes: 4 servings
time: 30 minutes

1 pound boneless, skinless chicken thighs

2 tablespoons olive oil

1 onion, chopped

Salt and pepper

2 teaspoons ground cumin

1 teaspoon ground coriander (optional)

½ teaspoon ground cinnamon

2 tablespoons tomato paste

1 cup couscous

¼ cup chopped fresh parsley, plus more
    for garnish

Lemon wedges

1. Cut the chicken into ½-inch pieces. Put the oil in a large skillet over medium-high heat. When it's hot, add the chicken and onion and sprinkle with salt and pepper. Cook, stirring occasionally until the onion is soft and the chicken is cooked through, 10 to 15 minutes.

2. Stir in the cumin, coriander if you're using it, and cinnamon and cook until fragrant, just a few seconds. Add the tomato paste and cook, stirring often, until the tomato paste darkens, 2 to 3 minutes.

3. Add the couscous and 1½ cups water, bring to a boil, then cover and turn off the heat. Let the skillet sit until the couscous is tender and the liquid is absorbed, about 5 minutes. Add the parsley and fluff with a fork. Taste, adjust the seasoning, and serve hot or at room temperature, garnished with more parsley and passing the lemon wedges at the table.

● WHOLE WHEAT COUSCOUS
with charred eggplant

makes: 4 servings
time: 45 minutes

1 pound eggplant, cut into ½-inch slices

7 tablespoons olive oil

Salt and pepper

2 red bell peppers

1 cup whole wheat couscous

½ cup fresh orange juice (from about 2 oranges)

½ cup chopped Kalamata olives

3 tablespoons fresh lemon juice, or as needed

½ cup chopped fresh mint

1. Prepare a charcoal or gas grill for direct cooking or turn on the broiler and position the rack 4 inches from the heat. Put the eggplant slices in a large bowl with 3 tablespoons oil and sprinkle with salt and pepper. If broiling, line a rimmed baking sheet with foil and add the eggplant slices in a single layer. Grill or broil the eggplant, watching closely and turning occasionally. The eggplant is done when browned, tender, and as charred in spots as you like, 5 to 15 minutes, depending on the size. As slices finish, transfer them to a cutting board.

2. Line another rimmed baking sheet with foil if broiling. Grill or broil the peppers, checking frequently and turning occasionally until they've collapsed and the skin is blistered and black in places, 15 to 20 minutes. Transfer the peppers to another piece of foil (or a bowl) as they finish; wrap (or cover) and let them sit for at least 10 minutes.

3. Put 1 tablespoon oil in a small saucepan over medium heat. When it's hot, add the couscous and cook, shaking the pan occasionally, until golden and fragrant, 2 to 3 minutes. Add the orange juice and 1 cup water and bring to a boil. Cover and remove from the heat. Steep until the couscous is tender, 10 to 15 minutes, then fluff with a fork.

4. When the peppers are cool enough to handle, remove and discard the skin, seeds, and stems (don't worry if the peppers fall apart). Chop the peppers and place in a large bowl. Cut the eggplant into bite-sized pieces and add to the bowl with the peppers.

5. Add the couscous, olives, lemon juice, remaining 3 tablespoons oil, and the mint to the eggplant and peppers and sprinkle with salt and pepper. Stir to combine, taste, and adjust the seasoning, adding more lemon juice if you like. Serve warm or at room temperature.

ROASTED RED PEPPERS

These add bright, intense pepper flavor to antipasti and bruschetta, salads, and sandwiches, or puree them into soups and sauces. Bookmark this recipe for later and consider roasting extra. (Hint: the same process works for green or any color sweet pepper as well as for chiles.) Prepare the grill or broiler as described above in Step 1, then jump to Step 2. Once peeled, the peppers will keep in the refrigerator for up to a week or the freezer for up to 2 months.

● PERFECT COUSCOUS
with braised lamb

makes: 4 to 6 servings
time: at least 4 hours, largely unattended

Salt

2½ cups couscous (about 1 pound; see the headnote, page 130)

1 cup milk

Pepper

2 tablespoons olive oil

2 pounds boneless lamb shoulder, cut into 2-inch chunks

1 pound leeks, trimmed and sliced

2 cups fruity red wine (like Beaujolais or Burgundy)

1 pound carrots, cut into chunks

12 dates, pitted and halved

About 1 pound ripe plums, pitted and quartered

2 tablespoons chopped fresh oregano

¼ cup chopped fresh cilantro, for garnish

1. Fill a large pot with 2 inches water, bring to a boil, and salt it. Rinse the couscous in a fine mesh sieve until the grains are saturated. Spread the couscous on a rimmed baking sheet and let it dry for 10 to 15 minutes, then use your fingers to break up any lumps.

2. Put the couscous back in the sieve (or another mesh steamer basket), set it over the bubbling water, and steam, uncovered, stirring a few times so the kernels on the bottom don't overcook, until the couscous is warmed through and has started to swell, 35 to 40 minutes. (Turn off the heat but leave the steamer set up.) Put the couscous back on the rimmed baking sheet and use a fork to break up any lumps and stir while you gradually (a few drops at a time) add the milk to the mixture. Sprinkle with salt and pepper. Let it rest, stirring occasionally and breaking up any lumps, until the couscous is no longer sticky, 1 to 2 hours.

3. Put 2 tablespoons oil in a large pot over medium-high heat. When it's hot, add half the lamb and sprinkle with salt and pepper, taking care not to crowd the pot. Cook, turning occasionally, until browned on all sides, 5 to 10 minutes. Transfer the lamb to a plate as it finishes and repeat with the remaining pieces. Pour off all but 3 tablespoons of fat, then add the leeks. Cook, stirring occasionally, until the leeks begin to soften and turn golden, 5 to 8 minutes.

4. Add the wine and cook, scraping any browned bits off the bottom of the pan. Add 3 cups water and bring to a boil, then return the lamb to the pan. Adjust the heat so the mixture bubbles steadily but not vigorously. Cook, stirring every 30 minutes or so, until the meat is almost done but not quite fork-tender, 1½ to 2 hours.

5. Add the carrots, dates, plums, and oregano to the lamb and continue cooking until the vegetables are tender and the meat is just about falling apart, another 25 to 35 minutes. Use a slotted spoon to transfer the meat and vegetables to a bowl and turn the heat to high. Reduce the cooking liquid to about a cup or even less. Taste and adjust the seasoning and remove from the heat. (At this point you can cool and refrigerate the lamb for up to 3 days.)

6. Meanwhile, put fresh water in the steaming pot and return to a boil. Put the couscous back in the strainer (or steamer basket) and steam for 20 minutes. Return it to the rimmed baking sheet and stir with a fork, slowly adding ½ cup cold water the same way you did the milk. Make sure there are no lumps, taste, and adjust the seasoning. Let the couscous dry until it is no longer sticky, another 1 to 2 hours.

7. Reheat the lamb mixture if necessary. Fluff the couscous with a fork and form it into a mound with a shallow well in the center. Put the lamb mixture in the center and spoon the warm sauce over it. Serve hot, garnished with the cilantro.

One-Pot Pasta

Cooking the sauce and noodles together is always easy. Exhibit A: Orecchiette, stirred with leeks to form a silky sauce and finished with salmon and its crisp baconlike skin to turn a weeknight pasta into something memorable. Likewise, Succotash and Shells depends on the key American vegetable combo to sauce the pasta as both cook together. Starting with homemade noodles and a stockpile of Parmesan rinds makes the All Out concept more of a project, but you plan ahead and I give you a break on the prep time with the shaved artichoke technique so the recipe is more inviting. That and the fact that it's a show-stopper should inspire you to give the recipe a try.

● ORECCHIETTE
with salmon and leeks

makes: 4 servings
time: 30 minutes

2 tablespoons olive oil

2 skin-on salmon fillets (about 12 ounces total)

Salt and pepper

1 pound leeks, trimmed, sliced crosswise and well rinsed

½ cup dry white wine

1 pound orecchiette or other small-cut pasta

2 tablespoons chopped fresh chives, for garnish

1. Put the oil in a large pot over medium-high heat. When it's hot, add the salmon skin side down, and sprinkle with salt and pepper. Cook until the skin is crisp and releases easily, 3 to 5 minutes; turn the fish and lower the heat to medium. Continue cooking until the salmon is not quite opaque all the way through, just another minute or 2.

2. Transfer the fish to a plate. Carefully peel off the skin and return it to the pot. Cook, turning occasionally, until browned and crisp, 3 to 5 minutes. Transfer to the plate with the filets and sprinkle with salt.

3. Add the leeks to the pot, sprinkle with salt and pepper, and cook, stirring occasionally, until soft, 3 to 5 minutes. Add the wine, pasta, and 1 cup water. Bring to a boil and scrape up any browned bits on the bottom of the pan. Reduce the heat so the mixture bubbles enthusiastically and cook, stirring frequently and adding more water ¼ cup at time to keep the mixture saucy, until the pasta just begins to get tender, no more than 10 minutes.

4. Chop the salmon skin. Use a fork to flake the salmon into large pieces. Add it to the pasta and cook until the salmon is heated through and the pasta is tender but still has some bite, another 2 to 3 minutes. Taste, adjust the seasoning, garnish with the chives and salmon skin, and serve.

● SUCCOTASH AND SHELLS

makes: 4 servings
time: 30 minutes

3 tablespoons olive oil

1 red onion, chopped

1 tablespoon minced garlic

Salt and pepper

12 ounces whole wheat shells or other cut pasta

2 cups frozen lima beans

1 red bell pepper, cored and chopped

2 cups corn kernels (frozen is fine)

1 tablespoon chopped fresh sage

1. Put the oil in a large pot over medium-high heat. When it's hot, add the onion and garlic, sprinkle with salt and pepper, and cook, stirring occasionally, until soft, 3 to 5 minutes.

2. Add the pasta, lima beans, bell pepper, and 1 cup water. Bring to a boil, scraping up any bits that might be stuck to the bottom of the pan. Reduce the heat so the mixture bubbles enthusiastically and cook, stirring frequently and adding more water ¼ cup at a time so the mixture stays saucy, until the pasta just begins to get tender, no more than 10 minutes.

3. Stir in the corn and sage and cook until the corn is warmed through and the pasta is tender but still has some bite, another 3 to 5 minutes Taste, adjust the seasoning, and serve hot or warm.

● PARMESAN-INFUSED NOODLES
with shaved artichoke hearts

makes: 4 servings
time: about 2 hours

8 ounces Parmesan rind, plus ½ cup grated Parmesan cheese (about 2 ounces)

1 onion, quartered (don't bother to peel)

2 garlic cloves, crushed

4 bay leaves

1 teaspoon black peppercorns, plus ground pepper as needed

About 2 cups flour, or more as needed

1 teaspoon salt, or more as needed

2 eggs, plus 3 egg yolks

2 lemons

3 medium or 6 small artichokes (about 1½ pounds)

3 tablespoons unsalted butter

1 tablespoon chopped fresh thyme

1. Put the Parmesan rind, onion, garlic, bay leaves, and peppercorns in a pot with 6 cups water. Bring to a boil, then reduce the heat so the mixture bubbles gently. Cook, stirring every few minutes to prevent the rinds from sticking to the pot, until the liquid is rich and flavorful, 30 to 40 minutes. Strain the stock and discard the solids. Return the stock to the pan over medium-low heat and cook, stirring occasionally, until it has reduced to about 2 cups, 20 to 25 minutes. Taste and adjust the seasoning. Keep warm. (Or you can cool it and refrigerate for a few days or freeze for a few weeks.)

2. Combine the flour and 1 teaspoon salt in the container of a food processor and pulse once or twice. Add the eggs and yolks and turn the machine on. Process just until a ball begins to form, about 30 seconds. Add a few drops of water if the dough is dry and grainy; add a tablespoon of flour if the dough sticks to the side of the bowl. (If you don't have a food processor, see page 117 for how to make the pasta dough by hand.)

3. Sprinkle the dough with a little reserved flour and cover with plastic or a cloth; let it rest for about 30 minutes. (At this point, you can refrigerate the dough, wrapped in plastic, until you're ready to roll it out, for up to 24 hours.)

4. Set up your pasta machine and sprinkle the work surface lightly with flour. Cut off about one-third of the dough and wrap the rest in plastic or cloth while you work. Roll the dough lightly in the flour and use your hands to flatten it into a rectangle about the width of the rollers. Set the machine to its thickest setting and feed the dough through the rollers. If it sticks, dust it with a little more flour. Repeat. Set the machine to its next-thinnest setting and repeat. Each time, if the pasta sticks, sprinkle it with a little more flour, and put the dough through each setting twice.

5. Continue to roll the dough thinner, moving the thickness only one setting each time (if you try to rush the process, the dough will tear). If at any point the dough tears badly, bunch it together and start again. Use only as much flour as you need to prevent sticking, added in small amounts each time. Continue to pass the dough through the machine until it's just a bit thicker than you might normally make (usually that's the third-thinnest setting.) Repeat 2 more times (by this time it will be going quickly), then flour the dough lightly, cover it, and set it aside. Repeat the process with the remaining dough.

6. Cut each dough sheet into rectangles roughly 16 inches long; trim any rough edges. Use a sharp knife to cut the sheets perpendicularly into long, wide noodles, or attach the broadest (tagliatelle) cutter to your machine and run each sheet through. Cover with a towel while you prepare the artichokes.

7. Fill a bowl with cold water and the juice of 2 lemons. Cut off the pointed tips of the artichoke leaves with scissors or cut off the whole top third using a large knife. Use a paring knife to peel around the base and cut off the stem and bottom ¼ inch; pull off and discard the toughest exterior leaves. Halve the artichoke lengthwise, pry open the central petals, and scrape out the fuzzy choke with a spoon. Keep the trimmed artichokes in the lemon water while you work. When all the artichokes have been trimmed, use the thinnest slicing blade of a food processor or a mandoline to slice cross-sections of artichoke. Put them back in the acidulated water as quickly as possible.

8. Put the butter in a large pot over medium heat. When it melts, add the noodles, quickly followed by 1½ cups Parmesan stock and all but a handful of the artichoke slices. Adjust the heat so the mixture bubbles enthusiastically and cook, stirring constantly and carefully and adding more stock ¼ cup at time to keep the mixture saucy, until the pasta is tender but still has some bite, 3 to 5 minutes. Add the grated Parmesan and thyme and sprinkle with salt and pepper. Cook, stirring constantly, until everything is mixed together and the sauce is silky. Taste and adjust the seasoning, then garnish with the remaining shaved artichokes and lots of pepper and serve.

Pasta Marinara

As basic as it gets: pasta with tomatoes. Or so you thought. For Pasta with One-Can Tomato Sauce I break a couple of my main pasta rules to deliver a delicious, super-creamy bowl of noodles in no time. For the Vegan option, the tomatoes get a boost from the anise flavor of fennel and the sweetness of raisins, adding in turn an element of surprise to the heartiness of the whole wheat pasta. And often the best way to make something simple "fancier" is to upgrade the ingredients, as in Spaghetti with Fresh Marinara and Fried Basil, so consider making this only in summer.

● PASTA
with one-can tomato sauce

makes: 4 servings
time: 25 minutes

Salt

4 tablespoons unsalted butter, or more as needed

4 garlic cloves, peeled

¼ teaspoon red chile flakes, or to taste

One 14-ounce can pureed tomatoes

Pepper

1 pound dried pasta (any kind you like)

½ cup grated Parmesan cheese (about 2 ounces), plus more for serving

1. Bring a half-full pot of water to a boil and salt it. Melt the butter in a large skillet over medium heat. Add the garlic and red chile flakes if you're using them. Cook, stirring occasionally, until golden and fragrant, 2 to 3 minutes. Add the tomatoes and sprinkle with salt and pepper.

2. Adjust the heat so the sauce bubbles enthusiastically and cook, stirring occasionally, until the tomatoes thicken and you can smash the garlic a bit, 5 to 10 minutes. Taste, adjust the seasoning, and adjust the heat so the sauce stays hot but doesn't boil.

3. Add the pasta to the boiling water, and cook, stirring occasionally, for 5 minutes, then start tasting. When the pasta is tender but still has some bite, scoop out 2 cups cooking water, then drain the pasta and return it to the pot.

4. Add the sauce and cheese to the pasta; swirl ½ cup cooking water in the skillet to loosen every last drop of sauce and add that to the pot too. Toss with tongs to coat the noodles, adding more cooking water or butter, a little at a time, to make the pasta creamy. Taste and adjust the seasoning and serve, passing more cheese at the table.

WHOLE WHEAT LINGUINE
with fennel-tomato sauce

makes: 4 servings
time: 30 minutes

Salt

2 large fennel bulbs (about 1½ pounds)

1 small red onion

3 tablespoons olive oil

Pepper

One 6-ounce can tomato paste

8 ounces whole wheat linguine

¼ cup golden raisins

1. Bring a pot of water to a boil and salt it. Trim the fennel down to the bulb and reserve some of the most tender fronds for garnish. Halve the bulbs top to bottom, then slice each half in either direction as thin as you can manage (a mandoline works well). Peel the onion, then halve and slice it the same way.

2. Put the oil in a large skillet over medium-high heat. When it's hot, add the fennel and onion and sprinkle with salt and pepper. Cook, stirring occasionally, until soft and golden, 8 to 10 minutes. Add the tomato paste and stir to coat the vegetables. Cook, stirring constantly, until the paste caramelizes, 2 to 3 minutes. Add water ¼ cup at a time, about ½ to 1 cup total, to make a thick sauce. Cook the sauce down until it is reduced slightly, 5 to 7 minutes. Adjust the heat so the sauce bubbles gently.

3. Add the pasta to the boiling water, and cook, stirring occasionally, for 5 minutes, then start tasting. When the pasta is tender but still has some bite, scoop out 1 cup cooking water, then drain the pasta.

4. Add the pasta to the skillet and toss to coat, adding a little cooking water if necessary to create a slightly creamy sauce. Taste, adjust the seasoning, then toss with the golden raisins. Garnish with the reserved fennel fronds and serve.

● SPAGHETTI
with fresh marinara and fried basil

makes: 4 servings
time: 45 minutes

Salt

4 pounds ripe Roma (plum) tomatoes, cored and chopped

Pepper

6 tablespoons unsalted butter

3 small shallots or 1 large, thinly sliced

Olive oil, for frying

16 to 20 whole fresh basil leaves

1 pound spaghetti or any other long pasta

½ cup grated Parmesan cheese (about 2 ounces), plus more for serving

1. Bring a pot of water to a boil and salt it. Put the tomatoes in a large skillet over medium heat and sprinkle with salt and pepper. Cook, stirring occasionally, until the tomatoes have completely broken down, 10 to 15 minutes. Working in batches, run the tomatoes through a food mill or press through a mesh sieve to separate the flesh from the seeds and skin; discard the solids.

2. Wipe out the skillet and return it to the stove over medium heat; add the butter. When the butter has melted, add the shallots. Cook, stirring occasionally, until golden and soft, 5 to 10 minutes. Sprinkle with salt and pepper, then add the pureed tomatoes. Adjust the heat so the sauce bubbles gently and cook, stirring occasionally, until the mixture begins to thicken and appear more uniform in texture, 5 to 10 minutes. Taste, adjust the seasoning, and keep the sauce hot but do not boil.

3. Put 2 inches of oil in a medium saucepan over medium-high heat. When it's hot but not smoking, add the basil leaves (put them in the oil one at a time so they don't clump and work in batches) and cook until crisp and deeper green, less than 30 seconds. Remove with a slotted spoon and transfer to a paper towel–lined plate to drain. Repeat with the remaining leaves.

4. Add the pasta to the boiling water, and cook, stirring occasionally, for 5 minutes, then start tasting. When the pasta is tender but still has some bite, scoop out 1 cup cooking water, then drain the pasta.

5. Immediately add the pasta and about ½ cup cooking water to the skillet and toss to coat. Add the cheese and a little more liquid a little at a time if necessary to create a creamy sauce. Taste and adjust the seasoning. Garnish with the fried basil leaves and serve, passing more cheese at the table.

Pasta Bolognese

There are as many ways to make this famous pasta as there are *nonnas*. For a true use-what-you've-got meal, make the first recipe with any ground meat and Italian seasoning that's handy. I've adapted the technique for making a finely chopped luxurious vegetable sauce for the Rigatoni with Ratatouille Bolognese. And everyone should spend more Sundays making fresh pappardelle with this pretty traditional sauce; as a reward, you're left with extra Bolognese for another meal.

● PASTA
with use-what-you've-got bolognese

makes: 4 servings
time: 30 minutes

Salt

2 tablespoons olive oil, or more as needed

1 pound ground beef or other ground meat

1 onion, chopped

1 tablespoon minced garlic

Pepper

1 teaspoon dried herb (like oregano, thyme, or marjoram)

1 teaspoon spices (like fennel seeds, ground coriander, or celery seeds)

¼ cup tomato paste

1 cup dry red wine or water

½ cup milk or heavy cream

1 pound any pasta

1 cup grated Parmesan or pecorino cheese (about 4 ounces)

1. Bring a large pot of water to a boil and salt it. Put the oil in a large skillet over medium-high heat with the beef, onion, and garlic and sprinkle with salt and pepper. Cook, stirring frequently and breaking the meat up until it's browned and the vegetables are soft, 5 to 10 minutes.

2. Add the herbs, spices, and tomato paste and stir until fragrant and the tomato paste has caramelized, 2 to 3 minutes. Add the wine, raise the heat a bit, and cook, stirring occasionally and scraping any browned bits off the bottom. Add the milk and adjust the heat so the sauce bubbles gently and cook until thickened, 5 to 10 minutes. Cover and keep warm.

3. Add the pasta to the boiling water, and cook, stirring occasionally, for 5 minutes, then start tasting. When the pasta is tender but still has some bite, scoop out 2 cups cooking water, then drain the pasta. Immediately add the pasta and ½ cup cheese to the skillet and toss to coat; if it's too dry, add enough of the reserved cooking water to coat the noodles in sauce. Taste and adjust the seasoning, toss again, and serve, passing the remaining cheese at the table.

RIGATONI
with ratatouille bolognese

makes: 4 servings
time: 45 minutes

Salt

1 pound eggplant, peeled if you like and
cut into chunks

1 onion, peeled and cut into chunks

1 fennel bulb, trimmed and cut into chunks

1 zucchini, cut into chunks

1 red or yellow bell pepper, cored and
cut into chunks

6 garlic cloves

¼ cup and 2 tablespoons olive oil

1 cup tomato paste

One 28-ounce can crushed tomatoes

Pepper

1 pound whole wheat rigatoni or other cut pasta

¼ cup chopped fresh parsley, for garnish

1. Bring a large pot of water to a boil and salt it. Put the eggplant, onion, fennel, zucchini, bell pepper, and garlic in a food processor with the ¼ cup oil. Pulse, stopping to scrape down the sides once or twice, until finely chopped but not pureed.

2. Put the remaining 2 tablespoons oil in a large skillet over medium-high heat. When it's hot, add the vegetables and cook, stirring often, until the onion becomes translucent, 3 to 5 minutes. Add the tomato paste, turn the heat to medium-low, and cook, stirring frequently, until the tomato paste caramelizes, 3 to 5 minutes. Add the crushed tomatoes and sprinkle with salt and pepper. Bring the mixture to a boil, and then reduce the heat so it bubbles gently but steadily. Cook, stirring occasionally until the sauce thickens and the vegetables are tender, 15 to 20 minutes.

3. Add the pasta to the boiling water, and cook, stirring occasionally, for 5 minutes, then start tasting. When the pasta is tender but still has some bite, scoop out 2 cups cooking water, then drain the pasta.

4. Immediately add the pasta and a splash of the cooking water to the skillet and turn the heat to medium-high. Toss to coat in the sauce, adding a little more reserved pasta water if necessary to create a slightly creamy, but not soupy, sauce. Taste and adjust the seasoning; then garnish with the parsley and serve.

FRESH PAPPARDELLE
with bolognese

makes: 4 servings
time: 3 to 4 hours

2 tablespoons olive oil

1 small onion, chopped

1 carrot, chopped

1 celery stalk, chopped

4 ounces pancetta, chopped

6 ounces boneless beef chuck, cut into
1-inch chunks

6 ounces boneless pork shoulder, cut into
1-inch chunks

6 ounces boneless veal shoulder, cut into
1-inch chunks

Salt and pepper

1 cup milk

One 28-ounce can whole Roma (plum) tomatoes

1 cup beef or chicken stock
(see page 47 or 43)

1 cup dry white wine

2 cups flour, or more as needed

2 eggs, plus 3 egg yolks

½ cup grated Parmesan cheese (about 2 ounces)

1. Put the oil in a large pot over medium-low heat. When it's hot, add the onion, carrot, celery, and pancetta. Cook, stirring occasionally, until the vegetables are tender, 8 to 10 minutes.

2. Meanwhile, put the meat into a food processor (in batches, if necessary) and pulse until coarsely ground—finer than chopped, but not much. Add the ground meat to the pot and sprinkle with salt and pepper. Cook, stirring and breaking up any clumps, until no longer pink, 5 to 10 minutes. Add the milk, raise the heat a bit, and cook, stirring occasionally and scraping any browned bits off the bottom, until most of the liquid has evaporated, 3 to 5 minutes.

3. Crush the tomatoes with your hands and add them to the pot; stir, then add the stock and wine. Adjust the heat so the mixture just barely bubbles and cook, stirring occasionally and breaking up the tomatoes, until the liquid has evaporated and the sauce is very thick, another 1 to 1½ hours. Taste and adjust the seasoning. (At this point, you can refrigerate the sauce for a day or so or freeze it for several weeks. Reheat before proceeding.)

4. While the sauce is cooking, make the pasta. Combine 2 cups flour and 1 teaspoon salt in a food processor and pulse once or twice. Add the eggs and yolks and turn the machine on. Process just until a ball begins to form, about 30 seconds. Add a few drops of water if the dough is dry and grainy; add a tablespoon of flour if the dough sticks to the side of the bowl. (To make pasta by hand, see the directions on page 117.)

5. Sprinkle the dough with a little flour and cover; let it rest for about 30 minutes. (At this point, you can refrigerate the dough, tightly wrapped in plastic, for up to 24 hours. Let it sit out for 15 minutes before proceeding.)

6. Set up your pasta machine and sprinkle the work surface lightly with flour. (To roll the pasta by hand, see page 117.) Cut off about one-third of the dough and wrap the rest in plastic or a dishtowel while you work. Roll the dough lightly in the flour and use your hands to flatten it into a rectangle about the width of the rollers. Set the machine to its thickest setting and roll the dough through. If it sticks, dust it with a little more flour. Repeat. Set the machine to its next-thinnest setting and repeat. Each time, if the pasta sticks, sprinkle it with a little more flour, and put the dough through each setting twice.

7. Continue to roll the dough thinner, changing the thickness only one setting each time (if you try to rush the process, the dough will tear). If at any point the dough tears badly, bunch it together and start again. Use only as much flour as you need to. Pass the dough through the machine's second-thinnest setting. Repeat 2 more times (by this time it will be going quickly), then flour the dough lightly, and cover. Repeat with the remaining dough.

8. Bring a large pot of water to a boil and salt it. Heat the sauce in a large pot if it isn't hot already, then remove half the sauce and reserve. Cut each pasta sheet into rectangles roughly 16 inches long and trim any rough edges. Roll the dough into cigars and cut crosswise to make wide noodles, or attach the broadest (tagliatelle) cutter to your machine and run each sheet through. Use right away or hang the strands to dry for up to a couple of hours.

9. Add the pasta to the boiling water, and cook, stirring occasionally, for 1 minute, then start tasting. When the pasta is tender but still has some texture (it will take less than 3 minutes, probably less than 2), scoop out 2 cups cooking water, then drain the pasta. Immediately add the pasta and a splash of the cooking water to the pot with the sauce and turn the heat to medium-high. Toss to coat, adding a little more cooking water if necessary to create a slightly creamy, but not soupy sauce. Add more of the reserved sauce to your liking, and save the rest for another use. Taste and adjust the seasoning; then toss with the cheese and serve right away.

Pasta Carbonara

Who says you can't honor tradition on a weeknight? After all, the sauce is only bacon, eggs, and Parmesan. Instead of eggs, the Vegan version features *aquafaba,* a trendy name for something that is usually thrown out: the water left behind after draining cooked or canned chickpeas. Spaghetti with Champagne Zabaglione isn't at all a true spaghetti carbonara. Instead, it exaggerates the concept with a rich, savory, and boozy custard sauce.

● CLASSIC SPAGHETTI CARBONARA

makes: 4 servings
time: 30 minutes

Salt

4 slices bacon, chopped

1 pound spaghetti or other long pasta

3 eggs

1 cup grated Parmesan cheese (about 4 ounces)

Pepper

1. Bring a pot of water to a boil and salt it. Heat the oven to 200°F and put the serving bowl on the middle rack. Line a plate with paper towels. Put the bacon in a medium skillet over medium heat and cook, stirring occasionally, until browned and crisped, 5 to 10 minutes. Transfer the bacon to the plate to drain. Remove the pan from the heat and reserve 2 tablespoons fat.

2. Add the pasta to the boiling water, and cook, stirring occasionally, for 5 minutes, then start tasting. When the pasta is tender but still has some texture, scoop out 1 cup cooking water, then drain the pasta.

3. Carefully remove the bowl from the oven, crack the eggs into it, add the cheese and lots of pepper, and beat the mixture with a fork. Immediately toss in the pasta, bacon, and the reserved fat; if it's too dry, add a tablespoon or so of the pasta water. Taste, adjust the seasoning, and serve right away.

CREAMY BUCATINI
with chickpea crumble

makes: 4 servings
time: 1 hour

Salt

One 15-ounce can chickpeas

2 tablespoons and ¼ cup olive oil, or more as needed

1 teaspoon paprika

Pepper

1 tablespoon nutritional yeast

1 large red onion, peeled, halved, and sliced

1 pound bucatini or other long pasta

¼ cup chopped fresh parsley, for garnish

1. Bring a pot of water to a boil and salt it. Heat the oven to 400°F. Drain the chickpeas into a colander set in a bowl to reserve the canning liquid. Rinse the chickpeas, and drain again; spread them on a rimmed baking sheet and mash lightly with a fork or potato masher. Drizzle with 2 tablespoons oil and sprinkle with the paprika, salt, and pepper; toss to coat. Roast, turning with a spatula once or twice, until crisp and lightly browned, 15 to 20 minutes. Sprinkle with the nutritional yeast and toss to coat.

2. Put the onion in a large dry skillet over medium heat. Cover and cook, stirring every 5 minutes or so, until the onion is dry and beginning to stick to the pan, 15 to 20 minutes. Add the remaining ¼ cup oil and a large pinch of salt and turn the heat down to medium-low. Cook uncovered, stirring occasionally and adjusting the heat as necessary to prevent burning, until the onion is soft and darkened, another 5 to 10 minutes. Keep warm.

3. Add the pasta to the boiling water, and cook, stirring occasionally, for 5 minutes, then start tasting. While the pasta is cooking, put the chickpea liquid into a medium bowl and beat it into a foamy sauce with a whisk or mixer.

4. When the pasta is tender but still has some texture, scoop out 1 cup cooking water, then drain the pasta. Immediately toss the pasta with the onion mixture and the chickpeas in the skillet; if it's too dry, add a little cooking water. Add lots of pepper, the foamy sauce, and the parsley; gently toss, then taste, adjust the seasoning, and serve.

● SPAGHETTI CARBONARA
with champagne zabaglione

makes: 4 servings
time: 40 minutes

Salt

4 ounces pancetta, chopped

2 shallots, chopped

2 egg yolks

¼ cup champagne or other sparkling wine

Pepper

¼ cup heavy cream

½ cup grated Parmesan cheese (about 2 ounces), or more to taste

1 pound spaghetti or other long pasta

1. Bring a pot of water to a boil and salt it. Put the pancetta in a large skillet over medium heat. Cook, stirring occasionally, until browned and crisped, 5 to 10 minutes. Pour off all but 2 tablespoons of the fat and add the shallots. Cook, stirring occasionally, until the shallots are soft and golden, 5 to 8 minutes. Remove from the heat.

2. Put the egg yolks in the top of a double boiler with the champagne and a sprinkle of salt and pepper. Turn on the heat and whisk constantly until thick. Keep beating; eventually the mixture will become light and frothy, 8 to 10 minutes total. Turn off the heat. In a separate bowl, beat the cream until it holds soft peaks, then fold the cream and half the cheese into the beaten yolks. Keep warm.

3. Add the pasta to the boiling water, and cook, stirring occasionally, for 5 minutes, then start tasting. When the pasta is tender but still has some texture, scoop out 1 cup cooking water, then drain the pasta.

4. Immediately toss the pasta with the custard and the pancetta mixture in the skillet; if it's too dry (unlikely), add a little of the cooking water. Taste and add more salt if you want, then add black pepper, mix in the remaining ¼ cup cheese, and serve right away.

● Roasted Beet Gnudi
with Pistachio Pesto,
page 153

Pasta with Pesto

The touchstone version of pesto is sublime, but it's been done to death, including by me. So let's explore new territory with these three recipes. The color contrast of the All Out dish is indisputably gorgeous, and the combination of earthy dumplings and herbaceous sauce is unbeatable. Linguine with Deconstructed Pesto lives at the other end of the time-work continuum, since there's no fretting over pureeing the sauce. And the leaf-to-root approach makes perfect sense for Whole Wheat Pasta with Carrot-Top Pesto.

● LINGUINE
with deconstructed pesto

makes: 4 servings
time: 30 minutes

Salt

4 garlic cloves

⅓ cup olive oil

½ cup pine nuts

2 cups loosely packed fresh basil leaves

1 pound linguine or other long, thin pasta

1 cup grated Parmesan cheese (about 4 ounces)

1. Bring a large pot of water to a boil and salt it. Smash the garlic cloves with the flat side of a knife and discard the skins; chop. Put the oil, pine nuts, and garlic in a large skillet over medium-low heat and sprinkle with salt. Cook, stirring occasionally, until the pine nuts and garlic just turn golden, 2 to 4 minutes. Turn off the heat and stir in the basil leaves.

2. Add the pasta to the boiling water, and cook, stirring occasionally, for 5 minutes, then start tasting. When the pasta is tender but still has some bite, scoop out 1 cup cooking water, then drain the pasta.

3. Immediately add the pasta to the skillet along with half the cheese and a splash of the cooking water and turn the heat to medium. Toss to coat the pasta evenly, adding a little more cooking water if necessary to create a creamy—but not soupy—sauce. Taste, adjust the seasoning, adding more cheese if you like, and serve, passing the remaining cheese at the table.

● WHOLE WHEAT PASTA
with carrot-top pesto

makes: 4 servings
time: 30 minutes

Salt

1 pound carrots with tops, rinsed and trimmed

½ cup fresh parsley, tough stems removed

½ cup walnuts

2 garlic cloves, chopped

2 tablespoons white miso

2 tablespoons lemon juice, or to taste

½ cup olive oil, or more as needed

1 pound whole wheat spaghetti or other
    long pasta

1. Bring a large pot of water to a boil and salt it. Peel the carrots, then starting at the top of each carrot, make ribbons with a vegetable peeler, turning it as you work. Pick off the frilly carrot tops, discarding any tough stems, and reserve 1½ loosely packed cups for the pesto.

2. Put the carrot tops, parsley, walnuts, garlic, miso, lemon juice, and about ¼ cup oil in a food processor or blender and sprinkle with salt. Turn the machine on and gradually add the remaining ¼ cup oil. Continue processing or blending, stopping a couple of times to scrape down the sides of the container, until you have a relatively smooth, thick sauce (you can add more oil if you need to, but remember that it will be thinner when mixed with pasta water). Taste and adjust the seasoning.

3. Add the pasta to the boiling water and cook, stirring occasionally, for 5 minutes, then start tasting. When the pasta is tender but still has some bite, add the carrots, and cook until pliable but not mushy, 1 to 2 minutes. Scoop out 1 cup cooking water, then drain the pasta. Immediately put the pasta back into the pot and add the pesto. Toss, adding more cooking water if necessary to make a creamy sauce. Taste, adjust the seasoning, and serve.

● ROASTED BEET GNUDI
with pistachio pesto

makes: 4 servings
time: 2 to 4 hours

About 2 pounds beets

1 cup shelled pistachios

1 cup fresh breadcrumbs (see page 173)

2 eggs, plus 1 yolk

1 cup ricotta cheese

1 cup grated Parmesan cheese (about 4 ounces),
    plus more for serving

Salt and pepper

⅓ to ½ cup semolina flour, as needed

2 cups loosely packed fresh basil

2 garlic cloves

1 teaspoon grated lemon zest

1 cup olive oil

1. Heat the oven to 400°F. Scrub the beets; wrap them individually in foil and put them on a baking sheet. Roast until a thin-bladed knife pierces one with little resistance, 45 to 90 minutes (they may cook at different rates; remove each as it is done).

2. While the beets are roasting, put the pistachios on a rimmed baking sheet and toast in the oven, shaking the pan every few minutes and watching like a hawk, until they are golden and fragrant, 3 to 5 minutes.

3. When the beets are cool enough to handle, peel them. Cut the beets into chunks and puree in a food processor until completely smooth; transfer to a bowl and wash the food processor.

4. Combine the breadcrumbs in a bowl with the eggs, ricotta, ¾ cup Parmesan cheese, and 1 cup beet puree. Sprinkle with salt and pepper. Stir the mixture until combined, then let it sit for about 10 minutes. Add semolina flour a little at a time until the mixture wants to stick to your hands but won't quite; it should feel like fresh play dough. Take care not to overmix. With floured hands, form the dough into tiny balls about 1 inch in diameter and put on a platter in a single layer. Refrigerate for at least 30 minutes and up to overnight, covered.

5. Bring a large pot of water to a boil and salt it. Combine the basil, pistachios, garlic, lemon zest, a sprinkle of salt, and ½ cup oil in a food processor or blender. Puree, stopping to scrape down the sides of the container if necessary and adding the remaining ½ cup oil gradually. Stir in the remaining ¼ cup Parmesan. Taste and adjust the seasoning.

6. When the water boils, cook the gnudi, a dozen or so at a time, until they come to the surface, about 3 minutes; remove with a slotted spoon and keep warm. Scoop out a cup of cooking water and use it to thin the pesto; start with just a tablespoon so you don't overdo it; you're looking for the pesto to coat the back of a spoon. To serve, spoon some pesto onto the bottom of 4 plates or shallow bowls, top with the gnudi, and sprinkle with more grated (or shaved) Parmesan.

Pasta with Cream Sauce

I love pasta too much to not include both carbonara and another three luxurious creamy sauces. Gina is a former babysitter for our family who used to make noodles with ham and peas for my kids; adults love it too, especially this way. There are no shortcuts with Tagliatelle with Lemon Crème Fraîche and Shaved Bottarga; I can only assure you the hunt for the fish and the homemade cream and pasta are totally worth the effort. The delightful sauce with Whole Wheat Spaghetti with Oven-Roasted Tomatoes and Almond Cream requires a leap of faith. Work through any doubts you might have and it all comes together in the end.

● GINA NOODLES
with ham and peas

makes: 4 servings
time: 30 minutes

ENRICHING MILK You need fat to make this sauce work. If you only have reduced-fat milk, add another 2 tablespoons butter in Step 2.

Salt

4 tablespoons unsalted butter

1 onion, chopped

8 ounces thick-cut ham, chopped

Pepper

¾ cup milk

1 pound long pasta (like spaghetti or linguine), or any other pasta

1 cup peas (frozen are fine)

1 cup grated Parmesan cheese (about 4 ounces), plus more for serving

1. Bring a large pot of water to a boil and salt it. Put 2 tablespoons butter in a large skillet over medium heat. When it melts, add the onion and ham, sprinkle with salt and pepper, and turn the heat up to medium-high. Cook, stirring occasionally, until the onion is soft and the ham is beginning to brown, 5 to 8 minutes.

2. Add the milk and remaining 2 tablespoons butter and scrape up any browned bits from the bottom of the pan. Adjust the heat so the sauce barely steams and cook, stirring frequently, until it thickens enough to coat the back of a spoon, about 5 minutes. Cover the pan and remove from the heat.

3. Add the pasta to the boiling water, and cook, stirring occasionally, for 5 minutes, then start tasting. When the pasta is tender but still has some bite, scoop out 1 cup cooking water, then drain the pasta.

4. Return the sauce to medium-low heat, add the peas, and stir. Immediately add the pasta to the skillet along with the cheese and toss to coat, adding a little more cooking water to create a creamy sauce. Taste and adjust the seasoning, then add lots of pepper, and serve, passing more cheese at the table.

Tagliatelle with Lemon Crème Fraîche
and Shaved Bottarga, page 157

● WHOLE WHEAT SPAGHETTI
with oven-roasted tomatoes and almond cream

makes: 4 servings
time: about 1 hour

7 tablespoons olive oil

2 pounds ripe Roma (plum) tomatoes (about a dozen), cored and halved lengthwise

Salt

1 cup raw almonds

12 ounces silken tofu

2 teaspoons minced garlic

1 teaspoon red chile flakes or cayenne, or to taste

Pepper

1 pound whole wheat spaghetti or any other long pasta

½ cup chopped fresh basil, for garnish

1. Heat the oven to 325°F. Grease a large baking sheet or roasting pan with 1 tablespoon oil. Scoop the seeds out of the tomatoes if you like. Put the tomatoes on the pan cut side down and drizzle with 2 tablespoons oil. Roast until they start to brown and shrivel (there's no need to turn), 25 to 35 minutes. When the tomatoes are halfway through cooking, bring a large pot of water to a boil and salt it.

2. Put the almonds in a large dry skillet over medium-heat. Toast, shaking the pan almost constantly, until they are golden and fragrant, 3 to 5 minutes. Transfer to a food processor and add the tofu, garlic, red chile flakes, and remaining 4 tablespoons oil and sprinkle with salt and pepper. Process until the mixture is smooth and creamy. Taste and adjust the seasoning, making sure there's enough salt and pepper.

3. Add the pasta to the boiling water, and cook, stirring occasionally, for 5 minutes, then start tasting. When the pasta is tender but still has some texture, scoop out 2 cups cooking water; drain the pasta.

4. Put the roasted tomatoes, any accumulated juices, and almond cream in the pot over medium-low heat. Cook, stirring occasionally, until steaming. Add the pasta and a splash of the cooking water and toss, adding a little more cooking water if necessary to create a creamy—but not soupy—sauce. Taste and adjust the seasoning, garnish with the basil, and serve.

● TAGLIATELLE
with lemon crème fraîche and shaved bottarga

makes: 4 servings
time: 13 to 25 hours, largely unattended

1 cup heavy cream

2 tablespoons buttermilk or yogurt

Zest of 1 lemon, cut into strips

Salt

3 to 4 ounces bottarga

3 tablespoons unsalted butter

1 large shallot, minced

Pepper

1 pound dried tagliatelle or other wide egg noodles

2 tablespoons chopped fresh chives, for garnish

1. Mix the cream and buttermilk in a small glass bowl and cover. Let the mixture sit at room temperature until it's the consistency of sour cream, anywhere from 12 to 24 hours (start checking after 12 hours). Cover tightly, refrigerate, and use within 5 days.

2. Heat the crème fraîche and lemon zest in a small saucepan over low heat until steaming but not boiling. Bring a large pot of water to a boil and salt it. Grate half the bottarga finely.

3. Put the butter in a large skillet over medium heat. When the butter melts, add the shallot and sprinkle with salt and pepper. Cook, stirring occasionally, until the shallot is soft and translucent, 3 to 5 minutes. Pour the crème fraîche into the skillet through a fine-mesh sieve; discard the lemon zest.

4. Add the pasta to the boiling water, and cook, stirring occasionally, for 5 minutes, then start tasting. When the pasta is tender but still has some bite, scoop out 2 cups cooking water, then drain.

5. Immediately add the pasta to the skillet with a splash of the cooking water and toss to coat, adding a little cooking water if necessary to create a creamy—but not soupy—sauce. Sprinkle no more than half the bottarga over the pasta to start; toss, taste, and add more incrementally until you achieve the right balance of umami to saltiness. Then taste and add a little salt and pepper if you'd like. Garnish with the chives and a pinch more grated bottarga if you'd like and serve right away, passing the grater and remaining bottarga at the table.

● Lobster Tortelloni
in Brown Butter
Brodo, page 160

Pasta with Seafood

Nothing soaks up the flavors of the sea like pasta. Enter Lobster Tortelloni in Brown Butter Brodo, an elegant play on lobster and drawn butter. Orzo with Shrimp and Dill comes together in a flash since you're working the stove and the broiler simultaneously. You can always depend on seaweed to bring the brine to Vegan recipes (I obviously do). But have you ever tried it in tomato sauce? Amazing.

● ORZO WITH SHRIMP AND DILL

makes: 4 servings
time: 20 to 30 minutes

Salt

1½ pounds peeled shrimp (thawed frozen is fine)

4 tablespoons olive oil

1 tablespoon chopped garlic

1 teaspoon grated lemon zest

1 teaspoon red chile flakes, or to taste

Pepper

2 cups orzo (about 1 pound) or any small-cut pasta

¼ cup fresh lemon juice, or to taste

¼ cup chopped fresh dill

1. Bring a large pot of water to a boil and salt it. Turn on the broiler and position the rack 4 inches below the heat. Put the shrimp on a rimmed baking sheet with 2 tablespoons oil, the garlic, lemon zest, and red chile flakes, and sprinkle with salt and pepper. Toss to coat. Broil the shrimp, shaking the pan once or twice, until just opaque at the center, 3 to 5 minutes; remove from the broiler immediately.

2. Add the orzo to the boiling water, and cook, stirring occasionally, for 5 minutes, then start tasting. When the pasta is tender but still has some bite, scoop out 1 cup cooking water, then drain the pasta.

3. Return the orzo to the pot with the shrimp, and add the lemon juice, dill, and remaining 2 tablespoons oil. Add a splash of cooking water and set over medium heat. Toss to coat, adding a little more cooking water if necessary to create a sauce. Taste, adjust the seasoning, and serve.

PENNE
with tomato and seaweed sauce

makes: 4 servings
time: 30 minutes

Salt

⅓ cup dried seaweed (like arame, dulse, or wakame)

3 tablespoons good-quality vegetable oil

1 small red onion, chopped

One 28-ounce can diced tomatoes

3 tablespoons soy sauce, or more as needed

Pepper

1 pound penne or other cut pasta

2 sheets nori

1 tablespoon dark sesame oil

1. Bring a large pot of water to a boil and salt it. Cover the seaweed with warm water by at least 2 inches and soak until tender, 5 to 8 minutes; drain and if it's large, chop into bite-sized pieces.

2. Put the vegetable oil in a large skillet over medium-high heat. When it's hot, add the onion. Cook, stirring occasionally, until soft, 3 to 5 minutes. Add the tomatoes, the seaweed, and the soy sauce, and sprinkle with salt and pepper. Bring the mixture to a boil, then adjust the heat so the sauce bubbles steadily and cook, stirring occasionally, until the tomatoes break down and the mixture begins to thicken and appear more uniform in texture, 10 to 15 minutes. Taste, adjust the seasoning, adding more soy sauce if you like, and adjust the heat so the tomato sauce stays hot but doesn't boil.

3. Add the pasta to the boiling water, and cook, stirring occasionally, for 5 minutes, then start tasting. When the pasta is tender but still has some bite, scoop out 1 cup cooking water, then drain.

4. While the pasta is cooking, toast the nori: Put a medium skillet over medium-high heat. Brush the nori sheets with some of the sesame oil and sprinkle with salt. Put a single nori sheet in the pan and toast it until it shrinks and darkens, about 15 seconds; turn it over and toast the other side for another 15 seconds. Repeat with the other sheet.

5. Add the pasta to the sauce. Add the remaining sesame oil and a splash of the cooking water and toss to coat; add a little more cooking water if necessary to create a slightly creamy sauce. Taste and adjust the seasoning. Crumble the nori sheets over the top and serve.

LOBSTER TORTELLONI
in brown butter brodo

makes: 4 servings
time: 4 hours

2 cups flour, or more as needed

1 teaspoon salt, or more as needed

2 eggs, plus 3 egg yolks

3 lobsters (about 1½ pounds each)

Three 1-inch strips orange zest, and 2 teaspoons grated orange zest, for garnish

Pepper

8 tablespoons (1 stick) unsalted butter

2 shallots, chopped

2 teaspoons chopped fresh tarragon

1. Combine the flour and 1 teaspoon salt in a food processor and pulse once or twice. Add the eggs and yolks and turn the machine on. Process just until a ball begins to form, about 30 seconds. Add a few drops of water if the dough is dry and grainy; add a tablespoon of flour if the dough sticks to the side of the bowl. Sprinkle the dough with a little flour and cover; let it rest for about 30 minutes. (At this point, you can refrigerate the dough, tightly wrapped in plastic, for up to 24 hours. Let it sit out for 15 minutes before proceeding.)

2. Bring 4 cups water in a large pot to a boil. Use tongs to put the lobsters in the pot one by one. Let the water return to a boil, then cook until an instant-read thermometer inserted into the tail meat between the body and the tail joint reads 140°F, 5 to 10 minutes. Use tongs to transfer the lobsters to a colander and let cool.

3. Separate the meat and shell, putting the pieces of shell back in the pot with the cooking water and the meat in a bowl. Twist off the claws and use a nut-cracker to split them and the knuckles. Use a pick to pull out the meat. Twist to separate the tail from the body. Cut through the soft side of the tail with kitchen shears and crack it open to remove the tail meat. Cut through the underside of the front part of the body to extract the meat there. Cut the meat into bite-sized pieces, then pulse in a food processor until finely chopped but not pureed.

4. Bring the cooking water to a boil, then adjust the heat so it bubbles gently and cook for 15 minutes. Strain through a fine-mesh sieve, gently pressing on the shells to extract as much liquid as possible, and discard the solids. Return the brodo to the pot and add the orange strips and sprinkle with salt and pepper. Cook over medium-low heat, until reduced by half. Taste and adjust the seasoning. Keep warm, or cool and refrigerate for up to a day.

5. Put 2 tablespoons butter in a medium skillet over medium heat. When it melts, add the shallots and sprinkle with salt and pepper. Cook, stirring occasionally, until the shallots are soft and jammy but have not colored, 5 to 8 minutes. Stir in the tarragon and remove from the heat. Add to the lobster and toss to coat. Taste and adjust the seasoning. Refrigerate until ready to use or up to 1 day, covered.

6. Set up your pasta machine and sprinkle the work surface lightly with flour. (Or for rolling by hand, see page 117.) Cut off about one-third of the dough and wrap the rest in plastic or a towel while you work. Roll the dough lightly in the flour and use your hands to flatten it into a rectangle about the width of the rollers. Set the machine to its thickest setting and roll the dough through. If it sticks, dust it with a little more flour. Repeat. Set the machine to its next-thinnest setting and repeat. Each time, if the pasta sticks, sprinkle it with a little more flour, and put the dough through each setting twice.

7. Continue to roll the dough thinner, changing the thickness only one setting a time (if you try to rush the process, the dough will tear). If at any point the dough tears badly, bunch it together and start again. Use only as much flour as you need to. Pass the dough through the machine's third-thinnest setting. Repeat 2 more times (by this time it will be going quickly), then flour the dough lightly, and cover. Repeat with the remaining dough.

8. Put a little water in a small bowl and lightly dust your work surface with flour. Cut the pasta sheets into thirty-two 4- to 5-inch squares. Dip your finger in water and dampen the edges. Drop a heaping tablespoon of the lobster in the center of each square. Fold the dough over onto itself into a triangle, pressing with your fingers to seal. Pick up the triangle and press the 2 bottom corners together around your middle fingers; make sure the top corner folds down and inward, toward the sealed tips.

9. Put the remaining 6 tablespoons unsalted butter in a small skillet over medium heat. Cook, swirling the pan occasionally until the butter is browned and smells toasted, 3 to 5 minutes. Strain the brown butter through a coffee filter or cheesecloth to remove the solids. Pour the brown butter into the lobster brodo and stir to combine. Remove the orange peel, taste, and adjust the seasoning.

10. Bring a large pot of water to a boil and salt it. Bring the brodo to a gentle bubble. Add the tortelloni to the boiling water, and cook, stirring occasionally, until they rise to the surface, 2 to 3 minutes. Use a slotted spoon to transfer the pasta to serving bowls. Pour about ½ cup hot brodo in each bowl, garnish with orange zest, and serve.

Pasta with Vegetables

Lots of pastas include vegetables. I like them best when they show the noodles who's boss. The key to the Easy recipe is to cook the liquid out of the mushrooms; it doesn't add anything to the sauce, but the butter and milk do! Pasta with Garlicky Roasted Squash combines caramelized roasted squash and garlic with any cut shape and plenty of parsley. The All Out recipe is a real stunner to all the senses. There's spinach in both the dough and sauce—assisted by a generous crumble of Gorgonzola—so there are plenty of vegetables hidden in the decadence.

● FARFALLE
with mushrooms

makes: 4 servings
time: 30 minutes

Salt

2 pounds fresh mushrooms (like cremini, button, portobello, or shiitake, alone or in combination)

¼ cup olive oil

Pepper

1 small onion, chopped

½ cup dry red or white wine

⅓ cup milk

4 tablespoons unsalted butter

1 pound farfalle or other cut pasta

¼ cup grated Pecorino Romano or Parmesan cheese (about 1 ounce), plus more for serving

2 tablespoons chopped fresh parsley, mint, or basil, for garnish

1. Bring a large pot of water to a boil and salt it. Remove any tough stems (discard or save them for stock) and dark spots from the mushrooms and rinse. Cut the mushrooms into bite-sized pieces.

2. Put the oil in a large skillet over medium-high heat. When it's hot, add the mushrooms and sprinkle with salt and pepper. Cook, stirring occasionally as the mushrooms first release their liquid and then start to become dry, 5 to 10 minutes. Lower the heat so they sizzle but don't burn, add the onion, and continue to cook and stir once in a while, until the mixture begins to brown, 5 to 10 minutes. Add the wine and scrape up any browned bits from the bottom of the pan. When the pan is almost dry again, add the milk and butter, stir, and turn off the heat.

3. Add the pasta to the boiling water, and cook, stirring occasionally, for 5 minutes, then start tasting. When the pasta is tender but still has some bite, scoop out 1 cup cooking water, then drain the pasta. Add the pasta to the mushrooms in the skillet and toss together. Turn the heat to medium-high to warm through, adding a little of the cooking water if the noodles seem dry. Stir in the cheese, taste, and adjust the seasoning. Garnish with the herbs and serve, passing more cheese at the table.

● Homemade
Spinach Fettuccine
with Gorgonzola,
page 164

● PASTA
with garlicky roasted squash

makes: 4 servings
time: 1 hour

1 pound hard squash (like kabocha, pumpkin, or butternut), peeled, seeded, and cut into 1-inch chunks

6 tablespoons olive oil, or more as needed

Salt and pepper

10 garlic cloves, peeled (about 1 head)

1 pound small whole wheat pasta (like orecchiette, penne, ziti, or farfalle)

½ cup chopped fresh parsley

1. Heat the oven to 425°F. Put the squash on a large rimmed baking sheet, drizzle with 4 tablespoons oil, sprinkle with salt and pepper, and toss to coat. Spread the squash out in a single layer and transfer to the oven. Roast without stirring or opening the oven for 20 minutes. Add the garlic, then use a spatula to toss and turn the squash. Continue roasting until it smells toasted, 10 to 15 minutes more. Toss the squash again and try piercing a couple pieces with a fork. They're ready when they're well browned outside and tender to the center. If not, return them to the oven and keep checking every 10 minutes until they are.

2. Meanwhile, bring a large pot of water to a boil and salt it. When the squash is nearly done, add the pasta to the boiling water, and cook, stirring occasionally, for 5 minutes, then start tasting. When the pasta is tender but still has some bite, scoop out 1 cup cooking water, then drain the pasta.

3. Return the pasta to the pot along with the remaining 2 tablespoons oil and a splash of the cooking water. Add the roasted vegetables with any oil from the pan. Toss to coat, adding a little more oil or cooking water if necessary and breaking up the garlic to create a slightly creamy sauce. Taste and adjust the seasoning with more salt or pepper, then toss with the parsley and serve.

● HOMEMADE SPINACH FETTUCCINE
with gorgonzola

makes: 4 servings
time: 90 minutes

1½ pounds fresh spinach, stemmed and rinsed

3 eggs

3 cups flour, or more as needed

1 teaspoon salt, or more as needed

4 tablespoons unsalted butter

1 teaspoon grated lemon zest

Pepper

4 ounces Gorgonzola cheese, crumbled (about 1 cup)

1. Rig a steamer in a pot of simmering water. Add the spinach and cook until bright green and tender, 2 to 3 minutes. Run the spinach under cold water and when cool enough to handle, squeeze out as much moisture as possible. Put one-third of the spinach in a blender. Add the eggs and puree until smooth. Reserve the remaining spinach.

2. Combine the flour and 1 teaspoon salt in a food processor and pulse once or twice. Add the spinach and egg mixture and turn the machine on. Process just until a ball begins to form, about 30 seconds. Add a few drops of water if the dough is dry and grainy; add a tablespoon of flour if the dough sticks to the side of the bowl.

3. Sprinkle the dough with a little flour and cover; let it rest for about 30 minutes. (At this point, you can refrigerate the dough, tightly wrapped in plastic, for up to 24 hours. Let it sit out for 15 minutes before proceeding.)

4. Set up your pasta machine and sprinkle the work surface lightly with flour. Cut off about one-third of the dough and wrap the rest in plastic or cloth while you work. Roll the dough lightly in the flour and use your hands to flatten it into a rectangle about the width of the rollers. Set the machine to its thickest setting and roll the dough through. If it sticks, dust it with a little more flour. Repeat. Set the machine to its next-thinnest setting and repeat. Each time, if the pasta sticks, sprinkle it with a little more flour, and put the dough through each setting twice.

5. Continue to roll the dough thinner, changing the thickness one setting each time (if you try to rush the process, the dough will tear). If at any point the dough tears badly, bunch it together and start again. Use only as much flour as you need to. Pass the dough through the machine's second-thinnest setting. Repeat 2 more times (by this time it will be going quickly), then flour the dough lightly, and cover. Repeat with the remaining dough.

6. Cut each pasta sheet into rectangles roughly 16 inches long; trim the ends to make it neat. At this point the dough is ready to cut. By hand, fold the pasta into quarters and use a pastry or pizza wheel or sharp long knife to make long strips about ¼ inch wide. By machine, pass the dough through the broadest (tagliatelle or fettuccine) cutter. Cook right away or hang the strands over clean coat hangers, chopsticks, dowels, or a sheet-draped chair to dry for up to a couple hours.

7. When you're ready to eat, bring a large pot of water to a boil and salt it. Put the butter in a large skillet over medium heat. When the butter is melted, add the reserved spinach, turn the heat up to medium-high, and cook, stirring, until warmed through, 2 to 3 minutes. Stir in the lemon zest, sprinkle with salt and pepper, taste, and adjust the seasoning. Turn off the heat.

8. Add the pasta to the boiling water, and cook, stirring occasionally, for 1 minute, then start tasting. When the pasta is tender but still has some bite, scoop out 1 cup cooking water, then drain the pasta. Add the pasta to the skillet with the spinach along with a splash of the cooking water and half the cheese, and turn the heat to medium-low. Toss to coat, adding a little more cooking water if necessary to create a creamy sauce. Taste and adjust the seasoning, then top with the remaining Gorgonzola and serve.

Uovo and Homemade
Ricotta en Raviolo,
page 168

Stuffed Pasta

For the record, the packaged stuff sold as fresh at the supermarket is never, ever, worth your money. Make the Skillet Cannelloni when you can't spare an afternoon to roll pasta. You'll learn a new wrapper trick too. Phyllo might seem like an unusual choice for a "noodle" in Baked Phyllo Agnolotti, but it's always Vegan and certainly saves you time. But really, just look at the Uovo and Homemade Ricotta en Raviolo. You want to try that, right?

● SKILLET CANNELLONI

makes: 4 servings
time: 30 minutes

2 tablespoons olive oil

2 tablespoons chopped garlic

1 tablespoon dried oregano or Italian seasoning

½ teaspoon red chile flakes, or to taste

One 28-ounce can crushed tomatoes

Salt and pepper

2 eggs

2 cups ricotta cheese

½ cup grated Parmesan cheese (about 2 ounces)

16 egg roll wrappers

1. Put the oil in a large skillet over medium-high heat. When it's hot, add the garlic, oregano, and red chile flakes and cook, stirring, until fragrant, about 1 minute. Add the tomatoes and ½ cup water and sprinkle with salt and pepper. Bring the sauce to a boil, then adjust the heat so that it bubbles gently but steadily while you make the pasta.

2. Beat the eggs in a bowl with some salt and pepper; stir in the ricotta and Parmesan. Stack 2 egg roll wrappers on top of each other and about ¼ cup filling along one of the edges; roll. Repeat with the remaining wrappers to make 8 cannelloni total.

3. Carefully put the rolls in the sauce seam side down. Bring the sauce back to a boil, then adjust the heat so it bubbles gently and cover the pan. Cook, undisturbed, until the wrappers are tender and the filling is heated through, 4 to 5 minutes. Let the cannelloni stand off the heat to set, 5 to 10 minutes, then serve.

BAKED PHYLLO AGNOLOTTI

makes: 4 servings
time: 45 minutes

1½ pounds firm tofu, cut into chunks

½ teaspoon ground nutmeg

Salt and pepper

8 tablespoons olive oil

2 tablespoons chopped garlic

8 ounces baby spinach

6 sheets phyllo dough, preferably whole wheat, thawed in the refrigerator overnight

2 tablespoons drained capers

1 teaspoon red chile flakes, or to taste

½ cup pitted oil-cured black olives, chopped

One 28-ounce can pureed tomatoes

½ cup chopped fresh parsley

1. Heat the oven to 400°F. Line a baking sheet with parchment. Put the tofu and nutmeg in a food processor and sprinkle with plenty of salt and pepper. Pulse until finely chopped, but not pureed.

2. Put 3 tablespoons oil in a large skillet over medium-high heat. When it's hot, add 1 tablespoon chopped garlic and cook until fragrant, about 30 seconds. Add the spinach and cook, stirring often, until wilted, 3 to 5 minutes. Add the tofu mixture and cook, stirring occasionally, until warmed through, another 2 to 3 minutes. Turn off the heat, taste, and adjust the seasoning.

3. Put 3 tablespoons oil in a small bowl. Unroll the phyllo sheets and cut them into thirds lengthwise. Keep the sheets covered with a damp towel. Remove one strip, brush lightly with oil, then put 1 heaping teaspoon spinach filling in one corner of the dough. Fold the corner over to make a triangle. Continue to fold the phyllo, making triangles (as you would fold a flag). Brush the top with olive oil and put on the prepared baking sheet. Repeat with the remaining filling. Bake until the triangles are browned, 15 to 20 minutes.

4. Put the remaining 2 tablespoons oil in the large skillet over medium-high heat. When it's hot, add the remaining tablespoon garlic. Cook, stirring occasionally, until soft, 2 to 3 minutes. Add the capers, red chile flakes, and olives and stir. Add the tomatoes and sprinkle with salt and pepper.

5. Bring the mixture to a boil, then adjust the heat so the sauce bubbles steadily and cook, stirring occasionally, until the tomatoes break down and the mixture begins to thicken and the flavors come together, 25 to 30 minutes. Taste, adjust the seasoning, and keep warm. When ready to serve, divide the agnolotti among 4 shallow bowls. Stir the parsley into the sauce, then spoon over the stuffed pasta; serve right away.

UOVO AND HOMEMADE RICOTTA EN RAVIOLO

makes: 4 servings
time: about 3 hours

2 quarts milk

2 cups buttermilk

1 teaspoon salt, plus more as needed

2 cups flour, or more as needed

3 eggs, plus 11 yolks

1 cup grated Parmesan cheese (about 4 ounces)

Pepper

8 tablespoons (1 stick) unsalted butter

1 shallot, minced

2 tablespoons chopped fresh parsley

2 tablespoons chopped fresh basil

2 tablespoons chopped fresh mint

1 tablespoon chopped fresh chives

1 teaspoon chopped fresh rosemary

1. Put the milk in a large pot over medium-high heat. Cook, stirring often to avoid scorching, just until the milk bubbles around the sides of the pot,

10 to 15 minutes. Line a strainer with 3 layers of cheesecloth. Add the buttermilk to the steaming milk and stir a few times, then turn off the heat and let the mixture sit until it separates into solids (curds) and liquid (whey). Stir in a large pinch of salt.

2. Carefully ladle the mixture into the prepared strainer. Leave the ricotta in the strainer set over the large pot until much of the whey has drained off, but the cheese is still loose and easy to work with, about 30 minutes. Taste and adjust the seasoning. (At this point you can transfer the ricotta to an airtight container and refrigerate for up to 2 days.) Discard the whey or reserve for another use.

3. Combine the flour and 1 teaspoon salt in a food processor and pulse once or twice. Add 2 eggs and 3 yolks and turn the machine on. Process just until a ball begins to form, about 30 seconds. Add a few drops of water if the dough is dry and grainy; add a tablespoon of flour if the dough sticks to the side of the bowl. Sprinkle the dough with a little flour and cover; let it rest for about 30 minutes. (At this point, you can refrigerate the dough, tightly wrapped in plastic, for up to 24 hours. Let it sit out for 15 minutes before proceeding.)

4. Set up your pasta machine and sprinkle the work surface lightly with flour. (Or to roll by hand, see page 117.) Cut off about one-third of the dough and wrap the rest in plastic or a dishtowel while you work. Roll the dough lightly in the flour and use your hands to flatten it into a rectangle about the width of the rollers. Set the machine to its thickest setting and roll the dough through. If it sticks, dust it with a little more flour. Repeat. Set the machine to its next-thinnest setting and repeat, putting the dough through each setting twice. Each time, if the pasta sticks, sprinkle it with a little more flour.

5. Continue to roll the dough thinner, changing the thickness only one setting each time (if you try to rush the process, the dough will tear). If at any point the dough tears badly, bunch it together and start again. Use only as much flour as you need to. Pass the dough through the machine's third-thinnest setting. Repeat 2 more times (by this time it will be going quickly), then flour the dough lightly, and cover. Repeat with the remaining dough.

6. Heat the oven to 200°F. Bring a large pot of water to a boil and salt it. Beat the remaining whole egg and ½ cup water in a small bowl and lightly flour your work surface. Cut as many of the pasta sheets as you need to make sixteen 5-inch squares (keep extra handy).

7. Bring the ricotta to room temperature if it isn't already. Mix the ricotta, ½ cup Parmesan, and lots of pepper and salt; taste and adjust the seasoning. Transfer to a pastry bag, or a zippered storage bag with one corner cut off to make a ½-inch opening. Dust a rimmed baking sheet generously with flour.

8. Brush one pasta sheet with the egg wash almost all the way to the center. Pipe a 2- to 2½-inch ring of ricotta in the center of a pasta square, leaving space for a yolk to fit snugly inside. Pipe another ring on top. Carefully put 1 egg yolk inside the ricotta ring without breaking. Drape another square of pasta on top, then very carefully press the top sheet onto the bottom, making sure the egg doesn't spill; it's okay if the edges don't line up but there should be no air bubbles or gaps in the seals. Repeat to make 7 more ravioli. Use a sharp knife, or large biscuit cutter or ring mold, to cut the ravioli into 4-inch circles. Discard the scraps and transfer the ravioli to the prepared pan. Refrigerate until ready to use, up to 8 hours.

9. Put the butter in a large skillet over medium heat. When it melts, add the shallot and cook, stirring occasionally, until the shallot is soft and translucent, 3 to 5 minutes. Remove from the heat, add the herbs, and sprinkle with salt and pepper. Taste and adjust the seasoning. Pour half the sauce into a large baking dish and transfer to the oven.

10. Lower the ravioli into the boiling water with a spatula 1 or 2 at a time, yolk side up, and boil until it floats, 2 to 3 minutes. Lift out the ravioli with a slotted spoon or strainer and transfer to the baking dish in the oven. Repeat with the remaining ravioli until all have been cooked. Warm the butter sauce remaining in the skillet over low heat and drizzle over the ravioli. Garnish with the remaining ½ cup Parmesan and serve right away.

Macaroni and Cheese

All three of these recipes are crowd-pleasers, whether you're a kid or a gourmand. Macaroni and Cheese in a Pot takes advantage of the starchiness of noodles to make a creamy cheese sauce without a roux or béchamel, while Creamy White Bean Pasta and Cauliflower delivers the goods with neither cheese nor mockery. The All Out recipe applies familiar technique to an unabashed focus on the cheese, so buy the best in your budget.

● **MACARONI AND CHEESE**
in a pot

makes: 4 servings
time: 30 minutes

1 tablespoon unsalted butter

1 cup breadcrumbs, preferably fresh
    (see page 173)

4 cups whole milk

1 pound elbow macaroni or other cut pasta

Salt

¼ cup cream cheese, softened

3 cups shredded cheddar cheese
    (about 12 ounces)

1. Melt the butter in a large pot over medium heat. Add the breadcrumbs and cook, stirring often, until they're golden and crisp, 3 to 5 minutes. Transfer to a bowl; wipe out the pot.

2. Put 3 cups milk and the pasta in the pot and sprinkle with salt. Bring the mixture to a boil, stirring often, then adjust the heat so it bubbles steadily. Cook, stirring constantly, for 5 minutes, then start tasting. You want the pasta to be tender but still with a tiny bit of crunch; it could take as long as 15 minutes. Meanwhile, the mixture should be neither soupy nor dry; add ¼ cup milk if necessary.

3. Stir in the cream cheese, cheddar, and enough of the remaining milk to make a thick sauce. Stir until the cheese is melted and fully incorporated. Taste and adjust the seasoning. Top with the bread-crumbs and serve hot.

CREAMY WHITE BEAN PASTA AND CAULIFLOWER

makes: 4 servings
time: 35 minutes

Salt

1 head cauliflower (about 1½ pounds), chopped

1 pound whole wheat macaroni or other cut pasta

2 cups cooked cannellini or navy beans, liquid reserved (see page 82; or one 15-ounce can, rinsed and drained)

⅓ cup nutritional yeast, or more to taste

1 tablespoon fresh lemon juice, or to taste

1 teaspoon hot sauce, or to taste

1 garlic clove

Pepper

½ cup whole wheat breadcrumbs (opposite)

3 tablespoons olive oil

2 tablespoons chopped fresh parsley

1. Turn on the broiler and position the rack 4 inches below the heat. Bring a large pot of water to a boil and salt it.

2. Add the cauliflower to the boiling water and cook until tender, 8 to 10 minutes. Transfer to a food processor with a slotted spoon and let the water continue boiling. Add the pasta to the boiling water and cook, stirring occasionally, for 5 minutes, then start tasting. When the pasta is tender but still has some bite, scoop out 1 cup cooking water and drain the pasta mixture.

3. Put the beans, nutritional yeast, lemon juice, hot sauce, and garlic in the food processor with the cauliflower and sprinkle with salt and pepper. Puree until smooth, adding water or bean cooking liquid 1 tablespoon at a time to make a thick sauce. Taste and adjust the seasoning, adding more yeast if you'd like. Mix the breadcrumbs, oil, and parsley in a small bowl and sprinkle with salt and pepper.

4. Put the sauce in a large ovenproof skillet over medium heat. Cook, stirring constantly and adding a splash of cooking water if the sauce is too thick, until it's bubbling, 5 to 10 minutes. Stir in the pasta and if the mixture is too thick, add cooking water a little at a time. Taste and adjust the seasoning and top with the breadcrumb mixture. Broil until the breadcrumbs are golden, 1 to 2 minutes, and serve.

ALL-ABOUT-THE-CHEESE MACARONI

makes: 4 servings
time: about 1 hour

4 tablespoons unsalted butter

Salt

1 pound medium-cut pasta (like elbow, shell, or ziti)

2½ cups whole milk

3 tablespoons flour

¾ cup grated Gruyère cheese (about 3 ounces)

¾ cup grated aged cheddar cheese (about 3 ounces)

½ cup grated Parmesan cheese (about 2 ounces)

Pinch ground nutmeg

Pepper

2 tablespoons chopped fresh chives

1. Heat the oven to 400°F and grease a 9 by 13-inch baking pan or 2-quart ovenproof dish with 1 tablespoon butter. Bring a large pot of water to a boil and salt it.

2. Add the pasta to the boiling water, and cook, stirring occasionally, for 5 minutes, then start tasting. When the pasta is tender but still needs another minute or 2 to be done, drain. Rinse under cold running water to stop the cooking, shake off any excess water, and transfer to a large bowl.

3. Put the milk in a small saucepan over medium-low heat. When tiny bubbles appear along the sides, turn off the heat. Put the remaining 3 tablespoons butter in a medium saucepan over medium-low heat; when it melts, add the flour and cook, stirring, until the mixture turns golden, 3 to 5 minutes. Add about ¼ cup milk to the hot flour mixture, whisking constantly until it's smooth. Keep whisking while you add the remaining milk a little at a time. The béchamel should be thick and smooth. Add the cheeses and nutmeg, and stir until combined.

4. Mix the sauce with the noodles, taste, then sprinkle with salt and pepper. Put the pasta mixture into the prepared pan and transfer to the oven. Bake until the sauce is bubbling and the top is browned in spots, 15 to 20 minutes. Serve hot, garnished with the chives.

BREADCRUMBS

In my recipes—especially the Vegan ones—I often call on breadcrumbs to do more than coat or bind other foods; they're an important ingredient for texture and heft. I don't expect you to make your own every time they're called for, but some explanation will help you decide what to buy when you need a quick fix or pantry staple.

Fresh breadcrumbs: These are slightly dried, coarse, and irregular, and almost impossible to find in stores. Panko is the closest approximation. To make them yourself, tear ½ large loaf of stale bread into pieces about 2 inches across. Put half the bread in a food processor. Pulse three or four times to break up the bread, then let the machine run for a few seconds to chop the bread to the desired texture: coarse, fine, or somewhere in between. Remove the crumbs and repeat with the remaining bread. Use right away or store at room temperature in an airtight container for up to 1 month or in the freezer for up to 3 months. Makes fresh breadcrumbs in 5 minutes.

Dried (or toasted) breadcrumbs: Grind fresh breadcrumbs more finely and take out almost all the moisture and you increase their shelf life exponentially. These are the common kind on supermarket shelves, though you can also make them yourself. Follow the directions above. After pulverizing, toast the crumbs on a rimmed baking sheet in a 350°F oven until lightly browned, about 15 minutes, depending on how fine they are.

Fried breadcrumbs: Not for breading, but great as a garnish. The recipe directions in this book walk you through the process when necessary. But I know you'll want to know how to make them: Put ¼ cup olive oil in a large skillet over medium heat. When it's hot, add the breadcrumbs and cook, stirring frequently, until they're golden and crisp, 3 to 5 minutes. Use right away.

Mediterranean
Gratin with Almond
Breadcrumbs,
page 176

Baked Pasta

Baked pastas have the added benefit of suspended animation: Assemble in advance and finish them whenever you're ready. The trick with Pasta Frittata alla Caprese? Assemble it on a rimmed baking sheet to decrease cooking time and maximize browned surface area. In Mediterranean Gratin with Almond Breadcrumbs, bitter greens, olives, and caramelized onions play well off nutty and hearty whole wheat pasta and bring the dish together without dairy. Spain-inspired Baked Fideos with Bacalao will remind you of paella (page 97), only the base is an angel hair pasta.

● PASTA FRITTATA ALLA CAPRESE

makes: 4 to 6 servings
time: 30 minutes

Salt

8 ounces angel hair pasta

4 tablespoons olive oil

8 eggs

4 large ripe Roma (plum) tomatoes, chopped

6 ounces fresh mozzarella cheese, chopped (about 1½ cups)

Pepper

¼ cup chopped fresh basil, for garnish

1. Bring a large pot of water to a boil and salt it. Heat the oven to 450°F. Add the pasta to the boiling water and cook, stirring occasionally, for 3 minutes, then start tasting. When the noodles become pliable but not yet edible, drain and immediately toss in the colander with 1 tablespoon oil; keep the pot handy. Use the remaining 3 tablespoons oil to grease a large rimmed baking sheet.

2. Beat the eggs in the pot until thoroughly combined. Add the tomatoes and cheese, and sprinkle with plenty of salt and pepper, then stir in the pasta. Pour the mixture into the prepared pan and use a fork to spread it out in an even layer. (It's okay if it doesn't quite get to all the corners.)

3. Bake until the eggs are set and the mixture is browned and bubbly, 8 to 12 minutes. Cut into squares or wedges and serve hot or at room temperature garnished with the basil and more pepper.

MEDITERRANEAN GRATIN
with almond breadcrumbs

makes: 4 to 6 servings
time: 1½ hours

Salt

7 tablespoons olive oil, plus more as needed

½ cup raw almonds

2 red onions, halved and sliced

2 thick slices stale crusty bread, torn into pieces

¼ cup fresh parsley

Pepper

12 ounces broccoli rabe, trimmed and cut into
    bite-sized pieces

½ cup pitted black olives, chopped

1 tablespoon chopped garlic

2 tablespoons tomato paste

1 cup dry white wine or water

1½ cups cooked cannellini beans (see page 82; or
    one 15-ounce can), drained

12 ounces whole wheat penne or other
    similar pasta

1. Bring a large pot of water to a boil and salt it. Heat the oven to 425°F and grease a 9-inch square baking dish or ovenproof 10-inch skillet with 1 tablespoon olive oil. Put the almonds in a large skillet over medium heat and cook, shaking the pan occasionally, until they are golden and fragrant, 3 to 5 minutes. Transfer to a food processor and wipe out the pan.

2. In the same skillet, cook the onions over medium heat, covering the pan and stirring once in a while, until they're dry and beginning to stick to the pan, 10 to 15 minutes. While the onions cook, add the bread to the food processor along with the parsley and 2 tablespoons oil and pulse until finely ground.

3. Uncover the onions and stir in 2 tablespoons oil and a large pinch of salt. Lower the heat so the mixture sizzles gently. Cook, stirring occasionally, until the onions are golden and soft, adding small amounts of oil if necessary to keep them from sticking without getting greasy, 15 to 20 minutes. Sprinkle with pepper; taste and adjust the seasoning. Transfer to a large bowl and return the pan to medium-high heat.

4. Add the remaining 2 tablespoons oil. Add the broccoli rabe, olives, and garlic and sprinkle with salt and pepper. Cook, stirring often, until the broccoli is crisp-tender, 5 to 10 minutes. Add the tomato paste and cook, stirring often, until it darkens, 2 to 3 minutes. Add the wine and beans and cook, stirring and scraping up any browned bits from the pan, until the wine is reduced by half. Add the vegetables to the onions, mix, taste, and adjust the seasoning.

5. Add the pasta to the boiling water and cook, stirring occasionally, for 5 minutes, then start tasting. When the noodles become pliable but not yet edible, drain and reserve ¼ cup cooking water. Add the penne and cooking water to the bowl with the rest of the ingredients and stir to combine.

6. Transfer the pasta to the prepared pan and top with the breadcrumb mixture. Bake until the pasta is tender but still has some bite and the breadcrumbs are browned, 10 to 15 minutes. Let sit for a couple minutes before cutting into squares or wedges and serve warm or at room temperature.

BAKED FIDEOS
with bacalao

makes: 4 to 6 servings
time: about 10 hours, largely unattended

8 ounces boneless salt cod

1 pound Yukon Gold potatoes, scrubbed and cut into 1-inch chunks

8 tablespoons olive oil, or more as needed

Salt and pepper

1 recipe aioli (see page 243), with more garlic as desired

1 teaspoon smoked paprika

½ teaspoon cayenne

3 to 4 cups chicken stock (see page 43)

8 ounces shallots (about 3 large), halved and sliced

4 garlic cloves, chopped

Large pinch saffron

12 ounces fideos, broken into 2-inch pieces

¼ cup chopped fresh parsley, for garnish

1. The morning you want to cook the pasta, cover the fish with cold water by at least 3 inches and soak for 8 to 12 hours, changing the water a few times.

2. Heat the oven to 425°F. Bring a large pot of water to a boil. Drain the salt cod and run your fingers over it to remove any bones or pieces of skin. When the water boils, add the cod, turn off the heat, and cover. Let stand for 15 to 20 minutes. Remove the fish from the pot, pat dry, and cut into 2-inch chunks.

3. Put the potatoes on a rimmed baking sheet, and toss them with 2 tablespoons oil and sprinkle with salt and pepper; spread them out in a single layer. Roast without stirring or opening the oven for 20 minutes. Use a spatula to toss and turn the potatoes, then continue roasting until they smell toasted, another 10 to 15 minutes. Toss the potatoes again and try piercing a couple with a fork. They should be browned outside and tender to the center. If not, return them to the oven and keep checking every 10 minutes until they are. Remove the potatoes from the oven, taste, and adjust the seasoning.

4. Put the aioli in a small bowl, add the smoked paprika and cayenne, sprinkle with salt and pepper, and mix. Taste and adjust the seasoning. (Use immediately or refrigerate for up to 3 days.)

5. Heat the chicken stock in a small saucepan over medium heat until steaming. Line a plate with paper towels. Put 4 tablespoons olive oil in a large oven-proof skillet over medium-high heat. When it's hot, add half the cod to the pan and cook, turning and rotating the pieces as necessary until well browned, 10 to 15 minutes total. Transfer to the prepared plate as they finish and repeat with the remaining fish.

6. If the pan is dry, add more olive oil. Add the shallots and chopped garlic to the pan and sprinkle with salt and pepper. Cook, stirring occasionally, until the shallots are soft and golden, 10 to 15 minutes. Stir in the saffron and scrape the mixture and pan juices into a bowl. Wipe out the skillet.

7. Add 2 tablespoons olive oil and turn the heat to medium. When it's hot, add the fideos and cook, stirring often, until the noodles are lightly browned, 2 to 4 minutes. Pour in the stock and bring the mixture to a boil. Spread the shallot mixture on top and nestle in the fried cod and the potatoes. If the mixture looks dry after you add the potatoes, add another ½ cup to 1 cup chicken stock.

8. Transfer the pan to the oven and bake uncovered until almost all the liquid has been absorbed and the top is golden and crisp, 8 to 12 minutes. Drizzle with the sauce, sprinkle with the parsley, and serve.

Lasagna

A noodle so good that there's a whole family of pastas named for it. (And, for the record, in Italian a single noodle is lasagna, and lasagne is the plural; it appears both ways everywhere in America.) I can't cut the time it takes tomato sauce and lasagna noodles cook, but you'll spend only 10 minutes assembling Lazy Lasagna—using real noodles and homemade sauce. Then you walk away. Tempeh Ragu Lasagna depends on silky vegetables—in the filling and on top—to give the noodles structure; it's probably the lightest lasagna you'll ever eat. The All Out lasagna, however, is plenty rich. And since Thousand-Layer Green Lasagna is all about the paper-thin homemade noodles, they're going to require your attention for a couple hours. Time very well spent.

● LAZY LASAGNA

makes: 6 to 8 servings
time: 1 hour, largely unattended

½ cup olive oil, plus more for the pan

1 large onion, cut into chunks

One 28-ounce can and one 14-ounce can crushed tomatoes (or three 14-ounce cans)

¼ cup tomato paste

1 tablespoon dried oregano or thyme

Salt and pepper

1 pound lasagna noodles

2 cups ricotta cheese (about 1 pound)

1½ cups grated Parmesan cheese (about 6 ounces)

1. Heat the oven to 400°F. Grease a 9 by 13-inch baking dish with oil. Put the onion in a food processor and pulse until finely chopped. Add the tomatoes, tomato paste, the ½ cup oil, the oregano, and 1½ cups water and season with salt and pepper. Pulse a few times just to combine, then taste and adjust the seasoning.

2. Put the prepared pan on a large rimmed baking sheet. Pour in about half the tomato sauce, then layer in half the noodles. Top with all the ricotta, 1 cup Parmesan, and the remaining noodles. Pour the rest of the sauce over the top. Cover the pan with foil and transfer the whole thing to the oven.

3. Bake until the noodles are tender and the sauce is bubbling and has mostly been absorbed, 35 to 40 minutes. Sprinkle the remaining Parmesan on top, and bake uncovered until it's melted, another 3 to 5 minutes. Let cool and set for at least 5 minutes before cutting and serving.

Tempeh Ragu Lasagna,
page 180

TEMPEH RAGU LASAGNA

makes: 4 servings
time: 1½ hours

8 tablespoons olive oil

8 ounces tempeh

Salt and pepper

1 onion, chopped

2 celery stalks, chopped

1 carrot, chopped

2 tablespoons chopped garlic

1 teaspoon red chile flakes, or to taste

2 tablespoons chopped fresh oregano,
    or 2 teaspoons dried

One 28-ounce can diced tomatoes, with
    their liquid

One 28-ounce can pureed tomatoes

10 ounces baby spinach

1 pound whole wheat lasagna noodles

2 ripe tomatoes, sliced

1. Heat the oven to 400°F. Put 3 tablespoons oil in a large pot over medium-high heat. When it's hot, crumble the tempeh into the pan and sprinkle with salt and pepper. Cook, stirring frequently and scraping up any browned bits, until the tempeh is browned and crisp, 5 to 10 minutes.

2. Lower the heat to medium and add the onion, celery, and carrot to the pot and sprinkle with salt and pepper. Cook, stirring occasionally, until the vegetables are soft and starting to turn golden, 5 to 8 minutes. Add the garlic, red chile flakes, and oregano and stir until fragrant, less than a minute. Add the diced and pureed tomatoes and bring to a boil. Adjust the heat so the mixture bubbles gently and cook, stirring occasionally until thickened and the flavors come together, 30 to 40 minutes. Stir in the spinach a handful at a time until all has been incorporated. Remove from the heat, taste, and adjust the seasoning. (You can make the ragu up to 3 days ahead.)

3. Bring a large pot of water to a boil and salt it. Add the pasta to the boiling water, and cook, stirring occasionally, for 4 minutes, then start tasting. When the pasta is halfway done, drain into a colander and toss with 1 tablespoon oil; you can drape the noodles over the sides to keep them separate.

4. Grease the bottom of a 9 by 13-inch baking dish with 1 tablespoon olive oil, then spread with about one-fourth of the ragu. Put in a layer of noodles, touching but not overlapping, and trim any overhanging edges. Spread the noodles with one-fourth of the ragu (there should be enough salt, but if you think it's underseasoned, add a little salt to each layer). Make three more layers, ending with lasagna noodles. Top with the sliced tomatoes, drizzle with the remaining 3 tablespoons olive oil, and sprinkle with salt and pepper.

5. Put the pan on a rimmed baking sheet and bake until the pasta is tender, browned on the edges, and a knife inserted into the center comes out hot, 20 to 30 minutes. Let the lasagna set for at least 5 minutes before cutting and serving.

THOUSAND-LAYER GREEN LASAGNA

makes: 6 to 8 servings
time: 4 to 5 hours

4½ cups flour, or more as needed

2 teaspoons salt, or more as needed

4 eggs, plus 6 egg yolks

1 pound baby arugula, chopped

8 tablespoons (1 stick) unsalted butter

4 to 6 cups milk

Pepper

2½ cups grated Parmesan cheese (about
    10 ounces)

Olive oil, for the pan

1. Combine 4 cups flour and the salt in the work bowl of a food processor and pulse once or twice. Add the eggs and yolks all at once and turn the machine on. Process just until a ball begins to form, about 30 seconds. Add a few drops of water if the dough is dry and grainy; add another tablespoon of flour if the dough sticks to the side of the bowl. (If you don't have a food processor, see page 117 for how to make the pasta dough by hand.)

2. Sprinkle the dough with a little flour and cover with plastic or a dishtowel; let it rest for about 30 minutes. (At this point, you can refrigerate the dough, wrapped in plastic, until you're ready to roll it out, for up to 24 hours.)

3. Bring a large pot of water to a boil and salt it. Set up your pasta machine and sprinkle the work surface lightly with flour. Cut off about one-third of the dough; wrap the rest in plastic or a dishtowel while you work. Roll the dough lightly in the flour and use your hands to flatten it into a rectangle about the width of the machine. Set the machine to its thickest setting and crank the dough through. If it sticks, dust it with a little more flour. Repeat. Set the machine to its next-thinnest setting and repeat. Continue to decrease the settings, running the dough through the machine twice each time, and sprinkling it with just a little more flour whenever it sticks.

4. When you've passed the dough through the thinnest setting (or next-thinnest, if the dough is too delicate) twice, flour the dough lightly, cover it, and set it aside. Repeat the process with the remaining dough. Cut each sheet into rectangles roughly 9 inches long; trim the ends to make them neat.

5. When the water boils, cook a few sheets of the pasta until they are tender but not mushy; start tasting after 1 minute (it will take less than 3 minutes, probably less than 2). As they are done, transfer them to a bowl with cold water and a little oil, then lay the noodles out on a dish towel, not touching. Cook the remaining pasta sheets in batches.

6. Put the arugula in a food processor (you might need to work in batches) and pulse until finely chopped. Put the butter in a large pot over medium-low heat. When the butter melts, use a wire whisk to incorporate the remaining ½ cup flour. Turn the heat to low and cook, whisking almost constantly, until the mixture turns tan, about 3 minutes. Stir in the milk a little bit at a time, whisking constantly. When about 4 cups milk has been added, the mixture will be fairly thick. Add more milk a little at a time until the consistency is just a little thinner than your desired end result. Stir in the arugula and 2 cups Parmesan and cook until the arugula has wilted and the Parmesan is incorporated. Sprinkle with salt and pepper, taste, and adjust the seasoning.

7. Grease a 9-inch springform pan with some oil. Cover the bottom with pasta, trimming as necessary so the pasta doesn't go too far up the sides (though a little is fine); save the scraps. Spread a very thin layer of sauce on top. Repeat, using the scraps to fill in spaces or create another layer, until you've used up all the pasta (you may have some sauce left over). The goal is to have as many layers as possible. End with a full layer of pasta and a last layer of sauce on top. Sprinkle with the remaining ½ cup Parmesan.

8. Put the baking dish on a rimmed baking sheet and bake until the pasta is tender, browned on the edges and separating from the pan, and a knife inserted into the center comes out hot, 20 to 25 minutes. Remove from the oven and let rest for 5 minutes before cutting into wedges and serving.

Polenta Party,
page 184

Polenta

I've never understood what all the complaining was about. So you've got to stir a little. But if that's really not your thing, then go for the baked polenta, which gives you time to enjoy making a lovely crudo-style tomato sauce and maybe a side or dessert. Fresh tomatoes and citrus take Lemon Polenta with Mushroom Ragu from a potentially stodgy winter dinner to a bright dish for any season. Polenta Party is based on *polenta alla spianatora*—which translates to "polenta spread flat"; this is a fun, communal dinner great for crowds and anyone who doesn't own a fancy tablecloth.

● BAKED CHEESY POLENTA
with spicy tomato crudo

makes: 4 servings
time: 30 minutes

1 cup polenta (medium-grind cornmeal; not instant)

2 tablespoons unsalted butter

4 tablespoons olive oil

Salt and pepper

8 ounces fresh mozzarella cheese, chopped (about 2 cups)

1 pound ripe tomatoes, cored and chopped

1 teaspoon chopped garlic

1 teaspoon red chile flakes, or 1 fresh red chile, seeded and chopped

½ cup chopped fresh basil

Grated Parmesan, for garnish

1. Heat the oven to 400°F. Mix 2½ cups water and the polenta in a large ovenproof skillet and whisk until smooth. Add the butter, 2 tablespoons oil, and sprinkle with salt and pepper. Bring to a boil over medium heat, whisking constantly.

2. Remove the skillet from the heat and fold in the mozzarella. Transfer to the oven and bake, undisturbed, until the polenta is firm, 20 to 25 minutes.

3. While the polenta bakes, mix the tomatoes, remaining 2 tablespoons oil, garlic, and chile in a bowl. Sprinkle with salt and pepper, mashing the tomatoes a bit as you stir. Taste, adjust the seasoning, and let sit (for up to 2 hours).

4. When the polenta is ready, slice it into wedges and mix the basil into the tomato mixture. Serve the polenta warm or at room temperature with the sauce and a sprinkle of Parmesan.

LEMON POLENTA
with mushroom ragu

makes: 4 servings
time: 1½ hours

½ ounce dried porcini mushrooms

2 cups boiling water

6 tablespoons olive oil

1 leek, halved, sliced, and rinsed well

1 tablespoon chopped garlic

1½ pounds fresh cremini mushrooms, sliced

Salt and pepper

¼ cup red wine

4 ripe Roma (plum) tomatoes, chopped
    (or whole canned tomatoes)

2 tablespoons chopped fresh thyme, or
    2 teaspoons dried

1 cup polenta (medium-grind cornmeal;
    not instant)

5 cups vegetable stock (see page 87) or water

2 teaspoons grated lemon zest

3 tablespoons fresh lemon juice, or to taste

¼ chopped fresh parsley, for garnish

1. Put the dried mushrooms in a medium bowl and add the boiling water. Make sure the mushrooms are submerged and soak until soft and pliable, 5 to 30 minutes, depending on the type. Lift the mushrooms from the liquid with a slotted spoon or your fingers, leaving any sediment in the bowl and reserve the soaking water. Chop the mushrooms.

2. Put 4 tablespoons oil in a skillet over medium heat. When it's hot, add the leek and garlic and cook until soft, 3 to 5 minutes. Add the fresh and dried mushrooms and sprinkle with salt and pepper. Cook, stirring occasionally, until the mushrooms are tender and the pan is dry, 10 to 15 minutes.

3. Pour in the wine and bring to a boil, scraping any browned bits off the bottom of the pan, then stir in the tomatoes, thyme, and 1 cup reserved soaking liquid, taking care to leave the sediment behind.

Cook until the liquid thickens a bit, another 3 to 5 minutes, then taste and adjust the seasoning. Remove from the heat.

4. Put the polenta in a medium pot with 1 cup stock and whisk into a smooth slurry. Put the pot over medium-high heat and add a large pinch of salt. Cook, whisking frequently, until the mixture boils, then adjust the heat so the mixture bubbles gently. Cook, whisking and adding more stock a little at a time to prevent lumps and keep the mixture fairly loose; it will take another 3 to 4 cups liquid before the polenta is ready. The polenta is done when it's thick and creamy, with just a little chew, and pulls away from the sides of the pan as you stir, 15 to 30 minutes, depending on the polenta. Stir in the lemon zest and juice and remaining 2 tablespoons olive oil; taste and adjust the seasoning.

5. Warm the mushroom ragu and serve over the polenta, garnished with the parsley.

POLENTA PARTY

makes: 8 servings
time: about 4 hours

8 tablespoons olive oil

4 ounces thick-sliced pancetta, chopped

2 pounds boneless pork shoulder, trimmed of
    excess fat and cut into chunks

Salt and pepper

4 carrots, chopped

1 large onion, chopped

5 garlic cloves, smashed

3 fresh thyme sprigs

1 fresh rosemary sprig

2 bay leaves

2 cups dry red wine

One 14-ounce can whole tomatoes

9 cups chicken stock or vegetable stock
    (see page 43 or 87)

2 fennel bulbs, trimmed but left whole

5 tablespoons unsalted butter

1 cup heavy cream

2 cups polenta (medium-grind cornmeal; not instant)

1 cup milk

1 cup grated Parmesan cheese (about 4 ounces)

2 oranges

10 ounces arugula, rinsed and dried

1 cup green olives, pitted and chopped

1. Put 1 tablespoon olive oil in a large pot over medium heat. Add the pancetta and cook, stirring occasionally, until it is crisp and has rendered most of its fat, 5 to 10 minutes. Remove with a slotted spoon and transfer to a paper towel–lined plate. Add some of the pork (taking care not to crowd the pan), and turn the heat up to medium-high. Cook, turning the cubes as they brown and sprinkling them with salt and pepper, until the meat is browned on all sides, 10 to 15 minutes. Remove with a slotted spoon and transfer to a plate. Repeat with the remaining pork.

2. Lower the heat to medium and add the carrots, onion, garlic, thyme, rosemary, and bay leaves, and sprinkle with salt and pepper. Cook, stirring occasionally, until the onion is soft, 3 to 5 minutes. Add the wine and let it bubble for a minute, scraping up any browned bits from the bottom of the pan, then add the tomatoes and return the pork to the pot. It should be almost submerged in liquid; if not, add a little water.

3. Adjust the heat so the mixture bubbles gently but steadily and cover. Cook, stirring once or twice for about an hour, then add the pancetta. Stir again, cover, and continue cooking, stirring occasionally and adding a little more liquid if the mixture seems dry, until the pork is fork-tender and almost falling apart. Depending on the fattiness of the meat, the stew could be done in as little as another 30 or as long as 90 minutes. Taste and adjust the seasoning, then keep warm. (Or cover and refrigerate for up to 2 days before reheating.)

4. Meanwhile, heat the oven to 375°F. Warm the stock over medium heat until steaming. Cut the trimmed fennel bulbs into ½-inch-thick slices, keeping the root intact. Put 3 tablespoons olive oil in a large ovenproof skillet over medium-high heat. Put the fennel slices in the pan in a single layer, working in batches if necessary, and sprinkle with salt and pepper. Cook until golden and partially tender, 2 to 3 minutes per side. Dot with 3 tablespoons butter and pour in the cream. Transfer to the oven and cook until the fennel is tender and most of the liquid has evaporated, 10 to 15 minutes. Taste and adjust the seasoning; keep warm.

5. Meanwhile, put the polenta in a large pot with 2 cups stock and whisk into a smooth slurry. Set over medium-high heat and add a large pinch of salt. Cook, whisking frequently, until the mixture boils, then whisk in the milk and adjust the heat so the mixture bubbles gently. Cook, whisking and adding more warm stock a little at a time to prevent lumps and keep the mixture fairly loose. It will take another 5 to 7 cups of stock before the polenta is ready. It should be creamy but still loose, with just a little chew, and it will pull away from the sides of the pan as you stir, 15 to 30 minutes, depending on the polenta. Stir in 2 tablespoons butter and the Parmesan; taste, adjust the seasoning, and keep warm.

6. Slice off about ¼ inch from each end of the oranges so you can stand them on the cutting board. Use a very sharp knife to cut as close to the flesh as possible, removing the skin and bitter white pith in long strips. Cut the oranges crosswise to make "wheels." When you are ready to serve, mix the oranges with the arugula, olives, 4 tablespoons olive oil, and plenty of salt and pepper; toss to combine, taste, and adjust the seasoning.

7. Make sure all your components except the arugula salad are hot. Serve all the ingredients family style or if you want, take the traditional Italian approach: Call everyone to the table. Spread the hot polenta on a large marble slab, the largest cutting board you have, or a giant platter or shallow bowl set in the middle of your table. Cover one-third of the polenta with some ragu, one-third with fennel, and one-third with salad. Then dig in.

Red Pizza

I couldn't write a book about iconic dinners with only three pizza recipes, so up first is the group of classic tomato-sauced pies. Start with a workhorse quick dough that can be repurposed into all sorts of easy meals, including Pepperoni Pan Pizza. For Mushroom and Pepper Pizza, I count on a big contrast of textures and colors to make for compelling gooey-less eating. Brick Oven–Style Margherita Pizza is the closest thing to pizza baked by professionals. The walk-away overnight dough accounts for 90 percent of the prep time. Once rolled, the pies come together fast.

● PEPPERONI PAN PIZZA

makes: 4 servings
time: 35 minutes

⅓ cup olive oil, plus more for the pan

One 28-ounce can diced tomatoes

1 teaspoon salt, or more as needed

Pepper

3 cups flour, or more if needed

1 tablespoon baking powder

2 cups grated mozzarella cheese (about 8 ounces)

3 to 4 ounces sliced pepperoni

2 teaspoons dried oregano or Italian herb blend

Pinch red chile flakes

1. Heat the oven to 500°F and position the rack in the lower third. Generously grease a 9 by 13–inch baking dish with olive oil. Put the tomatoes in a strainer set over a bowl and drain. Taste the tomatoes and sprinkle with salt if necessary and some pepper. Drain, shaking occasionally, while you prepare the other ingredients.

2. Put the flour, baking powder, and 1 teaspoon salt in a large bowl and stir to combine. Add the ⅓ cup olive oil and ¾ cup warm water, and mix just until the dough comes together (it should still be a little crumbly). If the dough is too dry, add water 1 tablespoon at a time and stir briefly after each addition. In the unlikely event the dough is too wet, add 1 tablespoon flour and stir.

3. Press the dough into the prepared pan all the way to the edge, making sure it's the same thickness everywhere. Scatter the drained tomatoes over the dough, leaving a ½-inch border all around, then sprinkle the cheese over the tomatoes. Transfer the pan to the oven and bake for 10 minutes.

4. Carefully put the pepperoni on the pizza and continue baking until the crust is golden and the cheese bubbles, another 3 to 5 minutes. Sprinkle with the herbs and red chile flakes and cool for at least 5 minutes before cutting into squares and serving.

● MUSHROOM AND PEPPER PIZZA

makes: 4 servings
time: 45 minutes

11 tablespoons olive oil, or more as needed

1 small onion, chopped

1 tablespoon chopped garlic

Salt and pepper

One 28-ounce can pureed tomatoes

1 pound cremini mushrooms, rinsed, trimmed, and sliced

⅓ cup fresh breadcrumbs (see page 173) or panko

1 tablespoon minced garlic

2 teaspoons nutritional yeast

1 batch Whole Wheat Pizza Dough (see page 195)

2 roasted red peppers (see page 132), cored and sliced

1. Heat 3 tablespoons oil in a medium saucepan over medium-high heat. Add the onion and garlic, sprinkle with salt and pepper, and cook, stirring occasionally, until soft, 3 to 5 minutes. Add the tomatoes and cook, stirring occasionally, until the sauce is almost as thick as tomato paste and has darkened a bit, 20 to 30 minutes. Let cool before using.

2. Heat the oven to 500°F and put the rack in the lower third, with the pizza stone on the rack if you're using one. Put 2 tablespoons oil in a large skillet over medium-high heat. Add the mushrooms, sprinkle with plenty of salt and pepper, and cook, stirring occasionally, until the pan is dry and the mushrooms are crisp, 10 to 15 minutes. Taste and adjust the seasoning and transfer to a bowl. Rinse and dry the skillet.

3. Put 2 tablespoons oil, the breadcrumbs, and garlic in the large skillet over medium heat. Cook, stirring often, until the breadcrumbs are golden and fragrant, 3 to 5 minutes. Add the nutritional yeast and stir, then transfer to a bowl.

4. Roll out the pizza dough according to the recipe directions. Drizzle each pizza with 2 tablespoons oil, then spread with a thin layer of the tomato sauce, leaving a 1-inch border all around. Scatter half the mushrooms and peppers on top of each pizza; sprinkle with salt and pepper. Put one of the baking sheets into the oven or slide one pizza onto the stone. Bake until the crust is crisp, 8 to 12 minutes. Sprinkle with the breadcrumbs, slice, and serve. Bake the second pizza while you eat the first.

● BRICK OVEN–STYLE MARGHERITA PIZZA

makes: 4 servings
time: about a day, almost entirely unattended

1½ pounds ripe Roma (plum) tomatoes

1 garlic clove

1 teaspoon dried oregano

½ onion, cut into chunks

7 tablespoons olive oil

Salt and pepper

1 batch Semolina Pizza Dough (see page 195)

1 pound fresh mozzarella cheese, sliced no more
than ⅛ inch thick

1 cup grated Parmesan cheese (about 4 ounces)

About 20 fresh basil leaves

1. Bring a large pot of water to a boil and fill a bowl with ice and water. Cut a small X in the bottom of each tomato. Put the tomatoes in the boiling water until the skin begins to loosen, about 30 seconds. Immediately transfer the tomatoes to the ice bath with a slotted spoon. When they are cool enough to handle, peel the tomatoes. Cut out the core, then halve the tomatoes and squeeze out the seeds.

2. Put the tomatoes in a blender with the garlic, oregano, onion, and 3 tablespoons olive oil. Sprinkle with salt and pepper. Puree until smooth; taste and adjust the seasoning.

3. Heat the oven to 500°F and put the rack in the lower third, with the pizza stone on the rack if you're using one.

4. Roll out the pizza dough according to the recipe directions. Drizzle each pizza with 2 tablespoons olive oil, then top with a thin layer of sauce, leaving a 1-inch border all around. Top each pizza with half the mozzarella and Parmesan; sprinkle with salt and pepper.

5. Put a baking sheet into the oven or slide one pizza onto the stone. Bake until the crust is crisp, anywhere from 5 to 12 minutes. As soon as the pizza comes out of the oven, rip a few basil leaves and scatter them on the surface. Let the pizza rest for 5 minutes before slicing and serving. Bake the second pizza while you eat the first.

White Pizza

Without the convention of tomato sauce, pizza gets pretty interesting. Aromatics and cheese on a quick cornmeal-spiked crust are enough for me in a basic Pizza Bianca, but go ahead and add some extras if you want; just don't overdo it. The sliced marinated potato on the Vegan pizza works double-time to supply the creaminess and the tang; the sautéed fennel balances with a little sweet. And as a nod to some formative years in New Haven, Connecticut, home of the famous clam pizza, witness my loose interpretation. I won't look if you sprinkle on some Parmesan when the pie is hot from the oven.

Clam Pizza, page 194

● PIZZA BIANCA

makes: 4 servings
time: 30 minutes

½ red onion

2¾ cups flour, or more as needed

¼ cup fine cornmeal

1 tablespoon baking powder

1 teaspoon salt, or more as needed

9 tablespoons olive oil

2 tablespoons chopped garlic

Pepper

1 cup grated Parmesan cheese (about 4 ounces)

1 small bunch fresh basil, leaves removed and left whole

1. Heat the oven to 500°F and put the rack in the upper third. Line a rimmed baking sheet with parchment or a silicone mat. Halve the onion top to bottom and slice crosswise as thinly as you can manage; separate the slices with your fingers.

2. Put the flour, cornmeal, baking powder, and 1 teaspoon salt in a food processor. With the machine running, slowly add 6 tablespoons olive oil, then 1 cup warm water. Process until the dough is a smooth, easy-to-handle ball, about 30 seconds. If the dough is too dry, add water 1 tablespoon at a time and process briefly after each addition. In the unlikely event the dough is too wet, add 1 table-spoon flour and pulse a few times.

3. Gently press the dough into the prepared pan all the way to the edge. Scatter the garlic and onion on top; press down gently. Drizzle the dough with the remaining 3 tablespoons oil and sprinkle with salt and pepper. Bake until the crust is golden and the onion is soft, 10 to 15 minutes. Sprinkle immediately with the cheese, then tear the basil and scatter over the pizza. Cool for 5 minutes before cutting and serving.

POTATO FENNEL PIZZA

makes: 4 servings
time: 45 minutes

1 pound small waxy potatoes, scrubbed

Salt

4 tablespoons fresh lemon juice

1 teaspoon grated lemon zest

7 tablespoons olive oil, plus more for greasing

Pepper

2 fennel bulbs; trimmed, halved, and sliced (about 1½ pounds), fronds reserved

½ cup white wine or water

1 batch Whole Wheat Pizza Dough (page 195)

1. Put the potatoes in a large pot with enough cold water to cover by 2 inches; add a large pinch of salt and bring to a boil. Cook until the potatoes can just be pierced with a fork, 10 to 25 minutes depending on their size. Drain and let them sit to dry out until they're cool enough to handle. Slice the potatoes as thin as you can manage, at most ¼ inch thick; transfer the potato slices to a bowl and gently toss with the lemon juice and zest, 4 tablespoons oil, and lots of salt and pepper.

2. Put the remaining 3 tablespoons oil in a large skillet over medium-high heat. When it's hot, add some of the fennel in a single layer, taking care not to crowd (you'll probably have to work in batches) and sprinkle with salt and pepper. Cook, stirring occasionally, until lightly browned and tender, 3 to 5 minutes. Transfer to a plate and repeat with the remaining fennel.

3. Return the fennel to the skillet and add the wine. Reduce the heat so the liquid bubbles gently and cook, stirring occasionally and scraping any browned bits from the bottom of the pan, until the fennel is quite tender and the pan is dry, 10 to 15 minutes. Taste and adjust the seasoning.

4. Heat the oven to 500°F and put the rack in the lower third, with the pizza stone if you're using one.

5. Roll out the pizza dough according to the recipe directions. Top each pizza with half the potato slices (it's okay if they overlap a bit), then scatter with half the braised fennel. Put one baking sheet into the oven or slide the pizza onto the stone. Bake until the crust is crisp, anywhere from 5 to 12 minutes. Chop the fennel fronds, sprinkle half over the pizza, slice, and serve. Bake the second pizza while you eat the first.

● CLAM PIZZA

makes: 4 servings
time: 1 hour

OPENING THE CLAMS If neither your fishmonger nor you is willing to shuck raw clams, just steam them first. The pizza is still a delight—just with slightly chewier, more concentrated seafood. Put the clams in a large pot with 1 cup white wine and sprinkle with salt and pepper. Cover, bring to a boil, and cook until most of the clams have opened, 5 to 10 minutes. Remove the meat and proceed with the recipe.

1 cup heavy cream

3 dozen littleneck clams, shucked by your fishmonger if possible, or rinsed

1 batch Semolina Pizza Dough (opposite)

10 garlic cloves, thinly sliced

2 fresh red chiles (like Thai or Fresno), thinly sliced, or 1 tablespoon red chile flakes

4 tablespoons olive oil

¼ cup chopped fresh parsley, for garnish

Lemon wedges

1. Heat the oven to 500°F and put the rack in the lower third, with a pizza stone if you're using one. Put the cream in a small saucepan over medium-low heat. Cook, stirring often to prevent scorching and never boiling, until the cream has reduced by half, 10 to 15 minutes.

2. If you bought whole clams, use a towel to protect your hand and hold a clam with its "hinge" facing you. Insert a sturdy paring or clam knife between the two shells (jiggle the knife if you have to). Once you get it in there, move it around to completely separate the shells, using the knife like a lever. Open the clam and, with the point of the knife, scrape the meat attached to the top shell into the bottom shell, repeat with the bottom shell, and put the meat and any liquid in a small bowl. Repeat with the remaining clams.

3. Prepare the pizza dough according to the recipe directions. Spread half the reduced cream over one pizza, leaving a 1-inch border all around, then scatter half the clams, garlic, and chiles on top; sprinkle with salt and pepper, and finally drizzle on 2 tablespoons olive oil. Put one baking sheet into the oven or slide the pizza onto the stone. Bake until the crust is crisp, anywhere from 5 to 12 minutes. Garnish with the parsley and let rest for 5 minutes before slicing and serving with the lemon wedges. Bake the second pizza while you eat the first.

PIZZA DOUGH

I have two go-to pizza doughs: a long-rising version made with some semolina flour and a quicker whole wheat dough. I've given suggestions in the recipes, but use whichever dough you like.

Semolina Pizza Dough Mix 2 cups all-purpose flour, 1 cup semolina flour, ¼ teaspoon instant yeast, and 2 teaspoons salt in a large bowl. Add 1½ cups water and 2 tablespoons olive oil and stir until combined. Cover the bowl with plastic wrap and let rise until doubled in size. Start checking after 12 hours; it should take about 18 hours, give or take a few hours based on the temperature of the room.

When the dough is ready and with floured hands and a generously floured workspace, turn the dough out and divide it into 2 equal bloblike pieces; it will be very wet. Cover the dough with plastic wrap or a towel and let rest until they puff slightly, 20 minutes or so.

Cut 2 pieces of parchment the size of a large rimmed baking sheet (or pizza stone if using). Line 2 baking sheets with the parchment and, using floured hands, transfer one piece of dough to the parchment with the help of a spatula or pastry blade; repeat with the other piece of dough. Let the pizzas sit for a few minutes; this will relax |the dough and make it easier to roll out. Lightly press or roll each dough ball into the pan to about ¼ inch thick, flouring the dough only as necessary to prevent sticking. (If you're using a pizza stone, roll or pat out the dough onto the parchment to ¼-inch thickness, then transfer to a peel.) Press gently on the pizzas to readjust and flatten them. Proceed with the recipe to top the pizza. Makes 4 servings in 14 to 20 hours.

Whole Wheat Pizza Dough Grease a large bowl with olive oil. Put 1½ cups all-purpose flour, 1½ cups whole wheat flour, 2 teaspoons instant yeast, and 2 teaspoons salt in a food processor. With the machine running, gradually add 1 cup water and 2 tablespoons olive oil, taking care not to overmix. Continue to run the machine, slowly adding ½ cup more water, until the dough forms a ball and is slightly sticky to the touch; about 30 seconds. If it's still dry, add 1 tablespoon water and process for another 10 seconds, but make sure the dough stays only a little sticky. (Unlikely, but if the mixture is too sticky to handle, add flour 1 tablespoon at a time and process for 10 seconds.) Transfer the dough onto a floured work surface and knead by hand until you have a smooth, round ball, just a few seconds. Put the dough in the prepared bowl, turn to coat in the oil, and cover with plastic wrap; let rise until doubled in size, 1 to 2 hours.

Cut the dough into 2 pieces. Cover the dough with plastic wrap or a towel and let rest until they puff slightly, 20 minutes or so.

Cut 2 pieces of parchment the size of your large rimmed baking sheet (or pizza stone if you have one). Line 2 baking sheets with the parchment and, using floured hands, transfer one piece of dough to the parchment with the help of a spatula or pastry blade; put the other piece of dough on the second sheet. Let the pizzas sit for a few minutes; this will relax the dough and make it easier to roll out. Lightly press or roll each dough ball into the pan to about ¼-inch thickness, flouring the dough only as necessary to prevent sticking. (If you're using a pizza stone, roll or pat out the dough onto the parchment, ¼-inch thick, then transfer to a peel.) Press gently on the pizzas to readjust and flatten them before topping. Makes 4 servings in 3 to 4 hours.

Quesadillas

Like a grilled cheese sandwich, but with way more potential for great fillings. To skip the dairy, you still need something to hold the tortillas together; Sweet Potato Quesadillas with Pepita Salsa will remind you of everything you love about melted cheese. Some nights, you probably wish you didn't have to stand over a stove, monitoring two skillets. Problem solved with these Chicken Quesadillas. From-scratch components make Chorizo Quesadillas Verdes with Homemade Flour Tortillas an event, so make sure you set the table to linger.

● CHICKEN QUESADILLAS

makes: 4 servings
time: 30 minutes

4 tablespoons good-quality vegetable oil

12 ounces boneless, skinless chicken thighs, cut into ½-inch slices

Salt and pepper

1 tablespoon chili powder

2 ripe tomatoes, cored and chopped

1 jalapeño, seeded and chopped, or to taste

4 scallions, chopped

½ cup chopped fresh cilantro

2 tablespoons fresh lime juice, or more as needed

1½ to 2 cups grated Mexican melting cheese (like Oaxaca, Asadero, or Chihuahua; 6 to 8 ounces)

Four 10- or 12-inch flour tortillas

Hot sauce

1. Heat the oven to 450°F and position 2 racks toward the middle. Put 2 tablespoons oil in a large skillet over medium heat. When it's hot, add the chicken and sprinkle with salt and pepper. Cook, stirring often, until the chicken is cooked through, 8 to 10 minutes. Add the chili powder and cook, stirring constantly, until fragrant, about 1 minute. Taste, adjust the seasoning, and remove from the heat.

2. Put the tomatoes, jalapeño, scallions, cilantro, and lime juice in a bowl and sprinkle with salt and pepper. Toss to combine; taste and adjust the seasoning.

3. Use the remaining 2 tablespoons oil to grease 2 baking sheets. Put 2 tortillas on each pan, turning them to rub both sides with some of the oil. Sprinkle the cheese evenly over the tortillas; scatter the chicken on top. Transfer the pans to the oven and bake until the cheese melts, 5 to 10 minutes.

4. Fold the tortillas in half. Continue to cook, turning once, until the tortillas are golden and crisp on both sides, about 2½ minutes on each side. Let the quesadillas sit for a few minutes, then cut them in wedges and serve with the salsa, passing the hot sauce at the table if you like.

● SWEET POTATO QUESADILLAS
with pepita salsa

makes: 4 quesadillas
time: about 1 hour, partially unattended

5 tablespoons good-quality vegetable oil

1 red onion, halved and sliced

4 tablespoons red wine vinegar

2 teaspoons salt, or more as needed

1 teaspoon turbinado sugar

1 large sweet potato (about 12 ounces), peeled
   and grated

Pepper

1 teaspoon ground cumin

1 chipotle chile and 1 teaspoon adobo sauce,
   or to taste

3 tablespoons fresh lime juice

Eight 6-inch whole wheat flour tortillas

⅓ cup raw pumpkin seeds (pepitas)

½ cup chopped fresh cilantro

1. Heat the oven to 350°F. Grease a large rimmed baking sheet with 1 tablespoon oil. Put the onion, vinegar, 2 teaspoons salt, and the sugar in a bowl with 4 tablespoons water and let sit until the onion has mellowed, at least 30 minutes, or refrigerate up to a few days.

2. Put 3 tablespoons oil in a large skillet over medium-high heat. When it's hot, add the sweet potato and sprinkle with salt and pepper. Cook, stirring occasionally, until it is just barely tender and still retains its shape, 10 to 15 minutes. If the potato threatens to burn, or hasn't softened at all, add ¼ cup water and cook until the liquid has evaporated, 1 to 2 minutes. Add the cumin and stir until fragrant, another minute more. Remove from the heat and toss occasionally with a fork to cool.

3. Drain the pickled onion, reserving the liquid. Put the chipotle, adobo, 2 tablespoons lime juice, and 2 tablespoons onion pickling liquid in a blender and process until smooth. Add to the sweet potatoes along with a spoonful of pickled onion; toss, taste, and adjust the seasoning, adding more onion if you like.

4. Put 4 tortillas on the baking sheet. Divide the sweet potato mixture among the tortillas and cover each with a second tortilla. Press gently to seal. Brush the tops with the remaining tablespoon oil. Bake, carefully turning the quesadillas once, until the tortillas are golden and crisp on both sides and the potatoes are fully tender, 10 to 15 minutes.

5. While the quesadillas are baking, put the pumpkin seeds in a dry medium skillet over medium heat. Cook, shaking the pan occasionally, until the seeds are puffed and browned, 3 to 5 minutes. Mix with ¼ cup pickled onion, the remaining tablespoon lime juice, and the cilantro and sprinkle with salt and pepper; taste and adjust the seasoning. Let the quesadillas sit for a few minutes, then cut them into wedges and serve with a spoonful of the salsa on top.

● CHORIZO QUESADILLAS VERDES
with homemade flour tortillas

makes: 4 servings
time: about 12 hours, largely unattended

1 pound boneless pork shoulder, cut into
    1-inch chunks

1 tablespoon chopped garlic

2 teaspoons cider vinegar

2 teaspoons ground ancho chile

1¾ teaspoons salt, or more as needed

1 teaspoon dried oregano

1 teaspoon pepper, or more as needed

1 teaspoon ground cumin

½ teaspoon ground coriander

1½ cups flour, plus more for dusting

2 tablespoons lard (or vegetable oil)

About ½ cup boiling water, or more as needed

8 tablespoons good-quality vegetable oil, or more
    as needed

2½ to 3 cups grated Oaxaca or other mild melting
    cheese (like Monterey Jack or mozzarella,
    10 to 12 ounces)

½ cup crema or thinned sour cream

2 scallions, chopped, for garnish

¼ cup chopped fresh cilantro, for garnish

¼ cup chopped radishes, for garnish

Lime wedges

1. Mix the pork shoulder, garlic, vinegar, ground chile, 1½ teaspoons salt, oregano, pepper, cumin, and coriander in a bowl. Cover and refrigerate for at least 8 or up to 12 hours.

2. Put the flour, lard, and remaining ¼ teaspoon salt in a food processor and pulse to combine. With the machine running, add the boiling water very gradually, processing just until the dough forms a ball. Turn the dough onto a lightly floured surface and knead until it becomes elastic and smooth, about 5 minutes. Wrap the dough in plastic and let rest for at least 30 minutes and up to 3 hours. (Or refrigerate for up to 3 days; bring to room temperature before proceeding.) Wash the food processor.

3. Transfer the pork to the food processor and pulse until coarsely ground. (You might need to work in batches.) Heat a large skillet over medium-high heat. When it's hot, add the meat and cook, stirring occasionally, until cooked through and crisp, 8 to 10 minutes. Transfer to a paper towel–lined plate to drain. Wash and dry the skillet.

4. Divide the dough into 8 pieces and lightly flour your work surface. Gently flatten the balls into disks, cover with plastic, and let rest for 5 minutes. Use a rolling pin (or a tortilla press) to roll (or flatten) out each disk into a tortilla about 8 inches in diameter, stacking them between sheets of parchment. Heat a dry cast-iron skillet or griddle over medium heat. When it's hot, cook the tortillas about 30 seconds on each side, until they are just set but not yet browned. (They'll crisp when you make the quesadillas but crack if you cook them too much at this point.) Transfer them to a wire rack as they finish and cover with a towel.

5. Heat the oven to 200°F and fit a wire rack in a rimmed baking sheet. Put 2 tablespoons oil in the large skillet over medium heat. When it's hot, carefully add 1 tortilla and scatter with one-eighth of the cheese and some pork. Cook until the bottom is toasted and the cheese is beginning to melt, 3 to 5 minutes. Gently fold the tortilla in half, press down on the quesadilla, and cook until the cheese has completely melted, 2 to 3 minutes. Keep warm in the oven on the prepared pan as you make the remaining quesadillas, using the remaining oil. Cut into wedges, drizzle with the crema, and garnish with the scallions, cilantro, and radishes. Serve, passing the lime wedges at the table.

Tacos a la Plancha

To make these recipes even more accessible, I'm loosening the Spanish translation here to mean seared, if not actually grilled. The Shrimp Tacos are like eating warm salad in tortillas, with the added benefit of one less thing to wash. Since the filling in Crunchy Peanut Tacos is cut into bits, have a little patience so all sides of the mushrooms and peanuts will be dry and crisp as advertised. And seared, marinated steak with salsa verde makes a heck of a taco with Carne Asada with Homemade Corn Tortillas.

● SHRIMP TACOS

makes: 4 servings
time: 30 minutes

¼ cup good-quality vegetable oil

2 tablespoons chopped garlic

1½ pounds raw medium shrimp, peeled, rinsed, and dried

1½ teaspoons ground chile (like ancho or chipotle)

1 teaspoon ground cumin

Salt and pepper

3 cups chopped or grated green cabbage (about 12 ounces)

2 limes, 1 halved and 1 cut into wedges

Twelve 6-inch corn tortillas

A couple dozen tender fresh cilantro sprigs, for garnish

Bottled hot sauce

1. Warm the oil in a large skillet over low heat. Add the garlic and cook, stirring once or twice, until golden, 2 to 3 minutes. Raise the heat to medium-high and add the shrimp, ground chile, and cumin and sprinkle with salt and pepper. Stir to combine and cook, shaking the pan once or twice and turning the shrimp once, until they're coated evenly, opaque, and sizzling, 5 to 10 minutes.

2. Remove the pan from the heat and add the cabbage. Squeeze in the juice from the halved lime and toss to soften the cabbage and combine with the sauce and shrimp. Taste and adjust the seasoning.

3. Warm the tortillas using one of the methods on page 207. Fill them with the shrimp mixture, top with cilantro, and serve right away, passing the lime wedges and hot sauce at the table.

Carne Asada with
Homemade Corn Tortillas,
page 203

CRUNCHY PEANUT TACOS

makes: 4 servings
time: 45 minutes

6 tablespoons good-quality vegetable oil

1 onion, chopped

Salt and pepper

2 pounds ripe tomatoes, peeled, cored, and chopped, with their liquid (about 3 cups; one 28-ounce can diced tomatoes is also fine)

2 canned chipotle chiles, chopped, plus their adobo sauce to taste

1 teaspoon sugar

¼ cup chopped fresh cilantro

3 tablespoons fresh lime juice, or to taste

2 cups roasted, unsalted peanuts

2 teaspoons ground cumin

½ teaspoon cayenne, or to taste

1 pound cremini mushrooms, rinsed, trimmed, and chopped

1 teaspoon chopped garlic

Twelve 6-inch corn tortillas

2 romaine hearts, shredded

1. Put 2 tablespoons oil in a medium saucepan over medium-high heat. When it's hot, add the onion and sprinkle with salt and pepper. Cook, stirring occasionally, until the onion is browned in spots, 10 to 15 minutes.

2. Add the tomatoes, chipotles, and sugar and bring the mixture to a boil. Adjust the heat so the mixture bubbles gently and cook, stirring occasionally, until the salsa thickens, 15 to 20 minutes. Stir in the cilantro and lime juice. Use an immersion blender to puree the mixture directly in the pot, or carefully transfer the mixture in batches to a blender to puree; thin with a little water if necessary. Taste and adjust the seasoning, adding some of the adobo sauce from the chipotles if you like. Keep warm or cool completely and refrigerate, covered, for up to 3 days (reheat gently before proceeding).

3. Put the peanuts in a food processor and pulse until chopped into bits. Put 2 tablespoons oil in a large skillet over medium-high heat. When it's hot, add the peanuts and sprinkle with salt and pepper. Cook, stirring frequently, until golden and crisp, 3 to 5 minutes. Add the cumin and cayenne and stir until fragrant, 30 seconds or so. Transfer to a bowl; don't bother to wipe out the skillet.

4. Put the remaining 2 tablespoons oil in the skillet and return it to medium-high heat. Add the mushrooms and garlic and sprinkle with salt and pepper. Cook, stirring occasionally, until browned and crisp and the pan is dry, 5 to 10 minutes. Return the peanuts to the pan and stir; taste, adjust the seasoning, and keep warm.

5. Warm the tortillas using one of the methods on page 207. To assemble the tacos, line the tortillas with lettuce, then a spoonful of warm salsa. Divide the peanut mixture among them. Serve right away, and pass the extra salsa at the table.

● CARNE ASADA
with homemade corn tortillas

makes: 4 servings
time: about 3 hours

½ cup fresh lime juice (from at least 4 limes)

2 tablespoons chopped garlic

½ teaspoon salt, or more as needed

Pepper

1½ pounds boneless flank or skirt steak

1½ cups masa harina (from blue corn, if you can find it)

2 tablespoons lard or good-quality vegetable oil

1 cup hot tap water

Flour or cornmeal, for kneading

1 pound tomatillos, husked but left whole

3 scallions, chopped

½ cup chopped fresh cilantro

6 ounces radishes, chopped

Lime wedges

1. Mix ¼ cup lime juice and 1 tablespoon garlic in a resealable plastic bag and sprinkle with salt and pepper. Add the steak, push out any air, and seal. Marinate for at least 30 minutes at room temperature, or up to 8 hours in the refrigerator.

2. Put the masa harina and ½ teaspoon salt in a bowl; stir in the lard or oil. Slowly pour in the water while mixing with a wooden spoon until the dough comes together into a ball. If the mixture is so dry it cracks when pressed, add water 1 tablespoon at a time. If it's too wet, add more masa harina 1 tablespoon at a time. Turn the dough out onto a lightly floured surface and knead until it is smooth and elastic, just a minute or 2. Wrap the ball in plastic and let it rest at room temperature for at least 30 minutes or refrigerate for up to 1 day.

3. Prepare a charcoal or gas grill for direct cooking. Or heat a large grill pan over 2 burners until smoking hot. Grill or broil the tomatillos, turning them with tongs as each side chars, until they are black and begin to burst. When they're cool enough to handle, chop. Put the tomatillos and any accumulated juices in a serving bowl and add the scallions, remaining tablespoon garlic, ¼ cup cilantro, and remaining ¼ cup lime juice; sprinkle with salt and pepper and stir to combine; taste and adjust the seasoning. Cover and refrigerate until ready to use (or for up to a day). Bring to room temperature before serving.

4. Divide the dough into 16 pieces, roll each into a slightly flattened disk, and flour lightly. Put a piece of dough between 2 pieces of plastic wrap or parchment. Use a heavy rolling pin, tortilla press, or heavy skillet to shape it into a disk about 6 inches in diameter. Stack the finished tortillas between sheets of plastic wrap or parchment.

5. Prepare the grill or grill pan again, if necessary. Remove the steak from the marinade and pat dry with a towel. Grill or broil the steak, moving it to the cooler side as necessary to prevent burning until it's browned on both sides but still rare in the thickest part, 5 to 10 minutes total. (To check, nick with a knife and peek inside; remove it from the heat when it's one stage rarer than you ultimately want it.) Let the meat rest while you fry the tortillas.

6. Put 2 large or medium dry skillets or griddle (preferably cast iron) over medium-high heat for 3 to 5 minutes. Cook the tortillas, 1 or 2 at a time, until browned in spots, about a minute. Turn and repeat on the other side. As the tortillas finish, wrap them in foil or a towel to keep warm.

7. Slice the steak thinly across the grain; then chop into small pieces. To serve family style, set out the warm tortillas, steak, salsa, radishes, lime wedges, and remaining ¼ cup cilantro and let everyone assemble his or her own tacos.

Cauliflower Tinga
Tacos, page 206

Saucy Tacos

Braised taco fillings have the advantage of built-in sauce, while fresh and crisp finishing touches provide necessary and welcome contrast. There's a reason north-of-the-border Tex-Mex tacos are so popular: ubiquitous ground beef. My interpretation is familiar but not at all ho-hum. Next, I call on *tinga*—the family of Mexican dishes where shredded meat is braised or tossed in chile sauce—to turn cauliflower into a hearty taco. And to go All Out, Tacos Borrachos—a culinary way of saying "drunk tacos" but meaning "cooked in alcohol"—are an ideal introduction to goat. (Or you can substitute boneless beef chuck, pork shoulder, or lamb shoulder.)

● TEX-MEX TACOS

makes: 4 servings
time: about 30 minutes

2 tablespoons olive oil

1 pound ground beef

1 small white onion, chopped

1 jalapeño, seeded and chopped

1 tablespoon chopped garlic

2 tablespoons chili powder

Salt and pepper

One 14-ounce can crushed tomatoes

12 preshaped crisp taco shells

3 cups shredded iceberg lettuce

2 ripe tomatoes, chopped

1 cup grated cheddar cheese (about 4 ounces)

Bottled hot sauce

1. Put the oil in a large skillet over medium-high heat. When it's hot, add the beef and cook, stirring often, until it's no longer pink and starting to crisp in places, 8 to 12 minutes. Add the onion, jalapeño, and garlic. Cook, stirring occasionally, until the onion is soft and the beef crisp, another 3 to 5 minutes.

2. Add the chili powder and sprinkle with salt and pepper. Cook, stirring constantly, until fragrant, about 1 minute, then add the tomatoes. Bring to a boil, then reduce the heat so the mixture bubbles gently. Cook, stirring once in a while until thickened and the flavors have had a chance to come together, 10 to 15 minutes. Taste and adjust the seasoning.

3. To assemble the tacos, spoon some of the filling into each shell and top with lettuce, tomatoes, and cheese. Serve right away, passing the hot sauce at the table.

CAULIFLOWER TINGA TACOS

makes: 4 servings
time: 2 hours

One 28-ounce can whole tomatoes, drained

4 tablespoons good-quality vegetable oil, plus more for frying

1 small white onion, chopped

2 tablespoons chopped garlic

Salt and pepper

1 tablespoon ground cumin

2 teaspoons dried oregano

1 canned chipotle chile, with 1 tablespoon adobo sauce, or to taste

2 cups vegetable stock (see page 87) or water

1 large head cauliflower (about 1½ pounds)

Eight 8-inch (or twelve 6-inch) whole wheat flour tortillas

6 ounces radishes, sliced

2 ripe avocados, pitted, peeled, and sliced

¼ cup chopped fresh mint, for garnish

1. Heat the oven to 375°F. Put the tomatoes in a baking dish and roast until they start to char and shrivel, 40 to 50 minutes.

2. Put the oil in a large pot over medium heat. When it's hot, add the onion and garlic and sprinkle with salt and pepper. Cook, stirring occasionally, until soft and starting to brown, 5 to 8 minutes. Add the cumin and oregano and cook, stirring constantly, until fragrant, about 1 minute. Add the roasted tomatoes, the chipotle, adobo, and stock and sprinkle with salt and pepper. Bring the mixture to a boil, then adjust the heat so it bubbles gently. Cook, stirring occasionally, until the tomatoes have broken down and the sauce has thickened a little, 25 to 30 minutes. Use an immersion blender to puree the mixture directly in the pot, or carefully transfer the mixture in batches to a blender to puree. Taste and adjust the seasoning.

3. Cut the core from the cauliflower, then roughly chop the florets into pieces about ½ inch in size. Add the cauliflower to the sauce and bring the mixture to a boil, then adjust the heat so the mixture bubbles gently. Cook, uncovered and stirring once in a while, until the cauliflower is tender, 10 to 15 minutes. Taste, adjust the seasoning, and keep warm.

4. Pour about ½ inch oil into a large skillet over medium-high heat. Put a wire rack on a large baking sheet. When it's hot, put a tortilla in the skillet and let it cook until it starts blistering but is still soft, less than 15 seconds. Carefully turn the tortilla with tongs, and immediately fold it over and hold it for a few seconds to form a taco shell. Once the tortilla holds its shape, turn it every few seconds, until it's crisp and golden all over, 15 to 30 seconds more. Transfer to the wire rack to drain. Repeat with the remaining tortillas, adjusting the heat and adding more oil as necessary.

5. To assemble the tacos, spoon the cauliflower into the crisp shells and top with radish slices, avocado, and mint.

TACOS BORRACHOS

makes: 4 servings
time: 3 hours

3 tablespoons good-quality vegetable oil

3 pounds bone-in goat stew meat, in 1-inch chunks (or about 1½ pounds boneless goat)

Salt and pepper

1 white onion, halved and sliced

6 garlic cloves, smashed

1 ounce mild dried chiles (like pasilla or guajillo)

12 ounces Mexican lager

¼ cup tequila

¼ cup fresh lime juice

¼ cup cider vinegar

2 teaspoons sugar

2 cups grated red cabbage

½ red onion, sliced

1 jalapeño

Twelve 6-inch corn tortillas (for homemade, see page 203)

1. Put the oil in a large pot over medium-high heat. When it's hot, add the goat meat, working in batches if necessary to avoid crowding the pan, and sprinkle with salt and pepper. Cook, turning when it releases, until the meat is well browned on most sides, 10 to 15 minutes total. Transfer to a plate.

2. Pour off all but 3 tablespoons fat, add the white onion, and cook over medium heat, stirring occasionally, until softened and golden, 8 to 10 minutes. Add the garlic and dried chiles and cook until fragrant, about 1 minute. Add the beer, tequila, and lime juice and sprinkle with salt and pepper. Return the meat to the pan, cover, and turn the heat to low.

3. Cook, stirring a couple of times, until the meat is fork-tender and nearly falling from the bone, 2 to 2½ hours. Remove the meat from the cooking liquid and transfer to a plate. When it's cool enough to handle, use 2 forks or your hands to remove the meat from the bones and shred it. Put the goat in a saucepan and dress with enough braising liquid to keep it moist but not submerged; reserve the rest. Taste and adjust the seasoning of both the meat and remaining sauce and keep warm.

4. While the goat is braising, make the garnishes: Put the vinegar, sugar, and 1 teaspoon salt in a small saucepan over medium heat. Cook, stirring often, until the sugar and salt have dissolved. Combine the cabbage and red onion in a bowl and toss with the brine; taste and adjust the seasoning. Refrigerate for at least 1 hour and up to 4 hours, stirring once in a while. Slice the jalapeño as thin as you can manage.

5. To serve, warm the tortillas (see below). Fill each with some goat and serve right away, topped with some of the pickled cabbage and a few jalapeño slices.

WARMING TORTILLAS

Cold corn tortillas are tricky—they won't fold, hold their shape, or taste good. Here are three easy ways to warm them up:

Flame (This only works on gas stoves.): Turn one or more burners to high and put the tortilla directly on the grate. Cook, watching carefully, until charred in spots, turning halfway through, 1 to 2 minutes total.

Oven: Heat the oven to 375°F. Stack the tortillas, wrap in foil, and bake until heated through, 5 to 10 minutes. Keep the tortillas wrapped in the foil until ready to serve.

Microwave: Stack the tortillas and wrap in a damp paper towel. Microwave until warmed through, 15 to 20 seconds.

Falafel

Lucky for us, the world's best street food is totally manageable for home cooks. (And it's vegan.) For the Easy way, meet Falafel Hash, not unlike the mish-mash of browned chickpea bits we associate with brunch. Slightly more advanced is the Vegan Baked Vegetable Falafel with Orange Tahini Sauce. For the All Out, the Falafel, Fixings, and Zhug—the last, a Yemeni hot sauce popular in Israel—takes falafel to a whole other level.

● FALAFEL HASH

makes: 4 servings
time: 20 minutes

¼ cup olive oil

1 onion, chopped

4 teaspoons chopped garlic

Salt and pepper

1 tablespoon ground cumin

1 teaspoon ground coriander

½ teaspoon cayenne, or to taste

1 cup yogurt

4 tablespoons lemon juice, or more as needed

3 cups cooked chickpeas (see page 82; or two 15-ounce cans), drained

1 teaspoon baking soda

½ cup chopped fresh parsley

1. Put the oil in a large skillet over medium heat. When it's hot, add the onion and 3 teaspoons garlic and sprinkle with salt and pepper. Cook, stirring occasionally, until the onion is soft and beginning to turn golden, 5 to 8 minutes. Add the cumin, coriander, and cayenne and stir until fragrant, less than a minute.

2. Put the yogurt, 2 tablespoons lemon juice, and remaining teaspoon garlic in a small bowl and season with salt and pepper. Whisk to combine, taste, and adjust the seasoning. Refrigerate until ready to use.

3. Put the skillet over medium-high heat and add the chickpeas and baking soda. Stir the mixture, and then crush half the chickpeas with a fork or potato masher. Cook, undisturbed and adjusting the heat as necessary to prevent burning, until the bottom is crisp and brown, 5 to 10 minutes. Remove from the heat, add the parsley and remaining 2 tablespoons lemon juice and stir gently, then taste and adjust the seasoning. Serve hot with the yogurt sauce drizzled over.

Falafel, Fixings, and
Zhug, page 210

BAKED VEGETABLE FALAFEL
with orange tahini sauce

makes: 4 servings
time: about 1 day, almost entirely unattended

1¼ cups dried chickpeas

8 ounces rutabaga, peeled and cut into chunks

2 garlic cloves, chopped

1 small onion, quartered

1 tablespoon ground cumin

¾ teaspoon cayenne, or to taste

1 cup chopped fresh cilantro, plus a little more
    for garnish

½ teaspoon baking soda

2 tablespoons lemon juice

1 teaspoon salt, or more as needed

Pepper

4 tablespoons olive oil

½ cup tahini

¼ cup fresh orange juice

1. Put the chickpeas in a large bowl and cover with water by at least 3 inches. Soak for 24 hours, checking once or twice to see if you need to add more water to keep the chickpeas submerged.

2. Heat the oven to 375°F. Grate the rutabaga with the shredding attachment on a food processor and transfer to a bowl. Fit the work bowl with the blade. Drain the chickpeas well and add to the rutabaga with the garlic, onion, cumin, cayenne, cilantro, baking soda, lemon juice, 1 teaspoon salt, and a pinch of pepper. Transfer the mixture to the food processor and pulse until almost smooth, scraping down the sides of the work bowl if needed; add 1 or 2 tablespoons water if necessary to help the machine, but keep the mixture as dry as possible. It should hold together when you pinch some in the palm of your hand. Taste and adjust the seasoning. Use right away or refrigerate, tightly wrapped, for up to 2 days.

3. Grease a rimmed baking sheet with 2 tablespoons oil. Roll the mixture into 20 balls, about 1½ inches each, then flatten them into thick patties. Put the falafel on the prepared pan and brush the tops with the remaining 2 tablespoons oil. Bake until golden all over, turning once, 10 to 15 minutes on each side. Remove from the oven and let cool on the pan for about 10 minutes to crisp.

4. Meanwhile, combine the tahini with the orange juice, ¼ cup water, and a large pinch of salt in a small bowl. Whisk until smooth; taste and adjust the seasoning and add a little more water if necessary to get the desired consistency. Serve the falafel warm drizzled with the sauce and garnished with cilantro.

FALAFEL, FIXINGS, AND ZHUG

makes: 4 to 6 servings
time: about 27 hours, largely unattended

1¾ cups dried chickpeas

2 cups chopped fresh cilantro

2 cups chopped fresh parsley

2 hot green chiles (like Thai bird or serrano), cut
    into chunks, or to taste

4 garlic cloves, peeled and lightly crushed

6 tablespoons olive oil, plus more for greasing

2 tablespoons lemon juice

4 teaspoons ground cumin

1½ teaspoons ground coriander

¼ teaspoon ground cardamom

3 cups flour, or more as needed

2 teaspoons instant yeast

2 teaspoons salt, or more as needed

½ teaspoon sugar

1 small onion, cut into chunks

½ teaspoon baking soda

¼ teaspoon cayenne, or more to taste

Pepper

4 tablespoons unsalted butter, melted

Good-quality vegetable oil, for frying

Chopped romaine lettuce, tomatoes, cucumbers, and red onions, for serving

1. Put the chickpeas in a large bowl and cover with water by at least 3 inches. Soak for 24 hours, checking once or twice to see if you need to add more water to keep the beans submerged.

2. Put 1½ cups each of the cilantro and parsley in a food processor with the chiles, 2 garlic cloves, 3 tablespoons olive oil, 1 tablespoon lemon juice, 1 teaspoon cumin, ½ teaspoon coriander, and the cardamom. Process until smooth and pourable (add water 1 tablespoon at a time if the mixture is too thick). Taste and adjust the zhug. (The sauce is best after refrigerating at least a day and keeps for 5; to serve, bring to room temperature.)

3. Put the flour, remaining 3 tablespoons olive oil, the yeast, 2 teaspoons salt, and the sugar in a food processor. With the machine running, add 1 cup water through the feed tube. Process for about 30 seconds, adding more water, a little at a time, until the mixture forms a ball that is just slightly sticky to the touch. If it's too dry, add another tablespoon of water and process for another 10 seconds. (In the unlikely event the mixture is too sticky, add flour, 1 tablespoon at a time.) Turn the dough out onto a floured work surface and knead by hand for a few seconds to form a smooth ball. Put the dough in a bowl and cover with plastic wrap; let it rise until the dough doubles in size, 1 to 2 hours. Clean the food processor.

4. Drain the beans thoroughly and transfer them to the food processor with the remaining ½ cup cilantro, ½ cup parsley, 2 garlic cloves, 3 teaspoons cumin, 1 teaspoon coriander, and 1 tablespoon lemon juice. Add the onion, baking soda, and cayenne. Season generously with salt and pepper and pulse until almost smooth, scraping down the sides of the work bowl if needed; add 1 or 2 tablespoons

water if necessary to help the machine, but keep the mixture as dry as possible. It should hold together when you pinch some in the palm of your hand. Taste and adjust the seasoning. Transfer the mixture to a bowl and refrigerate until ready to fry.

5. When the pita dough is ready, divide it into 6 or 8 pieces and roll each into a ball. Put the dough balls on a lightly floured surface, not touching, and sprinkle with a little flour. Cover with plastic wrap or a towel and let rest until they rise a bit again, about 20 minutes.

6. Lightly flour your work surface and roll each ball out to rounds of about ⅛-inch thickness. As you work, put the rounds on a floured surface so they don't touch and keep covered with a towel. Heat the oven to 350°F and let the dough rest for another 20 minutes. If you have a pizza stone, put it on a low rack in the oven; or, lightly oil a baking sheet and put it in the oven on a rack set in the middle.

7. To bake the pita on a stone, put the individual disks directly onto the stone without touching one another using a large spatula. Or put 2 disks at a time on the prepared baking sheet. Bake until the pitas are lightly browned on first side, then turn and brown on the other side, 2 to 3 minutes per side. As the pitas finish baking, remove them from the oven, brush with melted butter, and wrap in foil to keep warm.

8. Line a plate with paper towels. Put 2 inches of vegetable oil in a large pot over medium heat; bring to 350°F. Working in small batches to prevent crowding, scoop up heaping tablespoons of the falafel mixture and gently lower them into the hot fat, using another spoon to gently slide them in. Cook on all sides, flipping occasionally and adjusting the heat so the batter sizzles steadily without burning, until the falafel are brown and crisp, 3 to 5 minutes total. Drain on the paper towels and repeat with the remaining batter. Serve the falafel with the warm pita, passing the spicy zhug and any other fixings at the table.

Secret-Ingredient
Stovetop Burgers ,
page 214

Burgers

You know the quintessential American food is always better at home. Blow your mind by grinding meat fresh in the food processor for the Ultimate Cheeseburger with Tomato Chutney; each of the three different cuts of meat brings something to the party. When you have less time, go for Secret-Ingredient Stovetop Burgers. (I won't spoil the surprise here.) Like their meat counterparts, veggie burgers are now made a zillion ways. Here I borrowed the falafel method (see page 210) for Beet and Lentil Burgers, only with way less prep time.

Ultimate Cheeseburger
with Tomato Chutney,
page 215

Beet and Lentil
Burgers, page 214

SECRET-INGREDIENT STOVETOP BURGERS

makes: 4 servings
time: 20 minutes

4 oil-packed anchovies, or to taste

1 tablespoon Worcestershire sauce

1½ pounds good-quality, not-too-lean ground beef (no more than 90%)

Salt and pepper

4 kaiser rolls or other large rolls, split

2 tablespoons olive oil

Condiments

1. Turn on the broiler and position the rack 4 inches below it. Put the anchovies and Worcestershire sauce in a large bowl and mash with a fork until well blended. Add the beef to the bowl and sprinkle with salt and pepper. Use your hands to mix until just combined. To taste and adjust the seasoning, cook a small pinch of the meat in a pan or microwave.

2. With a light touch, shape the mixture into 4 burgers, about 1 inch thick. (You can make them ahead and refrigerate them, tightly covered, up to a few hours; bring back to room temperature before cooking.)

3. Put the hamburger buns cut side up on a baking sheet and, watching closely, broil until they are lightly toasted, just a few minutes.

4. Put a large skillet over medium-high heat until smoking hot. Add the burgers and drizzle with the olive oil. Cook the burgers until they release easily, about 4 minutes per side for medium-rare, and a minute more per side for each increasing stage of doneness, 5 for medium, and 6 for well done. Turn and repeat on the other side, checking frequently by peeking inside so you can remove them the second they're ready. Immediately transfer them to the buns to capture the juices. Serve with any condiments you like.

BEET AND LENTIL BURGERS

makes: 4 to 6 servings
time: 50 minutes, plus at least 8 hours soaking time

1 cup green or brown lentils

2 tablespoons vegetable oil

1 cup cooked brown basmati rice (see page 102)

½ cup chopped onion

2 teaspoons fennel seeds

2 tablespoons chopped fresh dill

Salt and pepper

1 medium or 2 small beets (about 6 ounces), scrubbed and peeled

4 whole wheat English muffins, split

½ cup vegan mayonnaise (see page 218)

2 tablespoons grainy mustard, or to taste

1. Put the lentils in a medium bowl with enough water to cover by 3 inches. Soak for at least 8 hours or up to 12; drain them well.

2. Heat the oven to 375°F and grease a rimmed baking sheet with the oil. Put the lentils, the rice, onion, fennel seeds, and dill in a food processor and sprinkle with salt and pepper. Pulse until finely ground but not pureed. Transfer to a large bowl.

3. Grate the beets in the food processor using the shredding disk or on the largest holes of a box grater. Measure 1 packed cup (save any extra for another use) and add to the bowl with the rice mixture. Stir to combine, taste, and adjust the seasoning.

4. Gently shape the mixture into 4 to 6 patties about 1 inch thick. Put on the prepared baking sheet and bake, undisturbed, until the bottom is crisp and releases easily from the pan, 10 to 15 minutes. Turn and brown the other side and insert a metal skewer or thin-bladed knife to make sure the center is piping hot, another 5 to 10 minutes. Put the English muffins on another baking sheet, and put them in the oven to toast when the burgers are almost done; they'll take 3 to 5 minutes (or just use a toaster).

5. Put the mayonnaise and mustard in a small bowl and sprinkle with salt and pepper. Stir to combine, then taste and adjust the seasoning, adding more mustard if you like. When the burgers are ready, spread the mayonnaise mixture on the muffins, top with the burgers, and serve.

● ULTIMATE CHEESEBURGER
with tomato chutney

makes: 4 servings
time: 45 minutes

1 cinnamon stick

6 whole cloves

3 dried Thai or other small, hot red chiles

3 tablespoons unsalted butter

1 large red onion, cut into ½-inch pieces

1 teaspoon curry powder (see page 299)

¼ teaspoon celery seeds

Salt

2 ripe large tomatoes, or 2 cups canned tomatoes, chopped

¼ cup cider vinegar, or more to taste

3 tablespoons tomato paste

3 tablespoons brown sugar

12 ounces boneless beef short ribs, cut into 1-inch chunks

6 ounces boneless beef sirloin, cut into 1-inch chunks

6 ounces boneless pork shoulder, cut into 1-inch chunks

½ white onion, chopped

Pepper

4 ounces aged sharp cheddar cheese, cut into 4 thin slices

4 brioche or other good-quality rolls, halved horizontally

1. Wrap the cinnamon stick, cloves, and chiles in cheesecloth and secure with string. Put the butter and red onion in a large skillet over medium heat and cook, stirring occasionally, until the onion is soft, 3 to 5 minutes. Add the wrapped spice bundle, curry powder, celery seeds, and a large pinch of salt and cook, stirring constantly, until the mixture is fragrant, about a minute.

2. Add the tomatoes, vinegar, tomato paste, and brown sugar and cook, stirring once in a while, until the tomatoes break down a bit and the sauce thickens, 5 to 10 minutes. Taste and adjust the seasoning, adding more vinegar if you like, then cool to room temperature. (You can make the chutney ahead and refrigerate it for up to 3 days. Bring to room temperature before proceeding.)

3. Put the meats and white onion in a food processor, working in batches if necessary. Sprinkle with salt and pepper and pulse until the mixture is ground slightly finer than chopped, but not anywhere near a paste. Transfer it to a large bowl. To taste and adjust the seasoning, cook a small pinch of the meat in a pan or microwave. With a light touch, shape the mixture into 4 burgers about 1½ inches thick. (Don't refrigerate them unless you won't be cooking for more than an hour.)

4. Prepare a gas or charcoal grill for direct cooking. Or, on the stovetop, heat a dry large, heavy skillet over medium-high heat until smoking hot, 2 to 4 minutes, and preheat the broiler. The grill or skillet is ready when you can only hold your hand 3 or 4 inches above it for a few seconds. Cook the burgers until they release easily, about 3 minutes per side for very rare, or longer if you like them more cooked, but no more than 5 minutes before turning.

5. As soon you turn the burgers, put a slice of cheese on each. Toast the insides of the rolls over the cool part of the grill or under the broiler until golden. When the burgers are ready, immediately transfer them to the buns to capture the juices. Top with a spoonful of tomato chutney and serve.

BLT

When you want one, you just do. So I'm including a bacon, lettuce, and tomato sandwich to get you through the ten months a year when tomatoes aren't worthy, and a couple of options for when they are. Primo ingredients and judicious excess make the Bacon Club special. The tomatoes must be perfectly ripe or you're better off using sliced orange or pear or whatever fruit is delicious and juicy at the moment. The Year-Round BLT has another solution: dried tomatoes. It's a compromise that's different, but never disappointing. For the EAT—Eggplant, Arugula, and Tomato sandwich—borrow from these strategies and either use vine-ripened garden or farmers' market tomatoes, or spike the vegan mayo with dried tomatoes.

● YEAR-ROUND BLT

makes: 4 sandwiches
time: 25 minutes

½ cup dried whole tomatoes (not packed in oil)

2 cups boiling water

16 bacon slices (about 1 pound regular cut)

8 slices sandwich bread

½ cup mayonnaise (recipe follows)

Salt and pepper

1 small head romaine lettuce, separated into
    whole leaves, rinsed, and dried

1. Heat the oven to 375°F. Put the tomatoes in a small bowl and cover with boiling water. Use a saucer to keep them submerged if necessary. Soak until they are pliable but not mushy, 5 to 10 minutes. Strain and shake well to dry.

2. Put the bacon in a large skillet over medium heat. It's okay if they overlap a little. Cook, turning with tongs so they cook evenly until crisp, 5 to 10 minutes. Transfer to a paper towel–lined plate.

3. Put the bread on a baking sheet in a single layer and toast, turning once, to the doneness you like, 5 to 10 minutes.

4. Put the tomatoes and mayonnaise in a blender with a pinch of salt and lots of pepper and puree until smooth, or mostly smooth, depending on your preference. Taste and adjust the seasoning. Spread a thin layer of the mayo mixture on each slice of toast, then divide the bacon and lettuce among 4 pieces and assemble the sandwiches. Serve, passing any remaining mayo at the table.

MAYONNAISE MADE QUICKLY

It'll take you about 10 minutes to make 1 cup: Put 1 egg yolk and 2 teaspoons Dijon mustard in a food processor or blender and turn the machine on. With the machine running, add 1 cup olive oil in a slow, steady stream. (Or use good-quality vegetable oil for a more neutral flavor). When the emulsion begins to form, it will become creamy; at this point you can start to add the oil a little faster. When the oil is completely incorporated and the mayonnaise is thick, sprinkle with salt and pepper, add 1 tablespoon sherry vinegar or lemon juice, and blend or process once more to combine. Taste and adjust the seasoning. Store in the refrigerator for up to a week.

● Bacon Club,
page 219

● EAT
eggplant, arugula, and tomato

makes: 4 sandwiches
time: about 1 hour, largely unattended

6 tablespoons olive oil

3 or 4 large eggplant (about 2 pounds)

2 teaspoons smoked paprika

Salt and pepper

8 slices whole wheat sandwich bread

Vegan mayonnaise, for serving (recipe follows; optional)

2 large ripe tomatoes, sliced

2 cups arugula, rinsed and dried

1. Heat the oven to 400°F. Line 2 baking sheets with foil and grease each with 1 tablespoon oil. Slice the eggplant as thin as you can manage and put the slices on the prepared pans in a single layer. Sprinkle with the paprika and generously season with salt and pepper.

2. Put the eggplant in the oven and roast until the slices released their liquid, the pan is dry again, and they start to shrivel, 20 to 30 minutes. Turn the heat to 325°F and cook until the eggplant is dry, barely pliable, and releases easily from the foil, 5 to 15 minutes, depending on their thickness. Transfer the eggplant slices to a rack to cool and keep the oven on.

3. Carefully remove the foil from the baking sheet and add the bread. Drizzle with the remaining 4 tablespoons olive oil. Cook, turning once or twice, until the bread is golden and toasted, 5 to 10 minutes.

4. To assemble the sandwiches, spread the bread with mayonnaise if you like. Sprinkle the tomatoes with salt and pepper, then layer them with the eggplant; top with arugula and the other piece of bread, and serve right away.

VEGAN MAYONNAISE

Put 1 pound medium-firm tofu, ½ cup olive oil, ¼ cup cider vinegar, 5 teaspoons Dijon mustard, 1 teaspoon salt, and a pinch of ground turmeric in a blender. Puree, stopping once or twice to scrape down the sides of the container with a flexible spatula, until the mayo is smooth. Taste and adjust the seasoning. Serve right away or store in a jar in the refrigerator for up to 1 week. Makes 2 cups in about 10 minutes.

● BACON CLUB

makes: 4 sandwiches
time: about 1 hour

1 pound thick-cut bacon

Pepper

2 tablespoons turbinado sugar

1 loaf good-quality brioche or challah, cut into
    12 slices (you might have bread left over)

Olive oil, as needed

1 egg yolk

1½ teaspoons Dijon mustard

1 teaspoon cider vinegar

Salt

8 ounces hearts of romaine, leaves separated,
    rinsed, and dried

1 pound ripe tomatoes (preferably an heirloom
    variety), thickly sliced

1. Heat the oven to 400°F and position one of the racks as high as it can go, with another rack in the middle of the oven. Line a large rimmed baking sheet with foil to help with cleanup and put a wire rack on top. Put half the bacon slices into a medium bowl; sprinkle with lots of pepper, toss, and spread out on the rack in a single layer. Repeat with the remaining bacon slices, sprinkling with just the sugar, and putting them on the rack as well.

2. Transfer the pan to the oven and roast, undisturbed, until the bacon is crisp and browned, 10 to 25 minutes, depending on the thickness. Put the bread slices on a baking sheet and toast in the oven on the middle rack, until both sides are as golden as you like.

3. When the bacon is ready, carefully lift the rack from the pan and transfer it to sit over paper towels to drain. Pour the rendered fat from the baking sheet into a heatproof measuring cup; you should have ½ cup; if not, add some olive oil until you do. Put the bacon on a platter, return it to the oven to stay warm, and turn it off.

4. Put the yolk and mustard in a medium bowl and beat with a wire whisk. Begin to add the bacon fat in dribbles as you beat, only adding more when the previous addition is incorporated. When a thick emulsion forms, then you can add the remaining fat a little faster. The whole process will take about 5 minutes. Whisk in the vinegar, sprinkle with salt and pepper, then taste and adjust the seasoning. (Use right away or refrigerate for up to 3 days.)

5. Spread one side of each slice of bread with mayonnaise. To assemble the sandwiches, start with one piece of bread, mayo side up, and layer with a little lettuce, tomatoes, and both kinds of bacon. Follow with another piece of toast mayonnaise side down, then spread a thin layer on the other side to help hold the sandwich together. Top with more lettuce, tomato, bacon, and the last slice of bread. Use a long toothpick or skewer to secure the sandwiches. Serve right away, passing any remaining mayo at the table.

Baked Mascarpone
French Toast with Cherries,
page 223

Sweet Breakfast

It's perfectly acceptable to eat breakfast for dinner. The only decision is whether you go savory (see the next section on page 224) or sweet. Or both. Nutty Quinoa-Blueberry Griddlecakes are the responsible option. On the other end of the decadence spectrum, witness Baked Mascarpone French Toast with Cherries—a custardy delight that isn't hard to make. For those nights when you have an insatiable waffle craving and no time, go for Ironed Toast—nothing short of a revelation.

● IRONED TOAST

makes: 4 servings
time: 15 minutes

4 tablespoons unsalted butter, or more as needed

2 eggs

1 cup milk

1 teaspoon vanilla extract (optional)

8 slices brioche bread or challah, or 4 English muffins (or white bread in a pinch); ½ inch thick is ideal

Maple syrup, jam, or any other topping you like

1. Heat the oven to 200°F. Heat the waffle iron. Microwave the butter for a few seconds (or heat in a small pot) to soften it without fully melting. Whisk together the eggs, milk, and vanilla, if using, in a shallow dish.

2. Brush both surfaces of the waffle iron with softened butter, using a brush or paper towels. Dunk a piece of bread in the egg mixture until saturated, then put it right onto the waffle iron. Close the lid and cook until golden and crisp. (The time depends on your appliance.) Keep the finished toast warm in the oven while you repeat with the remaining slices. Serve warm with maple syrup, jam, or any other toppings you like.

NUTTY QUINOA-BLUEBERRY GRIDDLECAKES

makes: 4 servings
time: about 1 hour

2 cups blueberries (frozen are fine)

1 cup quinoa, rinsed and drained

1 teaspoon salt

¼ cup unsweetened nut butter (any kind)

1 teaspoon ground cinnamon

1 ounce dark chocolate, chopped (optional)

Good-quality vegetable oil, for pan-frying

Maple syrup, sorghum syrup, or light molasses

1. If the blueberries are frozen, put them in a colander, run cold water over them for a few seconds, then drain.

2. Put the quinoa and salt in a large pot. Add enough water to cover by about 1½ inches. Bring to a boil, then adjust the heat so the mixture bubbles gently. Cook, stirring occasionally, until the kernels are no longer distinct and the mixture is thick, like mashed potatoes, 25 to 35 minutes. (The only way to mess up is if you don't let the grains absorb enough water to burst and get mushy.) As the quinoa cooks, adjust the heat and add small amounts of water to keep the bottom from burning but keep the mixture dry. When the quinoa is ready, cover, remove from the heat, and let it sit for at least 5 or up to 15 minutes.

3. Heat the oven to 200°F. Add the nut butter and cinnamon to the quinoa; stir with a flexible spatula, mashing a bit to make the grains even stickier, adding water 1 tablespoon at a time, until the batter is thick but drops easily from a spoon. Gently fold in the blueberries and chocolate if using.

4. Put a large skillet or griddle (well-seasoned cast iron or nonstick works best) over medium heat. When a drop of water glides on the surface, add a thin film of oil; the oil will shimmer when it's ready. Spoon the batter into the skillet by ½ cupfuls, spread each griddlecake evenly, and take care not to crowd the pan. Cook until the bottoms are crisp and golden, 2 to 3 minutes, then turn and cook the other side the same way, another minute or 2. Transfer the griddlecakes to a plate and keep warm in the oven as you continue to cook the rest of the batter. Serve warm, passing the syrup at the table.

BAKED MASCARPONE FRENCH TOAST
with cherries

makes: 4 servings
time: at least 3 hours, largely unattended

DAY-OLD BREAD IN NO TIME For French toast that's custardy but doesn't fall apart, you need stale—or at least dried-out—bread. Oven-drying fresh bread gets it there pretty quickly, and the results are worth the extra time. Heat the oven to 200°F and put the bread on a rimmed baking sheet in a single layer. Bake until the bread is dried on the outside but not browned, 5 to 20 minutes per side, depending on the thickness of your slices.

4 egg yolks

1 cup milk

½ cup mascarpone cheese

1 teaspoon vanilla extract

6 tablespoons granulated sugar

Salt

8 thick slices challah (stale or oven dried, see the note above)

4 tablespoons unsalted butter, plus more for greasing

6 cups frozen Bing cherries (no need to thaw)

½ cup chopped pecans

Confectioners' sugar, for garnish

1. Whisk together the egg yolks, milk, mascarpone, vanilla, 2 tablespoons of the sugar, and a pinch of salt in a bowl; it's fine if the mascarpone isn't completely incorporated. Put the bread in a 9 by 13-inch dish in a single layer. Pour the custard over the bread, wrap the dish tightly with plastic, and refrigerate for at least 2 hours or up to overnight.

2. Heat the oven to 375°F. Melt the butter in a saucepan over medium heat, then add the remaining 4 tablespoons sugar and the cherries and cook, stirring occasionally, until the cherries have given up most of their juice and the liquid is syrupy, 20 to 25 minutes.

3. Grease a large ovenproof dish or skillet with butter. Put one slice of bread in the center of your skillet, then overlap a ring of the remaining slices over it; pour any excess custard over the top. Bake the French toast until the bread is golden brown on top and springy to the touch and the bottom is caramelized, 40 to 50 minutes.

4. Put the pecans in a medium saucepan and cook, shaking the pan occasionally, until toasted and fragrant, 3 to 5 minutes. To serve, sprinkle the French toast with the nuts, dust with sugar, and spoon some of the cherries on top. Cut into wedges or just spoon it out, then pass the remaining sauce at the table.

Savory Breakfast

Eating eggs after dark is a time-honored tradition among busy parents, college students, or anyone with a nearly empty fridge. The Vegan recipe obviously doesn't include eggs, but I can make a convincing argument for calling a bowl of tortilla chips dinner, especially if they're coated in homemade salsa roja, as are the Chilaquiles with Black Bean Relish. For those nights when you have a hankering for eggs Benedict, but only the time and energy for toast, consider Fried Eggs Rarebit—a British dish of creamy, béchamel-like sauce broiled on bread and topped with easy-to-cook fried eggs. In Souffléd Hangtown Fry—a combination of eggs, oysters, and bacon traced to the Gold Rush—the eggs and oysters are so good together that for once the bacon plays second fiddle.

● FRIED EGGS RAREBIT

makes: 4 servings
time: 20 minutes

4 English muffins, split

4 tablespoons unsalted butter

2 cups grated Gruyère cheese (about 8 ounces)

2 tablespoons Dijon or English mustard

2 teaspoons Worcestershire sauce

8 eggs

Salt and pepper

1. Turn the broiler to high and position a rack 4 inches below the heat. Line a baking sheet with foil. Put the English muffins on the prepared pan cut side down and toast under the broiler until firm, just a minute or 2. Turn them over and return to the broiler until they're browned in spots, another minute or 2.

2. Put 2 tablespoons butter in a large skillet (preferably nonstick) over medium heat. When the butter has melted, tilt the pan to make sure the butter covers the bottom. Toss the cheese with the mustard and Worcestershire sauce and divide the mixture among the muffins. Return to the broiler just until the cheese is melted and browned in spots, a minute or 2, watching carefully to avoid burning.

3. When the butter stops foaming, crack 4 eggs into the skillet; it's fine if they all run into one mass. Cook until the whites just turn opaque, 1 to 2 minutes, then turn the heat down to low and sprinkle the eggs with salt and pepper. Continue cooking until the whites are completely firm, even around the yolk.

4. Use a spatula to cut between the eggs and carefully transfer them to an English muffin without breaking the yolk. Repeat with the remaining eggs and remaining 2 tablespoons butter. Sprinkle each with salt and pepper, and serve right away.

● CHILAQUILES
with black bean relish

makes: 4 servings
time: 1 hour

2 large guajillo or other medium-hot dried chiles

2 cups boiling water

¼ cup good-quality vegetable oil

1 large onion, chopped

1 tablespoon chopped garlic

2 pounds ripe tomatoes, cored, peeled, seeded, and chopped, with their liquid (about 3 cups; or canned are fine)

Salt and pepper

1 tablespoon sugar (optional)

1½ cups cooked black beans (see page 82; or one 15-ounce can), drained

2 ripe avocados, peeled and chopped

4 scallions, chopped

½ teaspoon ground cumin

½ cup chopped fresh cilantro

2 tablespoons fresh lime juice

12 ounces tortilla chips

1. Put the chiles in a bowl and cover with the boiling water. Soak until they are soft and pliable, 15 to 20 minutes. Drain and discard the stem, seeds, and tough skin; chop the chiles.

2. Put the oil in a large pot over medium-high heat. When it's hot, add the chiles, onion, and garlic and cook, stirring occasionally, until the onion softens, 3 to 5 minutes. Add the tomatoes and sprinkle with salt and pepper. Bring the mixture to a boil, then adjust the heat so it bubbles steadily. Cook, stirring occasionally, until the mixture has thickened, 15 to 20 minutes. Taste and adjust the seasoning, adding some or all of the sugar if you like; remove from the heat.

3. Combine the beans, avocados, scallions, cumin, cilantro, and lime juice in a medium bowl. Sprinkle with salt and pepper, then stir to combine; taste and adjust the seasoning.

4. Using an immersion blender, puree the tomato sauce right in the pot. (Or, working in batches, carefully transfer it to a blender or food processor and puree until smooth. Pour the sauce back into the pot.) Turn the heat to medium. Add the tortilla chips a handful at a time and stir gently to combine. Once all the chips are coated with sauce, divide the chilaquiles among 4 bowls, top with a spoonful of the black bean relish and serve right away.

● SOUFFLÉD HANGTOWN FRY

makes: 4 servings
time: 30 minutes

SHUCKING ADVICE Buy the briniest, freshest oysters you can find; in case that means teeny ones, get six extra. If you can pry open the shells without causing bodily harm—to you or the insides—go for it. Otherwise, better have your fishmonger do it and then use them right away.

4 ounces slab bacon, diced, or bacon slices cut into pieces 2 inches long

8 eggs, separated

Salt and pepper

¼ cup chopped fresh parsley

2 tablespoons unsalted butter

12 shucked oysters, drained (see the note above)

3 scallions, green and white parts separated and sliced

1. Heat the oven to 325°F. Fill a medium pot with 2 inches of water and bring it to a boil, then adjust the heat so it bubbles gently. Put a large ovenproof skillet over medium heat. When the pan is hot but not yet smoking, add the bacon. Cook, stirring occasionally and adjusting heat so the bacon browns and releases most of its fat without burning; it should still be a little soft. Take the pan off the heat and set aside.

2. Put the egg yolks in a metal bowl and set it over the pot of gently bubbling water; make sure the water doesn't touch the bottom of the bowl. Sprinkle the yolks with salt and pepper and whisk until thick and frothy but not yet scrambled, just a minute or 2; they'll be ready before you think they are, so err on the side of undercooking. Remove the bowl from the heat and keep whisking until the yolks cool; stir in the parsley.

3. In a large clean, dry bowl, beat the egg whites to stiff peaks, then gently fold in the yolk mixture; the mixture should be streaky.

4. Put the pan with the bacon over medium heat and add the butter. When it foams, add the oysters and scallion whites. Stir and cook until the oysters plump and become slightly firm, a minute or 2. Pour in the egg mixture and stir with a flexible spatula just enough to combine. Transfer the pan to the oven and cook, undisturbed, until the eggs are puffed and golden, but still a little jiggly in the center when you gently shake the pan, 15 to 20 minutes. Remove the pan from the oven and garnish with the scallion greens. Use a big spoon to scoop out portions from the pan.

● Potato Hash with Gravlax
and Creamy Horseradish,
page 231

Hash

The interplay between two textures defines a successful hash, the name for which comes from the French verb *hacher* ("to chop"). This treatment serves Broccoli and Bean Hash with Tomato Mostarda to a T. The bits of broccoli—both stems and florets—and whole beans, which are naturally bite-sized, are browned. The work toward Red-Eye Ham Hash with its quirky, old-school coffee-and-ketchup sauce is steady, well paced, and highly rewarding. Potato Hash with Gravlax and Creamy Horseradish is the Scandinavian variation on the theme. Curing fish is the kind of project that delivers the satisfaction of a big, difficult undertaking without much hands-on work. The potatoes do require babysitting to properly crisp, though. Be patient. Then stir in some of that amazing fish and sit down to the most luxurious hash you've ever had.

● RED-EYE HAM HASH

makes: 4 servings
time: 35 minutes

1½ pounds sweet potatoes, peeled

4 tablespoons unsalted butter, plus more for greasing the pan

1 red onion, chopped

8 ounces smoked ham, cut into matchsticks

Salt and pepper

½ cup brewed coffee

2 tablespoons ketchup

¼ cup sour cream

2 tablespoons chopped fresh chives, for garnish

1. Heat the oven to 400°F. Use the largest holes on a box grater or the shredding attachment on a food processor to grate the sweet potatoes. Grease a large rimmed baking sheet with a little butter.

2. Put 2 tablespoons of the butter in a large skillet over medium-high heat. When the butter melts, add the onion and ham and cook, stirring frequently, until the onion is soft and the ham is crisp in places, 3 to 5 minutes. Transfer the mixture to the prepared baking sheet.

3. Add another tablespoon of butter to the pan and return to medium-high heat. When it's hot, add half the sweet potatoes, sprinkle with salt and pepper, and cook without disturbing until the potatoes form some crust on the bottom, 5 to 7 minutes; adjust the heat as necessary so they sizzle without burning. Turn the potatoes in pieces with a spatula, and continue to cook until the potatoes start to soften, about 3 minutes more. Transfer them to the baking sheet with the ham, stir, and put in the oven. Put the remaining tablespoon of butter and remaining sweet potatoes in the skillet and cook as you did the first batch, then add them to the potatoes and ham on the baking sheet, and return to the oven.

4. Add the coffee and ketchup to the empty skillet and return to medium-high heat. Cook, stirring constantly and scraping up any browned bits from the bottom of the pan, until the coffee and ketchup are fully combined and reduced to the consistency of cream, 2 or 3 minutes. Pour over the potatoes and serve, garnished with sour cream and chives.

BROCCOLI AND BEAN HASH
with tomato mostarda

makes: 4 servings
time: 40 minutes

1 pound ripe Roma (plum) tomatoes, cored and chopped

1 tablespoon sugar

1 shallot, chopped

Salt and pepper

3 tablespoons grainy mustard

2 teaspoons fresh lemon juice, or to taste

1 tablespoon chopped fresh parsley, plus more for garnish

1½ pounds broccoli, stems and florets chopped into bite-sized pieces

2 cups cooked gigantes or butter beans (see page 82; or one 15-ounce can), drained

3 tablespoons olive oil

1. Heat the oven to 425°F. Put the tomatoes, sugar, and shallot in a small saucepan and sprinkle with salt and pepper. Bring to a boil over medium heat. Reduce the heat so the mixture bubbles gently and cook, stirring occasionally, until shallots are soft and the tomatoes are beginning to turn jammy, 15 to 20 minutes. Stir in the mustard, lemon juice, and parsley, taste, and adjust the seasoning. (You can make the mostarda up to 1 week in advance. Store in the refrigerator and bring to room temperature before serving.)

2. Put the broccoli and beans on a rimmed baking sheet, drizzle with the oil, and sprinkle with salt and pepper; taste and adjust the seasoning. Roast, stirring once or twice, until the broccoli is tender and browned and crisp in spots, 15 to 20 minutes. Garnish with parsley and serve hot or warm, passing the tomato mostarda at the table.

● POTATO HASH
with gravlax and creamy horseradish

makes: 4 to 6 servings
time: at least 24 hours, largely unattended

One 1- to 1½-pound salmon fillet

½ cup salt, plus more for seasoning

1 cup sugar

1 bunch fresh dill, chopped (including the stems is fine)

1 cup crème fraîche

¼ cup heavy cream

½ cup chopped mixed fresh herbs (like dill, parsley, chives, tarragon, and fennel fronds)

1 tablespoon fresh lemon juice, or as needed

1 teaspoon prepared horseradish, or to taste

Pepper

2 pounds starchy potatoes (like Idaho or other russets), scrubbed

8 tablespoons (1 stick) unsalted butter

1. Put the salmon, skin side down, on a large piece of plastic wrap. Run your hand against the grain of the flesh, and if you feel any pin bones, remove them with pliers or tweezers (or ask your fishmonger to do this).

2. Mix the salt, sugar, and dill. Pack the salt mixture onto the flesh, making sure it's completely covered, and putting a thicker layer on the thickest part of the fish. Wrap the fish tightly, put it on a rimmed baking sheet or plate, and refrigerate until the flesh is darkened and firm, some liquid has leeched out, and a sharp paring knife inserted into the thickest part of the fish meets some resistance, 24 to 36 hours.

3. Unwrap the salmon and rinse off the salt mixture. Pat dry with paper towels and refrigerate in an airtight container; don't slice until you're ready to serve. (You can make it a day or so in advance.)

4. Mix the crème fraîche, cream, herbs, lemon juice, and horseradish; season with salt and pepper and stir to combine. Taste and adjust the seasoning, adding more horseradish if you like, but keep in mind the flavor will intensify as it sits. (You can cover and refrigerate the crème fraîche mixture for up to 12 hours.)

5. Cut the potatoes into 1-inch cubes. Put the butter in a large skillet over medium heat and when it melts, add the potatoes and ¼ cup water. (It's okay if the pan is crowded.) Sprinkle with lots of salt, stir, cover, and cook undisturbed until the potatoes are just barely tender, 5 to 10 minutes. (Unlikely, but you may need to add a little more water, cover, and cook for another minute or 2.)

6. Uncover the pan, raise the heat to high, and cook undisturbed until the water has evaporated, the butter has started to brown, and the potatoes release easily from the pan, 20 to 25 minutes. (If they don't release easily from the pan, they aren't ready to be turned yet.) At this point, stir the potatoes and cook until browned on a second side, another 10 to 15 minutes.

7. Switch to a potato masher and a spatula, smashing and turning the potatoes once in a while without overworking them. Continue cooking until the potatoes clump up and brown in some spots, like fried mashed potatoes, 5 to 10 minutes; adjust the heat so the potatoes sizzle but don't burn. Taste and adjust the seasoning.

8. Holding the knife at a 45° angle, thinly slice as much of the gravlax as you like, leaving the skin behind. It's better to get smaller slices or ones with holes than to get a slice that's too thick. Remove the potatoes from the heat and fold in the gravlax. Serve drizzled with some of the sauce and pass the rest at the table.

Stir-Fry

The only way to slow down a stir-fry is to not be ready to stir. So this is the one time I suggest getting all the prep done—and the rice started (see page 102)—before cooking. What distinguishes the chicken stir-fry from the same-old same-old is the crisp-silky combination of celery and leeks. In Orange Beef, "velveting"—a tenderizing step that pushes the recipe into All Out territory—completely transforms a flavorful (but chewy) cut. And the tofu skin "noodles" in the Vegan stir-fry do double duty as a full-flavored protein and starch, to great effect.

● CHICKEN
with celery and leeks

makes: 4 servings
time: 30 minutes

2 tablespoons chopped fresh ginger

1 large leek, trimmed, chopped, and well rinsed

1 pound celery (leaves included), sliced diagonally into ½-inch pieces

3 tablespoons good-quality vegetable oil

1½ pounds boneless, skinless chicken thighs, cut into 1-inch pieces

Salt and pepper

1 tablespoon fish sauce (or soy sauce), or to taste

1 teaspoon dark sesame oil

1. Have the ginger, leek, and celery ready by the stove. Put a large skillet over high heat. When it's hot, add 2 tablespoons oil and swirl the pan.

2. Add half the chicken pieces, sprinkle with salt and pepper, and cook undisturbed until they release easily, about 3 minutes. Stir once with a spatula. Let the chicken sizzle for another minute or 2, again undisturbed, then cook, stirring occasionally, until it's no longer pink and is crisp in places, another 3 to 5 minutes. Transfer the chicken to a plate, add the remaining tablespoon oil to the pan, and repeat with the remaining chicken.

3. Return the pan to medium-high heat. Add the ginger and leek and cook, stirring constantly, for 30 seconds. Add the celery, sprinkle with salt, and cook, still stirring until it's crisp-tender, 1 to 2 minutes. Return the chicken and any juices to the pan, along with ¼ cup water and the fish sauce. Continue to cook until everything is coated and heated through, 1 to 2 minutes. Remove from the heat, drizzle with the sesame oil, and stir. Taste and adjust the seasoning, adding more fish or soy sauce, and serve.

Stir-Fried Snow Peas
and Tofu Skins, page 234

STIR-FRIED SNOW PEAS AND TOFU SKINS

makes: 4 servings
time: 25 minutes, not including soaking time

10 ounces fresh tofu skins (yuba; see page 254),
or 6 ounces dried

5 tablespoons good-quality vegetable oil

Salt and pepper

1 teaspoon red chile flakes, or to taste

1 small red onion, halved and sliced

2 tablespoons chopped fresh ginger

1 tablespoon chopped garlic

1 pound snow peas, trimmed

2 tablespoons soy sauce

Sesame seeds, for garnish

1. If you're using fresh tofu skins, put them in a bowl of tap water and carefully unfold the layers. (It's okay if they tear in places.) If you're using dried tofu skins, soak them in warm water until they are just pliable, 10 to 30 minutes. (Check them often so they don't get soggy.) Carefully roll the fresh or dried sheets into a tube and cut crosswise into ribbons about 2 inches wide to make "noodles."

2. Put a large skillet over high heat. When it's hot, add 4 tablespoons oil, swirl, then scatter the tofu skins around the pan, and sprinkle with salt and pepper. Cook, stirring occasionally, until they release easily from the pan and are golden and crisp, 5 to 7 minutes. Turn and repeat on the other side. Add the red chile flakes, stir once, then transfer to a plate.

3. Return the skillet to high heat, and add the remaining tablespoon oil along with the onion, ginger, and garlic. Stir until fragrant, about 1 minute. Add the snow peas and cook, stirring constantly, until crisp-tender and bright green, 1 to 2 minutes.

4. Return the tofu skins to the pan along with ¼ cup water and the soy sauce and toss to coat. Taste, adjust the seasoning, and serve sprinkled with sesame seeds.

● ORANGE BEEF

makes: 4 servings
time: about an hour

1½ pounds boneless beef flap meat
(a.k.a. sirloin tip), or hanger or skirt steak

4 oranges

3 tablespoons cornstarch

Salt

3 tablespoons and ¼ cup rice wine or dry sherry

2 tablespoons good-quality vegetable oil,
plus more for frying

¼ cup chopped fresh ginger

2 jalapeños, seeded and chopped

2 tablespoons chopped garlic

½ cup brown sugar

½ cup soy sauce

¼ cup rice vinegar

8 scallions, whites cut into 1-inch lengths and
greens chopped

5 to 10 dried chiles (like Thai or de arbol),
depending on your affinity for heat

1. Freeze the meat for 30 minutes or so to make it easier to slice. Cut the pieces across the grain into strips about ¼ inch thick. Grate 4 tablespoons zest from the oranges; cut a few narrow strips of zest for garnish. Squeeze as many oranges as needed to yield ½ cup juice. Whisk the cornstarch and a large pinch of salt into 3 tablespoons of the rice wine in a large bowl until they dissolve, then add the beef and toss to coat. Marinate at room temperature while you make the sauce.

2. Heat 2 tablespoons oil in a small saucepan over medium-high heat. When it's hot, add the ginger, jalapeños, and grated orange zest and stir. Cook, stirring constantly, until soft, 2 to 3 minutes, then add the garlic and continue cooking until it softens, 1 to 2 minutes. Add the ½ cup orange juice, the brown sugar, soy sauce, rice vinegar, and remaining ¼ cup rice wine to the pan and stir. Bring the mixture to a boil, then adjust the heat so it bubbles steadily and cook, stirring occasionally, until it is reduced by half and is thickened, 10 to 15 minutes. Remove from the heat.

3. Put 1 to 2 inches oil in a large pot and bring it to 375°F over medium heat. Line a rimmed baking sheet with paper towels. When the oil is ready (a pinch of cornstarch will sizzle but not immediately burn), carefully lower a few pieces of meat into the oil and cook, stirring so it doesn't clump, until the outsides are browned, 1 to 2 minutes. Transfer to the prepared pan and sprinkle with salt. Repeat with the remaining beef.

4. Transfer 2 tablespoons frying oil to a large skillet over high heat. Immediately add the scallion whites and chiles and cook, stirring constantly, until fragrant, about 30 seconds. Add the sauce and the beef and toss to coat. Cook, stirring constantly, until the sauce boils. Turn off the heat and serve, garnished with the scallion greens and strips of orange zest.

Scampi

Long story short, the small crustacean that lent its name to this dish has been almost entirely replaced by shrimp. The preparation—a quick sauté in some rich, often citrusy sauce—endures. My usual way to cook scampi has evolved over the years, but remains utterly simple, as in Shrimp with Olives. To make scampi without seafood, I found that tofu soaked in brine as salty as seawater infuses it with the taste of the ocean and satisfies that craving in a way plain tofu can't. And you *must* try the All Out version; sourcing the best seafood is all that's potentially time-consuming in Gulf Shrimp and Croutons with Vermouth and Herbs.

● SHRIMP with olives

makes: 4 servings
time: 20 minutes

¼ cup olive oil, or more as needed

4 garlic cloves, sliced

½ teaspoon red chile flakes, or to taste

Salt and pepper

1½ pounds peeled shrimp, any size, rinsed and drained

1 cup pitted Kalamata olives

1 lemon, halved

Chopped fresh parsley, for garnish

1. Put the olive oil in a large skillet over low heat. When it's hot, add the garlic and red chile flakes, sprinkle with salt and pepper, and cook, stirring often, until the garlic turns golden, a minute or 2.

2. Raise the heat to medium-high and add the shrimp and olives, and sprinkle with pepper. Stir to combine and cook, shaking the pan once or twice and turning the shrimp with tongs as necessary, until they are pink all over and the mixture is sizzling, 5 to 10 minutes.

3. Squeeze in the juice from half a lemon, taste the sauce, and adjust the seasoning, adding the rest of the lemon if you like; then garnish with the parsley and serve hot or at room temperature.

BRINY TOFU
with coconut crust

makes: 4 servings
time: 30 minutes, plus 8 to 12 hours for brining

¼ cup salt, plus more for seasoning

2 limes, halved

2 blocks firm tofu (about 2 pounds)

¼ cup unsweetened shredded coconut

6 tablespoons good-quality vegetable oil

2 tablespoons chopped garlic

2 tablespoons chopped fresh ginger

Pepper

1 tablespoon ground cumin

¼ teaspoon cayenne, or to taste

One 5.5-ounce can coconut milk, or about
    half of one 14-ounce can

2 tablespoons chopped fresh mint, for garnish

1. Pour 2 cups water into a large bowl; add ¼ cup salt and squeeze in the juice from the limes. Whisk until the salt is dissolved. Add the tofu and make sure it's completely submerged (you can weight it down with a plate, if you like). Marinate for 4 to 6 hours for barely briny, or up to 12 hours for a saltiness you'll taste.

2. Drain and rinse the tofu. Wrap the bricks in clean towels and press gently to extract as much water as possible; if the towels are quickly saturated, replace them and repeat. Cut the tofu into batons about 1 inch wide by 2 inches long.

3. Put the coconut in a large skillet over medium heat and cook, stirring often, until fragrant and golden, 3 to 5 minutes. Transfer to a plate to cool.

4. Put 3 tablespoons oil in a large skillet over medium heat. When it's hot, add half the tofu in a single layer and cook, undisturbed, until the bottom develops a brown crust and the pieces release easily, 5 to 10 minutes. Turn and cook the same way on another side. Transfer to a platter and repeat with the remaining tofu, using the remaining 3 tablespoons oil.

5. When the last batch is done, return the pan to medium heat and add the garlic and ginger; sprinkle with salt and pepper, and cook, stirring constantly, until the garlic softens, 3 to 5 minutes. Add the cumin and cayenne and cook, stirring constantly, until the spices are fragrant, less than a minute. Add the coconut milk and bring to a boil scraping any browned bits from the bottom of the pan.

6. Return the tofu to the pan, toss to coat in the sauce; taste and adjust the seasoning, and serve hot or at room temperature, garnished with the mint and toasted coconut.

GULF SHRIMP AND CROUTONS
with vermouth and herbs

makes: 4 servings
time: 30 minutes

BUYING SUSTAINABLE SHRIMP It's important to do a little research if you want to buy good-quality shrimp raised or caught sustainably. Most of what we get in supermarkets is imported and farmed in factory-like conditions. So read labels or talk to your fishmonger. Fresh isn't always best (or meaningful; it might have been frozen anyway). Flash-frozen shrimp will get to you at peak freshness, and can be thawed overnight in the refrigerator, or in cool running water. Buy shell-on and return the shells to the freezer to use for fish broth on another day (see page 251).

1 baguette, cut into thin slices

6 garlic cloves, 2 halved, 4 sliced

¼ cup olive oil

2 pounds large shell-on Gulf shrimp (frozen are fine; thaw in the refrigerator overnight)

3 tablespoons unsalted butter

Salt and pepper

½ cup dry vermouth

¼ cup heavy cream

2 tablespoons chopped fresh herbs (like parsley, tarragon, mint, chervil, chives, or a mixture)

1. Heat the oven to 400°F. Put the bread slices on a rimmed baking sheet in a single layer. Rub both sides of each slice with the halved garlic. Drizzle the olive oil over all of the slices and turn to coat in oil. Bake, turning halfway through, until golden and crisp, 10 to 15 minutes.

2. Peel the shrimp, reserving the shells (see the note at left). Rinse the shrimp, then drain them and pat dry. Put the butter in a large skillet over medium heat. When it foams, add the shrimp in a single layer (you might have to work in batches) and sprinkle with salt and pepper. Cook until the flesh is opaque on one side, less than 1 minute. Turn the shrimp and repeat until the other side is opaque. Transfer to a plate.

3. Add the sliced garlic to the skillet and cook, stirring frequently, until golden, 2 to 3 minutes. Pour in the vermouth. Cook, scraping any browned bits off the bottom of the pan, until the vermouth is reduced by half, 2 to 3 minutes.

4. Add the cream and bring to a boil, then lower the heat to medium-low. Add the cooked shrimp and stir to heat through, just a minute or 2. Turn off the heat, sprinkle with the herbs, and serve hot, spooned over the croutons.

The Big Reveal

The classic technique of wrapping food and a little liquid in a package—called *en papillote*—is still valuable, especially with some modern tweaks. Chicken Meunière Under Foil takes a shortcut to avoid precision folding, while lifting the signature French combination of butter, lemon, parsley, and capers for a quick bistro-style meal. Lots of ginger mingles with a coconut sauce to create the delightful topping for custardy Curried Tofu Flan. Salt-Baked Whole Fish with Aioli is another classic cooking-under-wraps preparation, only instead of seasoning the fish, I aggressively season the crust.

● CHICKEN MEUNIÈRE UNDER FOIL

makes: 4 servings
time: 25 minutes

2 tablespoons olive oil

4 small boneless, skinless chicken breasts (about 1½ pounds)

Salt and pepper

2 lemons, cut crosswise into 8 thin slices

3 tablespoons drained capers

2 tablespoons unsalted butter

2 tablespoons chopped fresh parsley, for garnish

1. Heat the oven to 450°F. Grease a 9 by 13–inch baking pan with the oil. Put the chicken in the pan, sprinkle with salt and pepper, and turn them a couple times to season them all over and coat in oil. Leave smooth side up and spread them out.

2. Remove as many of the seeds from the lemons as you can and spread the slices on top of (and in between) the chicken. Scatter with the capers and dot with the butter. Cover the top tightly with foil.

3. Transfer the pan to the oven (even if it's not fully heated yet) and cook undisturbed for 15 minutes. To check the chicken, nick the underside with a small sharp knife in the thickest place; it should be opaque and juicy. If it's still pink, cover again and check in another 3 minutes; repeat until they're no longer pink but not yet dry. Garnish with the parsley and serve each piece with a few lemon slices, drizzled with the pan juices.

Salt-Baked
Whole Fish
with Aioli,
page 243

CURRIED TOFU FLAN

makes: 4 servings
time: 45 minutes

CHOOSE THE WRAP Foil packages are the easiest to seal, but parchment is so much prettier. To have a go with paper, use 2 sheets for each serving: seal one, then turn the package at a 90° angle on top of the other sheet and secure it the same way to keep all the juices inside.

One 15-ounce can coconut milk

2 tablespoons curry powder (see page 299)

1 teaspoon garam masala (or another teaspoon curry powder)

2 tablespoons chopped fresh ginger

Salt and pepper

1 lime, halved

2 blocks firm silken tofu or medium regular tofu, each halved lengthwise

1 pound sweet potatoes, scrubbed and sliced

3 large celery stalks, sliced

2 carrots, sliced

1 red onion, halved and cut crosswise

½ cup chopped fresh cilantro or mint (or a combination), for garnish

1. Heat the oven to 450°F. Have a large rimmed baking sheet handy. Put the coconut milk in a small saucepan with the curry powder, garam masala, ginger, and a pinch of salt and pepper. Bring to a boil, then immediately lower the heat so it barely bubbles and cook, stirring occasionally, until the mixture darkens and the spices no longer taste raw, 5 to 10 minutes. Squeeze in the lime juice, taste and adjust the seasoning, and remove from the heat.

2. Cut four 1-foot-square pieces of aluminum foil and stack them. Put one-fourth of the tofu on one half of a square. Top with the vegetables, starting with the sweet potatoes and ending with the onion; sprinkle with salt and pepper and spoon one-fourth of the curry sauce on top. Fold the foil into a triangle and roll the edges to seal. (To use parchment, see the note above.)

3. Put the packets on the baking sheet and transfer to the oven. Bake until the potatoes are tender, 15 to 25 minutes, depending on their thickness. (Insert a toothpick or skewer into the vegetable topping; it should meet with no resistance.) To serve, put each package on a plate, cut an X in the top with scissors (mindful that steam will escape), and pull back the wrapper to reveal the vegetables; garnish with the cilantro.

SALT-BAKED WHOLE FISH
with aioli

makes: 4 servings
time: about an hour, largely unattended

6 bay leaves, broken into pieces

3 tablespoons black peppercorns

3 tablespoons fennel seeds

2 tablespoons coriander seeds

2 tablespoons brown mustard seeds

5 cups (about 3 pounds) kosher salt

2 egg whites, beaten

4 pounds whole white fish (see page 369), scaled and gutted, with head on

Lemon wedges

1 recipe Aioli, for serving (recipe follows)

1. Heat the oven to 400°F. Put the spices in a spice or coffee grinder and pulse a few times, working in batches if necessary. (If you don't have a spice grinder, put the spices in a sandwich bag, seal carefully, and whack with a rolling pin to crush the spices as best you can.) Put the salt in a large bowl, add the ground spices, and stir. Add the egg whites and mix thoroughly.

2. Line a large rimmed baking sheet with parchment. Put a layer of salt roughly the shape of the fish on the pan, then put the fish on top. Mound the rest of the salt on the fish, gently packing it onto the top and sides so the fish is completely enclosed and there are no gaps in the crust.

3. Bake undisturbed until you can smell the fish and the salt crust is hard and golden, 50 to 60 minutes. Bring to the table right away, and crack the crust with a serving spoon. Lift off the crust, then portion the fish and serve, passing the lemon wedges and aioli at the table.

AIOLI

Put 1 egg yolk and 1½ teaspoons Dijon mustard in a medium bowl. Beat together with a wire whisk. Begin to add 1 cup olive oil very slowly—just a few drops at a time—as you beat, adding more as each amount is incorporated. When a thick emulsion forms, you can begin to add it a little faster. Depending on how fast you beat, the whole process will take about 5 minutes. Use a microplane or the smallest holes on a box grater to grate 2 garlic cloves into the bowl, sprinkle with salt and pepper, then stir in 1½ teaspoons sherry vinegar. Taste and adjust the seasoning, adding more garlic if you like your aioli strong. Makes 1 cup in about 10 minutes.

Simmer Dinner

Cooking well with water is more nuanced than throwing a bunch of stuff in a pot, and so it deserves a sexier name than old-fashioned boiled dinner. Take the classic New Orleans Shrimp Boil. Then make it your own: Instead of water, choose your favorite beer for the cooking liquid—something not too dark or heavy. Pot-au-Feu is a traditional French one-pot show-stopper with endless variations, though they all have several kinds of meat; I borrowed the idea of adding turkey from Jacques Pépin. Now promise me you won't be tempted by store-bought seitan for the Vegan dinner; it's inferior in every way. Since making your own is easily incorporated into a boiled dinner—it's mixed and poached is all—why not?

● New Orleans Shrimp Boil, page 246

NEW ORLEANS SHRIMP BOIL

makes: 4 servings
time: 30 minutes

SUBSTITUTION IDEAS When summer corn on the cob is out of season, use green beans, fennel, celery, or cubed butternut squash instead.

One 12-ounce bottle beer, or 1½ cups water

1½ pounds waxy potatoes, cut into 2-inch chunks

1 large onion, cut into chunks

1 head garlic, halved horizontally

4 bay leaves

2 tablespoons black peppercorns

½ teaspoon cayenne

Salt

1½ pounds whole large shrimp (frozen are fine), peeled if you like

4 ears corn, husked and broken in half

Tabasco sauce or other hot sauce

Lemon wedges

1. Put the beer (or 1½ cups water) in a large pot with 8 cups water. Add the potatoes, onion, garlic, bay leaves, peppercorns, cayenne, and a couple big pinches of salt and bring to a boil. Adjust the heat so the liquid bubbles steadily and cook, stirring occasionally, until the potatoes are tender around the outsides but not quite done at the centers, 10 to 15 minutes.

2. Add the shrimp and corn and return the liquid to a boil. Immediately turn off the heat, cover, and let the pot sit until the shrimp are pink and opaque and the potatoes are fork-tender, just a minute or 2. Drain through a strainer set over a large bowl, reserving at least half the cooking liquid for serving (preferably in a pitcher or gravy boat).

3. Taste the shrimp and vegetables, and sprinkle with more salt if you like. Serve right away, passing the hot sauce, lemon wedges, and cooking liquid at the table.

SEITAN AND VEGETABLES
in miso broth

makes: 4 servings
time: about 2 hours, largely unattended

WITH A MACHINE Make the kneading in Step 1 easier by using a food processor fitted with the short plastic blade, or with a dough hook in the bowl of an upright mixer. If you have a large, wide pot, double the seitan ingredients so you can sock away leftovers in the freezer.

¾ cup vital wheat gluten

6 cups vegetable stock (see page 87) or water

¼ cup soy sauce

One 1-inch piece fresh ginger, cut into coins

1 pound carrots, cut into large chunks

¼ cup chopped walnuts

1 pound green beans, trimmed and cut into 2-inch pieces

¼ cup white or yellow miso

4 scallions, sliced

1. Put the gluten in a large bowl. Add ¾ cup water and stir until it is completely absorbed. Knead for a minute or 2. If any loose flour remains, add a few drops of water. Continue kneading the dough in the bowl until it becomes an elastic and rubbery mass, 3 to 5 minutes by hand, less with a machine. Cover the bowl with a clean damp cloth and let it relax for at least 20 and up to 30 minutes.

2. Put the stock, soy sauce, and ginger in a large pot. Pull or cut the dough into 2 equal portions and stretch and roll each piece into a log. Put them in the pot and bring to a boil. (It's okay if they aren't completely submerged.) Lower the heat so that the mixture bubbles gently and add the carrots to the pot; cover. Cook, undisturbed, until the seitan has expanded and it no longer leaves an impression when you gently press it with a spoon, 30 to 40 minutes.

3. Put the walnuts in a small skillet over medium heat and toast, shaking the pan occasionally, until golden and fragrant, 3 to 5 minutes. Transfer to a plate to cool.

4. Turn the seitan logs and scatter the green beans on top. Return the liquid to a steady bubble, cover, and cook without stirring until the vegetables are bright green and tender but not mushy, 3 to 5 minutes. Turn off the heat and carefully remove the seitan. Slice crosswise diagonally into ovals, about ½ inch thick.

5. Put the miso and 1 cup of the hot cooking liquid in a small bowl and whisk until smooth. Pour the miso mix into the pot (still off the heat) and stir, then return the seitan. Divide among 4 bowls, and serve hot, garnished with the walnuts and scallions.

● POT-AU-FEU

makes: 4 to 6 servings
time: 3 hours

1 pound beef oxtails

1 pound boneless beef rump roast

1 turkey leg or thigh (about 1 pound)

4 carrots, halved

4 celery stalks, halved

1 pound leeks, trimmed, well rinsed, and cut into 3-inch chunks

Salt and pepper

1 bunch fresh parsley

1 small bunch fresh thyme

4 bay leaves, preferably fresh

20 black peppercorns

10 whole cloves

4 medium waxy potatoes (about 1 pound), quartered

1 small green cabbage, trimmed and cut into quarters

24 cornichons, chopped (about 1 cup)

½ cup grainy mustard, or to taste

½ cup chopped fresh dill

2 tablespoons prepared horseradish, or to taste

¼ cup olive oil

2 tablespoons white wine vinegar, or to taste

1. Put the oxtails, rump roast, and turkey leg in a large stockpot, cover with cold water, and bring to a boil. Turn off the heat immediately, drain the meat, discarding the water, and wash the pot.

2. Put meat back in the clean pot with the carrots, celery, and leeks and 2 large pinches of salt. Reserve several of the parsley sprigs for the sauce, then put the rest in a large square of cheesecloth with the thyme, bay leaves, peppercorns, and cloves. Fold the corners to enclose the herbs and spices in a bundle, secure the top with a string, and add to the pot.

3. Add cold water to cover all the ingredients by 3 inches and bring to a boil. Adjust the heat so the mixture bubbles gently but steadily and cook, stirring once in a while, until all the meat is tender, 1½ to 2 hours.

4. Add the potatoes and cabbage. Taste the broth and adjust the seasoning. Cook until the potatoes and cabbage are tender, another 20 to 30 minutes, then turn off the heat.

5. While the pot-au-feu is cooking, make the relish: Mix the cornichons, mustard, dill, horseradish, olive oil, and vinegar and sprinkle with salt and pepper; taste and adjust the seasoning, making it as tart or spicy as you like.

6. Carefully remove the meat to a cutting board with tongs. Discard the seasoning bundle. Use a slotted spoon to transfer the vegetables to individual warm shallow bowls. Turn the heat to high and let the broth reduce a little while you carve the meat. Slice the roast and remove the meat from the turkey leg and oxtails, discarding the bones and skin. Top the vegetables with the meat and ladle over some of the hot cooking liquid. Serve right away, passing the relish at the table.

Bouillabaisse,
page 250

Bouillabaisse

What started as a way for French fishermen to use less desirable seafood evolved into an upmarket restaurant dish. Let's bring it back home. The All Out Bouillabaisse, a somewhat precise combination of fish and shellfish, homemade fish stock, and lovely red pepper mayonnaise, is the most elegant. If that sounds like fun for another time, make Fish Stew in a Skillet—same flavors with a fraction of the fuss. And when you want all vegetables, infusing the cooking liquid with the taste of kombu seaweed gives Vegetables in Saffron Broth with Almond Rouille a flavor reminiscent of the sea.

● FISH STEW IN A SKILLET

makes: 4 servings
time: 20 minutes

8 thick slices rustic bread

1 garlic clove, halved

5 tablespoons olive oil

1 onion, chopped

1 large carrot, chopped

Salt and pepper

2 teaspoons paprika

2 bay leaves

One 28-ounce can crushed tomatoes

1 cup dry white wine or water

1½ pounds firm white fish fillets (like cod or halibut)

¼ cup chopped fresh parsley, for garnish

1. Heat the oven to 425°F. Put the bread on a rimmed baking sheet and cook, checking occasionally, until as toasted as you like, 10 to 20 minutes. When the bread is toasted, rub it with the cut side of the garlic and drizzle with 2 tablespoons oil.

2. Put the remaining 3 tablespoons oil in a large skillet over medium-high heat. When it's hot, add the onion and carrot, and sprinkle with salt and pepper. Cook, stirring occasionally, until the vegetables soften, 3 to 5 minutes. Add the paprika and bay leaves and stir constantly until fragrant, less than a minute. Stir in the tomatoes, bring to a boil, then adjust the heat so it bubbles steadily.

3. Add the wine, stir to combine, and nestle the fish in the tomato sauce. Bring to a boil, then reduce the heat so the mixture bubbles gently. Cook, uncovered, until the fish is firm and just cooked through, 5 to 10 minutes. Break it into big pieces (which will reveal its doneness; cook for another minute or 2 if the middle isn't opaque). Taste the sauce and adjust the seasoning. Serve hot in shallow bowls, over or underneath the toast as you like and garnished with parsley.

VEGETABLES IN SAFFRON BROTH
with almond rouille

makes: 4 servings
time: 45 minutes

½ ounce kombu seaweed (2 or 3 large pieces)

2 fennel bulbs (about 1 pound)

6 tablespoons olive oil

2 large shallots, sliced

Salt and pepper

Big pinch saffron

Grated zest and juice of 1 lemon

1 dried red chile (like Thai or de árbol), or a pinch cayenne

1 tablespoon chopped garlic

2 cups chopped ripe tomatoes (diced canned are fine; include the juices)

1 pound fingerling or other small waxy potatoes, halved lengthwise

½ cup raw almonds

2 roasted red peppers (see page 132)

1 teaspoon sherry vinegar or white wine vinegar

½ teaspoon smoked paprika

¼ teaspoon cayenne, or to taste

1. Put the seaweed in a medium saucepan with 4 cups water over high heat. As soon as it comes to a boil, remove from the heat, cover, and let steep. Trim the fennel, reserving the fronds; halve the bulbs and slice them and the stalks thinly. Save a few of the tenderest fronds for garnish and add the rest to the pan with the seaweed.

2. Put 4 tablespoons oil in a large pot over medium heat. When it's hot, add the shallots and fennel, and sprinkle with salt and pepper. Cook, stirring occasionally, until soft, 5 to 10 minutes. Add the saffron, lemon zest, chile, and garlic and cook, stirring a few times, until fragrant, about a minute.

3. Add the tomatoes and strain the seaweed broth into the pot, discarding the solids. Add the potatoes, sprinkle with salt and pepper, and bring to a boil. Cook, stirring occasionally, until the potatoes are tender enough to pierce with a fork and the broth has thickened a bit, 20 to 30 minutes, depending on the size of the potatoes. Add the lemon juice and stir. (At this point, you can cool the soup and refrigerate for up to a day or so; reheat before proceeding.)

4. Put the almonds in a large skillet over medium heat. Cook, shaking the pan occasionally, until they are golden and fragrant, 3 to 5 minutes. Transfer to a food processor along with the red peppers, vinegar, smoked paprika, cayenne, and the remaining 2 tablespoons olive oil and sprinkle with salt and pepper. Let the machine run until the rouille is smooth, stopping to scrape down the sides as necessary; taste and adjust the seasoning.

5. Chop the reserved fennel fronds. Serve the stew with a dollop of the rouille, garnished with the fennel fronds.

BOUILLABAISSE

makes: 4 servings
time: about 2 hours

7 ripe Roma (plum) tomatoes

1 pound bones and/or cleaned heads from any firm, white fish (see page 369)

2 onions, 1 cut into chunks (don't bother to peel) and 1 chopped

2 fresh parsley sprigs

2 garlic cloves, 1 smashed and 1 chopped

1 carrot, cut into chunks

1 celery stalk, cut into chunks

½ cup dry white wine

1 bay leaf

1 egg yolk

1 teaspoon Dijon mustard, or to taste

1 tablespoon sherry vinegar or lemon juice

1 roasted red pepper (see page 132), chopped

½ teaspoon cayenne, or to taste

1 cup and 2 tablespoons olive oil

Salt and pepper

Grated zest and juice of 1 orange

1 tablespoon fennel seeds

Big pinch saffron

2 tablespoons Pernod liqueur (or other anise-flavored liqueur)

12 ounces halibut fillet, cut into 2-inch cubes

4 large (sea) scallops

4 ounces shrimp, unpeeled

1 dozen littleneck clams, scrubbed

1 dozen mussels, scrubbed

1 baguette, sliced on the bias

¼ cup chopped fresh chervil or chives

1. Make the fish broth: Chop 1 tomato and put it in a large pot with the fish bones, chunked onion, parsley, smashed garlic, carrot, celery, wine, bay leaf, and 4 cups water. Bring to just below a boil, then adjust the heat so the mixture bubbles gently and cook until very fragrant, 50 to 55 minutes. Cool slightly, then strain, pressing the vegetables and fish bones to extract as much liquid as possible. (Use immediately or refrigerate for up to 3 days or freeze for up to a few weeks.)

2. Make the rouille: Put the egg yolk, mustard, vinegar, roasted pepper, chopped garlic, and ¼ teaspoon cayenne in a blender or food processor; turn on the machine and, with the machine running, add 1 cup oil in a thin, steady stream. After you've added about half of it, the mixture will thicken; you can then begin adding the oil a bit faster. Sprinkle with salt and pepper, taste, and adjust the seasoning. (Refrigerate until ready to use or up to 2 days.)

3. Bring a small saucepan of water to boil. Fill a large bowl with ice and cover with water. Working with the remaining 6 tomatoes, one at a time, cut a small X in the bottom end. Put each tomato in the bubbling water and leave it until the skin begins to loosen, less than a minute. Immediately transfer the tomato to the ice bath; repeat with the remaining 5 tomatoes. Peel the tomatoes and squeeze out the seeds, then chop the tomatoes.

4. Put the remaining 2 tablespoons oil in a large pot over medium heat. When it's hot, add the chopped onion and sprinkle with salt and pepper. Cook, stirring occasionally, until softened, 3 to 5 minutes. Add the orange zest, fennel seeds, saffron, and remaining ¼ teaspoon cayenne and cook, stirring, for 1 minute.

5. Add the tomatoes, the Pernod, the orange juice, and all the fish stock and bring to a boil. Reduce the heat so the liquid bubbles enthusiastically and cook, stirring occasionally, until the tomatoes break down, 10 to 15 minutes. Add the halibut and when the broth starts to bubble again, add the scallops, shrimp, clams, and mussels. Cover and stand close by. When the broth boils again, reduce the heat and cook, checking every minute or 2, until the clams and mussels begin to open and the shrimp and scallops are opaque, 5 to 10 minutes. Remove any unopened shellfish. Taste and adjust the seasoning.

6. Make the croutons: Turn the broiler to high and position the rack 4 inches beneath it. Put the bread slices on a baking sheet and broil until browned on the edges and crisp, about a minute or 2. Spread some rouille on the croutons and serve with the hot bouillabaisse, garnished with the herbs.

Roll-Ups

The French—and fancy—word is *roulade*, and it describes a practical way to assemble and cook multiple ingredients simultaneously. The presentation is always impressive. See the Chicken Roulades with Goat Cheese and Asparagus. That's the Easy recipe. Cold and sliced crosswise, the roulades are a guaranteed hit for sandwiches. Then once I was cleaning out my fridge and in a moment of inspiration, I used thawed tofu skins to wrap leftovers, and Crisp Stuffed-and-Rolled Tofu Skins were born. (The filling is based on freekeh, cracked green "immature" wheat similar to bulgur.) The Marrow Bone Lamb Rolls with Berbere Tomato Sauce showcase a nontraditional use for a classic mix of warm spices. They're as dramatic as they are delicious.

● CHICKEN ROULADES
with goat cheese and asparagus

makes: 4 servings
time: 30 minutes

1 pound asparagus, tough bottoms trimmed

4 tablespoons olive oil

Salt and pepper

8 chicken tenders (about 1½ pounds)

4 ounces fresh goat cheese

½ cup dry white wine or water

2 tablespoons chopped fresh herbs (like parsley, chives, basil, or mint, or a mixture)

1 lemon, cut into wedges

1. Heat the oven to 450°F. Put the asparagus in a large ovenproof skillet. Drizzle with 2 tablespoons oil, sprinkle with salt and pepper, and toss to coat the spears. Remove the asparagus and divide into 4 equal portions.

2. Put 2 tenders flat on a plate so they overlap a little; dab a quarter of the cheese on top. Put one portion of asparagus perpendicularly on top of the chicken and cheese (it's fine if both ends are sticking out). Roll the chicken to enclose the asparagus and secure with 1 or 2 toothpicks. Transfer the roll to the pan and repeat with the remaining ingredients.

3. Sprinkle the rolls with salt and pepper and drizzle with the remaining 2 tablespoons olive oil. Roast until the asparagus is browned in places and the chicken is no longer pink inside, 20 to 30 minutes.

4. Transfer the chicken to serving plates and put the skillet over high heat. Add the wine and cook, scraping up any browned bits from the bottom of the pan. Add the herbs and as soon as the liquid starts to reduce, pour it over the chicken and serve, garnished with the lemon.

CRISP STUFFED-AND-ROLLED TOFU SKINS

makes: 4 to 6 servings
time: 45 minutes

UNPACKING TOFU SKINS These workhorses are sheets of thickened soy milk, skimmed off the top of tofu during processing. They come fresh, frozen, and dried. Sometimes fresh or frozen skins are a joy to work with and sometimes they take some finesse. (Dried skins are a good though utterly different substitute; see the vegan stir-fry recipe on page 234.) Since it's hard to know exactly how the fresh kind have been handled, you might need to put the whole bundle in a bowl of water to unroll them in one piece. Once you've got them spread out and are ready to work, keep them covered with a damp towel.

⅓ cup raisins

6 tablespoons olive oil

1 tablespoon chopped garlic

⅓ cup pine nuts

1 pound spinach, trimmed of tough stems and chopped

Salt and pepper

2 cups cooked freekeh, farro, bulgur, or short-grain brown rice (see page 92)

5 ounces fresh or defrosted frozen tofu skins

1. Soak the raisins in 1 cup hot tap water in a small bowl until soft, about 10 minutes. Put 3 tablespoons oil in a large skillet over medium heat. When it's hot, add the garlic and pine nuts and cook, stirring occasionally, until golden, 2 to 3 minutes. Transfer to a large bowl.

2. Raise the heat to high and add the spinach to the pan a handful at a time, stirring frequently until there's room in the pan for more. When all the spinach has been added, sprinkle with salt and pepper, and stir constantly until it's wilted and the pan is dry, 3 to 5 minutes.

3. Drain the raisins and add to the pan along with the freekeh and the reserved pine nut mixture and lower the heat to medium-high. Cook, stirring occasionally, until the filling is steaming, 3 to 4 minutes. Taste, adjust the seasoning, and transfer to the large bowl; wipe out the pan and leave it off the heat.

4. Heat the oven to 200°F. Carefully unfold 2 tofu skins one sheet at a time on a flat surface and keep covered under a damp cloth. If the skins are square, halve horizontally and cut each half into 3 even rectangles; if they're circles, cut into sixths like a pie. Spread each piece with about ⅓ cup of the spinach mixture, leaving a small border on all sides, and roll like sushi to enclose the mixture. (If your skins are wedge-shaped, start on the wider end and roll.) Transfer them to a platter seam-side down, pressing down gently to flatten them. If you need to stack them, separate the layers with wax paper, parchment, or foil. Repeat with the remaining tofu skins.

5. Put the remaining 3 tablespoons olive oil in the large skillet (preferably nonstick or well-seasoned cast iron) over medium-high heat. When it's hot, put as many rolls in the skillet as will fit without crowding. Fry until browned on one side, then turn and brown the other side, 5 to 10 minutes total. Transfer to an ovenproof plate and keep warm in the oven. Repeat with the remaining rolls, adding more oil if necessary. Sprinkle with lots of pepper and serve hot.

● MARROW BONE LAMB ROLLS
with berbere tomato sauce

makes: 4 servings
time: 1½ hours

LOOKING FOR LAMB CHOP First choice here is a bone-in arm chop, which is a relatively thin oval—like a ham steak—only with a small, circular marrow bone at one end. Stick with me; sometimes these are sold as shoulder chops. True shoulder chops will either be boneless or have a blade-shaped bone that runs along one side. The boneless chop will work here too, but you won't be able to roll the one with the long bone.

1 tablespoon black peppercorns

1 teaspoon cumin seeds

1 teaspoon coriander seeds

1 teaspoon cardamom seeds (from about 5 pods)

½ teaspoon fenugreek seeds

6 whole cloves

2 tablespoons minced garlic

3 tablespoons sweet paprika

1 tablespoon ground cinnamon

1 teaspoon ground ginger

Salt

2 cups green olives (like Castelvetrano or picholine), pitted and chopped

½ cup Quick Preserved Lemons (page 380); or use good-quality store-bought

½ cup chopped dried apricots

½ cup chopped fresh mint, plus more for garnish

4 bone-in lamb arm chops (about 10 ounces each)

3 tablespoons olive oil

½ cup dry red wine or water

One 28-ounce can whole Roma (plum) tomatoes

1. Heat the oven to 275°F. Cut 8 pieces of kitchen twine, each about 8 inches long. Put the peppercorns, cumin seeds, coriander seeds, cardamom seeds, fenugreek seeds, and cloves in a small skillet over medium-low heat. Cook, shaking the pan occasionally, until the spices are fragrant and toasted but not burned, 3 to 5 minutes.

2. Pulverize the toasted spices with a mortar and pestle or in a clean coffee grinder; transfer to a small bowl. Stir in the garlic, paprika, cinnamon, ginger, and a large pinch of salt. Combine the olives, preserved lemon, apricots, and ½ cup of the mint in another small bowl. Stir in 2 tablespoons of the spice mixture; taste and adjust the seasoning.

3. Put the chops on a rimmed baking sheet, sprinkle with salt, and cover with wax paper or parchment. Flatten the lamb around the bone with a meat pounder (or bottom of a can) until it's about ¼ inch thick; discard the paper. Spread the chops evenly with the olive mixture. Beginning at the boneless end, roll each into a football-shaped cylinder. Tie in 2 places with kitchen twine to secure.

4. Put the oil in a large lidded ovenproof pot over medium heat. When it's hot, add the lamb rolls and cook, turning as they release from the pan, until browned on all sides, 10 to 15 minutes. Remove them from the pan and pour off all but 3 tablespoons fat. Add the wine and cook, stirring to scrape up any browned bits. When it's almost completely bubbled away, add the tomatoes and the remaining spice mix and bring to a boil. Return the lamb to the pot, bone side up, cover, and transfer to the oven.

5. Braise the lamb undisturbed for 60 minutes. After that, check every 20 minutes or so until you can spear a roll with a fork and it slides right off. This could take another hour more. Transfer the rolls to a platter and carefully cut and remove the string. Taste the sauce and adjust the seasoning if necessary; stir to mash up any large tomato pieces. Spoon some of the sauce over the rolls and serve hot, garnished with the mint and passing the remaining sauce at the table.

● Duck Confit with
Warm Spices, page 259

Confit

The French technique for food "preserved in its own fat" traditionally is used for duck, goose, or other fatty meats. But confit has evolved to describe anything poached in fat. You'll get hooked on Duck Confit with Warm Spices, and anything you cook with the resulting fat tastes amazing—especially potatoes. For everyday luxury, try Olive Oil–Poached Chicken Breasts. Unlike a true confit, the meat is never fully submerged in oil and the only fussing you do is to turn and baste the chicken once. For a Vegan alternative, Garlic and Tomato Confit with White Bean Cakes will teach you how to intensify vegetables for this dish and many others, I hope.

● OLIVE OIL–POACHED CHICKEN BREASTS

makes: 4 to 6 servings
time: 40 minutes

2 whole bone-in chicken breasts, split
    (4 pieces total)
Salt and pepper
1 lemon, sliced crosswise and seeded
2 fresh thyme sprigs
4 large shallots, or 1 red onion, sliced
1 cup olive oil

1. Rub the chicken generously all over with salt and pepper. Put the lemon slices in a single layer into a medium skillet that will accommodate the chicken tightly. Scatter the thyme and shallots over the lemon and put the chicken pieces on top, skin side down.

2. Pour the olive oil over all and put the pan over medium-high heat. When the oil starts to shimmer, adjust the heat so the poaching mixture is barely bubbling. Cover and cook, undisturbed, until you can smell the chicken cooking, about 20 minutes.

3. Turn the chicken skin side up. Tip the pan slightly and spoon oil over the breasts to baste them a few times. Cover again and cook another 10 minutes. Again tip the pan and baste the chicken with oil. Make a cut close to the bone where the breast is the thickest. The chicken is done when it's easy to pierce with a thin-bladed knife and no longer pink inside. If it's not quite ready, continue cooking and check again in another 5 minutes.

4. You can serve the breasts whole, or cut between the bone and the breast to separate the meat and serve it in slices. Strain the poaching liquid, drizzle some over the chicken, and pass the lemon confit at the table.

GARLIC AND TOMATO CONFIT
with white bean cakes

makes: 4 servings
time: 2 hours

12 ripe Roma (plum) tomatoes

2 heads garlic, cloves separated and peeled

Salt and pepper

1 cup olive oil

1¾ cups cooked white beans (see page 82; or one 15-ounce can), drained

¾ cup rolled oats (not quick or instant)

2 teaspoons minced fresh rosemary, or 1 teaspoon dried

1. Heat the oven to 250°F. Halve the tomatoes vertically, and use a spoon to scoop out the seeds. Put the tomatoes cut-side down in a 9 by 13–inch baking dish so they overlap a bit. Scatter the garlic cloves around and among the tomatoes, and sprinkle with salt and pepper. Pour the oil into the dish, cover with foil, and bake, undisturbed, until the tomatoes and garlic are silky and tender, 1½ to 2 hours, stirring a few times during cooking. Cool to room temperature. (Refrigerate them and their oil in a covered container for up to 1 week.)

2. Put the beans, oats, and rosemary in a food processor and sprinkle with salt and pepper. Run the machine in long pulses, stopping to scrape down the sides, until the mixture is ground but not pureed, no more than 1 minute total. Taste and adjust the seasoning. Shape the bean mixture into 8 patties.

3. Pour 4 tablespoons of the confit oil in a large skillet over medium heat. When it's hot, add as many bean patties as you can fit without crowding and cook, undisturbed, until they are browned and crisp on the bottom, 5 to 8 minutes. Turn and cook until browned on the other side, 3 to 5 minutes more. Repeat with any remaining patties, adding more oil if necessary. Serve the cakes hot or at room temperature, with the tomato confit spooned over.

● DUCK CONFIT
with warm spices

makes: 8 servings
time: at least 1 day

6 star anise

2 tablespoons coriander seeds

1 tablespoon black peppercorns

1 large orange

1 cup salt

4 duck leg quarters (about 3½ pounds total)

One 3-inch piece ginger, peeled and cut into coins

6 cups rendered duck fat or olive oil, or a combination

Mesclun salad, for serving (optional)

1. Grind the star anise, coriander seeds, and peppercorns with a mortar and pestle or in a spice grinder (or put them in a plastic bag and bash them with a rolling pin). Use a vegetable peeler to remove the zest from the orange in long strips and scrape off any white pith from the underside with a paring knife. Mix the spices, zest, and salt in a bowl. Put the duck in a large bowl and rub all over with the salt mixture. Press the ginger and orange zest into the legs, cover, and refrigerate for 24 to 48 hours.

2. Heat the oven to 300°F. Remove the duck from the salt mixture and rinse off the salt; blot dry. Warm the duck fat in a saucepan over low heat just until it's pourable. Put the duck and ginger in a baking dish or roasting pan in one snug layer. Pour enough of the duck fat over the legs to just submerge them. (You may not need all of it; and if you don't have enough, add olive oil.) Transfer to the oven and cook, undisturbed, until you can easily insert a fork into the thickest part of the meat in a few of the legs and the fat becomes viscous, 3 to 4 hours.

3. Remove the legs from the fat but don't scrape off the excess. Discard the ginger and orange zest. When they're cool enough to handle, tightly wrap the legs individually or in pairs and refrigerate. Pour the fat into a separate storage container. (The legs will keep for up to 2 weeks; the fat will keep, refrigerated, for months. Freezing the legs and fat will extend the storage time to a year.)

4. To serve, heat a couple tablespoons of the fat in a skillet over medium-low heat. Add 1 or more legs at a time and cook, turning as necessary, until brown and crisp, 10 to 15 minutes. Serve with a mesclun salad, if desired.

Coq Au Vin

Braising chicken (or anything else) in wine has a way of exponentially developing big flavor. My Coq Au Vin with Shiitakes updates the classic chicken stew. It will take an afternoon to make, but has the depth of a dish that took much longer. For flexible everyday cooking, you can use either red or white wine to make Any-Wine Chicken. The seasonings will accommodate whatever half bottle you have lingering from dinners past. Artichokes and Shell Beans Braised in White Wine will be the brightest and lightest wine-sauced stew you'll ever eat.

● **ANY-WINE CHICKEN**

makes: 4 servings
time: 30 minutes

3 tablespoons unsalted butter

2 large boneless, skinless chicken breasts (about 1½ pounds)

Salt and pepper

1½ cups red or white wine

4 bay leaves

1 teaspoon grated orange zest

1. Put the butter in a large skillet over medium-high heat. When it melts, add the chicken and sprinkle with salt and pepper. Cook undisturbed until the chicken is browned and releases easily from the pan, 3 to 5 minutes. Turn and cook the other side the same way.

2. Move the breasts to the side of the pan and add the wine, bay leaves, and orange zest, then scrape any browned bits from the bottom of the pan. Return the chicken to the middle of the pan.

3. Bring the liquid to a boil and cook until the chicken is firm but still slightly pink at its thickest part and the wine has reduced slightly, 5 to 10 minutes. Remove from the heat, cover, and let sit for a couple minutes. Taste, adjust the seasoning, and serve warm.

Coq Au Vin with Shiitakes,
page 262

ARTICHOKES AND SHELL BEANS
braised in white wine

makes: 4 servings
time: at least 90 minutes

VEGAN WINE The process of making wine often includes animal products; strictly vegan options are increasingly easy to find, so be sure to look for a vegan label if it's important to you.

½ cup fresh lemon juice (from 3 or 4 lemons)

2 cups dry white wine

Salt

1½ pounds baby artichokes, 3 pounds large artichokes, or 1 pound defrosted frozen artichoke hearts

3 tablespoons olive oil

1 large shallot, sliced

1 tablespoon chopped fresh rosemary, or 1 teaspoon dried

3 cups frozen beans (like edamame, black-eyed peas, lima beans, or green fava beans)

1 tablespoon drained capers

Pepper

¼ cup chopped fresh parsley, for garnish

1. Put the lemon juice in a bowl with the wine and sprinkle with a little salt. Trim the tops, bottoms, and toughest outer leaves from the artichokes but leave the stalk and light-colored parts intact. Quarter them and scrape away the fibrous chokes with a spoon. As you finish each artichoke, toss it with the brine. (For large globes, trim the leaves and feathery chokes from the hearts and slice them. If using frozen, slice them into manageable pieces.)

2. Put the oil in a large skillet over medium-high heat. When it's hot, transfer the artichokes to the pan with a slotted spoon or tongs; save the liquid in the bowl. Cook, stirring occasionally, until they stop steaming and start sizzling, 3 to 5 minutes. Lower the heat to medium and cook, stirring occasionally with a spatula, until the leaves are tender and crisp all over, 10 to 15 minutes. Transfer to a plate with a slotted spoon.

3. Add the shallot to the pan and return to medium heat. Cook, stirring, until soft, 3 to 5 minutes. Add the rosemary, beans, and capers, and strain the wine mixture into the skillet; bring to a boil.

4. Cook, stirring frequently, until beans are warmed through and the sauce reduces by about one-third. Return the artichokes to the skillet, toss to coat, taste, and adjust the seasonings, adding some pepper. Garnish with the parsley and serve.

COQ AU VIN
with shiitakes

makes: 4 servings
time: at least 4 hours

1 whole chicken (3 to 4 pounds), cut into 8 pieces

Salt and pepper

1 bottle Pinot Noir or other fruity red wine

1 pound additional chicken wings, feet, or a combination

1 onion, cut into chunks

2 carrots, cut into chunks

2 celery stalks, cut into chunks

1 small bunch fresh parsley

Several fresh thyme sprigs

4 bay leaves

1 pound shiitake mushrooms

4 ounces slab bacon, cut into ½-inch pieces

8 garlic cloves, peeled

20 pearl onions, peeled (frozen are fine)

2 tablespoons chopped fresh tarragon

1. Put the chicken serving pieces in a large shallow bowl or baking dish and rub them generously all over with salt and pepper; pour the wine over and toss to coat. Keep the chicken submerged with a plate if necessary, cover tightly, and refrigerate for at least 1 hour and up to 24.

2. About 2 hours before you're ready to braise the chicken, heat the oven to 400°F. Put the chicken wings (and feet if you've got them) in a large roasting pan and sprinkle with salt and pepper. Cook, shaking the pan once or twice, until the meat is falling off the bone and the skin is browned, 45 to 55 minutes. Transfer the wings and all the fat and pan drippings to a large pot. Add a little water to the pan, scrape up any browned bits, and add that too. Add the onion, carrots, celery, several parsley sprigs (reserve the rest), thyme, and bay leaves. Trim the stems from the mushrooms and add them to the pot with 4 cups water; reserve the mushroom caps.

3. Lift the chicken from the wine marinade and transfer the pieces to a paper towel–lined plate and pat dry. Add the marinade to the pot with the wings and vegetables and bring to a simmer, then lower the heat so the mixture bubbles gently but steadily. Cook, skimming any foam from the top and stirring as necessary to prevent sticking, until the vegetables are quite soft and the stock is dark and fragrant, at least 1 hour but no longer than 2. Strain the stock, pressing on the solids to extract more juice; discard the solids and return the stock to the pot. Bring the liquid to a steady bubble, and let it reduce by about a third while you cook the chicken.

4. Put the bacon in a large skillet over medium heat and cook, stirring occasionally, until it renders fat and becomes brown and crisp, 10 to 15 minutes; remove it with a slotted spoon. Add half the chicken to the pan, skin side down. Cook, turning the pieces when they release easily from the pan and rotating them so they brown evenly, until the skin is crisp, 10 to 15 minutes. As they finish, transfer them to a plate and repeat with the remaining chicken.

5. Slice the shiitake caps and smash the garlic with the flat side of a knife blade. Pour off all but 4 tablespoons fat from the skillet and add the mushrooms, garlic, and pearl onions. Raise the heat to medium-high, sprinkle with salt and pepper, and cook, stirring frequently, until the mushrooms release their liquid and the pan is dry again, 10 to 15 minutes. Add 1 cup of the stock and the reserved bacon and scrape any browned bits from the bottom of the pan.

6. Nestle the chicken legs, thighs, and wings into the skillet skin side up. Add enough stock to almost submerge the meat, bring to a boil, then adjust the heat so the liquid bubbles gently and cover. Cook, checking once in a while to make sure nothing is scorching, until you can pierce the chicken easily with a fork, 30 to 40 minutes. Add the breasts to the pan and more stock if necessary. Sprinkle with the tarragon, and continue cooking until the chicken is tender and cooked through; an instant-read thermometer inserted into the thickest part of the breast should read between 150°F to 155°F. Chop 2 tablespoons of the remaining parsley leaves.

7. Transfer the chicken to a shallow serving bowl and use a slotted spoon to scatter the mushroom mixture on top; keep warm. Add whatever stock remains in the pot to the skillet and bring to a boil. Cook, stirring frequently until the mixture reduces and thickens, 3 to 5 minutes. Taste and adjust the seasoning. Spoon a little of the sauce on the chicken, garnish with the parsley, and serve, passing the remaining sauce at the table.

Cacciatore

If you're old enough to associate this classic with the midcentury Italian craze or a dining hall at college, I urge you to revisit the quintessential tomato braise with these new spins. And those of you too young to know what it is, allow me to introduce you. Italians might even approve of Drumstick Cacciatore, which creates enough crust on the skin for good flavor and texture without bogging down the clock. When you have a little more time, Hearty Vegetable Cacciatore delivers a saucy legume-based alternative. Since cacciatore translates to "hunter's stew" in Italian, the All Out recipe features rabbit, a mild, affordable, increasingly available, and environmentally friendly meat. The rustic elegance of this recipe might just convert you.

● DRUMSTICK CACCIATORE

makes: 4 servings
time: 30 minutes

2 tablespoons olive oil

8 chicken drumsticks (about 2 pounds)

Salt and pepper

¼ cup tomato paste

¼ cup balsamic vinegar

1 teaspoon dried sage (or dried oregano or thyme)

¼ teaspoon red chile flakes, or to taste

1 pound small button mushrooms, trimmed but left whole

1 tablespoon chopped garlic

1. Put the oil in a large skillet over medium heat. When it's hot, add the chicken and sprinkle with salt and pepper. Adjust the heat so it sizzles without burning, and cook, undisturbed, until it's browned and releases easily from the pan, 5 to 8 minutes.

2. Meanwhile, make the sauce. Put the tomato paste and vinegar in a medium bowl. Add 1½ cups water, the sage, red chile flakes, and a sprinkle of salt and pepper. Whisk with a fork until smooth.

3. Turn the chicken when it's browned on one side and releases easily, after about 5 minutes. Scatter the mushrooms and garlic onto the hot fat. Pour the sauce over the chicken and vegetables, then shake the pan once or twice to combine. Bring the mixture to a boil, then reduce the heat so it bubbles steadily without splattering. Cook uncovered, carefully shaking the pan a couple times more, until the chicken is just separating from the bone, about 20 minutes. Taste and adjust the seasoning, and serve.

HEARTY VEGETABLE CACCIATORE

makes: 4 servings
time: about 1 hour

4 tablespoons olive oil, or more as needed

1 pound portobello mushrooms, trimmed and sliced

Salt and pepper

1 large red onion, halved and sliced

1 red bell pepper, cored and sliced

1 cup green olives, pitted if you like

1 tablespoon chopped garlic

½ teaspoon red chile flakes, or to taste

One 28-ounce can whole tomatoes

1 cup dry white wine or water

1 pound fingerling potatoes

1 tablespoon chopped fresh oregano, or 1 teaspoon dried

1 cup frozen fava beans (or lima beans or edamame)

1. Put the oil in a large skillet over medium-high heat. When it's hot, add the mushrooms and sprinkle with salt and pepper. Lower the heat to medium-low and cover. Cook, undisturbed, for 5 minutes. Uncover the pan; the mushrooms should have released their liquid by this point, if not, cover and cook for another minute or 2. Turn the heat up to medium-high and cook, uncovered and watching carefully, until the pan is dry and the mushrooms are crisp and browned, about another 10 minutes. Transfer the mushrooms to a plate.

2. If the pan is dry, add more olive oil. Add the onion and bell pepper to the skillet and sprinkle with salt and pepper; return to medium heat. Cook, stirring occasionally, until the vegetables are beginning to soften, 3 to 5 minutes. Add the olives, garlic, and red chile flakes and cook until fragrant, less than a minute. Add the tomatoes, wine, potatoes, and oregano and bring to a boil. Adjust the heat so the mixture bubbles gently and cover. Cook until the potatoes are easily pierced with a fork, 20 to 30 minutes.

3. Add the mushrooms and favas to the pot and stir to coat in the sauce. Simmer until the beans are cooked through, 5 to 10 minutes. Serve hot or at room temperature.

● RABBIT CACCIATORE

makes: 4 servings
time: at least 10 hours, largely unattended

SUBSTITUTION IDEAS If you like, use eight skinless, bone-in chicken thighs instead of the rabbit.

1 rabbit (about 3 pounds), cut into 8 pieces

1 cup white wine vinegar

¼ cup salt, or more as needed

1 pound ripe Roma (plum) tomatoes

½ cup flour

5 tablespoons olive oil

Pepper

1 head garlic, cloves peeled and sliced

1½ cups dry white wine

1 fresh parsley sprig

1 fresh rosemary sprig

1 fresh thyme sprig

1 tablespoon drained capers

1. Put the rabbit pieces in a large bowl or pot. Mix 7 cups water with the vinegar and ¼ cup salt and stir until the salt is fully dissolved. Pour the brine over the pieces, making sure they are submerged; if not, use a plate to weight them. Cover and refrigerate for at least 8 or up to 24 hours.

2. Bring a large pot of water to a boil. Fill a large bowl with ice and cover with water. Cut a small X in the bottom end of each tomato. Put the tomatoes in the boiling water until the skin begins to loosen, about 30 seconds. Immediately transfer the tomatoes to the ice bath. When they are cool enough to handle, peel the tomatoes, remove the seeds, and chop them.

3. Remove the rabbit from the liquid and pat the pieces dry; discard the brine. Put the rabbit in a large bowl and toss with the flour to coat. Heat 3 tablespoons of the oil in a large pot over medium-high heat. When it's hot, add half the rabbit pieces and sprinkle with pepper. Cook, turning once, until browned on both sides, 10 to 15 minutes total. Transfer to a plate and repeat with the remaining pieces.

4. Add the garlic to the pot and cook, stirring frequently until fragrant, less than 1 minute. Pour in the wine and stir, scraping any browned bits off the bottom of the pan. When the pot is almost dry again, add the tomatoes and bring the mixture to a boil. Tie the herb sprigs together with kitchen twine and add to the pan along with the rabbit. Adjust the heat so the mixture bubbles gently and cover. Cook, turning the pieces once or twice, until the meat is tender and starting to separate from the bones, 1½ to 2 hours.

5. When the rabbit is nearly done, put the remaining 2 tablespoons oil in a small skillet over medium-high heat. Blot the capers dry and, when the oil is hot, add them to the pan. Cook, shaking the pan occasionally, until the capers are golden and crisp, 3 to 5 minutes. Transfer to a paper towel-lined plate.

6. When the rabbit is ready, transfer the meat to a warm serving platter. Discard the herbs. Boil the sauce over high heat for a few minutes to reduce, if you like. Serve the rabbit with the sauce spooned over and garnished with the fried capers.

Indian Curry

"Curry" is an inauthentic catchall for the richly nuanced food of India. Though this group of recipes doesn't untangle the confusion, it offers three completely different interpretations. The easy and fast lemon-butter pan sauce in Chicken Breasts with Curried Cucumber Raita ensures you'll never miss the long, slow braising. The Vegan recipe might not be quite what you expect from curry; brace yourself for an epiphany. Likewise, the seasoning for Lamb Shanks with Sambar Spinach is based on the blend used in a Southern Indian soup by the same name: sambar. The small pinch of asafetida—also called *hing*—will knock your socks off; it's a haunting taste you can't otherwise duplicate.

● CHICKEN BREASTS
with curried cucumber raita

makes: 4 to 6 servings
time: 45 minutes

1½ cups yogurt

2 tablespoons curry powder (see page 299)

Salt and pepper

4 tablespoons unsalted butter

4 small boneless, skinless chicken breasts
   (about 1½ pounds)

1 large cucumber

1 lemon, halved

1. Heat the oven to 325°F. Put the yogurt in a medium bowl. Sprinkle the curry powder in the bottom of a large dry ovenproof skillet and put over medium heat. Cook, stirring constantly with a spatula until the spices are fragrant but not burned, just a minute or 2. Scrape the spices into the yogurt, add some salt and pepper, and stir to combine the raita.

2. Rinse out the skillet and put over medium-high heat. Add the butter and when it's melted, add the chicken flat side down. Sprinkle with salt and pepper and lower the heat to medium. Cook until the breasts are browned and release easily from the pan, about 5 minutes. Turn and repeat on the other side. When that side is browned, turn the chicken again, then tip the pan and spoon the melted butter over the top. Transfer the skillet to the oven. Bake the chicken, undisturbed, until the thickest part is no longer pink but is still juicy, 10 to 15 minutes.

3. Peel and chop the cucumber and stir it into the curried yogurt; taste and adjust the seasoning. Slice the chicken thinly across the grain. Squeeze lemon juice into the pan the chicken cooked in and stir to scrape up any browned bits. Drizzle the chicken with the pan sauce. Serve the chicken with a spoonful of the curried raita.

Vegetable Masala with Turmeric
Tomato Sauce, page 270

● VEGETABLE MASALA
with turmeric tomato sauce

makes: 4 to 6 servings
time: 45 minutes

6 tablespoons good-quality vegetable oil

2 tablespoons chopped fresh ginger

1 teaspoon ground turmeric, or 2 tablespoons chopped fresh

One 28-ounce can diced tomatoes, or 3 cups chopped fresh

1 pound green beans, rinsed, trimmed, and chopped into ½-inch pieces

Salt and pepper

¾ pound all-purpose potatoes (like Yukon Gold), peeled and grated

1 red onion, chopped

1 teaspoon ground cumin

1 teaspoon fennel seeds

½ teaspoon ground cinnamon

¼ teaspoon ground cardamom

¼ teaspoon ground cloves

¼ teaspoon ground nutmeg

¼ cup chopped pistachios

¼ cup chopped fresh mint

1 fresh red chile (like Thai or Fresno), seeded if you like and minced

Toasted popadam (optional)

1. Put 1 tablespoon oil in a medium saucepan over medium-high heat. When it's hot, add the ginger (and the fresh turmeric, if using) and cook, stirring frequently, until it's golden, 3 to 5 minutes. Add the dried turmeric (if using) and cook and stir until fragrant, less than a minute. Add the tomatoes, stir, and bring the mixture to a boil. Reduce the heat so the sauce bubbles steadily, cover, and cook, stirring once in a while, until the tomatoes break down and the ginger softens, about 15 minutes.

2. Put 1 tablespoon of the oil in a large nonstick or well-seasoned cast-iron skillet over medium-high heat. When it's hot, add the beans, sprinkle with salt and pepper, and stir to coat with the oil. When they start to sizzle, add ¼ cup water to the pan and cook, tossing occasionally, until the water evaporates and the beans are crisp-tender, 3 to 5 minutes. Transfer them to a large bowl.

3. Return the skillet to medium-high heat. When it's dry and hot, add 2 tablespoons oil, swirl, then add the potatoes. Cook, tossing occasionally with a spatula, until the potatoes are lightly browned and tender but not mushy, 10 to 15 minutes. Transfer to the bowl with the beans but don't stir.

4. Put the remaining 2 tablespoons oil in the skillet and return to medium heat. When it's hot, add the onion and cook, stirring frequently, until it's soft and a little caramelized, 5 to 10 minutes. Add the cumin, fennel seeds, cinnamon, cardamom, cloves, and nutmeg; sprinkle with salt and pepper. Cook, stirring until the spices are fragrant, just a minute or 2.

5. Pour the spiced onion over the potato mixture and toss with 2 forks to combine. Taste and adjust the seasoning. (If you'd like the vegetables steaming hot, return them to the skillet and cook over low heat for a few minutes.) Serve the potato mixture nestled into some tomato sauce, garnish with the pistachios, mint, and chile, and have some popadam on the side if you like.

LAMB SHANKS
with sambar spinach

makes: 4 servings
time: 3 hours, largely unattended

SUBSTITUTION IDEA If you can only find large lamb shanks, buy 3 pounds total, cook as directed, then remove the meat from the bones in Step 5.

1 or 2 small dried hot chiles, or to taste

1 tablespoon coriander seeds

1 teaspoon yellow or brown mustard seeds

1 teaspoon fenugreek seeds

5 black peppercorns

2 tablespoons orange lentils

Pinch asafetida (optional)

4 tablespoons clarified unsalted butter
    (see page 335)

4 lamb shanks (about 12 ounces each)

Salt and pepper

1 large onion, chopped

2 tablespoons chopped fresh ginger

2 tablespoons chopped garlic

3 cups chicken stock (see page 43), or more
    as needed

2 pounds fresh spinach, trimmed but leaves
    left whole

One 14-ounce can coconut milk

¼ cup unsweetened shredded coconut

1. Heat the oven to 300°F. Make the sambar powder: Put a large pot over medium heat. Add the chiles, coriander seeds, mustard seeds, fenugreek seeds, peppercorns, and lentils. Cook, shaking the pan frequently, until fragrant, just a minute or 2. Transfer to a spice or coffee grinder and let cool a bit. Pulverize to a fine powder; add the asafetida (if using) and pulse to combine.

2. Rinse out the pot and put it over medium heat. When it's dry, add 2 tablespoons clarified butter and 2 lamb shanks; sprinkle with salt and pepper. Cook, turning occasionally, until browned on all sides, 10 to 12 minutes total. Transfer the shanks to a plate as they finish and repeat with the remaining butter and lamb shanks.

3. Pour off all but 3 tablespoons of fat from the pot and turn the heat down to medium-low. Add the onion, ginger, and garlic and cook, stirring occasionally, until soft and golden, 8 to 10 minutes. Add the sambar powder and stir until fragrant, less than 1 minute.

4. Add the chicken stock, stir, and return the lamb to the pot; if needed, add enough additional stock to halfway submerge the meat. Bring to a boil, cover, and transfer to the oven. Braise until the lamb is very tender and falling off the bone, 1½ to 2 hours, checking once or twice to make sure the liquid is bubbling gently and to turn the meat.

5. Remove the shanks from the pot. Skim the fat off the liquid and put the pot over high heat. Cook, stirring once in a while, until it's reduced by almost half, about 15 minutes. Add the spinach a handful at a time, stirring until it has wilted and there is room in the pan for more. When all the spinach is wilted, add the coconut milk and coconut and adjust the heat so the mixture bubbles gently. Cook uncovered, stirring occasionally until the spinach softens and the sauce thickens, 25 to 30 minutes. Taste and adjust the seasoning.

6. Return the lamb to the pot to rewarm. Serve the shanks with the spinach spooned over the top.

Tofu Curry, Massaman Style,
page 274

White Basmati Rice,
page 102

Green Fish Curry, page 274

Thai Curry

Named for the ingredient that defines the dish—curry paste—which is different from Indian curries. Not all Thai curries include coconut milk, but I'm partial to the versions that do. The quality of prepared curry pastes varies widely, so I always choose to make my own, even in a pinch. And, considering the food processor is the only other dirty piece of equipment besides the pot, Green Fish Curry comes together remarkably fast. Half of the long ingredient list in the recipe for Tofu Curry, Massaman Style, is for the seasoning paste, so don't be discouraged. Thai Curried Drumsticks are spectacular and ideal for a crowd; double or even triple this recipe and cook it in a deep roasting pan instead of a pot.

GREEN FISH CURRY

makes: 4 servings
time: 25 minutes

3 tablespoons good-quality vegetable or
    coconut oil

1 onion, halved and sliced

Salt and pepper

One 2-inch piece fresh ginger, peeled and
    chopped

4 garlic cloves, peeled and chopped

1 cup fresh cilantro, tough stems removed

1 jalapeño, seeded if you like and sliced, or to taste

2 teaspoons ground cumin

One 14-ounce can coconut milk

1½ pounds sturdy white fish fillets (like striped
    bass, halibut, or catfish), skin removed

2 limes, quartered

1. Put the oil in a large pot over medium heat. When
it's hot, add the onion, sprinkle with salt and pepper,
and cook, stirring occasionally, until soft and
golden, 5 to 8 minutes.

2. Meanwhile put the ginger, garlic, cilantro, jalapeño, and cumin in a food processor with a large
pinch of salt and pepper. Pulse until minced but
not pureed. Add the mixture to the onion and cook,
stirring, until fragrant, 1 or 2 minutes.

3. Pour in the coconut milk and stir until combined.
Bring the mixture to a gentle bubble (not a rolling
boil). Nestle the fish fillets in among the vegetables.
The liquid should almost submerge the fish; if not,
add a little water. Adjust the heat so the liquid again
bubbles gently, cover, and cook until the fish is just
cooked through, 5 to 10 minutes. Taste, adjust the
seasoning, and serve hot, with the lime quarters.

TOFU CURRY, MASSAMAN STYLE

makes: 4 servings
time: 45 minutes

1 star anise

1 mild fresh pepper (like red Anaheim or bell),
    cored and chopped

1 lemongrass stalk, trimmed and cut into
    2-inch pieces

3 fresh, frozen, or dried lime leaves, or
    2 teaspoons grated lime zest

2 tablespoons chopped garlic

2 tablespoons chopped fresh ginger

1 teaspoon ground coriander

1 teaspoon ground cinnamon

½ teaspoon ground turmeric

Salt and pepper

2 tablespoons coconut oil

1 onion, chopped

One 14-ounce can coconut milk

1 pound sweet potatoes, peeled and cut
    into chunks

1 pound pressed tofu, cubed

2 ripe tomatoes, chopped

½ cup chopped roasted, unsalted peanuts

2 tablespoons soy sauce

2 limes, quartered

¼ cup chopped fresh cilantro, for garnish

1. Pulverize the star anise in a spice grinder or with a mortar and pestle. Transfer to a blender and add the pepper, lemongrass, lime leaves, garlic, ginger, coriander, cinnamon, and turmeric; sprinkle with salt and pepper. Run the machine, stopping as necessary to scrape down the sides and adding water 1 teaspoon at a time just to help the machine do its job, until the mixture is completely smooth.

2. Put the oil in a large pot over medium heat. Add the onion, and sprinkle with salt and pepper. Cook, stirring often until soft, 3 to 5 minutes. Add the curry paste and cook, stirring constantly, until fragrant, about 30 seconds. Add the coconut milk and ½ cup water and bring to a simmer.

3. Add the sweet potatoes and tofu and another sprinkle salt and pepper. Bring the mixture to a boil, then reduce the heat so it bubbles gently. Cover and cook, stirring once in a while and adding a splash of water if the mixture starts to scorch, until the potatoes are barely fork-tender, 20 to 25 minutes.

4. Add the tomatoes and peanuts and stir until warmed through. Stir in the soy sauce and the juice from a couple lime wedges. Taste and adjust the seasoning, and serve garnished with the cilantro and the remaining lime wedges.

● THAI CURRIED DRUMSTICKS

makes: 4 servings
time: 1 hour

10 Thai or other medium to hot dried red chiles, seeded, or to taste

¼ cup dried shrimp

4 dried fresh lime leaves, or 1 tablespoon grated lime zest

2 cups boiling water

Seeds from 2 cardamom pods

2 teaspoons coriander seeds

1 teaspoon cumin seeds

4 large shallots

6 garlic cloves, peeled

1 bunch fresh cilantro

2 lemongrass stalks, peeled, trimmed, and roughly chopped

One 2-inch piece fresh galangal or fresh ginger, peeled and cut into coins

4 tablespoons good-quality vegetable oil, plus more for frying

8 chicken drumsticks (about 2 pounds)

1 teaspoon ground turmeric

One 14-ounce can coconut milk

Salt

Fish sauce

Lime wedges

2 or more fresh Thai or other red chiles, sliced, for garnish

1. Soak the dried chiles, shrimp, and lime leaves in the boiling water until pliable, about 15 minutes. Put the cardamom seeds, coriander seeds, and cumin seeds in a small dry skillet over medium heat. Cook, shaking the pan frequently, until darkened and fragrant, 2 to 3 minutes. Cool, then pulverize the spices to a powder in a spice or coffee grinder.

(recipe continues)

2. Slice the shallots crosswise into thin rings; separate them and reserve about ½ loosely packed cup of the larger rings. Smash the garlic with the flat side of a knife. Trim the cilantro and chop about ½ packed cup of stems. (Save the tender sprigs for garnish.)

3. Drain the chiles, shrimp, and lime leaves, reserving the soaking liquid. Put them in a blender or food processor along with the ground spices, the lemongrass, the smaller slices of shallots, the garlic, the galangal, and the cilantro stems; grind to a paste, stopping the machine to scrape down the sides as necessary. Gradually add 2 tablespoons oil while blending to make a fairly smooth, thick paste. (Use the curry paste immediately or cover tightly and refrigerate for up to a week.)

4. Heat the oven to 350°F. Put 1 tablespoon oil in a large pot over medium-high heat. When it's hot, add half the drumsticks and cook, turning until browned on all sides, 5 to 10 minutes total; transfer to a plate and repeat with the remaining chicken and remaining tablespoon oil.

5. Spoon off all but 2 tablespoons of the fat, turn the heat to medium, and add the curry paste. Cook, stirring frequently, until the mixture darkens and no longer smells raw, 5 to 8 minutes. Add the turmeric and continue stirring for 30 seconds, then return the chicken to the pot and toss to coat.

6. Add the coconut milk and enough of the reserved chile soaking water to submerge the chicken a little more than halfway (or just use tap water, depending on your affinity for heat). Adjust the heat so the mixture bubbles gently and carefully transfer the pot to the oven. Braise uncovered, stirring once or twice to prevent a skin from forming, until the chicken is fork-tender, 45 to 50 minutes.

7. While the curry is cooking, put about 2 inches of oil in large pot and bring to 325°F (a piece of shallot will sizzle immediately without burning). Line a plate with paper towels. When the oil is ready, fry the shallot rings, tossing with tongs until evenly golden, 2 to 3 minutes. Transfer to the prepared plate and sprinkle with salt.

8. Put the fried shallots, fish sauce, lime wedges, cilantro sprigs, and sliced fresh chiles in small bowls and set on the table for garnishing. When the chicken is done, taste the sauce, adjust the seasoning, and serve hot.

Adobo

There are almost as many variations of Filipino Adobo as home cooks. The defining characteristic is seasoned vinegar; the rest is up for debate. To get the true Coconut Chicken Adobo experience, it's worth tracking down a few special ingredients, but even with the suggested substitutions it's pretty darn great. Chicken Tenders Adobo has a well-balanced sauce that glazes irresistibly when grilled. For the Vegan version, I find roasted crumbled tempeh and carrots provide just the right texture.

● CHICKEN TENDERS ADOBO

makes: 4 servings
time: 20 minutes

4 garlic cloves, peeled

½ cup soy sauce

¼ cup rice vinegar

1 tablespoon brown sugar

2 bay leaves

Pepper

1½ pound chicken tenders

3 tablespoons good-quality vegetable oil

Salt

2 scallions, sliced, for garnish

1. Turn on the broiler and position the rack about 4 inches below the heat. Smash the garlic on a cutting board with the flat side of a knife and put it in a large skillet with the soy sauce, vinegar, sugar, bay leaves, and a pinch of pepper. Stir in ½ cup water and bring to a boil.

2. Add the chicken, turn to coat in the sauce, and adjust the heat so the liquid barely bubbles. Cover and cook, undisturbed, until the meat is opaque outside but still slightly pink inside, 5 to 10 minutes.

3. Grease a large rimmed baking sheet with 1 tablespoon oil. Remove the chicken from the braising liquid with tongs and transfer to the prepared pan, drizzle with the remaining 2 tablespoons oil, and

sprinkle lightly with salt. Broil on one side only, until the top is browned, 3 to 5 minutes. Meanwhile turn the heat up under the sauce and cook until syrupy and reduced, 3 to 5 minutes. Cut into one tender to make sure the chicken is cooked all the way through, then taste and adjust the seasoning. Serve garnished with the scallions, passing the reduced sauce at the table.

● TANGY BRAISED TEMPEH AND VEGETABLES

makes: 4 servings
time: 1 hour

12 ounces carrots, cut into 1-inch pieces

8 ounces tempeh

¼ cup good-quality vegetable oil

Salt and pepper

½ cup soy sauce

¼ cup rice vinegar

2 tablespoons chopped garlic

2 bay leaves

1 to 3 small dried chiles, depending on your affinity for heat

12 ounces green cabbage, chopped

1 onion, chopped

¼ cup chopped fresh cilantro, for garnish

(recipe continues)

● Coconut Chicken Adobo

1. Heat the oven to 425°F. Put the carrots on a rimmed baking sheet and crumble the tempeh onto it. Add the oil, season with salt and pepper, and toss to coat. Roast, stirring once or twice, until the tempeh is browned and crisp and the carrots are tender, 15 to 20 minutes.

2. Combine the soy sauce, vinegar, garlic, bay leaves, chiles, cabbage, onion, and lots of black pepper with ½ cup water in a large pot. Bring to a boil; reduce the heat to medium-low so the mixture bubbles gently, and cook, covered, until the cabbage is just barely tender, 10 to 15 minutes.

3. Add the roasted carrots and tempeh to the cabbage mixture and turn the heat to medium-high. Bring to a boil and cook, stirring occasionally, until the vegetables are tender and the sauce has thickened and reduced a little so it glazes everything, 15 to 20 minutes. Garnish with the cilantro and serve.

● COCONUT CHICKEN ADOBO

makes: 4 servings
time: at least 3 hours

THE RIGHT SOY SAUCE A Filipino brand of soy sauce is helpful to get the right sodium level. If that's not possible, use a brand you know is not overly salty, since the flavors concentrate during cooking.

1 tablespoon black peppercorns

5 garlic cloves

1 cup soy sauce (see the note above)

½ cup palm vinegar, or ½ cup cider vinegar mixed with 1 tablespoon honey

One 14-ounce can coconut milk

2 bay leaves

1 hot red chile (like serrano or Thai), sliced

1 whole chicken (3 to 4 pounds), cut into 8 pieces

3 tablespoons good-quality vegetable oil

2 scallions, sliced, for garnish

¼ cup chopped fresh cilantro, for garnish

1. Using a mortar and pestle, crack the peppercorns (or put them in a plastic bag and crush with a rolling pin). Smash the garlic on a cutting board with the flat side of a knife and peel it. Combine the peppercorns, garlic, soy sauce, vinegar, coconut milk, bay leaves, and chile in a large roasting pan. Add the chicken in a single layer and turn to coat with the marinade. Cover and refrigerate for at least 2 hours and up to 12.

2. Put the chicken and marinade in a large pot and bring to a boil. Reduce the heat so the mixture bubbles gently. Cover and cook, turning once or twice, until the chicken is no longer pink inside but not falling apart, 30 to 35 minutes, removing pieces as they finish (keep an eye on the chicken breast, especially).

3. Prepare a grill for direct cooking or turn on the broiler and position the rack 4 inches below the heat source.

4. Remove the chicken from the sauce and drain on paper towels. Turn the heat under the pot to high and cook the sauce until reduced to about 1 cup. Discard the bay leaves, taste and adjust the seasoning, and keep the sauce warm.

5. While the sauce reduces, pat the chicken dry and coat the pieces with the oil. Grill or broil the chicken until the skin is brown and crisp, 4 to 5 minutes per side. To serve, spoon the sauce over the chicken and garnish with the scallions and cilantro.

Ma Po

You don't have to have a pantry full of special ingredients to make this classic Chinese sauce—just Szechuan peppercorns. What Almost-Ma Po Chicken lacks in authenticity is more than compensated by its familiar flavor and convenience. Fresh chiles and fermented black beans deliver the right seasonings for Szechuan Mushroom Ragu. If you're leery of tofu, the freezing method here eliminates all the common textural complaints and turns it into an entirely different food. The All Out recipe is a tribute to tradition with ground pork and tofu. You even make a chile-bean paste—a spin on *doubanjiang*. I draw the line at asking anyone to ferment his or her own so-called broad beans, so check out my method for getting a similar tang.

● ALMOST-MA PO CHICKEN

makes: 4 servings
time: 30 minutes

3 tablespoons good-quality vegetable oil

1½ pounds ground chicken

Salt and pepper

1 pound green beans, trimmed

¼ cup cooked black beans (see page 82; or one 15-ounce can), drained

2 tablespoons ketchup

2 tablespoons cider vinegar

1 tablespoon cornstarch

1 teaspoon dark sesame oil

1 teaspoon red chile flakes, or to taste

1 teaspoon ground Szechuan peppercorns

1. Put the oil in a large skillet over medium-high heat. Add the chicken, sprinkle with salt and pepper, and cook, stirring occasionally, until it's browned and crisp in places, 5 to 10 minutes. Chop the green beans into bite-sized pieces.

2. While the chicken cooks, mash the black beans with a fork in a small bowl. Add the ketchup, vinegar, cornstarch, sesame oil, red chile flakes, and Szechuan peppercorns; sprinkle with salt and pepper. Stir and mash until a thick paste forms.

3. Add the mixture to the browned chicken, stirring until coated and fragrant, just a minute or 2. Add ½ cup water and the green beans and stir. Bring to a boil, then reduce the heat so the mixture bubbles steadily and cover. Cook, stirring once or twice, until the sauce thickens and the beans are as tender as you like, 5 to 10 minutes. Taste, adjust the seasoning, and serve hot.

Szechuan Mushroom Ragu,
page 282

● SZECHUAN MUSHROOM RAGU

makes: 4 servings
time: 30 minutes, plus 24 hours for the tofu

SUBSTITUTION IDEA If you don't have time—or you forget—to freeze the tofu, it's better to use 1 pound firm silken tofu (usually 1½ packages) instead of unfrozen firm blocks. Break it into small pieces in Step 5.

1 block firm tofu (about 14 ounces)

½ ounce dried shiitake mushrooms

1½ cups boiling water

8 ounces sliced fresh shiitake mushrooms, rinsed, dried, and trimmed

8 ounces button or cremini mushrooms, rinsed, dried, and trimmed

4 tablespoons good-quality vegetable oil, or more as needed

Salt and pepper

2 tablespoons chopped garlic

2 tablespoons chopped fresh ginger

1 or 2 small hot fresh red chiles (like Thai or Fresno), minced

2 tablespoons fermented black beans

1 teaspoon ground Szechuan peppercorns, or to taste

1 teaspoon Chinese five-spice powder

2 scallions, chopped

Soy sauce

1. At least 1 night (and up to 2 weeks) before you plan on serving, drain the tofu, put it in a plastic bag, and press out the air; put in the freezer for at least 8 hours, until frozen solid. The morning you plan to make the dish, remove the tofu from the bag, put it on a plate, and let it thaw in the refrigerator.

2. Put the dried mushrooms in a small bowl with the boiling water and soak until pliable, up to 20 minutes. Lift them from the water, careful to leave any sediment behind; reserve the liquid. Slice the fresh and rehydrated mushrooms.

3. Put 2 tablespoons oil in a large skillet over high heat. When it's hot, add the mushrooms and sprinkle with salt and pepper. Cook, stirring occasionally, until the mushrooms release their liquid and the pan becomes dry, 5 to 10 minutes. Lower the heat so they sizzle without burning and cook, stirring once in a while until the mushrooms are browned, 10 to 15 minutes. Transfer to a bowl.

4. Put the remaining 2 tablespoons oil in the pan on high heat. When it's hot, add the garlic, ginger, and chiles and cook, stirring, until fragrant, about 30 seconds. Add the fermented black beans and ground Szechuan peppercorns and five-spice powder, and cook, stirring and mashing them constantly, until a dark, rough paste forms, about 1 minute. Taste; the paste should be sharp and relatively salty; adjust the seasonings accordingly.

5. Return all the mushrooms and any accumulated juices to the pan, plus 1 cup of the mushroom soaking liquid. Cook, stirring often, until the sauce thickens, 5 to 10 minutes. Squeeze as much water out of the thawed tofu as you can manage; it's fine if it breaks up a bit. Crumble the tofu into the pan, and cook until heated through, 1 to 2 minutes. Taste, and adjust the seasoning, garnish with the scallions, and serve right away, passing the soy sauce at the table.

● MA PO TOFU

makes: 4 to 6 servings
time: about 90 minutes

4 cardamom pods

8 small dried chiles (like Thai or de árbol),
stems removed

1 star anise

2 bay leaves

One 1-inch cinnamon stick

4 whole cloves

1 tablespoon black peppercorns

1 tablespoon Szechuan peppercorns

¼ cup cooked fava beans (see page 82; or
one 15-ounce can)

2 tablespoons fermented black beans

2 tablespoons cider vinegar, preferably
unpasteurized

Salt

2 teaspoons dark sesame oil

1 pound boneless pork shoulder (a little fat is
desirable), cut into 2-inch pieces

3 tablespoons good-quality vegetable oil

2 tablespoons chopped garlic

2 tablespoons chopped fresh ginger

4 scallions, white and green parts separated
and chopped

2 cups chicken stock (see page 43), or water

2 tablespoons cornstarch

2 pounds firm tofu, chopped

1 fresh red chile (like serrano or Thai), seeded if
you like and sliced

1 cup tender fresh cilantro sprigs

1. Split the cardamom on a cutting board with the flat side of a knife; remove the seeds and discard the husks. Put a dry medium skillet over medium heat. When it's hot, add the chiles and toast, shaking the pan frequently, until they brown in spots, just a minute or 2. Remove the pot from the heat and add the cardamom seeds, the star anise, bay leaves, cinnamon stick, cloves, black peppercorns, and Szechuan peppercorns; stir until warmed. Transfer the mixture to a clean spice or coffee grinder and process until pulverized.

2. Mash the fava and black beans in a small bowl with the vinegar and a large pinch of salt. Add the spice blend and sesame oil, mashing and stirring to form a rough paste. Pulse the pork in a food processor until chopped but not fully ground; you want some texture.

3. Put the vegetable oil in the large pot over medium-high heat. When it's hot, add the pork, sprinkle lightly with salt, and cook, stirring occasionally, until it's no longer pink and begins to brown, 5 to 10 minutes.

4. Lower the heat to medium, add the garlic, ginger, and scallion whites and stir. Add the chile-bean paste and cook, stirring frequently, until the pork is coated, sizzling, and fragrant, just a minute or 2. Stir in the stock and bring to a boil. Reduce the heat so the mixture bubbles gently but steadily, cover, and cook, stirring now and then, until the pork is crumbly and the liquid thickens a little, 20 to 30 minutes.

5. Transfer ½ cup of the cooking liquid to a small bowl and whisk in the cornstarch to make a smooth slurry. Stir the mixture back into the pot. Adjust the heat to maintain a steady gentle bubble and cook, stirring frequently, until the sauce thickens, 2 or 3 minutes. Add the tofu and stir until heated through, 2 or 3 minutes more. Taste, adjust the seasoning, and serve right away, garnished with the scallion greens, fresh chile slices, and cilantro.

Vietnamese Caramel

Few techniques are as magical as cooking in a sweet and savory caramel sauce, a technique I first learned while traveling in Vietnam. Melting sugar stresses people out, but the directions in all the recipes are detailed so as to give you confidence. If you're still nervous, adding an extra tablespoon or two of water at the very beginning will slow the pace. Caramel Salmon is a good place to start since the process is straightforward. Pairing jackfruit with piquant caramel sauce and winter squash for a meatless spin is an excellent way to balance the sharpness of the fruit. Buy jackfruit in water or brine, not syrup (see page 306 for more about this increasingly popular food). For the addictive Candied Ribs, baby backs are my first choice since you can easily cut between the bones.

● CARAMEL SALMON

makes: 4 servings
time: 30 minutes

SUBSTITUTION IDEA If you like fish sauce but not in the amounts in these recipes, replace some of it with water or a combination of water and soy sauce.

½ cup fish sauce

1 cup sugar

1 red onion, halved and sliced

1 teaspoon pepper, or more as needed

¼ cup rice vinegar, or to taste

1½ pounds salmon fillets or steaks

¼ cup chopped fresh cilantro, for garnish

1. Mix the fish sauce with ½ cup water in a measuring cup with a pour spout. Put the sugar in a large skillet over medium heat, add 2 tablespoons water, and stir to combine. Cook, gently shaking the pan occasionally but not stirring, until the sugar liquefies and begins to bubble. When the sugar is all melted, continue to cook and shake until the caramel darkens to the color of iced tea, a minute or 2. Remove from the heat.

2. Carefully and slowly, standing away from the pan to avoid any spatters, pour in the fish sauce mixture. Return the skillet to medium heat and cook, stirring constantly, until the caramel melts into the liquid. Add the onion and cook, stirring occasionally, until it softens, 3 to 5 minutes. Add the pepper and vinegar and mix.

3. Nestle the salmon in the sauce (skin side down, if using fillets). If necessary, add enough water to bring the sauce about halfway up the sides of the fish. Adjust the heat so it bubbles very gently and cook, using a spoon to baste the top of each piece with sauce occasionally until the fish is almost opaque at the center and flakes without looking dry, 5 to 10 minutes, depending on the thickness.

4. Remove the fish from the pan with a spatula. Taste the sauce and adjust the seasoning, adding more vinegar or pepper if necessary. Pour the sauce over the fish, garnish with the cilantro, and serve.

CARAMEL-BRAISED WINTER SQUASH
with jackfruit

makes: 4 to 6 servings
time: 45 minutes

CHOOSING A SQUASH My favorites for this recipe are delicata or acorn squash, since the skin is so thin it crackles. Second choice are any of the crazy-looking winter squashes at the farmers' markets. They're harder to work with, but you can usually eat the skins after roasting; they'll just be a little thicker. Good ol' butternut is always an option.

1½ pounds any winter squash (see the note above)

Salt

3 tablespoons good-quality vegetable oil

⅓ cup soy sauce

3 tablespoons fresh lime juice, or to taste

¾ cup sugar

2 tablespoons chopped garlic

2 shallots, halved and sliced

8 ounces canned jackfruit, rinsed, patted dry, and cut into chunks (see page 306)

1 teaspoon pepper

½ cup chopped raw cashews

1 fresh red chile (like serrano or cayenne), minced, or to taste

1. Trim the squash and remove the seeds; if thick-skinned, peel it. Cut the squash into 1½-inch chunks; you should have about 4 cups. Put 1 cup water in a large skillet over medium-high heat. Add the squash, sprinkle with salt, and bring to a boil. Reduce the heat so the water bubbles gently, cover, and cook, stirring once or twice, until you are just barely able to pierce the squash with a fork, 5 to 15 minutes, depending on the type; do not over-cook. Drain the squash and let it sit in the colander. Rinse the skillet.

2. Mix the soy sauce and lime juice with ¼ cup water in a small bowl. Put the sugar in the large skillet with ⅓ cup water, and stir. Cook, gently shaking the pan occasionally but not stirring, until the sugar liquefies and begins to bubble. When the sugar is melted, continue to cook, swirling and shaking the pan, until the caramel darkens to the color of iced tea, a minute or 2.

3. Lower the heat and add the garlic and shallots and cook, stirring occasionally, until they soften, 3 to 5 minutes. Return the squash to the skillet along with the jackfruit, soy sauce mixture, and the pepper, and stir to coat. Turn the heat down to medium-low, cover, and cook, undisturbed, until heated through, 2 or 3 minutes.

4. While the vegetables are cooking, put the cashews in a small skillet over medium heat. Toast, shaking the pan occasionally, until golden and fragrant, about 3 minutes. Taste the squash, adjust the seasoning, adding more lime juice if you like, and serve garnished with the cashews and chile.

● CANDIED RIBS

makes: 4 servings
time: 10 hours, largely unattended

2 tablespoons minced lemongrass

2 tablespoons chopped garlic

Salt

2 pounds pork baby back ribs, separated into
    individual ribs

1¼ cups brown sugar

½ cup fish sauce

3 limes, halved

3 large shallots, sliced

4 star anise

2 teaspoons pepper

1 small bunch fresh cilantro

1. Combine the lemongrass and garlic in a big bowl with a big pinch of salt. Add the ribs and rub the mixture all over and toss to coat. Cover and refrigerate at least 8 hours or overnight.

2. Heat the oven to 450°F. Line a baking sheet with foil to help with clean up. Shake off any excess marinade, then put the ribs on the prepared pan in a single layer. Roast, turning once or twice, until the pork renders some fat and is browned, 15 to 20 minutes total.

3. Put the brown sugar in a large pot over medium heat and add 1¼ cups water. Cook, gently shaking the pan occasionally, until the sugar dissolves. Stir in the fish sauce and squeeze the limes into the pot. Add the shallots, star anise, pepper, and cilantro and stir to combine.

4. Transfer the ribs to the large pot with the sauce. Cover tightly and transfer to the oven. Braise, undisturbed, for 1 hour. If the ribs aren't fork-tender, continue to cook, covered, until they are, checking every 5 minutes.

5. Reheat the oven to 275°F and reline the baking sheet with fresh foil. Remove the ribs to the prepared pan and transfer to the oven. Strain the sauce into a medium saucepan and cook until thick and syrupy, 5 to 10 minutes. Taste, adjust the seasoning, and serve the ribs hot or warm, passing the extra sauce at the table.

Teriyaki

You want it to be sweet, salty, glossy, and thicker than soy sauce. But you don't want it to come from a bottle. Skillet Teriyaki proves that searing meat on just one side is perfectly acceptable. Skirt steak is ideal for a quick braise; it's got plenty of fat for tenderness and flavor, and it melts away quickly over high heat because the meat is so thin. I use the sweetness of teriyaki as an advantage in the Vegan recipe, where the sauce is first used to marinate portobello mushrooms before passing them under a broiler for gentle charring. Then with more moderate heat, the remaining sauce is reduced and used to glaze the mushrooms. And there's only one thing to say about Braised Beef Teriyaki with Shallots: The aroma as it cooks will drive you wild.

● SKILLET TERIYAKI

makes: 4 servings
time: 20 minutes

SUBSTITUTION IDEAS This recipe also works for boneless, skinless chicken thighs or pork sirloin steaks, cut into narrow strips.

1½ pounds skirt steak

2 tablespoons good-quality vegetable oil

Salt and pepper

1 tablespoon chopped garlic

1 tablespoon chopped fresh ginger

¼ cup honey

½ cup soy sauce

2 scallions, sliced, for garnish

1. If you have time, put the steak in the freezer for up to 30 minutes. Put a large skillet over medium-high heat. Slice the steak against the grain as thin as you can manage. When the pan is smoking hot, add 1 tablespoon oil and swirl to coat. Add half the beef to the skillet, sprinkle with salt and pepper, turn the heat to high, and cook undisturbed until it's browned on the bottom and releases easily from the pan, 3 to 5 minutes. Transfer to a bowl and repeat with the remaining tablespoon oil and the beef.

2. Add the garlic and ginger to the pan and cook, stirring frequently until soft, 2 to 3 minutes. Stir in the honey, soy sauce, and ½ cup water. Bring to a boil. Reduce the heat so the mixture bubbles gently and cook, stirring occasionally, until the sauce thickens and lightly coats the back of a spoon, 2 to 3 minutes.

3. Return the steak to the pan and toss to coat with the sauce. Garnish with the scallions and serve right away.

● TERIYAKI MUSHROOMS

makes: 4 servings
time: 25 minutes, plus time to marinate

MAKING MIRIN If you don't have mirin (which keeps practically forever), substitute a scant ½ cup water mixed with a splash of vodka and 2 tablespoons brown sugar and mix until the sugar is dissolved.

8 large portobello mushrooms

½ cup soy sauce

½ cup mirin (see the note above)

Salt and pepper

1 tablespoon dark sesame oil

2 tablespoons sesame seeds

2 tablespoons good-quality vegetable oil

2 tablespoons chopped fresh ginger

1 tablespoon chopped garlic

1. Carefully separate the stems from the mushrooms; rinse both well and drain the caps on towels. Put the soy sauce, mirin, and mushroom stems in a small saucepan over medium-low heat. Bring to a boil, then strain and discard the mushroom stems. Put the mushrooms in a wide dish and pour the sauce over them. Cover and refrigerate for at least 1 hour and up to 8 hours.

2. Turn on the broiler and position the rack 4 inches below the heat. Remove the mushrooms from the marinade and let any excess drip off. Put the mushrooms on a large rimmed baking sheet lined with foil, sprinkle both sides with salt and pepper, and brush the tops with the sesame oil.

3. Broil the mushrooms cap side up until they begin to brown, 5 to 8 minutes, then turn, and cook until the gills dry out a little, 3 to 5 minutes. Turn once more to finish browning and drying the tops, another 3 to 5 minutes. Watch carefully and remove the mushrooms as soon as the pan is dry and sauce has caramelized, or they will burn. Transfer the mushrooms to a cutting board; when they're cool enough to handle, slice them into 1-inch strips.

4. Put a large dry skillet over medium heat. Add the sesame seeds and cook, shaking the pan almost constantly, until they're golden and toasted. Transfer them to a small bowl and return the pan to medium heat. Add the vegetable oil; when it's hot, add the ginger and garlic and cook, stirring frequently, until soft and slightly golden, 3 to 5 minutes. Stir in the marinade and ½ cup water, and bring the sauce to a boil. Reduce the heat so the mixture bubbles gently. Cook, stirring occasionally, until the sauce is a little syrupy, 5 to 8 minutes.

5. Add the mushroom strips to the skillet and toss to coat with sauce and heat them through. Taste and adjust the seasoning, garnish with the toasted sesame seeds, and serve right away.

● BRAISED BEEF TERIYAKI
with shallots

makes: 4 to 6 servings
time: about 2½ hours

½ ounce dried shiitake mushrooms

2 tablespoons good-quality vegetable oil, or more as needed

2 pounds boneless beef chuck or brisket, cut into 2-inch cubes

Salt and pepper

4 large or 6 small shallots, peeled and halved

6 garlic cloves, peeled

One 2-inch piece fresh ginger, sliced

½ cup mirin (see the note opposite)

½ cup soy sauce

2 tablespoons cornstarch

2 tablespoons sesame seeds, for garnish

4 scallions, sliced, for garnish

1. Pour 4 cups boiling water over the dried mushrooms and soak until they're pliable, 20 to 30 minutes. Lift the mushrooms from the water with a slotted spoon to leave any grit behind; discard the stems. Chop the caps and reserve the soaking liquid.

2. Put 1 tablespoon of the oil in a large pot over medium-high heat. Working in batches to avoid overcrowding, add a few pieces of the beef and sprinkle with salt and pepper. Cook, turning the meat as it browns and releases easily from the pan, until dark and crisp on all sides, about 10 minutes per batch. Transfer to a shallow bowl with a slotted spoon and repeat with the remaining beef and remaining tablespoon oil, adding more oil if the pot looks dry.

3. Lower the heat to medium and add the shallots, garlic, ginger, and mushrooms. Cook, stirring occasionally, until the vegetables soften, 5 to 10 minutes. Add the mirin and bring to a boil, scraping up any browned bits from the bottom of the pot, just a minute or 2. Return the meat, along with the soy sauce, mushrooms, and enough of the mushroom soaking liquid to come halfway up the meat. Reduce the heat so the liquid bubbles gently. Cover and cook until the meat is easy to pierce with a fork and the sauce looks glossy, 1½ to 2 hours.

4. Remove ½ cup braising liquid and mix in a small bowl with the cornstarch until smooth. Pour the slurry back into the pot and bring to a boil. Cook, stirring occasionally, until the sauce thickens, just a few minutes.

5. Put the sesame seeds in a small dry skillet over medium heat, and cook until golden, shaking the pan occasionally, 3 to 5 minutes. Taste the beef and adjust the seasoning, then serve garnished with the scallions and sesame seeds.

Tamarind Tempeh Kebabs,
page 294

Kebabs

There's no denying the universal appeal of crisp grilled food on a stick. Even if you don't actually skewer the food before cooking, as with Skewer-less Minty Chicken Kebabs, which skips the chore of threading and unthreading—no one will even notice. The tamarind and tempeh meld in meatless kebabs like they were born together, while the All Out recipe is utterly different, inspired by the Greek stuffed grape leaves ubiquitous to mezze tables throughout the Mediterranean.

● SKEWER-LESS MINTY CHICKEN KEBABS

makes: 4 servings
time: 40 minutes

1 cup yogurt

¼ cup olive oil

2 tablespoons fresh lemon juice

1 tablespoon chopped garlic

2 tablespoons chopped fresh mint (or dill, basil, or chives), plus more for garnish

Salt and pepper

1½ pounds boneless, skinless chicken thighs, cut into strips about 1 inch wide

2 bell peppers (any color or colors)

1 large onion

8 ounces cremini mushrooms

1. Put the yogurt, oil, lemon juice, garlic, mint, and a sprinkle of salt and pepper in a large bowl. Whisk with a fork, pressing the mint and garlic against the side of the bowl to bruise them a bit; taste and adjust the seasoning. Add the chicken to the bowl and toss to coat. Marinate the chicken at room temperature for at least 15 minutes and up to 1 hour (or refrigerate overnight) while you prepare the vegetables.

2. Turn on the broiler and position the rack 4 inches below the heat. Core and seed the peppers and cut into 1-inch pieces. Halve the onion, then cut it into 1-inch chunks. Trim the stem bottoms and any discolored or soft spots from the mushrooms.

3. Pull the chicken from the marinade, shaking off the excess. Spread the strips on a rimmed baking sheet and broil, turning once or twice, until the chicken is brown in spots and cooked through, 10 to 15 minutes. Transfer the chicken to a platter with tongs, leaving the juices behind. Keep the chicken warm.

4. Put the vegetables on the baking sheet with the pan drippings, and toss to coat. Return the pan to the broiler and cook until the vegetables are soft and browned in spots, 5 to 8 minutes, shaking the pan once or twice. Spoon the vegetables and any juices over the chicken and serve, garnished with more mint.

TAMARIND TEMPEH KEBABS

makes: 4 servings
time: at least 3 hours, largely unattended

KINDS OF TAMARIND Prepared tamarind is needlessly difficult to source. What you want is a product that is nearly pure tamarind (most have preservatives, which is unavoidable) and not any sort of prepared chutney, candy, or other food. If you buy the dried, shelf-stable, pressed concentrated block, which is almost like fruit leather, hydrate it in a little hot water, then strain and measure.

2 tablespoons tamarind concentrate

½ cup soy sauce

½ cup mirin (see page 290)

⅓ cup good-quality vegetable oil, plus more
    for brushing

¼ cup minced fresh ginger

Salt and pepper

1 pound tempeh, cut into 16 pieces

8 long or 16 short wooden or metal skewers

1 large red onion, cut into 1-inch pieces

16 cherry tomatoes

1 broccoli crown, cut into large florets
    (about 8 ounces)

2 tablespoons rice wine vinegar

2 teaspoons Dijon mustard

1. Stir the tamarind, soy sauce, mirin, oil, and ginger together in a small bowl and season with salt and pepper. Reserve 1 cup in a small saucepan, and mix the rest with the tempeh in a shallow dish. Marinate for at least 2 hours, and up to overnight.

2. Heat the oven to 425°F. If you're using wooden skewers, submerge them in hot tap water in a rimmed baking sheet for at least 10 minutes. Drain.

3. Thread a few pieces of onion onto a skewer, then add tomato, broccoli, onion again, and tempeh; repeat on the same stick (or, if using small skewers, start a new one). Repeat with the remaining skewers and put them on a baking sheet; brush them all over with oil, and sprinkle with salt and pepper.

4. Roast the skewers until the vegetables soften and the tempeh develops a crust, 5 to 10 minutes; turn and roast another 5 to 10 minutes on the second side. Brush the skewers with the sauce and return to the oven for 5 minutes to glaze the tempeh and vegetables; turn and repeat at least once more, until the skewers are golden brown in spots and the vegetables are crisp-tender, another 5 to 10 minutes.

5. Add the vinegar, mustard, and ½ cup water to the saucepan with the reserved tamarind sauce. Bring to a boil and cook, stirring often, until slightly reduced and syrupy. Cool slightly, then taste and adjust the seasoning. Serve the kebabs hot or at room temperature, passing the warm sauce at the table.

● DOLMA KEBABS with saffron yogurt

makes: 4 servings
time: at least 1 hour

8 long wooden or metal skewers

1 cup yogurt

1 teaspoon minced garlic

½ teaspoon saffron threads, or a few more to taste

Salt and pepper

2 lemons, halved and seeded

16 jarred grape leaves (or fresh if you can find them), plus several extras

1½ pounds boneless beef chuck or lamb shoulder, cut into 1-inch chunks

½ onion, cut into chunks

2 tablespoons chopped fresh thyme

1 tablespoon ground cumin

1 tablespoon sumac

1 teaspoon ground Aleppo or other medium chile, or to taste

6 tablespoons olive oil

1 tablespoon toasted sesame seeds (see page 112), for garnish

¼ cup chopped fresh parsley, for garnish

1. If you're using wooden skewers, submerge them in hot tap water in a rimmed baking sheet for at least 10 minutes. Whisk together the yogurt and garlic. Rub the saffron between your fingers so it crumbles into the yogurt. Sprinkle with salt and pepper and add the juice of half a lemon and stir. Taste and adjust the seasoning, adding more saffron or lemon if you'd like.

2. Bring a large pot of water to a boil; salt it only if you're using fresh grape leaves. Blanch the leaves, a few at a time, until tender: up to several minutes for fresh and just 15 seconds or so for jarred. Rinse under cool water; lay out on a dish towel to dry. Remove any thick stems or hard veins near the base of the leaves with scissors.

3. Put the meat and onion into a food processor, working in batches if necessary, and pulse until coarsely chopped. Transfer to a large bowl and add the thyme, cumin, sumac, and ground chile, and sprinkle with salt and pepper. Mix with your hands until just barely combined. (To taste, cook a pinch in a skillet or the microwave, then adjust the seasoning.)

4. Put the olive oil on a rimmed baking sheet and keep it handy. Working with one grape leaf at a time, open it on a work surface with the veiny side up and the flat end closest to you. Put 2 tablespoons or so of the beef in the middle of the leaf and gently pinch it to form a horizontal log. Fold the stem end up over the meat, then fold in the sides to enclose the filling. Roll toward the tip, making a tight little package. Put the dolma in the prepared pan and repeat until the filling is used up.

5. Gently roll the dolmas to coat them in the oil. Line up 4 dolmas and carefully insert a skewer about ¾ inch from one end through all 4. Insert another skewer about ¾ inch from the other end, so the weight of the dolmas is fully supported; make sure the dolmas aren't quite touching. (You can prepare the dolmas up to several hours ahead. Tightly cover and refrigerate, then bring to room temperature before proceeding.)

6. Prepare a grill for indirect cooking and position the rack 4 inches above the heat source. (Or, heat the oven to 375°F.) Start the kebabs over the cool part of the fire and grill, turning occasionally, until cooked through, then move them back and forth over the flame until they're firm and charred in places, 10 to 20 minutes total. If roasting, cook until the meat filling is firm and cooked through, 15 to 20 minutes.

7. To serve, spread a little of the sauce on the bottom of serving plates or a platter and put the dolmas on top. Sprinkle with toasted sesame seeds and chopped parsley and serve hot or warm, passing the extra yogurt sauce at the table.

Tandoori

Like Tagine on page 378, this dish is named for the cooking vessel—an oven found in India called a tandoor. Few folks have access to one, but at home you can approximate the spiced yogurt marinade, the charred onions, and the tender meat. Charred whole cauliflower has become a vegetarian phenomenon, with good reason. My technique keeps the drama to one pan. The Tandoori-Style Shrimp is so fast you've got to snatch them from under the broiler in a flash, so be sure the rest of your meal is ready to roll. And I won't say that you must grind your own curry powder for Tandoori Chicken and Charred Onions, but you'll be happy if you do.

● TANDOORI-STYLE SHRIMP

makes: 4 servings
time: 10 minutes

¼ cup yogurt

2 tablespoons unsalted butter, melted

2 teaspoons paprika

1 teaspoon smoked paprika

Salt and pepper

1½ pounds large shrimp, peeled

¼ cup chopped fresh cilantro, for garnish

2 limes, cut into wedges

1. Turn the broiler to high and position the rack 4 inches below the heat. Line a rimmed baking sheet with foil to help with cleanup, if you like.

2. Combine the yogurt, melted butter, and both paprikas in a large bowl and sprinkle with salt and pepper. Taste and adjust the seasoning. Add the shrimp to the bowl and toss to coat.

3. Spread the shrimp on the prepared baking sheet in a single layer. Broil until the shrimp are pink and opaque in the center and charred around the edges, about 5 minutes total; shake the pan once or twice and move the shrimp around if they're not cooking evenly. Garnish with the cilantro and serve immediately, passing the lime wedges at the table.

Charred Whole Cauliflower
with Mustard Seeds, page 298

CHARRED WHOLE CAULIFLOWER
with mustard seeds

makes: 4 servings
time: about 90 minutes

1 large head cauliflower (about 2 pounds)

8 tablespoons coconut oil

Salt

2 tablespoons chopped garlic

2 tablespoons chopped fresh ginger

¼ cup yellow mustard seeds

1 tablespoon paprika

½ teaspoon cayenne, or to taste

Pepper

1 lime, halved

1. Heat the oven to 450°F and position the rack in the middle. Put a kettle of water on to boil. Trim any discolored leaves from the cauliflower and cut off the bottom but leave the core intact. Rub the cauliflower all over with 2 tablespoons of the coconut oil and a generous pinch of salt. Put it in an ovenproof medium skillet and cover the pan tightly with aluminum foil.

2. Transfer the skillet to the oven, carefully pull the rack out, lift up a corner of foil, and pour ½ inch boiling water into the skillet. Reseal tightly and roast the cauliflower until a knife inserted near the core meets only some resistance, 35 to 40 minutes. Remove the foil, pour off all but a thin film of water from the pan, and continue roasting until the cauliflower is deeply browned and tender to the core, 25 to 35 minutes, always making sure there is a little water in the pan.

3. Meanwhile, put the remaining 6 tablespoons oil in a small saucepan with the garlic and ginger over medium-low heat. When it starts to sizzle, cook, stirring frequently until the garlic and ginger puff a little and turn golden, 5 to 10 minutes. Stir in the mustard seeds and cook until they pop, a minute or 2. Remove from the heat and add the paprika, cayenne, and a sprinkle of salt and pepper. Let the mixture steep while the cauliflower roasts.

4. When the cauliflower is ready, carefully remove the skillet from the oven and let it cool a bit. Put the saucepan with the seasoned oil over medium-low heat to rewarm and squeeze in the lime; taste and adjust the seasoning. Quarter the cauliflower and open it up into wedges. Drizzle the oil over all and serve.

TANDOORI CHICKEN AND CHARRED ONIONS

makes: 4 to 6 servings
time: at least 5 hours

IN THE OVEN If you don't have a grill, place a rack on a rimmed baking sheet and cook the pieces in a 425°F oven until no longer pink inside, 30 to 40 minutes.

2 cups yogurt

2 tablespoons curry powder (recipe follows)

2 tablespoons chopped fresh ginger

2 tablespoons chopped garlic

Salt and pepper

1 whole chicken (3 to 4 pounds), cut into 8 pieces, or an equal weight of combined parts

2 large sweet onions, peeled and cut crosswise into thick slices

2 lemons, cut into wedges

1. Put the yogurt in a food processor with the curry powder, ginger, garlic, and big pinches of salt and pepper. Puree, scraping down the sides as necessary; taste and adjust the seasoning.

2. Remove the skin from the chicken pieces. Make 2 or 3 diagonal slashes in the flesh of each piece, almost down to the bone. Put the chicken in a 9 by 13–inch baking dish and add 1½ cups of the yogurt mixture. Rub the marinade into the cuts and all over the chicken, then spread the pieces in a single layer.

3. Put the remaining marinade in a small bowl with the onions and toss, careful to keep the slices from separating too much into rings. Cover both the chicken and onions and refrigerate for at least 4 hours or overnight.

4. Heat a charcoal or gas grill to medium heat for indirect cooking and put the rack about 4 inches from the heat source. Put the chicken and onions on the cool side of the grill with the bonier side down and as flat as you can manage. Cover and cook, adding more coals if necessary to keep the fire steady at moderate heat, until most of the fat has been rendered and the chicken looks pretty much cooked, 20 to 25 minutes.

5. Move the chicken and onions directly over the fire and brown, turning frequently. If the fire flares up, move the pieces back to the cool part of the grill. When the chicken is browned and a thermometer inserted into the thickest part of a thigh reads at least 155°F, 40 to 60 minutes total, remove the pieces from the grill. The onions are done when they are charred and tender. Let the chicken rest for a few minutes, then serve with the onions and lemon wedges.

CURRY POWDER

Put a dry medium skillet over medium heat. Add 2 small dried Thai or other small dried chiles, 2 tablespoons black peppercorns, 2 tablespoons coriander seeds, 2 tablespoons cumin seeds, and 2 teaspoons fennel seeds, then crumble in 4 dried bay leaves. Cook, shaking the pan constantly, until fragrant, just a minute or 2. Transfer to a spice or coffee grinder and add 2 tablespoons ground ginger, 1 tablespoon ground turmeric, and 2 teaspoons ground fenugreek if you can find it. Let the machine run until the spices are pulverized and combined. Store out of the sunlight in an airtight container for up to several months. Makes about ¾ cup in 5 minutes.

Korean BBQ
at Home,
page 303

Korean BBQ

You know it when you taste it. That unique funky, tangy taste you can't quite place in many Korean dishes is *gochujang*—a condiment that includes fermented soybeans, chiles, and ground starchy rice. You can make the All Out Korean BBQ at Home *after* you pay a visit to your butcher for pork belly and for spare ribs cut crosswise, or "flanken style." They'll look like cross-sections of small marrow bones held in a line with meat. Small pickled or cold vegetable sides (called *banchan*) round out the meal. For Roasted BBQ Brisket, you need neither special meat nor a weekend. The trick is to slice the fatty cut very thin so it cooks up tender, juicy, extremely flavorful, and lightly caramelized. The Vegan recipe is based on chewy, dense Korean rice cakes. There's no substitute; rice cakes come whole or sliced, fresh, frozen, or dried, and in all shapes and sizes. Use what you can find; the instructions in the recipe are flexible enough to accommodate different thicknesses.

● ROASTED BBQ BRISKET

makes: 4 servings
time: 20 minutes

1½ pounds boneless beef chuck

½ cup soy sauce

2 tablespoons brown sugar

2 tablespoons dark sesame oil

2 tablespoons minced garlic

2 tablespoons chile paste (like gochujang or sriracha)

Salt and pepper

1. Heat the oven to 400°F. Put the meat in the freezer for a few minutes. Whisk together the soy sauce, brown sugar, sesame oil, garlic, and chile paste with 1 cup water in a large bowl and season with salt and pepper.

2. When the beef has firmed up a bit, slice it against the grain as thin as you can manage. Add it to the bowl with the sauce and toss to coat. Lift the beef from the marinade, letting any excess drip back into the bowl, and spread it on a rimmed baking sheet. Transfer to the oven and cook until the beef is crisp and caramelized on the edges and just barely cooked through, 5 to 7 minutes.

3. Meanwhile, put the remaining marinade in a saucepan and bring to a boil; cook for 5 minutes, then remove from the heat and keep warm. Add the beef to the pot to reglaze, let the excess drip off, and serve immediately, passing the extra cooked marinade at the table.

● SEARED RICE CAKES

makes: 4 servings
time: 90 minutes

Salt

1 pound cylindrical Korean rice cakes (*dok*)

¼ cup gochujang

2 tablespoons soy sauce

1 tablespoon dark sesame oil

1 tablespoon brown sugar

2 tablespoons good-quality vegetable oil, or more as needed

1 bunch scallions, trimmed and cut into 2-inch pieces

Salt and pepper

8 ounces bean sprouts

1 tablespoon sesame seeds, for garnish

¼ cup chopped fresh Thai basil, for garnish

1. If you are using dried or frozen rice cakes, bring a large pot of salted water to a boil and follow the package instructions, boiling for 5 to 10 minutes. Drain thoroughly. Whisk together the gochujang, soy sauce, sesame oil, and brown sugar.

2. Put the vegetable oil in a cast-iron skillet over high heat. Dry the rice cakes well and slice diagonally into 1-inch pieces. When the oil is hot, add the rice cakes in one layer (you'll have to work in batches) and fry, turning once, until golden brown, 3 to 4 minutes per side. Transfer to a bowl as you finish. Repeat with the remaining rice cakes, adding more oil as necessary.

3. Add the scallions, sprinkle with salt and pepper, and cook, stirring occasionally, until browned in spots, 1 to 2 minutes. Transfer to the bowl with the rice cakes. Put the bean sprouts in the pan, sprinkle with salt and pepper, and cook until just wilted, 1 to 2 minutes.

4. Return the rice cakes to the pan along with the scallions and sauce. Cook, stirring constantly, until everything is nicely glazed, 1 to 2 minutes. Serve hot, sprinkled with the sesame seeds and basil.

KOREAN BBQ AT HOME

makes: 6 to 8 servings
time: at least 10 hours, largely unattended

CONTROLLING FLARE-UPS Be vigilant so you char without burning. Prepare hot and cool sides of the fire, and turn the meat often, moving it to the cold side of the grates (or to the edges of the grill pan) if any fat drips down and ignites or the sweet marinades threaten to burn.

1 pound skinless pork belly

2 tablespoons chopped garlic

2 tablespoons chopped fresh ginger

1 Asian pear, peeled and grated

1¾ cups soy sauce

4 tablespoons dark sesame oil

3 to 5 pounds spareribs, cut into ½-inch slices across the bone (flanken style)

1 cup mirin (see page 290)

Salt and pepper

1 cup boiling water

3 dates, pitted

½ cup gochujang

¼ cup toasted sesame seeds

2 tablespoons rice vinegar

1 tablespoon sugar

1 tablespoon soju or vodka (optional)

¼ cup chopped scallions

1. Heat the oven to 300°F. Put the pork belly in an ovenproof skillet and roast, uncovered, until at least ¼ inch of fat has accumulated in the skillet, 1½ to 2½ hours, depending on how fatty the belly is.

2. Meanwhile, whisk 1 tablespoon of the garlic, the ginger, pear, ¼ cup soy sauce, and 1 tablespoon sesame oil in a large bowl. Add the spareribs and toss to coat. Cover the bowl and refrigerate for at least 8 hours or up to overnight.

3. Reserve the rendered fat for another use and let the pork belly cool slightly, then cut it into slices ¼ to ½ inch thick. Whisk together 1 cup soy sauce and the mirin and sprinkle with salt and pepper in a medium bowl. Add the pork belly and toss to coat. Cover and refrigerate for at least 8 hours or up to overnight.

4. Prepare a gas or charcoal grill for direct and indirect cooking. Or heat a large grill pan over 2 burners until smoking hot. Make the sauces: Pour 1 cup boiling water over the dates. When they're soft, chop them, and add to a blender or food processor with the gochujang and 1 tablespoon sesame oil. Puree until smooth. Put the sesame seeds in a dry medium skillet over medium heat. Toast, shaking the pan occasionally, until they are golden and fragrant, 3 to 5 minutes. In a bowl, combine the remaining ½ cup soy sauce, the rice vinegar, remaining 2 tablespoons sesame oil, the sesame seeds, sugar, soju if using, 1 tablespoon garlic, remaining tablespoon ginger, and the scallions; whisk until the sugar dissolves.

5. When the grill is ready, cook the meat: Let any excess marinade drip off the ribs, then put them directly over the heat. Cook, turning them as soon as they release easily, until both sides are charred and the meat is just barely cooked through, 4 to 5 minutes per side. Transfer to a plate and brush the grill grates. Shake off any excess marinade from the pork belly and put them directly over the heat. Cook, turning occasionally and transferring the pieces to the cool part of the grill during any flare-ups, until cooked through and the edges are charred, 10 to 20 minutes. (The exact time will depend on how often you have to move the belly.) Serve the meats hot, with both sauces for dipping.

Something Smoky

For times you want the experience of eating classic, slow-cooked American barbecue, here are my newest offbeat solutions. Boozy BBQ Jackfruit Sandwich—the least traditional of the group—puts the power of barbeque sauce to work on a stringy, chewy tropical fruit. The combo can be so reminiscent of meat it freaks out some all-the-time vegans. Not surprising, jackfruit is having a moment right now. Since you can't actually smoke anything for Tuesday night dinner, Smoky Ham Steaks with Greens makes the most of already-smoked meat in a stir-fry, then doubles down with bacon and smoked paprika. The real barbecue project is Smoked Spareribs with My Spin on Three Sauces, which forgoes the rub in favor of last-minute basting. That way, the flavor of the meat comes through too.

● SMOKY HAM STEAKS
with greens

makes: 4 servings
time: 30 minutes

2 tablespoons olive oil

1½ pounds ham steaks (½ to 1 inch thick)

1 red onion, chopped

4 ounces bacon (6 to 8 slices, depending on the thickness), chopped

1½ pounds collard greens, leaves and stems separated, rinsed, and chopped

1 teaspoon smoked paprika

1 cup beer, or more as needed

Salt and pepper

1. Heat the oven to 200°F. Put the oil in a large skillet over medium-high heat. Cut the ham if necessary so it fits in the pan in a single layer. When the oil is hot, add the ham and cook, turning once, until nicely browned, 2 to 3 minutes per side. Remove to a plate and transfer to the oven. (If you're not pressed for time, don't cut the ham and cook it in 2 batches.)

2. Return the skillet to medium-high heat and add the onion and bacon; let sizzle for minute, then add the collard stems. Cook, stirring occasionally, until the stems are just barely tender and the bacon has released most of its fat, 3 to 5 minutes.

3. Add half the collard leaves, the paprika, and beer and sprinkle with salt and pepper; when the leaves begin to soften and make room in the pan, add the remaining leaves. Bring the mixture to a boil, then adjust the heat so that it bubbles steadily. Cook, stirring occasionally and adding more beer if the mixture gets too dry, until the greens are tender and the liquid has reduced to a sauce, 8 to 12 minutes. Taste and adjust the seasoning. Slice the ham and serve with the greens.

Boozy BBQ Jackfruit Sandwich,
page 306

● BOOZY BBQ JACKFRUIT SANDWICH

makes: 4 servings
time: 1 hour

THE JACK OF ALL FRUITS A few tips for buying: You want "young" or "green" canned jackfruit, not the fully ripe, stinky fruit. Stay away from the kind packed in syrup; choose a brand canned in water or brine and rinse it thoroughly to remove as much of the vinegary taste as possible. If you see frozen plain jackfruit, grab some. To use, thaw under cold running water (or in the fridge), squeeze it dry, and proceed. The sauced jackfruit will be even better reheated the next day.

2 cups ketchup

½ cup scotch, bourbon, or other whiskey

5 tablespoons cider vinegar

1 tablespoon soy sauce

1 large red onion, chopped

2 garlic cloves, chopped

2 teaspoons chili powder

1 teaspoon smoked paprika

Salt and pepper

Two 15-ounce cans jackfruit in water or brine, drained (see the note above)

4 tablespoons olive oil

1 tablespoon Dijon mustard, or to taste

1 teaspoon chopped fresh chile (like jalapeño or Thai), or to taste

2 cups cored and shredded cabbage, any type (about 1 pound)

1 tart, crisp apple, cored and chopped

¼ cup raisins

1 large loaf ciabatta bread (about 1 pound), or 4 ciabatta rolls

1. Combine the ketchup, whiskey, 4 tablespoons vinegar, and the soy sauce in a medium saucepan; add three-fourths of the onion, most of the garlic, and all the chili powder and paprika. Cook, stirring occasionally, until the vegetables soften and the sauce thickens slightly, 10 to 15 minutes. Taste and add salt and pepper if necessary. (Use right away or cool, cover, and refrigerate for up to a week.)

2. Rinse and drain the jackfruit in a colander, pressing down to extract as much water as possible. Run your hands through the pieces, pulling and separating them into shreds with your fingers.

3. Put 2 tablespoons oil in a large skillet over medium-high heat. When it's hot, add the jackfruit and cook, stirring occasionally, until browned and crisp in places, 2 to 3 minutes. Add the sauce and bring to a boil, then adjust the heat so the mixture bubbles gently. Cook, stirring once in a while, until the sauce has thickened and the jackfruit has absorbed some of the flavor, 20 to 30 minutes.

4. Whisk together the mustard and remaining tablespoon vinegar in a large bowl, along with the rest of the garlic and the chile. Add the remaining 2 tablespoons oil a little at a time, whisking all the while. Add the cabbage, apple, remaining onion, and the raisins and sprinkle with salt and pepper; toss to coat with the dressing. Taste and adjust the seasoning, then refrigerate until ready to serve. (It's best to let the slaw rest for a few minutes so the cabbage can soften and exude some juice to plump the raisins, but it will start to brown after about 1 hour.)

5. When you're ready to eat, cut the ciabatta (if you're using it) crosswise into squares, then slice each piece in half horizontally to create a sandwich bun; if using the rolls, simply slice them for sandwiches. Divide the jackfruit among the bread, top with some of the slaw and a second slice of bread, and serve.

● SMOKED SPARERIBS
with my spin on three sauces

makes: 8 servings
time: at least 3 hours, largely unattended

2 racks spareribs, 4 to 6 pounds total
Salt and pepper
Wood chips (like hickory, apple, or cherry)
Sauce or sauces of your choice (recipes follow)

1. A day or two before the meal, decide on your sauces (recipes follow) and allow enough time to let them rest as needed. The night before you plan to cook, sprinkle the meat generously with salt and pepper, rubbing all over, including in and around all the cracks and crevices. Cover loosely and refrigerate.

2. The next day, take the ribs out of the refrigerator. Start a gas grill, using the burners on only one side to get a heat of 250°F to 300°F. Put enough wood chips in a 9 by 13–inch disposable roasting pan to cover the bottom; add enough water to create a very shallow pool and just moisten them without letting them drown. Set this pan over the burners that are on, leaving one side cool and empty. (Or prepare a live fire with lump charcoal and some of the wood chips for indirect cooking in a covered grill. But be prepared: You'll need to add a lump or two and a few chips every 30 minutes to maintain the heat without letting the fire get too hot. It's worth the attention, though.)

3. Put the pork on the cool side of the grill and close the cover. Check about 15 minutes later to make sure the chips are smoking and the heat is below 300°F. Check and turn the ribs every half hour or so to make sure the heat hasn't escalated too much and the chips or charcoal (or water!) don't need replenishing. The ribs are done when most of their fat melts away, the bones feel a little loose when you wiggle them, and they look irresistibly ready to eat, anywhere from 2 to 4 hours (or even a little more).

4. Remove the meat from the grill. Turn off the burners under the wood chips and turn the rest to high. (Or add a bunch more charcoal to the live fire, spread it out a bit, and wait a few minutes for them to turn mostly gray.) When the grill is hot, put the meat directly over the fire to brown it on both sides. Leave the ribs uncovered, watch them constantly, and move them frequently; they should still have enough fat on them to flare up and burn, ruining all your hard work in, literally, a flash. Expect it to take 3 to 5 minutes to give both sides on both racks the right char. Brush them on both sides with some sauce if you like, turning once. Then remove them to a cutting board to rest for a few minutes while you finish setting up the spread. Cut the racks between the ribs and serve, passing the sauce at the table.

PICK A SAUCE

It's impossible not to offend some region of the U.S., so I'm narrowing the field and throwing the choice over to you:

Kansas City, Ketchup–Based: See the BBQ jackfruit Step 1, opposite. You can customize this by adding curry powder, mashed chipotle chiles, molasses, or wine or beer instead of whiskey.

Classic North Carolina, Vinegar–Based: Stir together 4 cups cider vinegar (save the bottle), 1/3 cup red chile flakes, and large pinches of coarsely ground black pepper and salt. I also like the nontraditional addition of 1 tablespoon minced garlic. Funnel the sauce back into the vinegar bottle and refrigerate for at least 4 hours.

South Carolina-Style, Mustard–Based: Whisk together 3/4 cup yellow mustard (yes, the bright yellow stuff, not coarse-ground mustard), 1/2 cup honey, 1/4 cup cider vinegar, 1 tablespoon brown sugar, 1 tablespoon Worcestershire sauce, and 1 teaspoon (or more) hot sauce. Refrigerate for at least 1 day and up to a week.

● Korean Fried
  Chicken Wings,
  page 311

● Buffalo
  Celery Root,
  page 310

Wings

Back in the day, you had no choice but to disjoint chicken wings with a sharp knife to break them down into their parts—the mini-drumstick-looking drumettes, the flat, and the tip (which is best saved for stock). Now you can buy them done for you. This is the way to go for the Easy Hot Sweet-and-Sour Wings. Give them some elbow room on two baking sheets in a very hot oven and they'll get just as crisp as if you fried 'em. It may not be pretty, but the Vegan-ized blue cheese sauce for Buffalo Celery Root is *that* close to the real thing, without relying on anything too wacky. Use it for dipping these hot-sauce-spiced celery-root fritters. First, Korean BBQ (see page 301) and now Korean Fried Chicken Wings. Here's a big secret: double-frying equals double-crispness. And here's another: dredge in cornstarch instead of flour. You almost don't need the amazing glaze, but you'll want to make some now that I've told you about it.

HOT SWEET-AND-SOUR WINGS

makes: 4 servings
time: 30 minutes

2 pounds split chicken wings

Salt and pepper

2 tablespoons olive oil

1 teaspoon red chile flakes, or to taste

½ cup cider vinegar

1 tablespoon chopped garlic

½ cup honey

1 teaspoon cornstarch

4 scallions, chopped

1. Heat the oven to 450°F. Put the wings on a rimmed baking sheet, sprinkle with salt and pepper, drizzle with oil, and toss to coat. Spread them out evenly in the pan and roast for 10 minutes, undisturbed.

2. Put 1 teaspoon red chile flakes, the vinegar, garlic, and honey in a small saucepan over medium heat and sprinkle with salt and pepper. Whisk until thoroughly combined, then taste and add more chile flakes if you like a spicier sauce. Bring to a boil, then adjust the heat so the mixture bubbles steadily. Cook, stirring occasionally, until the sauce has thickened, 10 to 15 minutes. Whisk the cornstarch with 1 tablespoon water until smooth, then add to the sauce. Stir to incorporate.

3. Check the wings. If they don't release easily from the pan, cook for another 3 to 5 minutes; when they do, turn and roast undisturbed until crisp and the juices run clear when pricked with a fork, another 5 to 10 minutes.

4. Drizzle the wings with the glaze and toss with a spatula to coat. Return the pan to the oven and cook until hot and sizzling but not burning, 3 to 5 minutes more. Sprinkle the scallions on the wings, toss again, and serve hot or at room temperature (leftovers are also great cold).

BUFFALO CELERY ROOT

makes: 4 servings
time: 45 minutes

1 tablespoon fermented black beans

1½ teaspoons cider vinegar

1 teaspoon tahini

1 teaspoon nutritional yeast

Salt

¼ cup vegan mayonnaise (see page 218)

1½ pounds celery root

½ cup flour

½ cup cornstarch

½ cup Louisiana-style hot sauce

Pepper

Good-quality vegetable oil, for frying

1. Heat the oven to 350°F. Soak the fermented black beans in the vinegar until slightly plumped, 10 to 15 minutes. Add the tahini, nutritional yeast, and a pinch of salt and mash with a fork. Stir the mixture into the vegan mayonnaise to give it the look and consistency of blue cheese dressing. Taste and adjust the seasoning.

2. Peel the celery root with a sharp knife, and cut into sticks about ½ inch wide and 3 to 4 inches long. Whisk the flour, cornstarch, ⅔ cup water, ¼ cup hot sauce, and a pinch of salt and pepper in a large bowl until no lumps remain. Add the celery root to the batter and toss to coat thoroughly.

3. Put ½ inch oil in a large skillet over medium-high heat. When it's hot (a drop of batter should sizzle enthusiastically), lift the celery root from the bowl 1 piece at a time, letting any excess batter drip off, and add to the skillet, cooking just a few pieces at a time. Cook, turning once or twice and adjusting the heat to prevent burning until the celery root is golden brown on all sides, 5 to 10 minutes total. Transfer the pieces to a baking sheet in a single layer as you cook additional batches, adding more oil to the skillet as necessary to maintain the depth.

4. When all the pieces are fried, roast in the oven without turning until the outside is crisp and browned in spots and the inside is tender, 8 to 12 minutes. Drizzle the remaining ¼ cup hot sauce in a spiral into the dressing and serve with the hot celery root.

● KOREAN FRIED CHICKEN WINGS

makes: 4 servings
time: about 1 hour

2 tablespoons sesame seeds

Good-quality vegetable oil, for frying

½ cup gochujang

¼ cup brown sugar

¼ cup mirin (see page 290)

2 tablespoons fresh lemon juice

1 tablespoon chopped garlic

1 tablespoon chopped fresh ginger

1 cup cornstarch

Salt and pepper

2 pounds split chicken wings

1. Put the sesame seeds in a large pot over medium-low heat and toast, stirring often, until golden and fragrant, 3 to 5 minutes. Transfer to a bowl. Fill the pot with at least 3 inches of oil and bring to 325°F over medium-high heat. Adjust the heat as necessary. If the oil starts to smoke, remove it from the heat immediately to cool a bit.

2. Put the gochujang, sugar, mirin, lemon juice, garlic, and ginger in a small saucepan and bring to a boil over medium heat. Reduce the heat so the mixture bubbles gently and cook, stirring occasionally, until the sugar has dissolved and the mixture has thickened to the consistency of barbeque sauce, 15 to 20 minutes. Taste and adjust the seasoning.

3. Put the cornstarch in a large bowl; sprinkle with salt and pepper. Add the wings and toss to coat.

4. When the oil is ready, shake off any excess cornstarch from the wings a few pieces at a time. Working in batches to avoid crowding the pan, carefully drop the wings into the oil. Cook, turning the pieces as necessary with a slotted spoon, for 5 minutes. Transfer the wings to a wire rack set over a rimmed baking sheet as they finish.

5. Bring the oil up to 375°F. Stir 2 tablespoons hot water into the gochujang sauce. When the oil is up to temperature, fry the wings again, until cooked through, crisp, and golden, 5 to 10 minutes. Transfer back to the rack and immediately brush with the sauce. If the sauce has thickened too much after cooling, stir in a tablespoon or so of water, but remember that the heat from the wings will help loosen it too. Sprinkle with the toasted sesame seeds and serve immediately, passing any extra sauce at the table.

Whole-Bird
Jerk Chicken,
page 315

Jerk

Skip the store-bought spice mixes—I've tailored the traditional blend for each recipe—and enjoy the iconic flavors of Jamaica at home. The project is as close to the real deal as you can get without smoking the chicken over laurel branches, as is typical. I've accounted for that subtle taste by adding more allspice and bay leaves to the spice rub. As a counterpoint, the Easy fix is to cook sliced boneless thighs with a quick pantry pan sauce fragrant with just a few spices. For a credible Vegan jerk, add a can of tomatoes to a spicy seasoning paste and use it to sauce another import from the Caribbean—crisp-fried tostones. The sauce is best fresh, but the chances of leftovers are low.

● SAUCY JERK CHICKEN

makes: 4 servings
time: 30 minutes

2 tablespoons vegetable oil

1½ pounds boneless skinless chicken thighs, cut into bite-sized pieces

Salt and pepper

1 bunch scallions, chopped

1 habanero or Scotch bonnet chile, seeded and chopped

1 tablespoon minced fresh ginger

1 tablespoon minced garlic

1 tablespoon chopped fresh thyme

1 teaspoon ground allspice

¼ cup fresh lime juice

2 tablespoons brown sugar

1. Put 2 tablespoons oil in a large skillet over medium-high heat. When it's hot, add the chicken in a single layer, taking care not to overcrowd (you may need to work in batches). Sprinkle the chicken with salt and pepper, stir once, then cook, undisturbed, until it starts to sizzle and brown, another minute or 2. Continue cooking, stirring occasionally, until the chicken is no longer pink, another 3 to 5 minutes. Transfer to a bowl, leaving the fat in the pan, and repeat with the remaining chicken.

2. Add the scallions and chile and cook, stirring often, until starting to soften, 2 to 3 minutes. Add the ginger, garlic, thyme, allspice and lots of black pepper, and sprinkle with salt. Cook, stirring constantly, until fragrant, about 30 seconds. Add the lime juice and sugar and cook, stirring often, until the sugar has dissolved and the mixture has reduced slightly, a minute or 2.

3. Return the chicken to the pan and turn off the heat. Toss to coat in the sauce. Taste, adjust the seasoning, and serve hot or at room temperature.

● CRISP PLANTAINS
with jerk-spiked tomato sauce

makes: 4 servings
time: 45 minutes

3 tablespoons good-quality vegetable oil, plus more for frying

2 tablespoons chopped garlic

2 tablespoons chopped fresh ginger

Salt and pepper

1 teaspoon ground allspice

¼ teaspoon ground nutmeg

2 teaspoons dried thyme

1 teaspoon cayenne, or to taste

1 tablespoon paprika

One 28-ounce can crushed tomatoes

1 tablespoon turbinado sugar

2 green-yellow plantains (not the blackened, ripe kind)

2 tablespoons fresh lime juice, or to taste

¼ cup chopped fresh cilantro, for garnish

1. Put the 3 tablespoons oil in a large pot over medium heat. When it's hot, add the garlic and ginger and sprinkle with salt and pepper. Cook until soft and just starting to turn golden, 2 to 3 minutes. Add the allspice, nutmeg, thyme, cayenne, paprika, and 1 teaspoon pepper and cook, stirring constantly, until fragrant, about 30 seconds. Add the tomatoes and sugar. Bring to a boil, then reduce the heat so the mixture bubbles gently. Cook until the sauce has thickened and the flavors come together, 25 to 30 minutes.

2. Cut both tips off the plantains, then cut each into three sections. Use a sharp knife to make three lengthwise slits in the skin of each section, peel off each piece of the skin, then trim any remaining skin from the plantain with a paring knife. Cut the plantains into ½-inch rounds.

3. Put a thin film of oil in a large skillet over medium heat. When it's hot, add the plantains, taking care not to crowd the pan and cooking in batches if necessary, and sprinkle with salt and pepper. Cook, undisturbed, until golden on one side, then turn and repeat until golden on the other, 3 to 5 minutes per side. Transfer to a paper towel–lined plate and let them cool a bit.

4. Put a plantain between 2 sheets of wax paper and pound with the side of your fist or the palm of your hand until it flattens and just about doubles in diameter; it will look squashed and might split a little around the edges, which is fine. (This step can be done an hour or so in advance.) Repeat with the remaining plantains.

5. Make sure there is still a thin film of oil in the skillet and add more if necessary. Turn the heat to medium, and when the oil is hot, cook the tostones again on each side (working in batches) until crisp and browned, 3 to 5 minutes per side. Reheat the sauce if necessary and add the lime juice. Taste, and adjust the seasoning. Serve the tostones hot, with the hot tomato sauce spooned over and garnished with cilantro.

● WHOLE-BIRD JERK CHICKEN

makes: 4 servings
time: about 1½ hours, plus 12 hours marinating

1 tablespoon allspice berries

¼ teaspoon nutmeg pieces (crack a whole nutmeg with a hammer)

4 bay leaves

1 teaspoon black peppercorns

1 tablespoon paprika

1 tablespoon brown sugar

4 scallions, chopped

1 tablespoon minced garlic

1 tablespoon minced fresh ginger

3 habanero or Scotch bonnet chiles, or to taste, seeded if you like and minced

2 tablespoons chopped fresh thyme

1 tablespoon salt, or more to taste

1 whole chicken (3 to 4 pounds)

1. Put the allspice, nutmeg, bay leaves, and peppercorns in a small skillet over medium-low heat. Cook, shaking the pan often, until toasted and fragrant, 3 to 5 minutes. Transfer the spices to a spice or coffee grinder and grind to a fine powder. Transfer to a bowl, add the paprika, sugar, scallions, garlic, ginger, chiles, thyme, and 1 tablespoon salt and stir to combine.

2. Butterfly the chicken: With the bird on a cutting board, breast facing up, use a heavy knife or sharp scissors to cut inside the cavity along each side of the backbone, working from the neck down. Once the backbone is removed (freeze it for making stock if you like), spread the chicken out (skin side up), and flatten it by pressing on either side of the breastbone with your hands. Put the chicken in a nonreactive dish large enough to hold it laid flat and rub the marinade on all surfaces on the chicken. Cover tightly with plastic. Refrigerate for at least 12 and up to 24 hours.

3. Set up a charcoal or gas grill for indirect cooking over medium heat and put the rack about 4 inches from the heat source. Or heat a large grill pan over 2 burners until smoking hot. Put the chicken on the cool side of the grill, skin side up and as flat as you can manage. Cover and cook, adding more coals if necessary to keep the fire steady at medium until most of the fat has been rendered and the bird looks pretty much cooked, 20 to 25 minutes. At this point, move the chicken directly over the fire and brown, turning frequently. Grill the lime halves the same way. If the fire flares up, return the bird to the cooler part of the grill.

4. When the chicken is browned and a thermometer inserted into the thickest part of the thigh reads at least 155°F, 40 to 60 minutes total, remove it from the grill. Let it rest for a few minutes. To carve, put the bird on a sturdy cutting board and with a cleaver, boning knife, or heel of a large knife, free the wings from the carcass at the joint and discard the wing tips; separate the thighs and drumsticks, then halve the thighs horizontally and cut off the bony end of the drumstick and discard; finally, separate the breasts, cut each into 3-inch wide pieces crosswise, and serve on a platter.

Escabeche

Cooks in Spain, the Caribbean, and some South American countries have this excellent technique of marinating food *after* cooking. If you're not in a huge hurry, you can hold off on the garnish and refrigerate Chicken Escabeche for as little as 1 hour or up to 24 hours, but even 10 minutes of marinating in the tangy, slightly hot dressing will be noticeable. Breaded-and-fried food can benefit from long marinating, with the right coating; Green Tofu Escabeche does the job with a lovely coconut-herb sauce. When you can put time on your side, Bluefish Escabeche with Fresh Tomatoes is simple but the details are important.

● CHICKEN ESCABECHE

makes: 4 servings
time: 30 minutes

2 large boneless, skinless chicken breasts (about 1½ pounds)

6 tablespoons olive oil

Salt and pepper

1 large red onion, halved and sliced

Juice from 1 orange

1 cup cider vinegar

1 jalapeño, seeded if you like less heat and chopped, or to taste

¼ cup chopped fresh cilantro, for garnish

1. Heat a grill over moderate heat or turn on the broiler and position the rack 4 inches below the heat source. Halve the chicken breasts horizontally to make 2 thin cutlets each. Flatten each by pressing with your hand.

2. Rub the cutlets with 2 tablespoons oil, sprinkle with salt and pepper, and grill or broil until they begin to firm and turn golden, 2 to 5 minutes. Turn and cook the other side until the center is white or only slightly pink, another 2 to 5 minutes. (The chicken might cook through before it starts to color; be careful not to let it overcook.) Transfer to a cutting board to rest.

3. Put the remaining 4 tablespoons oil in a large skillet over medium-high heat. When it's hot, add the onion and sprinkle with salt and pepper. Cook, stirring occasionally, until soft, 3 to 5 minutes. Add the orange juice, vinegar, jalapeño, and ¼ cup water and bring to a boil, then immediately turn off the heat. Sprinkle with salt and pepper.

4. Slice the chicken and transfer it to a shallow serving bowl. Pour the vinaigrette over the chicken. Let it marinate for as long as you can, then serve warm or at room temperature, garnished with cilantro.

GREEN TOFU ESCABECHE

makes: 4 servings
time: at least 1½ hours, largely unattended

One 15-ounce can coconut milk

1 cup fresh mint

½ cup coconut vinegar or rice vinegar

3 large garlic cloves, lightly smashed

1 fresh green chile (like jalapeño or serrano),
    seeded if you like less heat and chopped

1 tablespoon turbinado sugar, or to taste

Salt and pepper

½ cup unsweetened shredded coconut

Good-quality vegetable oil, for frying

2 blocks firm tofu (about 2 pounds), patted dry

½ cup cornstarch

1. Put the coconut milk, mint, vinegar, garlic, chile, and sugar in a blender or food processor and sprinkle with salt and pepper. Process until smooth, stopping to scrape down the sides as necessary. The sauce should coat the back of a spoon. If it's too thick, add water 1 tablespoon at a time. Stir the shredded coconut into the marinade. Taste and adjust the seasoning.

2. Put 2 to 3 inches oil in a large pot over medium heat; bring the oil to 350°F. Cut 1 tofu block diagonally, then cut each triangle in half horizontally to make 4, each about 1 inch thick; cut each triangle in half again so you end up with eight ½-inch-thick triangles and then halve horizontally again to end up with sixteen ¼-inch-thick triangles. Repeat with the other tofu block and transfer to a large bowl. Sprinkle with the cornstarch and toss gently to coat. When the oil is hot, carefully and slowly add the tofu to the pot—working in batches—and fry, turning once or twice, until golden brown and puffy, 2 to 4 minutes per side. Remove with a slotted spoon, drain on paper towels, and sprinkle with salt.

3. Put the tofu in a serving dish and pour the marinade over it. Refrigerate for at least 1 hour, or up to 8, and serve cold or at room temperature.

● BLUEFISH ESCABECHE
with fresh tomatoes

makes: 4 to 6 servings
time: 45 minutes, plus 12 to 24 hours marinating

1 pound ripe Roma (plum) tomatoes

3 garlic cloves, smashed

2 tablespoons chopped fresh oregano

1 cup dry white wine

2 tablespoons olive oil, plus more for pan-frying

About 2 pounds bluefish steaks, skin on if you like (or try fillets of mackerel or other rich sustainable fish)

Salt and pepper

1 cup flour

2 tablespoons chopped fresh chives, for garnish

1. Bring a pot of water to a boil; fill a large bowl with ice and cold water. Cut a wedge around the stem of each tomato and remove it; cut a small X in the opposite end. Drop each tomato into boiling water and cook until the skin begins to loosen, 30 seconds or less; then use a slotted spoon or tongs to immediately transfer to the ice bath. Remove the skin with a paring knife. Repeat with the rest of the tomatoes. Halve each lengthwise, then squeeze and shake out the seeds or remove them with your finger. Chop the tomato flesh.

2. Combine the chopped tomatoes, garlic, oregano, wine, and oil in a small saucepan over medium heat. Whisk as it heats, mashing the tomatoes lightly. When it boils, turn off the heat, taste, adjust the seasoning, and let cool.

3. Put about ¼ inch of oil in a large skillet over medium heat. Line a baking sheet with paper towels. Sprinkle salt and pepper on both sides of the fish. Put the flour on a large plate, season with salt and pepper, and mix. Dredge both sides of the fish in the flour.

4. When the oil is hot but not yet smoking, start adding the fish in batches (skin side down), taking care not to crowd the pan. Cook, undisturbed, adjusting the heat so the fish sizzles without burning, until the fillets are browned and release easily from the pan, 3 to 5 minutes. Turn, adding more oil if necessary, and cook the second side until the interior is opaque and flakes a little, another 2 to 3 minutes. Drain on the paper towels. Add more oil to the pan again if it's dry, and repeat with the remaining fish.

5. Put the fillets in a 9 by 13–inch baking dish in a single layer and pour the marinade over them. Let cool to room temperature, cover, and refrigerate for at least 12 hours or up to 24. To serve, transfer the fish to a serving platter, top with as much of the marinade as you like, garnish with the chives, and serve.

Agrodolce

Take the concept of sweet-and-sour in a different direction, give it a sexy Italian name, and you know the recipes will play on intense but balanced contrasts. Tomatoes bring extra brightness to Chicken Agrodolce; this shortcut method leaves you with a generous amount of an unusual and amazing sauce. Sweet and Sour Dumplings will be familiar to fans of Manchurian-style dishes—they're named for the Indo-Chinese sauce most commonly paired with cauliflower. And you can't rush the searing step in Short Ribs Braised with Balsamic and Cherries, or you'll shortchange the intensity of the sauce. So promise me you won't!

● CHICKEN AGRODOLCE

makes: 4 servings
time: 30 minutes

TYPES OF TOMATOES When tomatoes are ripe and in season, go with fresh—any kind—and figure 1 pound is about 1½ cups chopped.

2 tablespoons olive oil

1½ pounds boneless, skinless chicken thighs

Salt and pepper

1 red onion, halved and sliced

2 celery stalks, chopped

One 15-ounce can diced tomatoes

⅓ cup red wine vinegar

2 tablespoons sugar

Polenta, for serving (optional; see page 183)

1. Put the oil in a large skillet over medium-high heat. When it's hot, add the chicken and sprinkle with salt and pepper. Cook until it's browned and releases easily from the pan, 5 to 8 minutes. Turn and brown the other side. Transfer the chicken to a plate.

2. Pour off all but 2 tablespoons of the fat and return the pan to medium-high heat. Add the onion and celery and sprinkle with salt and pepper. Cook, stirring occasionally, until the vegetables soften, 3 to 5 minutes. Add the tomatoes, vinegar, and sugar and cook, scraping up any browned bits from the pan, until the sugar dissolves and the mixture boils, just a couple minutes.

3. Return the chicken to the pan and cook until the chicken is no longer pink inside and the sauce has thickened a bit, 10 to 15 minutes. Taste and adjust the seasoning, then serve the chicken hot, on the polenta if you like, with the sauce spooned over.

● SWEET AND SOUR DUMPLINGS

makes: 4 servings
time: 40 minutes

5 tablespoons good-quality vegetable oil

½ cup rolled oats

2 tablespoons chopped garlic

8 ounces cremini mushrooms, rinsed and trimmed

½ cup walnuts

1 teaspoon chili powder

2 tablespoons red or yellow miso

Salt and pepper

1 cup ketchup

¼ teaspoon cayenne, or to taste

2 tablespoons rice vinegar, or to taste

1. Heat the oven to 425°F. Grease a rimmed baking sheet with 2 tablespoons oil. Pulse the oats in a food processor until they're ground to a coarse meal; transfer to a large bowl. Put 1 tablespoon garlic and the mushrooms in a food processor and pulse until the mixture is finely chopped but not pureed. Add to the bowl with the oats. Put the nuts in the food processor and run until they're ground to a thick paste, scraping down the sides as needed. Add water 1 teaspoon at a time only if necessary to help the machine do its job; be careful not to make the mixture too wet. Add the nut butter to the bowl along with the chili powder and miso. Season with a little salt and lots of pepper and stir until the ingredients are distributed evenly.

2. Shape the mixture by the heaping tablespoon into small dumplings and put them on the prepared baking sheet. Carefully roll them around to coat them in the oil. Bake the dumplings, undisturbed, until they're crisp and brown, 15 to 20 minutes.

3. Put the remaining 3 tablespoons oil and remaining tablespoon garlic in a large skillet over medium heat. Cook until fragrant but not colored, a minute or 2, then add the ketchup and cayenne and ½ cup water. Cook, stirring frequently, until the sauce bubbles, thickens, and starts to caramelize around the edges of the pan, about 5 minutes. Add the vinegar, taste, and adjust the seasoning.

4. Add the cooked dumplings to the sauce and turn gently to coat evenly. Serve hot or at room temperature, passing any extra sauce at the table.

SHORT RIBS BRAISED
with balsamic and cherries

makes: 4 servings
time: about 3 hours

2 tablespoons olive oil

About 3 pounds meaty beef short ribs

Salt and pepper

1 large red onion, chopped

1 cup chicken stock (see page 43), or more
　　as needed

1 cup balsamic vinegar

½ cup dried cherries

1 cup pitted fresh cherries (frozen are fine)

1 teaspoon grated orange zest

1. Put the oil in a large pot over medium-high heat. When it's hot, add a few short ribs, taking care not to crowd the pan. Sprinkle with salt and pepper and cook, turning them so they brown on all sides and adjusting the heat so they sizzle without burning, about 15 minutes. As they're ready, transfer them to a plate and add more to the pot until all the ribs are browned.

2. Pour off all but 2 tablespoons of the fat and turn the heat to medium. Add the onion and cook, stirring occasionally and scraping up the browned bits from the bottom of the pot, until soft and golden, 5 to 10 minutes. Stir in the stock and vinegar, and season with salt and pepper. Return the ribs to the pot and bring to a boil. Adjust the heat so the liquid bubbles gently but steadily, cover, and cook, stirring once in a while, until the meat is tender, 1 to 1½ hours.

3. Add the dried and fresh cherries to the pot, and stir. Return the mixture to a steady bubble, cover again, and cook, stirring and checking the ribs every 15 minutes or so; add a little more stock or water if the sauce is scorching. The meat is done when it's fork-tender and almost falling off the bone, at least another 30 minutes and up to 45 minutes. Stir in the orange zest, taste and adjust the seasonings, and serve hot.

Southern Fried

You'll be licking your fingers while you eat any one of these recipes, no matter how much time they take to cook. When I go All Out to fry, I start with an overnight buttermilk soak, double-dredge the chicken for extra crunch, and deep-fry in plenty oil. Once you go that far, fluffy waffles and peach butter make perfect sense. For everyday crispness, you can get pretty close to the real thing by coating chicken tenders in a simple batter and shallow-frying. And since I won't rob vegans of a similar golden fried opportunity, Nashville Hot Okra Cakes answer the call.

● CRISP AND TANGY CHICKEN TENDERS

makes: 4 servings
time: 30 minutes

1½ pounds chicken tenders

5 tablespoons cider vinegar

½ teaspoon cayenne, or to taste

Salt and pepper

½ cup Dijon mustard

2 tablespoons honey

1 cup flour

1 egg

3 tablespoons good-quality vegetable oil, or more as needed

1. Heat the oven to 200°F. Combine the chicken, 4 tablespoons vinegar, and cayenne in a large bowl and sprinkle with salt and pepper; toss to coat. Put the mustard, remaining tablespoon vinegar, and the honey in a small bowl and whisk to combine. Put a wire rack on a rimmed baking sheet.

2. Put the flour in a large bowl and season with salt and pepper. Beat the egg in a small bowl and add ½ cup warm water, then pour into the flour mixture; stir until thoroughly combined and smooth.

3. Put the oil in a large skillet over medium-high heat. Toss the chicken tenders in the batter, and when the oil is hot, lift them out of the batter one by one, shaking off any excess, and carefully lower them into the skillet. Take care not to crowd the pan (you'll probably have to work in batches). Cook, turning and rotating and adjusting the heat as necessary so the chicken sizzles without burning, until each side is crisp and browned and the chicken is cooked through, 5 to 8 minutes total per batch.

4. Transfer the finished tenders to the prepared pan and keep warm in the oven while you fry the remaining chicken. Serve hot, passing the honey mustard at the table.

● Double-Dipped Fried Chicken
and Waffles, page 327

NASHVILLE HOT OKRA CAKES

makes: 12 fritters
time: 30 minutes

1 cup rice milk, oat milk, or other nonsweetened
    grain milk

8 ounces fresh okra, trimmed and cut
    into ½-inch slices

Salt

½ cup flour

¾ cup fine cornmeal

½ cup drained bread-and-butter pickles, chopped

Pepper

Good-quality vegetable oil, for frying

1 tablespoon cayenne

1 tablespoon brown sugar

1 teaspoon paprika

1. Heat the oven to 200°F and put a wire rack on a rimmed baking sheet. Pour the rice milk into a large bowl, add the okra, sprinkle with a little salt, and stir. Let sit for 10 minutes. Put the flour, cornmeal, and pickles in a shallow bowl; sprinkle with salt and pepper, and stir well. Drain the okra and reserve the soaking liquid. Fold the vegetables into the flour mixture. Add the soaking liquid 1 tablespoon at a time until the batter is thick like cookie dough.

2. Put ¼ inch oil in a large skillet over medium-high heat. Carefully shape the batter into 12 patties. When the oil is hot, add the patties, taking care not to crowd the pan (you might need to work in batches) and fry until cooked through and browned all over, 3 to 5 minutes per side. Transfer to the baking sheet, sprinkle with salt, then put in the oven to keep warm. Repeat until all the patties are cooked, adding more oil as necessary.

3. Remove the skillet from the heat and drain off all but 3 tablespoons of the oil. Add the cayenne, brown sugar, and paprika to the hot oil and stir to combine. Return the cakes to the skillet and spoon the pan sauce over to glaze them; serve right away.

DOUBLE-DIPPED FRIED CHICKEN AND WAFFLES
with peach butter

makes: 4 to 6 servings
time: at least 24 hours, largely unattended

1 whole chicken (3 to 4 pounds), trimmed of excess fat and cut into 8 pieces, or any combination of parts

Salt and pepper

3¾ cups buttermilk

2 fresh rosemary sprigs

5 cups flour

2 tablespoons sugar

1½ teaspoons baking soda

2 eggs, separated

12 tablespoons (1½ sticks) unsalted butter, 8 softened and 4 melted

½ teaspoon vanilla extract (optional)

1 tablespoon paprika

1 teaspoon cayenne

1 cup chopped very ripe peach, or thawed frozen

Good-quality vegetable oil, for frying

Hot sauce

1. Put the chicken in a large bowl or plastic bag and sprinkle generously with salt and pepper. Add 2 cups buttermilk and the rosemary, and toss to coat. Cover and refrigerate for at least 12 hours or up to 24.

2. When you're ready to eat, make the waffles: combine 2 cups flour, ½ teaspoon salt, the sugar, and baking soda in a large bowl. In another bowl, whisk together the remaining 1¾ cups buttermilk and the egg yolks. Mix in the melted butter and the vanilla if you're using it. Stir the wet ingredients into the dry. Beat the egg whites with a whisk or electric mixer until they hold soft peaks. Fold them gently into the batter.

3. Line a baking sheet with parchment or foil. Put the remaining 3 cups flour, the paprika, and cayenne in a shallow dish and season with salt and pepper; whisk to combine. Working in batches, take a few chicken pieces out of the buttermilk mixture, let the excess drip off, then coat in the flour mixture; put on the prepared baking sheet. Once all the chicken has been breaded once, work in batches to again dip the chicken in the buttermilk mixture, then coat in flour, and return the pieces to the baking sheet. Let sit for 10 minutes.

4. Heat the oven to 200°F; heat your waffle iron. Put the stick of softened butter and chopped peach in a small bowl and sprinkle with salt and pepper. Mash with a fork until incorporated and mostly, but not entirely, smooth.

5. Put 2 to 3 inches of oil in a large pot over medium heat and bring to 350°F. Put a wire rack on a rimmed baking sheet. When the oil is ready, add the chicken pieces, one at a time, working in batches so as not to crowd them. Cook, undisturbed, but adjusting the heat so the oil bubbles without smoking, until a crust begins to form, 5 to 7 minutes. Turn the pieces as they're ready to cook on the other side. Continue to fry, turning a couple more times, until the chicken is golden all over and cooked through, 5 to 10 minutes more. (To check for doneness, cut into a piece close to the bone; the juices should run clear.) As the pieces finish, transfer them to the wire rack, sprinkle with salt, and keep them warm in the oven.

6. Spread only enough batter onto the waffle iron to barely cover it; close the lid and bake until the waffle is cooked through and crisp, 3 to 5 minutes, depending on your iron. Transfer to the platter in the oven while you cook the remaining batter. Serve the waffles right away, topped with the warm chicken and pass the peach butter and hot sauce at the table.

Friday Fry

A mixed bag of fried food—mostly fish—in keeping with the Italian intention. Deep-fried anything is best eaten soon after it emerges from the hot oil. So I like to make this an informal meal, often served in the kitchen as fast as I can cook it. You can indulge the urge to fire up a pot of hot oil any time with the Fried Calamari and Onion Rings; the Bloody Mary–like sauce comes together while the oil heats. Mushroom Tempura with Orange-Soy Dipping Sauce is so good you might even prefer it over the other options. The reigning king of the fish fry is Beer-Battered Fish and Chips with Tartar Sauce.

● FRIED CALAMARI AND ONION RINGS
with cocktail sauce

makes: 4 servings
time: 15 minutes

Good-quality vegetable oil, for frying

1½ pounds cleaned squid, sliced into rings, tentacles cut in half lengthwise if large

Salt and pepper

1 large onion

1 cup flour, or more as needed

½ cup ketchup

2 tablespoons Worcestershire sauce

1 tablespoon fresh lemon juice

1 tablespoon Dijon mustard

1. Put 2 to 3 inches oil in a deep pot over medium heat and bring to 350°F. Line a plate with paper towels. Blot the squid completely dry with additional paper towels and sprinkle with salt and pepper.

2. Peel and trim the onion, cut it crosswise into ½-inch-thick slices, and separate the slices into rings. Put the flour in a large bowl. Whisk the ketchup, Worcestershire sauce, lemon juice, and mustard in a small bowl and sprinkle with salt and pepper; taste and adjust the seasoning.

3. When the oil is hot, toss half the squid and onion rings in the flour, then transfer to a sieve and shake over the bowl to remove the excess.

4. Add the dredged squid and onion to the oil, adjusting the heat as necessary so the temperature remains nearly constant. Fry, turning with a slotted spoon as necessary to cook evenly, until the squid and onions are lightly browned and cooked through, 2 to 5 minutes. Do not overcook. Remove with a slotted spoon and drain on the prepared plate; sprinkle with salt. Repeat with the second batch and serve with the dipping sauce.

MUSHROOM TEMPURA
with orange-soy dipping sauce

makes: 4 servings
time: 30 minutes

THE BACON OF SEAWEED Dulse is a dried seaweed, less well known than kombu, that's often smoked. Look for the flakes that don't need to be soaked and are handy for dressings and sauce.

1 teaspoon sesame seeds

1 tablespoon dulse flakes, or one 3- to 5-inch piece kombu

½ cup soy sauce

3 tablespoons mirin (see page 290)

¼ cup fresh orange juice

1 tablespoon fresh lime juice

Good-quality vegetable oil, for frying

¾ cup rice flour

Salt and pepper

1 cup ice-cold sparkling water

½ cup all-purpose flour

4 portobello mushroom caps, cut into 1½-inch-thick strips

1. Put the sesame seeds in a small pot over medium heat. Cook, shaking the pan occasionally, until golden and fragrant, 3 to 5 minutes. Transfer to a small bowl.

2. Put the dulse, soy sauce, and mirin in the small pot. Heat gently over medium-low heat just until steaming—do not boil—then turn off the heat and let cool to room temperature. Remove the dulse and stir in the orange and lime juices.

3. Heat the oven to 200°F. Put 2 to 3 inches oil in a large pot over medium heat and bring to 350°F. Fit a rimmed baking sheet with a wire rack. Put the rice flour in a large bowl and season with salt and pepper. Pour in the sparkling water and stir 2 or 3 times with a fork. You want the batter to be just barely mixed and a few lumps are fine; the less you stir, the lighter the batter. Put the all-purpose flour on a plate or in a shallow bowl.

4. When the oil is hot, take a few pieces of mushrooms, dredge them in the flour, then dip them in the batter, letting any excess drip off. Lower carefully into the oil. Cook, working in batches and turning once if needed, until the pieces are golden all over, just a few minutes. As they finish, transfer them to the rack to drain and sprinkle with salt. Keep warm in the oven. Add the sesame seeds to the sauce and serve with the tempura for dipping.

BEER-BATTERED FISH AND CHIPS
with tartar sauce

makes: 4 servings
time: about 1 hour

1½ pounds large starchy potatoes, peeled if you like and cut into long sticks

1 cup mayonnaise (see page 216)

2 tablespoons chopped pickles

1 tablespoon drained capers, chopped

1 teaspoon Dijon mustard

Salt and pepper

2 cups flour

1 teaspoon baking powder

1 cup beer, not too dark

1 egg, beaten

Good-quality vegetable oil, for frying

About 1½ pounds firm, large-flake white fish (like cod, ocean perch, sea bass, or tilefish)

Malt vinegar

1. Soak the potatoes in water while you prepare the other ingredients, changing the water once or twice.

2. Mix the mayonnaise, pickles, capers, and mustard, and season with salt and pepper; taste and adjust the seasoning. Refrigerate the tartar sauce until ready to use.

3. Put 1 cup flour and the baking powder in a bowl and mix. Add the beer and egg and sprinkle with salt and pepper. Stir until just combined (some lumps are fine). Put the remaining 1 cup flour in a shallow dish. Fit a wire rack inside a rimmed baking sheet.

4. Heat the oven to 200°F. Put 2 to 3 inches oil in a large pot over medium heat and bring to 300°F. Line a plate with paper towels. Drain the potatoes and pat them dry. When the oil is hot, fry the potatoes in 2 batches, stirring occasionally with tongs, until tender and beginning to turn golden, 5 to 10 minutes, depending on the size of the fries. As they finish, transfer them to the paper towel–lined plate. (You can do this up to an hour ahead; remove the oil from the heat until you're ready to continue.)

5. Raise the temperature of the oil to between 350°F and 375°F. Cut each long fillet into 3- or 4-inch lengths and dredge in the flour, shaking off the excess. Dip into the batter, allowing any excess to drip off. Fry 3 or 4 pieces at a time until puffed and golden, 3 to 5 minutes. Transfer to the rack and sprinkle with salt and pepper, then transfer the baking sheet to the oven to keep warm while you finish the fries.

6. Line another plate with paper towels. Return the oil to 350°F to 375°F. Fry the potatoes again in manageable batches until crisp and deeply colored, just a few minutes. (Try to maintain a constant oil temperature.) Drain on the paper towels and sprinkle with salt. Serve the fish and chips as soon as you can, keeping them in the warm oven for no more than 10 minutes. Pass the malt vinegar and tartar sauce at the table.

Fab-Cakes

Savory and crunchy pan-fried cakes make such good appetizers, why not expand the concept for dinner? One way to elevate them for special occasions is to use spirited seasonings, as in Curried Crab Cakes with Mango Salsa, with lime leaf, lemongrass, and fresh turmeric. Crab is an easy option, but can be an expensive one for an everyday meal. Instead I turn to the most reliable crustacean and put together the Shrimp Melts—admittedly unorthodox, but a winner. The Double Black Bean Cakes with Spicy Mayo double-down on savory, with the pleasant and funky ingredients common to Chinese cooking working wonders.

● SHRIMP MELTS

makes: 4 servings
time: 20 minutes, plus chilling

1 egg

4 scallions, trimmed and cut into 1-inch pieces

1½ pounds peeled shrimp, any size, rinsed and drained

1 teaspoon grated lemon zest

Salt and pepper

1 tablespoon hot sauce, or to taste, plus more for serving

½ cup breadcrumbs (see page 173) or panko

3 tablespoons olive oil, or more as needed

4 slices provolone or other mild melting cheese

Lemon wedges

1. Lightly beat the egg with a fork in a large bowl. Put the scallions in a food processor and pulse to chop into small pieces. Add about 1 pound of the shrimp and the lemon zest and season with salt and pepper. Pulse to chop the shrimp, but not too finely. Add the mixture to the egg, but don't stir.

2. Put the remaining shrimp in the food processor with the hot sauce and let the machine run until a paste forms. Add it to the bowl, then add the breadcrumbs and stir with a flexible spatula until combined. Taste and adjust the seasoning. (If you like, cook a small amount in a skillet and then taste.) Use your hands to gently shape the mixture into 4 cakes about 1 inch thick. If you have the time, refrigerate them for 30 minutes.

3. Put the oil in a large skillet over medium-high heat. When it's hot, add the shrimp cakes. Cook undisturbed, adjusting the heat as necessary so they sizzle without burning, until the bottoms have browned and the cakes release easily from the pan, 3 to 5 minutes. Turn, put a slice of provolone on each cake, and cover the pan. Cook until the bottoms have browned, the cake is cooked through, and the cheese has melted, another 3 to 5 minutes. Serve with lemon wedges and pass more hot sauce at the table.

● Curried Crab
Cakes with
Mango Salsa,
page 335

DOUBLE BLACK BEAN CAKES
with spicy mayo

makes: 4 servings
time: 30 minutes

1½ cups cooked black beans (see page 82; or one 15-ounce can), drained

½ cup fermented black beans

¾ cup old-fashioned rolled oats (not quick or instant)

1 small red onion, cut into chunks

1 tablespoon chopped fresh ginger

2 teaspoons chopped garlic

1 fresh red chile (like Thai or Fresno), seeded if you like less heat, and chopped

1 tablespoon soy sauce

½ cup vegan mayonnaise (see page 218)

1 tablespoon sriracha or chile paste, or to taste

1 teaspoon rice vinegar

2 tablespoons vegetable oil, or more as needed

1. Heat the oven to 200°F. Put 1 cup of the black beans, the fermented beans, oats, onion, ginger, garlic, chile, and soy sauce in a food processor and pulse, stopping occasionally to scrape down the sides, until the ingredients are chopped and thoroughly combined but not pureed, no more than 1 minute total. Transfer the mixture to a large bowl and stir in the remaining whole black beans. Taste and adjust the seasoning, then let the mixture sit for a few minutes. (You can make the recipe to this point up to 1 day in advance; cover tightly and refrigerate.) Shape the bean mixture into 8 patties, 1 inch thick.

2. Whisk together the mayo, chile paste, and vinegar. Taste and adjust the seasoning, adding more chile paste or vinegar to taste.

3. Put the oil in a large skillet over medium heat. When it's hot, add the cakes, taking care not to crowd them (you might need to work in batches). Cook undisturbed, adjusting the heat as necessary to keep them sizzling without burning, until the bottoms are browned and crisp, 5 to 8 minutes. Turn and cook until the second side is crisp and the bean cakes are cooked through, 5 to 8 minutes.

4. As they're ready, transfer the cakes to a heatproof platter to keep warm in the oven. Repeat with the remaining cakes if working in batches, adding more oil as necessary. Serve with the mayo.

CURRIED CRAB CAKES
with mango salsa

makes: 4 servings
time: about 1 hour

8 tablespoons (1 stick) unsalted butter

1½ pounds fresh lump crabmeat, picked over for cartilage

1 tablespoon chopped fresh turmeric, or ½ teaspoon ground

2 tablespoons fresh breadcrumbs (see page 173)

2 teaspoons fish sauce

One 2-inch piece lemongrass stalk, chopped

1 lime leaf, torn into pieces, or 1 teaspoon grated lime zest

1 fresh Thai red chile

1 tablespoon chopped fresh ginger

½ cup chopped fresh cilantro and ¼ cup chopped stems

Salt and pepper

1 egg, beaten

1 mango, peeled and chopped

¼ cup chopped fresh mint

1 small shallot, minced

2 limes

½ cup flour, for dredging

1. Melt the butter in a small saucepan over medium heat. Cook undisturbed, adjusting the heat to avoid burning, until the butter separates and the milk solids sink to the bottom of the pan and begin to turn golden. (This happens in just a few minutes, so watch it like a hawk.) Skim the foam off the top with a spoon or strainer, then carefully pour the golden clarified butter into a small bowl, and discard the solids.

2. Heat the oven to 200°F. Put 8 ounces of the crab and the turmeric in the food processor and puree until smooth. Put the crab paste in a large bowl and add the breadcrumbs.

3. Put 1 teaspoon of the fish sauce, the lemongrass, lime leaf, chile, ginger, and cilantro stems in the food processor and season with salt and pepper. Pulse until finely chopped, but not yet pureed. Add the mixture to the bowl and stir in the remaining crab and the egg. Cook a small amount in a skillet to taste and adjust the seasoning, then refrigerate the mixture for 30 minutes.

4. Mix the mango, chopped cilantro, mint, remaining teaspoon fish sauce, the shallot, and juice from 1 lime in a small bowl and sprinkle with salt and pepper. Taste and adjust the seasoning, adding more lime juice if you like. Let the salsa sit and macerate while you cook the crab cakes.

5. Shape the chilled crab mixture into twelve 1-inch-thick patties. Put the flour on a plate, season with salt and pepper, and mix. Put 2 tablespoons clarified butter in a large skillet over medium-high heat. Dredge each patty in flour and add to the skillet, taking care not to crowd the pan (you will probably have to work in batches).

6. Cook, carefully turning once, until browned on both sides and cooked through, about 10 minutes total. As they're ready, transfer to a heatproof platter in the oven to keep warm. Cook the remaining cakes, adding more clarified butter to the pan as needed. Serve hot with the mango salsa.

CLARIFIED BUTTER

Once you heat butter to remove the solids and water, the liquid left behind is intensified and can be heated to a relatively high temperature. If you have some clarified butter in the refrigerator—it keeps for up to a week—you can use it for pasta, stir-fries, and sauces. It's easy to make. Step 1 of the recipe above explains how to do it.

Schnitzel

For anyone concerned I'd skip breaded and fried pork or beef—or vegetable—cutlets, schnitzel has you covered. The Japanese cousin, *katsu,* is usually prepared in almost the same way, only with panko. You're going to love the Easy burgerlike method and want to bathe in the accompanying sauce. Squash Schnitzel with Fresh Vegetable Relish works around the challenges of cutting, breading, and frying enough squash to feed a family by breading the cutlets in a way that's both offbeat and terrific. To make Wiener Schnitzel with Green Sauce correctly, you need either a meat pounder or a willing butcher to do the deed. Invest in the gadget—you'll use it; you probably don't want to call the meat market every time you want to crush ice.

● PORK KATSU

makes: 4 servings
time: 20 minutes

⅔ cup ketchup

¼ cup soy sauce

1 tablespoon Dijon mustard

½ teaspoon ground ginger

2 cups panko

1½ pounds ground pork

Salt and pepper

Good-quality vegetable oil, for frying

1. Heat the oven to 350°F. In a small bowl, mix the ketchup, soy sauce, mustard, and ginger. Taste and adjust the seasoning. Keep the sauce at room temperature while you make the katsu.

2. Put the panko in a dish. Shape the ground pork into four ½-inch-thick patties and sprinkle them generously with salt and pepper. Press each patty into the panko to coat and flatten more.

3. Put about ⅛ inch oil in a large skillet over medium-high heat. When it's hot, add the patties and cook until the panko are golden, 2 to 3 minutes; turn and brown the other side. Transfer the skillet to the oven and roast until the pork is cooked through, 8 to 10 minutes. Drizzle each patty with some sauce and pass the rest at the table.

SQUASH SCHNITZEL
with fresh vegetable relish

makes: 4 servings
time: 45 minutes

¾ cup cider vinegar

¼ cup turbinado sugar

1 tablespoon salt, or more as needed

1 cucumber, seeded and cut into chunks

2 scallions, cut into chunks

1 red bell pepper, cored and cut into chunks

1 carrot, cut into chunks

1 tablespoon chopped fresh tarragon

2 cups puffed brown rice cereal or whole wheat breadcrumbs (see page 173)

Pepper

8 ounces silken tofu

¼ cup soy milk

¼ cup Dijon mustard

2 tablespoons white or yellow miso

1 sugar pumpkin, hubbard squash, or kabocha squash (about 2 pounds), peeled

3 tablespoons olive oil

1. Heat the oven to 425°F. Put the vinegar, sugar, salt, and ¾ cup water in a small saucepan and bring to boil, then transfer to a heatproof bowl. Put the cucumber in a food processor and pulse until chopped; transfer to the bowl with the brine. Repeat with the scallions, red pepper, and carrot. Add the tarragon, taste, and adjust the seasoning. Rinse and dry the food processor.

2. Put the puffed rice in the food processor and process until it's the consistency of fine cornmeal. Transfer to a plate and season with salt and pepper. Wipe out the food processor and add the tofu, soy milk, mustard, and miso and a pinch of salt and pepper; process until smooth; pour into a wide shallow bowl or baking dish.

3. Halve the squash lengthwise and use a spoon to scoop out the seeds. Put the squash on a cutting board cut-side down and slice into 12 crescents no more than 1 inch thick. (If you have extra, save the rest for another use.) Grease a baking sheet with 1 tablespoon oil and put the slices on the pan in a single layer. Drizzle with the remaining 2 tablespoons oil and sprinkle with salt and pepper. Bake, turning once, until just fork-tender, 15 to 20 minutes. Set aside to cool.

4. When the squash is cool enough to handle, dip one side of a squash slice in the tofu mixture, then in the rice, pressing so the crumbs adhere. Put it on the baking sheet crumb side up. Repeat with the remaining squash. Bake until the squash slices are tender and the breading is golden, 15 to 25 minutes depending on their thickness. Serve the schnitzel hot, passing the relish at the table.

● WIENER SCHNITZEL
with green sauce

makes: 4 servings
time: about 1½ hours, with resting time

4 bone-in veal chops (about 12 ounces each)

½ large loaf (about 8 ounces) French or Italian bread (preferably a day or two old)

1 cup flour

½ teaspoon ground nutmeg

Salt and pepper

2 eggs

¼ cup sour cream

2 cups fresh parsley, tough stems removed

½ cup fresh dill, tough stems removed

4 scallions

¼ cup fresh lemon juice, or more as needed

4 anchovy fillets

2 garlic cloves

1 tablespoon drained capers

½ cup olive oil

Good-quality vegetable oil, for frying

Lemon wedges

1. Heat the oven to 375°F; put a rack on a rimmed baking sheet. Either have the butcher prepare the veal or do it yourself: Put each chop between 2 pieces of wax paper or plastic and use a meat pounder to pound to no more than ¼-inch thickness, leaving the bone intact. Keep them separated with pieces of wax paper.

2. Tear the bread into pieces and put about half in a food processor. Pulse a few times, then let the machine run for a few seconds until coarsely chopped. Transfer to a shallow dish and repeat with the remaining bread. Mix the flour, nutmeg, and a pinch of salt and pepper in another shallow dish. Use a third shallow bowl to beat together the eggs, sour cream, and a sprinkle of salt and pepper until smooth. Clean the food processor.

3. Line another rimmed baking sheet with wax paper. Coat one chop in flour, then dip in the egg mixture, then the breadcrumbs, and put on the prepared baking sheet. Repeat with the remaining chops. (The breaded chops can be refrigerated for up to 2 hours.)

4. Put the parsley, dill, and scallions in a food processor and pulse a few times. Add the lemon juice, anchovies, garlic, and capers. With the machine running, slowly pour in the olive oil. Taste and adjust the seasoning; cover and refrigerate until ready to serve.

5. Put ½ inch vegetable oil in a large skillet over medium-high heat. When it's hot, carefully lower 2 chops into the pan and cook until the crust is crisp and golden on the bottom and the meat around the bone begins to turn opaque, 3 to 5 minutes. Turn and repeat on the other side. Transfer to the pan and rack. Repeat with the remaining 2 chops.

6. Put the chops in the oven and bake until the veal is very lightly pink or opaque all the way through, another 5 to 10 minutes. (You can check by taking a peek at the meat closest to the bone.) Serve hot with lemon wedges and pass the sauce at the table.

Parmigiana

There's your red-checkered-tablecloth-restaurant red-sauce standard, and then there are these three. Skillet Chicken Parm with Spicy Breadcrumbs has all the components of the original dish, minus the pounding or frying. When you go vegan, lots of breadcrumbs are an asset: Some cook on the eggplant and some brown in the pan for a spectrum of textures. (Up the ante with a grain-packed bread.) For times when I go to the trouble to make a big production of an Italian-American red gravy for Best Chicken Parmigiana, there had better be plenty of it. Maybe more than you need, but the leftovers won't go to waste, right?

● SKILLET CHICKEN PARM
with spicy breadcrumbs

makes: 4 servings
time: 30 minutes

4 tablespoons olive oil

1 cup breadcrumbs (see page 173), preferably panko

Salt and pepper

¼ teaspoon red chile flakes, or to taste

½ cup grated Parmesan cheese (about 2 ounces)

4 garlic cloves, sliced

One 28-ounce can diced tomatoes

½ cup dry white wine

2 large boneless, skinless chicken breasts (about 1½ pounds)

1½ cups grated mozzarella cheese (about 6 ounces)

1. Put 2 tablespoons oil in a large skillet over medium heat. When it's hot, add the breadcrumbs, sprinkle with salt and pepper, and cook, stirring often, until golden, 3 to 5 minutes. Add the red chile flakes and stir to combine, then transfer the bread-crumbs to a bowl and stir in the Parmesan. Taste and adjust the seasoning.

2. Put the remaining 2 tablespoons oil in the skillet and return to medium heat. When it's hot, add the garlic and cook until fragrant but not browned, about 1 minute. Add the tomatoes and wine and a sprinkle of salt and pepper. Bring to a boil, then adjust the heat so the mixture bubbles steadily. Cook, stirring occasionally, until the tomatoes break down a bit while you prepare the chicken.

3. Put the chicken on a flat surface and put your hand on top of one. Carefully slice the breast in half parallel to the cutting board to make 2 thin cutlets; repeat with the other breast.

4. When the sauce has thickened, nestle the cutlets into the skillet, adjust the heat to a steady but gentle bubble, and cover. Cook, undisturbed, until the chicken is opaque around the edges, 3 to 5 minutes. Turn, top each with some cheese, and cover again. Cook until the chicken is no longer pink inside and the cheese has melted, another 3 to 5 minutes. Taste and adjust the seasoning of the sauce. Serve the chicken topped with sauce and sprinkled with breadcrumbs.

EGGPLANT PARMESAN
with creamy vodka sauce

makes: 4 servings
time: 50 minutes

SUBSTITUTION IDEA To adjust the recipe for the long, narrow Asian varieties of eggplant—which I prefer when I can find 'em—there's no need to peel; after trimming, just halve lengthwise and start them in Step 1 cut-side down. Everything else remains the same.

8 tablespoons olive oil

2 pounds large eggplant, cut into rounds about 1½ inches thick

Salt and pepper

1 onion, chopped

One 28-ounce can whole tomatoes

2 cups fresh breadcrumbs (made from whole-grain bread; see page 173)

6 ounces soft silken tofu (about ½ package)

¼ cup vodka

¼ cup chopped fresh parsley, for garnish

1. Heat the oven to 350°F. Coat a large rimmed baking sheet with 2 tablespoons oil. Put the eggplant in the pan (it's okay if the slices touch, but don't overlap them) and sprinkle with salt and pepper. Drizzle the top with 2 tablespoons oil and rub all over the slices. Transfer to the oven and bake until the eggplant can just be pierced easily with a fork, 25 to 30 minutes.

2. While the eggplant bakes, put 2 tablespoons oil in a large skillet over medium-high heat. When it's hot, add the onion and cook, stirring frequently, until soft, 2 or 3 minutes. Add the tomatoes and a sprinkle of salt and pepper. Cook, stirring occasionally, until the tomatoes break down and the mixture comes together and thickens, 25 to 30 minutes. Taste, adjust the seasoning, and remove from the heat. (You can make the sauce up to this point and refrigerate for a few days.)

3. Toss the breadcrumbs in a small bowl with the remaining 2 tablespoons oil and a sprinkle of salt and pepper. Remove the eggplant from the oven and raise the heat to 425°F. Turn the pieces, and mash each lightly with a fork or a spatula until their skins split. Sprinkle the breadcrumbs over the whole pan as evenly as you can and press gently into the eggplant. Return the pan to the oven and bake until the breadcrumbs are browned, 5 to 10 minutes.

4. Carefully transfer the sauce to a blender, add the tofu, and puree until smooth. Return the sauce to the skillet and cook over medium heat, stirring occasionally, until it's bubbling again, 3 to 5 minutes. Stir in the vodka; taste, adjust the seasoning, and keep warm. To serve, spoon some of the sauce into 4 plates or a platter, put the eggplant and crumbs on top, and garnish with the parsley. Serve right away, passing the remaining sauce at the table.

● BEST CHICKEN PARMIGIANA

makes: 4 to 6 servings
time: at least 2½ hours, largely unattended

2 tablespoons olive oil, plus more for frying and drizzling

4 ounces pancetta, chopped

2 carrots, chopped

2 celery stalks, chopped

1 large onion, chopped

3 tablespoons chopped garlic

Salt and pepper

2 bay leaves

2 tablespoons chopped fresh thyme

1 tablespoon chopped fresh oregano

Two 28-ounce cans whole tomatoes

1 cup dry red wine

1 cup flour

2 eggs, beaten

2 cups fresh breadcrumbs, finely ground (see page 173)

½ cup grated Parmesan cheese (about 2 ounces), plus more for serving

1 ball fresh mozzarella cheese (about 8 ounces)

8 large boneless, skinless chicken thighs (about 2 pounds)

1 cup fresh basil

1. Put a large pot with the oil over medium heat. When it's hot, add the pancetta. Cook, stirring occasionally, until it has released most of its fat and browned in spots, 5 to 10 minutes. Add the carrots, celery, onion, and garlic; sprinkle with salt and pepper. Cook, stirring occasionally, until the vegetables are soft but not browned, 8 to 10 minutes. Add the bay leaves, thyme, and oregano and stir to combine.

2. Add the tomatoes and wine, bring the sauce to a boil, then lower the heat so the mixture bubbles very gently. Partially cover the pot and cook, stirring occasionally to mash the vegetables and make sure they're not sticking, until the mixture darkens and develops a smooth texture and intense flavor, 1½ to 2 hours. Taste, adjust the seasoning, and keep warm. (You can make the sauce up to 3 days ahead of time, if you like; rewarm it over low heat before proceeding.)

3. Put the flour in a shallow dish and the eggs in another; sprinkle both with salt and pepper. Mix the breadcrumbs and Parmesan in a third similar dish. Slice the mozzarella as thin as you can. Heat the oven to 425°F.

4. Put about ½ inch olive oil in a large skillet over medium-high heat. Set a wire rack inside a rimmed baking sheet. Sprinkle the chicken thighs with salt and pound them to an even thickness between pieces of plastic or wax paper with a meat pounder. Dredge each piece in the flour on both sides; shake to remove the excess. Dip it the same way in the eggs, then coat all over with breadcrumbs. (Keep the chicken thighs separated on a plate with wax paper if the oil isn't hot enough to cook yet.)

5. The oil is ready when a pinch of flour sizzles vigorously but doesn't brown immediately. Working in batches to avoid crowding and adding oil as necessary, put the chicken in the skillet. Cook until the coating browns and the cutlets release from the pan, 2 to 5 minutes; turn and cook the other side, 2 to 3 minutes usually. As they finish, drain on the rack while you bread and cook the remaining chicken.

6. Spread about one-third of the sauce in a 9 by 13-inch baking dish, and put the chicken in the pan; it's okay if the pieces overlap a little. Cover with the mozzarella, and bake until the sauce is bubbling and the cheese melts and browns in spots, 5 to 10 minutes.

7. As soon as the pan comes out of the oven, scatter the basil on top, drizzle with olive oil, and sprinkle with black pepper. Serve right away, passing more sauce and Parmesan cheese at the table.

Bitter Greens
Gratin, page 346

Gratin

The name describes a specific cooking method in France—au gratin—essentially anything browned in a shallow dish with a crisp topping of crumbs and grated cheese. Remember this when you make Bitter Greens Gratin, an undeniably rich dinner that's also packed full of virtuous vegetables. Socca Gratin, based on a thick batter made from chickpea flour—also known as besan, or gram flour—is a wonderful vegan alternative with a sort of unbelievable custardy texture. The difference between Sweet Potato Gratin with Pancetta and Taleggio and other gratins is that the potatoes aren't completely submerged in cheesy cream. Without question, it's still quite deluxe.

BITTER GREENS GRATIN

makes: 4 servings
time: 25 minutes

2 pounds bitter greens (like kale, escarole, collards, or a mix)

2 tablespoons unsalted butter

1 onion, chopped

1 tablespoon chopped garlic

Salt and pepper

1 cup heavy cream

4 eggs

½ cup grated Parmesan cheese (about 2 ounces)

½ cup breadcrumbs, preferably fresh (see page 173)

1. Turn on the broiler and position the rack 4 inches below the heat source. Separate the greens from their stems, if applicable, and chop the stems; tear the leaves into large pieces.

2. Put the butter in a large ovenproof skillet over medium heat. When it melts, add the onion, garlic, and chopped stems and sprinkle with salt and pepper. Cook, stirring occasionally, until the onion is soft, 3 to 5 minutes.

3. Add the greens a handful at a time, stirring as they wilt, and make room in the pan for more; continue until all the greens have been added, 3 to 5 minutes. Pour in the cream and adjust the heat so it bubbles steadily. Cook, stirring frequently, until the mixture thickens and the cream coats the back of a spoon, 3 to 5 minutes. Taste and adjust the seasoning.

4. Carefully crack the eggs onto the greens. Transfer the skillet to the broiler. Cook, watching like a hawk, until the whites have just set, 2 to 3 minutes. Sprinkle the Parmesan and breadcrumbs over the gratin and return to the broiler. Cook, still watching, until the cheese has melted and the topping is golden, 3 to 5 minutes. Serve hot or warm.

SOCCA GRATIN

makes: 4 servings
time: at least 1 hour, largely unattended

SUBSTITUTION IDEAS   Instead of green beans and tomatoes, try an approximate quantity—say 3 cups—of virtually any cooked vegetable. To make this more like a traditional gratin, see page 173 for some ways to use breadcrumbs, then sprinkle them over the top for the last 10 to 15 minutes of baking.

7 tablespoons olive oil

2 cups chickpea flour

Salt and pepper

1½ pounds green beans, trimmed and cut into 1-inch pieces

2 ripe tomatoes, chopped

1 tablespoon chopped garlic

2 cups cooked chickpeas (see page 83; one 15-ounce can, rinsed and drained, is fine)

1. Heat the oven to 400°F. Grease a 9 by 13-inch baking dish with 2 tablespoons oil. Put the chickpea flour and 2 cups water in a large bowl and whisk until combined. Add 2 tablespoons oil, a big pinch of salt, and some pepper. Whisk until the batter is smooth; let sit for at least 30 minutes (or cover and refrigerate for up to 12 hours).

2. Put the remaining 3 tablespoons oil in a large skillet over high heat. When it's hot, add the green beans, tomatoes, and garlic and sprinkle with salt and pepper. Cook, stirring frequently, until the pan is dry and the green beans are tender, 5 to 10 minutes. Taste, adjust the seasoning, and transfer to the prepared baking dish. Mash the chickpeas with a fork until most are broken and scatter them over the green beans.

3. Pour the chickpea batter evenly over the vegetable mixture. Bake until the gratin is golden brown, firm in the center, and separates from the sides of the pan, 25 to 35 minutes. To serve, cut the gratin into squares and serve hot or at room temperature.

● SWEET POTATO GRATIN
with pancetta and taleggio

makes: 4 servings
time: 1½ hours

1 pound sweet potatoes, peeled

1½ cups heavy cream

¼ teaspoon ground nutmeg

Salt and pepper

¼ cup chopped hazelnuts

1 tablespoon olive oil

8 ounces pancetta, chopped

8 ounces taleggio cheese

1. Heat the oven to 375°F. Slice the sweet potatoes crosswise about ⅛ inch thick (a food processor or mandoline makes this quick work). Put the cream in a pot with the nutmeg and pinch of salt and pepper; warm over medium heat just until steaming. Put the hazelnuts in a dry medium skillet over medium heat. Toast, shaking the pan occasionally, until they are golden and fragrant, 3 to 5 minutes. Transfer to a bowl.

2. Line a plate with paper towels. Put the oil in the skillet over medium heat. When it's hot, add the pancetta and cook, stirring occasionally, until cooked through and crisp, 5 to 10 minutes. Transfer the pancetta to the towels to drain. Remove and discard the rind from the cheese and chop.

3. Layer the potatoes, pancetta, and cheese in a 2-quart gratin or similar ovenproof dish, making sure to end with cheese. Pour the hot cream over all. Bake, undisturbed, until the potatoes are tender (a thin-bladed knife can be inserted easily) and the top is browned and bubbly, 40 to 50 minutes. Sprinkle with the hazelnuts and serve hot.

Baked Panzanella,
page 350

Casserole

The concept of a hot dish, a covered dish, or however you know casseroles, is begging for an update. Often the sauce comes from cream-of-something soup or, better still, homemade béchamel, as with the Easy Scalloped Scallops, which require hardly any prep after you make the sauce. To get to that luxurious warmth—I try to avoid the word *comfort* but it undeniably applies here—without dairy, the Vegan Baked Panzanella combines day-old bread with vegetable stock, baked into a custardlike backdrop for tomatoes and beans. Or with only a tad more work you can try this glorious and familiar rice and mushroom casserole, which has a few twists, like goat, the world's most popular meat.

● SCALLOPED SCALLOPS

makes: 4 servings
time: 30 minutes

3 tablespoons unsalted butter

3 tablespoons flour

2 cups milk, or more as needed

10 ounces baby spinach

1 cup grated fontina cheese (about 4 ounces)

Salt and pepper

1½ pounds sea scallops, patted dry

½ cup grated Parmesan cheese (about 2 ounces)

1. Turn the broiler to high and position the rack 4 inches below it. Melt the butter in a large ovenproof skillet over medium-low heat. Add the flour to the pan and whisk until smooth. Turn the heat to low and cook, whisking constantly, until the mixture darkens a bit, 2 to 3 minutes.

2. Add the milk and cook, whisking constantly, until the mixture has thickened slightly and coats the back of a spoon. Add a handful of spinach and cook until wilted; repeat until all the spinach is incorporated. Stir in the fontina cheese and season with salt and pepper. Cook until the cheese has melted, another 2 to 3 minutes. You want the consistency to be like creamed spinach; in the unlikely case that it's too thick, stir in more milk 1 tablespoon at a time.

3. Put the scallops in the sauce, in a single layer, giving each enough space to cook properly and sprinkle with salt and pepper. Transfer the skillet to the oven. Broil, watching like a hawk, until the sauce is bubbling and the scallops are just barely cooked, 3 to 5 minutes.

4. Carefully pull the skillet out, sprinkle the Parmesan cheese over the sauce and scallops, and return to the oven until the cheese is browned in spots, 2 to 3 minutes. Serve right away.

● BAKED PANZANELLA

makes: 4 to 6 servings
time: 1 hour

6 ounces crusty whole wheat bread (about ⅓ loaf)

6 tablespoons olive oil

8 ounces leeks, trimmed, well rinsed, and chopped

Salt and pepper

¾ cup vegetable stock (see page 87), or water

1½ pounds ripe Roma (plum) tomatoes, chopped

½ cup chopped fresh basil

2 cups cooked white beans (see page 82; or one 15-ounce can), drained

1 tablespoon chopped garlic

1. Heat the oven to 350°F. Cut the bread into ½-inch cubes; you should have about 4 cups. Put them on a baking sheet and drizzle with 2 tablespoons oil. Bake until golden brown and crisp, 15 to 20 minutes.

2. Put 2 tablespoons oil in a large skillet over medium heat. Add the leeks and sprinkle with salt and pepper. Cook, stirring occasionally, until very soft and silky, 15 to 20 minutes. Remove from the heat and stir in the stock, tomatoes, bread cubes, and basil. Taste and adjust the seasoning. Transfer the skillet to the oven and bake for 10 minutes while you make the bean topping.

3. Put the beans and garlic in a bowl and mash with a fork until crumbled but not pureed. Stir in the remaining 2 tablespoons oil and season with salt and pepper. Scatter the bean mixture on top of the casserole in an even layer and return the skillet to the oven. Continue baking until the top is browned and the stock has been completely absorbed, another 35 to 40 minutes. Serve hot or warm.

● CABRA CASSEROLE

makes: 4 servings
time: at least 2 hours, largely unattended

FINDING GOAT Look for boneless goat leg or shoulder—the best sources are farmers' markets, natural food stores, and Halal or other specialty butchers. It might be called goat "stew meat." Talk to your source about getting an equivalent; do not use rack or loin. If you still can't find boneless, buy 2 pounds bone-in goat leg or shoulder and cut the meat off the bone yourself. For a substitute, try boneless beef chuck or beef "stew meat."

3 tablespoons olive oil

1 pound boneless goat leg or shoulder, cut into 1-inch pieces

Salt and pepper

6 tablespoons unsalted butter

3 large or 4 medium shallots

1 pound fresh mushrooms (like cremini, shiitake, miatake, or a mix), cleaned and sliced

1½ cups wild rice

2½ cups chicken stock (see page 43) or water

1 cup fresh orange juice

½ cup heavy cream

4 ounces brioche or challah, torn into large chunks

¼ cup chopped fresh parsley

1 tablespoon chopped fresh thyme, or 1 teaspoon dried

1. Heat the oven to 350°F. Put the oil in a large ovenproof pot over medium-high heat. When it's hot, add the goat meat, working in batches if necessary to avoid crowding, and sprinkle with salt and pepper. Cook until the meat is well browned all over, 3 to 5 minutes per side, transferring the pieces to a plate as they finish.

2. Turn the heat to medium and add 2 tablespoons butter to the pot. When it's hot, add the shallots, sprinkle with salt and pepper, and cook until soft, 3 to 5 minutes. Add the mushrooms and cook, scraping up any browned bits from the bottom of the pan, until the mushrooms are browned, the liquid has evaporated, and the pan is dry again, 10 to 15 minutes.

3. Add the wild rice and stir to coat with the fat. Pour in 2 cups stock, the orange juice, and cream and season with salt and pepper. Return the meat to the pot and bring to a boil. Cover the pot and transfer to the oven. Cook for 1 hour, then if the cooking liquid has nearly cooked away, add the remaining ½ cup stock. Bake until the goat is fork-tender and the rice is just cooked through, another 30 to 45 minutes.

4. When the casserole is almost done, make the topping: Put the bread in a food processor and pulse three or four times, then let the machine run for a few seconds until the bread is coarsely chopped. Put the remaining 4 tablespoons butter in a large skillet over medium heat. When the butter melts, remove the pan from the heat and add the breadcrumbs, parsley, and thyme.

5. Raise the oven temperature to 400°F and uncover the pot. Sprinkle the breadcrumbs on top of the casserole and cook until the breadcrumbs are browned and crunchy, 5 to 10 minutes. Serve hot.

Moussaka

There are countless versions of this lasagna-like Greek eggplant dish, but I'm not crazy about the kind with the custard on top. Stewed Lamb Moussaka takes a different tack with a creamy cheese sauce, and is the perfect party food since you can assemble and then refrigerate for up to two days. All the flavors and ingredients of the classic are captured in Miracle Moussaka without needing to cook and assemble a bunch of separate components. And moussaka meets shepherd's pie with a nifty crackling nut sauce in the Vegan (and eggplant-free) mushroom and sweet potato version.

● MIRACLE MOUSSAKA

makes: 4 servings
time: 40 minutes

4 tablespoons olive oil

12 ounces eggplant, unpeeled, cut into 1-inch cubes

Salt and pepper

1 red onion, chopped

1 tablespoon chopped garlic

One 14-ounce can diced tomatoes, drained

1 pound ground lamb (or ground chuck)

2 tablespoons flour

1 teaspoon ground cinnamon

1 teaspoon dried oregano

⅔ cup milk

2 egg yolks

¼ cup chopped fresh parsley, for garnish

1. Heat the oven to 425°F. Grease a large ovenproof skillet with 2 tablespoons oil. Add the eggplant, sprinkle with salt and pepper, and toss to coat. Scatter the onion and garlic over the eggplant, followed by the tomatoes.

2. Generously season the lamb with salt and pepper. Dot the tomatoes evenly with dollops of ground lamb; sprinkle again with salt and pepper. Transfer the pan to the oven and bake, undisturbed, until the mixture sizzles, and browns in spots, 10 to 15 minutes.

3. Put the remaining 2 tablespoons oil and the flour in a small saucepan over medium-low heat. Cook, whisking almost constantly, until the flour turns golden and begins to stick, 8 to 12 minutes. Stir in the cinnamon, oregano, and a sprinkle of salt and pepper, and keep cooking and whisking until fragrant, less than a minute more. Remove from the heat and add the milk, whisking constantly until smooth. Whisk in the egg yolks.

4. Remove the skillet from the oven and drizzle the sauce over the meat and vegetables; shake the pan to distribute the liquid. Continue baking until the moussaka is hot and bubbly but the sauce is still a little loose, 7 to 10 minutes. Remove from the oven and let the moussaka set for 10 minutes. Garnish with the parsley and serve.

Stewed Lamb
Moussaka,
page 354

MUSHROOM–SWEET POTATO MOUSSAKA

makes: 4 to 6 servings
time: 6 hours, largely unattended

1 cup raw cashews

2 pounds mushrooms (preferably an assortment), trimmed and sliced

4 tablespoons olive oil

Salt and pepper

1 tablespoon chopped garlic

2 tablespoons chopped fresh oregano, or 2 teaspoons dried

1 large onion, chopped

2 teaspoons ground cinnamon

½ teaspoon ground nutmeg

One 28-ounce can crushed tomatoes

2 pounds sweet potatoes, peeled and cut into chunks

1. Soak the cashews in 2 cups water for at least 4 hours. Drain and reserve the liquid. Puree the cashews in a blender, adding the reserved water 2 tablespoons at a time until they become the consistency of buttercream, 6 to 8 tablespoons total.

2. Heat the oven to 400°F. Line a rimmed baking sheet with parchment and add the mushrooms and 2 tablespoons oil. Sprinkle with salt and pepper and toss to coat. Transfer to the oven and bake, stirring every 5 minutes, until the mushrooms are crisp and the pan is dry, 20 to 25 minutes. Stir in the garlic and oregano; taste and adjust the seasoning. Reduce the temperature to 350°F.

3. Put the remaining 2 tablespoons oil in a large pot over medium heat. When it's hot, add the onion and sprinkle with salt and pepper. Cook, stirring occasionally, until the onion softens and starts to turn golden, 5 to 8 minutes. Add the cinnamon and nutmeg and stir until fragrant, about 30 seconds, then pour in the tomatoes. Bring to a boil, then adjust the heat so the mixture bubbles gently.

Cook, stirring once in a while, until the sauce has thickened and the flavors have combined, 30 to 35 minutes; taste and adjust the seasoning.

4. Put the potatoes in a large pot with enough cold water to cover by about 1 inch. Add a generous pinch of salt and bring it to a boil. Keep the water bubbling steadily until the potatoes are fork-tender, anywhere from 10 to 25 minutes depending on the size of the pieces. Drain them, reserving some of the cooking water.

5. Mash the potatoes right in the pot with a potato masher or spatula. Add two-thirds of the cashew cream and about ¼ cup reserved cooking water, and sprinkle with salt and pepper. If the potatoes are too thick, add cooking water 1 tablespoon at a time until they are creamy. Taste and adjust the seasoning.

6. Put half the tomato sauce in an 8- or 9-inch square baking dish. Add the mushrooms in an even layer. Carefully spread the mashed potatoes on top to completely cover the dish. Spoon the remaining cashew sauce on top and spread it around. Transfer the pan to the oven and bake until the sauce is bubbling and the top is browned, 45 to 50 minutes. Let the moussaka rest for a few minutes, then serve.

STEWED LAMB MOUSSAKA

makes: 4 to 6 servings
time: 3 hours

2 pounds large eggplant

Salt

1½ cups milk

2 bay leaves

Grated zest of 1 lemon

5 tablespoons olive oil

1½ pounds boneless lamb shoulder, cut into 1-inch chunks

Pepper

1 red onion, chopped

2 tablespoons minced garlic

One 28-ounce can whole tomatoes

½ cup dried currants

One 3-inch cinnamon stick

4 whole cloves

4 allspice berries

Several fresh thyme sprigs

2 tablespoons unsalted butter, plus more for greasing the pan

2 tablespoons flour

1 cup grated Kefalotyri or Pecorino Romano cheese (about 4 ounces)

2 tablespoons chopped fresh dill, for garnish

1. Slice the eggplant lengthwise between ¼ and ½ inch thick. Put the slices in a colander, sprinkle generously with salt, rub it into all sides, and set in the sink to drain. Put the milk, bay leaves, and lemon zest in a small saucepan over medium heat and cook, stirring once or twice just until steaming, about 5 minutes. Let the mixture steep while you make the lamb sauce.

2. Heat 2 tablespoons oil in a large pot over medium-high heat. Add half the lamb, sprinkle with salt and pepper, and cook, turning the pieces as they release, until browned on all sides, 5 to 10 minutes. As they cook, transfer the pieces to a plate and add the remaining lamb to the pot until all has been browned.

3. Spoon off all but about 2 tablespoons of the fat. Add the onion to the pot and raise the heat to medium-high. Cook, stirring occasionally, until the onion is soft and starting to turn golden, 5 to 8 minutes. Add the garlic and cook for 30 seconds. Return the lamb to the pot and add the tomatoes and currants. Season with salt and pepper. Bring to a boil, then adjust the heat so the mixture bubbles gently.

4. Tie the cinnamon stick, cloves, allspice, and thyme in a square of cheesecloth. Add the bundle to the sauce, cover, and cook, stirring once in a while, until the lamb is fork-tender and the sauce has thickened, 1½ to 2 hours. Heat the oven to 400°F.

5. Rinse the eggplant and pat it dry. Smear 1 tablespoon oil on a rimmed baking sheet, and put the eggplant on the sheet in a single layer. Drizzle the remaining 2 tablespoons oil over the top, and sprinkle with salt and pepper. Bake until the eggplant is browned and the pan is dry, 20 to 30 minutes. Reduce the oven temperature to 350°F. (Both the eggplant and lamb can be made ahead to this point and refrigerated for up to a day.)

6. When you're ready to assemble the moussaka, grease a deep 2-quart baking dish with some butter. Put the 2 tablespoons butter in a small saucepan over medium-low heat. When it foams, whisk in the flour. Lower the heat so the mixture doesn't burn and cook, whisking almost constantly, until the mixture turns tan, 2 to 3 minutes. Strain in the steeped milk a little bit at a time, whisking constantly. Cook, still over low heat and whisking frequently, until the mixture thickens, just a couple minutes. Stir in the cheese and sprinkle with salt and pepper, cover, and remove from the heat.

7. Discard the seasoning bundle from the lamb sauce. Transfer the meat to a cutting board and shred it with a knife and fork; return it to the sauce.

8. Line a large baking dish with one-third of the eggplant and cover with half the lamb sauce. Top with another layer eggplant, the rest of the lamb, and finally the remaining eggplant. Spoon the cheese sauce over the top. Bake until the moussaka is bubbling and the top is golden brown, 45 to 50 minutes. Sprinkle with the dill, let the moussaka set for a few minutes, then serve hot.

The Whole Enchilada

The texture of enchiladas is incredible; getting there can be a bit of a journey. That's the fun if you decide to go for the Chicken Enchiladas Verde. Either devote an afternoon to the project or tackle the components incrementally. Or go the polar-opposite route and take the road to Cheese Enchiladas, which seem like utter heresy until you pull the pan out of the oven. The Vegan recipe is flexible for all seasons: Use frozen corn and canned tomatoes most of the year, and fresh produce in the summer.

Cheese
Enchiladas,
page 358

CHEESE ENCHILADAS

makes: 4 servings
time: 30 minutes

1 red onion, halved and thinly sliced

Salt

3 tablespoons olive oil

2 tablespoons chopped garlic

1 tablespoon chili powder

2 teaspoons ground cumin

¼ teaspoon cayenne, or to taste

One 28-ounce can crushed tomatoes

Pepper

2½ cups grated mild melting cheese (like casero, Chihuahua, or Jack, about 8 ounces)

Eight 8-inch flour tortillas

½ cup sour cream

¼ cup chopped fresh cilantro

2 limes, quartered

1. Put the onion in a small bowl. Add a large pinch of salt and enough cold water to cover and let sit while you prepare the rest of the dish.

2. Heat the oven to 450°F. Put the oil in a small saucepan over medium heat. When it's hot, add the garlic and cook, stirring once in a while until soft, 2 to 3 minutes. Add the chili powder, cumin, and cayenne and stir until fragrant, 30 seconds or so, then add the tomatoes and sprinkle with salt and pepper. Bring to a boil, then turn off the heat; taste and adjust the seasoning.

3. Spread ½ cup of the tomato sauce on a rimmed baking sheet. Reserve ½ cup of the grated cheese. Top each tortilla with a ¼ cup cheese and roll to enclose the filling. Put the enchilada on the baking sheet, seam side down.

4. Fill and roll the remaining tortillas, pour the remaining sauce on top, and sprinkle with the remaining ½ cup cheese. Bake until the cheese has melted and the sauce is heated through, 10 to 15 minutes. Drain the onion. Let the enchiladas set for a couple minutes, then serve, garnished with sour cream, cilantro, and the onion and passing the lime wedges at the table.

SWEET POTATO AND CORN ENCHILADAS
with guacamole

makes: 4 servings
time: 2 hours, largely unattended

2 large guajillo or other medium-hot dried chiles

5 tablespoons good-quality vegetable oil

2 large yellow onions, chopped

2 tablespoons chopped garlic

Two 28-ounce cans whole peeled tomatoes, with their liquid

1 tablespoon sugar

Salt and pepper

½ cup chopped fresh cilantro

5 tablespoons lime juice

1 pound sweet potatoes, peeled and cut into ½-inch pieces

2 cups corn kernels (frozen are fine; no need to defrost)

1 tablespoon chopped fresh oregano, or 1 teaspoon dried

Eight 8-inch whole wheat tortillas

2 ripe avocados

1 jalapeño, seeded if you like and chopped

1 teaspoon ground cumin

1. Heat the oven to 425°F. Put the chiles in a small skillet over medium heat and cook, turning occasionally, until fragrant, 3 to 5 minutes. Transfer to a bowl and cover with boiling water and a small plate to keep them submerged. Soak until soft and pliable, about 30 minutes. Drain and reserve the soaking liquid, then remove the stems and as many seeds as you like from the chiles and chop them.

2. Put 4 tablespoons oil in a large pot over medium heat. When it's hot, add the chiles, onions, and garlic and cook, stirring occasionally, until the onions soften, 3 to 5 minutes. Add the tomatoes and sugar and season with salt and pepper. Adjust the heat so the mixture bubbles gently and cook, stirring occasionally, until the mixture has thickened and come together, 20 to 30 minutes. Add a little soaking water if the sauce gets too thick.

3. Stir in ¼ cup of the cilantro and 3 tablespoons of the lime juice. Use an immersion blender to puree the sauce in the pan. Or cool the mixture, and working in batches, carefully puree in a blender or food processor. Taste and adjust the seasoning. (You can make and refrigerate the sauce up to 2 days in advance.)

4. Put the sweet potatoes on a large rimmed baking sheet. Drizzle with 1 tablespoon oil, sprinkle with salt and pepper, and stir to combine. Roast until they brown a bit and release from the pan, 15 to 20 minutes, then turn with a spatula. Scatter the corn and oregano around the potatoes, and return to the oven, stirring with the spatula once or twice, until the potatoes are tender and the corn is browned in spots, about 15 minutes.

5. Spread 1 cup of the sauce in a 9 by 13-inch baking dish. Put a thin layer of sauce on a plate. Drag a tortilla through the sauce on the plate, turning to coat both sides. Let it sit for moment to become pliable. Fill with a heaping ¼ cup vegetable mixture and roll to enclose the filling. Nestle the rolled tortilla in the baking pan, seam side down. Repeat with the remaining tortillas and filling, adding more sauce to the plate if necessary, and pour any leftover sauce on top. Bake until the top is browned in places and bubbling, 25 to 30 minutes.

6. Let the enchiladas cool a bit while you make the guacamole. Halve the avocados, scoop out the flesh, and add to a medium bowl. Roughly mash it with a fork until it starts to become creamy. Stir in the remaining ¼ cup cilantro, remaining 2 tablespoons lime juice, the jalapeño, and cumin, mix, then taste and adjust the seasoning. Serve the enchiladas with a spoonful of guacamole.

● CHICKEN ENCHILADAS VERDE

makes: 4 to 6 servings
time: 3 hours

1 whole chicken (3 to 4 pounds), trimmed of excess fat

4 large onions, 2 quartered and 2 chopped

4 bay leaves

1 cinnamon stick

Salt

1½ pounds tomatillos, husked and left whole

2 medium poblano or other mild fresh green chiles

1 or 2 serrano or other hot fresh green chiles

3 tablespoons olive oil, plus more for frying the tortillas

2 tablespoons chopped garlic

1 teaspoon dried oregano (preferably Mexican)

Pepper

½ cup chopped fresh cilantro

¼ cup fresh lime juice

Twelve 6-inch corn tortillas

4 ounces cotija cheese, crumbled

(recipe continues)

1. Put the chicken, quartered onions, bay leaves, and cinnamon stick in a large pot with 8 cups water (the chicken won't be completely submerged); add a large pinch of salt. Bring to a boil, then reduce the heat so the liquid bubbles steadily but gently and skim any foam that rises to the surface. Cover and cook, checking once or twice, until an instant-read thermometer inserted into the thickest part of the thigh reads 155° to 165°F, or the juices run clear when cut to the bone, 35 to 45 minutes. Remove the chicken from the pot to cool in a shallow bowl and save the cooking liquid.

2. Heat the oven to 450°F. Put the tomatillos and chiles on a large rimmed baking sheet lined with foil and roast until the skins are lightly browned and blistered, 15 to 20 minutes. Wrap the chiles in foil immediately to steam. When they're cool enough to handle, remove the skin, seeds, and any membranes. Chop the chiles and tomatillos, saving their juices.

3. When the chicken is cool enough to handle, remove the meat from the bones (pulling off the skin), chop or shred enough to make 3 cups, and save the rest for another use. Put the 3 cups chicken in a large bowl. Return the carcass and any scraps to the pot without adding more water. (If the bones aren't submerged, break them up a bit.) Bring the stock back to a boil and reduce the heat so the liquid bubbles steadily. Cook, stirring occasionally, until it's reduced by an inch or so and is fragrant, 40 to 60 minutes. Strain into a wide pot, discarding the solids. Bring the liquid to a boil, and reduce until you have about 1½ cups, another 15 to 30 minutes.

4. Put the oil in a large deep skillet over medium heat. When it's hot, add the chopped onions and the garlic and cook, stirring occasionally, until very soft and lightly browned, 10 to 15 minutes. Add the chopped tomatillos, chiles, the oregano, 1 cup of the reduced chicken stock, and a large pinch of salt and pepper; stir and bring to a low bubble. Cook, stirring occasionally, until the mixture is slightly thickened, 10 to 15 minutes. Stir in the cilantro and lime juice and taste and adjust the seasoning.

5. Use an immersion blender to puree the finished sauce in the pan. Or cool the mixture slightly and working in batches, transfer to a blender or food processor, and puree carefully. Stir a little sauce into the chopped chicken to moisten it. Transfer the remaining sauce to a bowl and wipe out the skillet.

6. Preheat the oven to 400°F. Line a large baking sheet with kitchen towels. Put ½ inch oil in the skillet over medium-high heat. When it's hot, use tongs to dip the tortillas in the oil one at a time until they're just pliable, about 10 seconds. Add more oil to the pan as needed. Drain the tortillas on the prepared pan.

7. Spread ½ cup of the tomatillo sauce in a 9 by 13–inch baking dish. Put a layer of sauce on a plate. Add a tortilla and turn to coat both sides with sauce. Fill with 2 tablespoons or so chicken and roll to enclose the filling. Nestle the tortilla into the baking pan, seam side down. Repeat with the remaining tortillas. Make a row of 8 enchiladas in the center of the pan; put the remaining 4 along the sides to fill the gaps in the pan. Pour any leftover sauce on top of the enchiladas.

8. Bake until bubbly and browned, 25 to 30 minutes. Let the enchiladas set for a couple minutes, then sprinkle with the cotija cheese and serve.

Tamales

Extreme projects take extreme measures to make them accessible. So I focused on the common thread: the dough. The secret ingredient in the Vegan tamale pie is millet, a whole grain that looks and tastes a lot like corn. The Easy tamale—another pie known as a picada—tops a quick fajita stir-fry with a crisp corn crust. For the real deal, dig into Carnitas Tamales with Smoky Salsa, which takes advantage of a classic technique to leave one end of the corn husk open. A little less fussy and a lot more fluffy.

● BEEF FAJITAS PICADA

makes: 4 servings
time: 40 minutes

6 tablespoons unsalted butter or lard, cut into pieces

1 cup masa harina

1 teaspoon baking powder

Salt

1 egg

¾ cup boiling water

2 tablespoons good-quality vegetable oil, or more as needed

1 pound boneless beef sirloin steak, sliced

Pepper

1 large onion, halved and sliced

1 bell pepper, any color, cored and sliced

1 tablespoon chopped garlic

1 tablespoon chili powder

4 ripe Roma (plum) tomatoes, chopped (canned whole tomatoes are fine)

½ cup chopped fresh cilantro

1. Put the butter in a large skillet (preferably non-stick or well-seasoned cast iron) on the middle rack of the oven and turn the heat to 400°F. Combine the masa harina, baking powder, and a big pinch of salt in a large bowl. Use a fork to whisk in the egg and boiling water. The picada batter should have the consistency of drop-cookie dough.

2. When the butter in the skillet melts, carefully remove the pan from the oven and add all but 2 tablespoons into the masa batter. Stir once more and if the batter doesn't drop easily from a spoon, whisk in tap water, 1 tablespoon at a time. Scrape the batter into the skillet and spread into an even layer. Bake until the top is firm and the bottom and sides are golden, 15 to 20 minutes. Remove the pan from the oven, carefully turn the whole picada, and let it sit in the hot pan.

3. While the picada is in the oven, put the oil in a large skillet over medium-high heat. When it's hot, add half the beef. Sprinkle with salt and pepper, turn the heat to high, and cook, stirring occasionally, until it's lightly browned, 3 to 5 minutes. Transfer to a bowl and repeat with the remaining beef, adding more oil if necessary to keep the meat from sticking.

4. Add the onion, bell pepper, and garlic to the pan and sprinkle with salt and pepper. Cook, stirring often, until the vegetables are soft and browned in spots, 5 to 7 minutes. Add the chili powder, stir a couple times, then add the tomatoes. Return the beef to the pan and stir to combine; cook just until the beef and tomatoes are heated through. Stir in the cilantro, taste, and adjust the seasoning. Cut the picada into 4 wedges and serve hot with the fajita mixture spooned on top.

● MILLET TAMALE PIE

makes: 4 servings
time: 2 hours, largely unattended

12 ounces poblano chiles

12 ounces green bell peppers

6 tablespoons olive oil

1 cup millet

Salt

¼ cup oat or rice milk, or more as needed

1½ cups cooked black beans (see page 82; or one 15-ounce can), drained

4 scallions, chopped

2 tablespoons chopped fresh oregano

1 tablespoon chopped garlic

1 tablespoon ground cumin

2 teaspoons ground coriander

Pepper

3 limes, 2 cut into quarters

1. Heat the oven to 450°F. Put the poblano and bell peppers on a rimmed baking sheet lined with foil. Roast, turning once or twice, until the skins blister, 50 to 60 minutes. When they're done, wrap them in the foil and let them steam until cool.

2. Lower the oven to 400°F. Grease a medium ovenproof skillet or 9-inch square baking dish with 2 tablespoons oil. Put the millet in a large saucepan with a big pinch of salt. Add water to cover by about 1½ inches. Bring to a boil, then adjust the heat so the mixture bubbles gently. Cover and cook, stirring occasionally, until the grains are overcooked and begin to burst, 30 to 40 minutes. If the grains get too dry before they're overcooked, add just enough water to keep them from burning. They're ready when they're no longer independent kernels, look more like thick mashed potatoes, and are pretty dry; remove the pot from the heat. Add the milk and 2 tablespoons oil, stir with a fork, taste, and adjust the seasoning, then cover the pot again.

3. Remove the skin, seeds, and stems from the chiles and bell peppers and slice them. Put them in a large bowl with the beans, scallions, oregano, garlic, cumin, and coriander and sprinkle with salt and pepper. Drizzle with the remaining 2 tablespoons oil and squeeze in the juice of 1 lime. Toss to combine, taste, and adjust the seasoning, adding more lime juice if you like.

4. Transfer the poblano filling to the prepared pan. Check the millet mixture; it should drop from a spoon like cookie dough. If not, stir in more milk 1 tablespoon at a time. Dot the top of the filling with the millet mixture, then spread it around a little with the back of a spoon, allowing some of the filling to show. Bake until the top is golden brown, 40 to 50 minutes. Cut the pie into quarters and serve with the remaining lime wedges.

CARNITAS TAMALES with smoky salsa

makes: 24 tamales
time: 4 hours, largely unattended

24 dried corn husks

2 pounds boneless pork shoulder, with fat, cut into 1-inch chunks

1 white onion, quartered

5 garlic cloves, lightly crushed

2 bay leaves

Salt and pepper

1 cup and 2 tablespoons lard, cubed

1 teaspoon baking powder

2 pounds ground fresh masa, or 3½ cups masa harina

2¼ cups chicken stock (see page 43), or more as needed

2 shallots, chopped

1 fresh green chile (like jalapeño or serrano), seeded and chopped

2 chipotle chiles in adobo, chopped, or to taste

1 pound ripe Roma (plum) tomatoes, cored and chopped (about 2 cups)

¼ cup chopped fresh cilantro leaves

3 tablespoons cider vinegar

1. Soak the corn husks in water for at least 3 hours. Put the pork, onion, garlic, bay leaves, and a pinch of salt and pepper in a large pot and add water to cover. Turn the heat to high, bring to a boil, and skim any foam that comes to the surface. Partially cover and adjust the heat so the mixture bubbles steadily. Cook until the meat is quite tender, about an hour, then let stand until cool enough to handle.

2. Chop the meat into bite-sized pieces, return to the pan, and cook over medium-high heat until all the liquid is evaporated. You want the meat to fry in the fat until it's crisp and brown.

3. With an electric mixer with the whisk attachment, beat the 1 cup cubed lard with 1 teaspoon salt and the baking powder until fluffy. If you're using fresh masa, add one-third of the masa and one-third of

the stock alternately, beating continuously. If you're using the masa harina, mix with the stock a little at a time just until combined and stop when the mixture is crumbly, then add the masa harina mixture to the lard. With either method, beat until the dough is light and fluffy, adding more stock if the mixture is too dry. The mixture is ready when a small ball of the dough floats in water.

4. Drain the husks and pat dry with paper towels. With the wide end of the husk nearest to you, put 2 tablespoons of the masa dough on a husk near the wide edge, then use the back of a spoon to spread the dough into a 4 by 3-inch rectangle along the right edge of the husk, leaving at least ½ inch on each side. Spoon 1 tablespoon crispy pork lengthwise down the center of the dough rectangle. To wrap the tamales, fold the sides in over the dough, then fold up the tapered end (the wider end will remain open during steaming) and secure the package around the center with kitchen string. Repeat with the remaining ingredients.

5. Prepare a large steamer by setting a steamer rack about 2 inches above gently boiling water. Stand the tamales on the rack, open side up. Cover all the tamales with another corn husk, cover, and steam until done, 40 to 50 minutes. To test for doneness, remove a tamale and open the husk—the filling should be firm and come away easily from the husk. Let the tamales rest for at least 15 minutes.

6. While the tamales are steaming, put the remaining 2 tablespoons lard in a medium saucepan or skillet and turn the heat to medium. When the fat melts, add the shallots and fresh chile, and cook, stirring occasionally, until the shallots begin to brown at the edges, 5 to 8 minutes.

7. Add the chipotles, tomatoes, and ½ cup water and adjust the heat so the mixture bubbles steadily but not violently. Cook until the tomatoes have broken down, 10 to 15 minutes. Stir in the cilantro and vinegar. Taste and adjust the seasoning. Cool for a few minutes, then put the mixture in a blender and puree until smooth. To serve, open each tamale a little and spoon in some salsa.

Mole

The quick answer: *Mole* is a generic term for a style of rich, complex Mexican sauces and the dishes made with them. Most are characterized by a long list of ingredients. Sometimes they contain chocolate, but they would never be confused with dessert. Turkey with Black Bean Mole is obviously a distilled version that hits the notes you want to deliver in a highly seasoned sauce. Though green mole is lighter than the darker sauces, Fried Tofu with Vegetable Mole Verde makes the point that the stew can still be hearty and dramatically seasoned. *Manchamanteles* means "one who stains tablecloths" and it contains a laundry list (get it?) of ingredients that come together in a fruity, not too dark mole. You'll want a big stack of tortillas with any of them; see pages 203 and 207.

● TURKEY with black bean mole

makes: 4 servings
time: 25 minutes

One 28-ounce can crushed tomatoes

2 cups cooked black beans (see page 82; or one 15-ounce can), drained

2 ounces good dark chocolate (at least 80% cacao)

1 garlic clove, chopped

½ cup raw almonds

1½ teaspoons ground cumin

1 teaspoon paprika

½ teaspoon ground cinnamon

4 tablespoons olive oil

8 small turkey breast cutlets (about 1½ pounds)

Salt and pepper

1 lime, cut into wedges

½ cup Mexican crema or sour cream, for garnish

1. Turn the broiler to high; position the rack 4 inches below the heat. Put the tomatoes and beans in a blender with the chocolate, garlic, almonds, cumin, paprika, and cinnamon, and puree until smooth. The sauce should be thick but pourable; if not, add water 1 tablespoon at a time.

2. Put 2 tablespoons oil in a large skillet over medium-high heat. When it's hot, slowly pour in the mole sauce (careful: it will splatter a bit). Stir constantly until it darkens and begins to boil. Adjust the heat so that the mixture bubbles gently but steadily, cover, and cook, stirring occasionally, while you cook the turkey, 10 minutes.

3. Put the turkey on a rimmed baking sheet in a single layer. Drizzle with the remaining 2 tablespoons oil and sprinkle with salt and pepper. Broil until the turkey is opaque and golden on top, 5 to 10 minutes, depending on your broiler. It won't be cooked through.

4. Uncover the sauce and add a little water if it looks too thick. Transfer the partially browned turkey along with any juices from the baking sheet to the skillet with the sauce in a single layer, browned side up., Return the sauce to a gentle bubble and cover again. Cook, spooning sauce over the turkey once or twice and checking to make sure it's not sticking, until the cutlets are no longer pink in the thickest parts, 5 to 10 minutes. Taste the sauce and adjust the seasoning. Serve hot with the lime wedges and a dollop of crema.

Manchamanteles,
page 368

FRIED TOFU
with vegetable mole verde

makes: 4 servings
time: about 1 hour

1 pound tomatillos, husked and rinsed

1 cup hulled pumpkin seeds (pepitas)

6 tablespoons good-quality vegetable oil, or more
   as needed

2 large onions, chopped

2 tablespoons chopped garlic

1 jalapeño, seeded and chopped

1 tablespoon chopped fresh epazote
   (or 1 tablespoon each chopped fresh oregano
   and mint)

1 cup vegetable stock (see page 87) or water

Salt and pepper

1½ blocks firm tofu (about 1½ pounds)

8 ounces chayote

1½ cups corn kernels (frozen is fine)

½ cup chopped fresh cilantro leaves, plus more
   for garnish

3 limes, halved

1. Heat the oven to 450°F. Put the tomatillos on a rimmed baking sheet and roast, shaking the pan occasionally, until the skins are lightly browned and blistered, 15 to 20 minutes. Let the tomatillos cool in the pan.

2. While the tomatillos are roasting, put the pumpkin seeds in a large dry pot over medium heat. Cook, stirring often, until they are puffed and golden, 5 to 10 minutes. Transfer to a food processor or blender and pulse a few times to chop. Add the tomatillos and their juices and pulse once or twice just to break them into bite-sized chunks.

3. Add 3 tablespoons oil to the pot and return to medium heat. When it's hot, add the onions and garlic and cook, stirring occasionally, until very soft and lightly browned, 10 to 15 minutes. Raise the heat so the mixture sizzles, add the jalapeño and epazote and cook, stirring constantly until fragrant, just a minute or 2. Add the tomatillo mixture, stock, and a large pinch of salt and pepper; stir and bring to a boil. Reduce the heat so the mixture bubbles gently but steadily, and cook, stirring occasionally, until the mole thickens, 10 to 15 minutes. Cover and keep warm.

4. Cut the tofu crosswise into slices ½ inch thick. Spread the pieces out on towels to drain; pat them dry. Put the remaining 3 tablespoons oil in a large skillet over medium heat. Line a baking sheet with paper towels. When the oil is hot, put some of the tofu into the pan, taking care not to crowd the pieces, and cook until they're browned and release easily, 6 to 8 minutes; turn and repeat with the other side, 3 to 5 minutes more. As they finish, transfer the pieces to the prepared pan to drain and sprinkle with salt and pepper. Repeat with the remaining tofu; add more oil to the pan if necessary to keep the tofu from sticking.

5. Use the largest holes on a box grater to grate the chayote around the seed. Add the corn and chayote to the oil remaining in the skillet you used for the tofu and sprinkle with salt and pepper. Cook for 2 minutes, undisturbed, then continue cooking, stirring occasionally, until the vegetables are browned in places and tender, another 5 to 10 minutes.

6. Add the vegetables to the mole along with ¼ cup of the cilantro and the juice from 2 limes; taste, and adjust the seasoning, adding more lime juice if you like, and make sure the sauce is still bubbling. Add the tofu, toss gently to coat, and heat through, 2 to 3 minutes. Serve the tofu and mole hot, garnished with more cilantro.

● MANCHAMANTELES

makes: 6 to 8 servings
time: about 4 hours, largely unattended

2 ounces mild to medium dried chiles (like pasilla,
   guajillo, ancho, or a combination)

1 cup boiling water

½ cup raw almonds

¼ cup roasted, unsalted peanuts

2 tablespoons tahini

2 tablespoons unsweetened cocoa powder

1 large onion, chopped

1 head garlic, cloves separated and peeled

About 12 ounces ripe Roma (plum) tomatoes,
   cored (one 14-ounce can, drained, is fine)

1 thick slice stale white bread

¼ cup good-quality vegetable oil, plus more
   for frying

3 or 4 bay leaves

One 3-inch cinnamon stick

2 tablespoons ground cumin

1 tablespoon ground coriander

1 teaspoon ground allspice

1 teaspoon ground cloves

Salt and pepper

2 cups pineapple juice

1 pound boneless pork shoulder, cut into
   2-inch pieces

4 boneless, skinless chicken thighs, cut into strips
   (about 12 ounces)

2 cups chopped fresh pineapple (about ½ large
   pineapple)

1 cup dried apricots, chopped

½ cup raisins

1 black-ripe plantain

Lime wedges

1. Put the chiles in a medium skillet over medium heat and cook, shaking the pan occasionally, until toasted and fragrant, 3 to 5 minutes. Transfer them to a small bowl, pour in the boiling water, and top with a small plate to keep them submerged. Soak until soft, 20 to 30 minutes. Strain and reserve the soaking liquid, then remove the stems and seeds from the chiles.

2. Working in batches if necessary, put the chiles, almonds, peanuts, tahini, cocoa, onion, garlic, tomatoes, and bread in a blender or food processor with just enough of the soaking liquid to get the machine running and puree until smooth.

3. Put the oil in a large pot over medium heat. Add the puree, the bay leaves, cinnamon stick, cumin, coriander, allspice, and cloves, and sprinkle with salt and pepper. Cook, stirring frequently and scraping the bottom of the pan, until it begins to color and become fragrant, 3 to 5 minutes. Turn the heat to low and continue cooking, stirring occasionally, until the mixture is deeply colored and nearly dry, another 15 to 20 minutes.

4. Slowly stir in the pineapple juice and 2 cups water and add the pork. Bring to a boil, then reduce the heat so the mixture bubbles gently. Cook until the pork is fork-tender, 1½ to 2 hours. Add the chicken, pineapple, and dried fruit, and cook, covered, until chicken is cooked through, 15 to 20 minutes.

5. Cut both tips off the plantain, then cut it into 3 sections. Use a sharp knife to make 3 lengthwise slits in the skin of each section, peel off each piece of the skin, then trim any remaining skin from the plantain with a paring knife. Cut the plantains into ½-inch rounds.

6. Put about ⅛ inch oil in a large skillet over medium heat. Line a plate with paper towels. When the oil is hot, add the plantains, working in batches if necessary to avoid crowding. Cook, undisturbed, until they brown and release easily from the pan, 3 to 5 minutes. Turn and repeat with the other side. As they're done, transfer them to the prepared plate and repeat with the remaining pieces, adding more oil as necessary to keep them from sticking. Stir the plantains into the mole. Serve the mole hot and pass the lime wedges at the table

MY APPROACH TO SOURCING MEAT AND FISH

Nothing is more personal than choosing the food you buy and eat. Since these decisions can affect the health of you *and* the planet, it's important to consider ways to shift the balance in our diets toward a wide variety of fruits and vegetables, which have less impact on the land than meat and fish. Vegan dinners—like the recipes in this book—are one way. Another is to seek out animal products that are raised and harvested sustainably, without antibiotics and environmental deterioration.

To the extent that you are able, buy sustainably and humanely raised meat. The best source is usually the nearest farmers' market, where you can talk to the people making the animal welfare decisions. Smaller farms are much less likely to rely on industrial soy and corn for feed, or to pollute waterways; the animals are less likely to be stressed out or abused.

If you don't have a local farmers' market, do your best at the grocery store. "Natural" and "free-range" are nearly meaningless terms, watered down by food conglomerates ("organic" at least requires certification, though it's not a guarantee of humane conditions). However, these options are still a step up from conventionally raised animals, so choose them when you can. And if you're really stuck for humane, additive-, and antibiotic-free options, well, go with a vegan recipe—that's what they're for.

Fish is a particular challenge to source with an eye for sustainability. Fish farming practices have the same set of problems as livestock and wild fish can be caught with no regard for mercury levels or endangered species status. If your grocery store has a fish counter, someone there might be able to help identify at least what's been farmed, where the wild seafood came from, and how it was caught. The best fishmongers will be able to suggest what fish to buy based on your planned recipe as well as environmental practices. If you don't have a dedicated staff to talk to, you can always check my recommendations against those of the Monterey Bay Aquarium's Seafood Watch—even from your phone—for the most up-to-date information.

Winter Stew

Slow braising typically defines stew, whether it's made with meat, poultry, or vegetables. The Beef Stew with Baked Potatoes pictured here is streamlined for immediate gratification. When you crave something substantial yet plant-based, turn to Bean and Parsnip Stew with Oregano Pistou, with a bright French-style pesto. For special-occasion cooking, Osso Buco's long braising time with a mix of garlic, anchovies, and white wine work wonders on veal shanks to coax unsurpassed tenderness and an amazing sauce.

● BEEF STEW with baked potatoes

makes: 4 servings
time: about an hour, largely unattended

2 large starchy potatoes (like Idaho or other russets)

4 tablespoons olive oil

Salt

1½ pounds boneless beef chuck or round, cut into ½-inch pieces

Pepper

1 onion, chopped

2 large carrots, chopped

3 celery stalks, chopped, with leaves reserved

2 tablespoons flour

1 tablespoon Worcestershire sauce

¼ cup ketchup

1. Heat the oven to 425°F and line a baking sheet with parchment. Cut the potatoes in half lengthwise, put them on the prepared pan, rub all over with 2 tablespoons oil, sprinkle with salt, and turn cut side down. Transfer to the oven, even if it's not hot yet. Roast, undisturbed, until the potatoes are browned and a skewer or sharp knife inserted meets almost no resistance, 30 to 40 minutes.

2. Put 1 tablespoon oil in a large pot over medium-high heat. When it's hot, add half the beef, sprinkle with salt and pepper, and cook without moving the pieces until browned on one side, 3 to 5 minutes. Remove from the pot, add the remaining tablespoon oil, and repeat with the remaining meat. When the second batch of meat is done, return the first batch to the pot (with any accumulated juices).

3. Add the onion, carrots, and celery to the pan. Cook, stirring occasionally, until the vegetables just begin to soften, 3 to 5 minutes. Sprinkle in the flour and cook, stirring constantly, until the flour absorbs the fat and colors a bit, 2 to 3 minutes.

4. Add enough water just to cover the beef and vegetables; stir in the Worcestershire sauce and ketchup. Bring to a boil, then adjust the heat so the mixture bubbles gently. Cover and cook, stirring occasionally, until the beef and vegetables are tender, 25 to 30 minutes. To thicken the stew more, turn the heat to medium-high and cook, uncovered, stirring frequently for a minute or 2, until the liquid reduces slightly. Taste and adjust the seasoning. Divide the potatoes among 4 shallow bowls, split each potato to open it more, then ladle the stew on top. Garnish with the celery leaves and serve right away.

● BEAN AND PARSNIP STEW
with oregano pistou

makes: 4 servings
time: about 2 hours, largely unattended

5 tablespoons olive oil, plus more for drizzling

2 pounds leeks, trimmed, chopped, and
    well-rinsed

1 tablespoon chopped garlic

1 pound dried gigantes or large white lima beans,
    rinsed and picked over

1 tablespoon chopped fresh rosemary,
    or 1 teaspoon dried

1 teaspoon red chile flakes (optional)

1 pound parsnips, peeled

2 tablespoons white wine vinegar

2 tablespoons chopped fresh oregano

Salt and pepper

1. Put 3 tablespoons oil in a large pot over medium heat. When it's hot, add the leeks and garlic. Cook, stirring occasionally, until the vegetables are soft and start to turn golden, 5 to 8 minutes.

2. Add the beans, rosemary, red chile flakes if using, and enough water to cover by about 2 inches. Bring to a boil, then turn the heat down so the mixture bubbles steadily but gently. Cover and cook, stirring occasionally, and adding a little water if the stew gets too thick, until the beans are as tender as you like, 60 minutes to 2 hours, depending on the beans.

3. Meanwhile, grate the parsnips with the shredding attachment on the food processor or the largest holes on a box grater and cover. In a separate bowl combine the vinegar, remaining 2 tablespoons oil, and oregano and sprinkle with salt and lots of black pepper. Taste and adjust the seasoning. Refrigerate the pistou until ready to use.

4. When the beans are ready, add the parsnips and a good sprinkling of salt and pepper. Adjust the heat so the mixture bubbles gently, cover again, and cook, stirring once in a while until the vegetables soften a little, 3 to 5 minutes. Taste and adjust the seasoning, then serve hot, garnished with the oregano pistou.

● OSSO BUCO

makes: 4 servings
time: at least 2 hours

Four ½-inch-thick pieces center-cut veal shank
  (2 pounds total)

2 tablespoons olive oil

Salt and pepper

4 anchovy fillets

1 onion, chopped

3 carrots, chopped

2 celery stalks, chopped

1 tablespoon and 1 teaspoon minced garlic

2 bay leaves

3 fresh thyme sprigs

1 cup dry white wine

1 cup chicken stock (see page 43) or beef stock
  (see page 47), or water

1 teaspoon grated lemon zest

2 tablespoons chopped fresh parsley

Polenta (see page 183) or cooked white rice

1. Tie the shanks around the circumference with a piece of kitchen string to keep the meat on the bone during cooking. Put the oil in a large pot over medium-high heat. When it's hot, add the veal, sprinkle with salt and pepper, and cook, turning and rotating the pieces as necessary, until well browned all over, 10 to 15 minutes total. Transfer the veal to a plate and turn off the heat.

2. Let the pot cool a bit, then return it to medium heat. Add the anchovies and cook, stirring occasionally, until they break up, a minute or 2. Add the onion, carrots, celery, 1 tablespoon garlic, the bay leaves, and thyme, and cook, stirring occasionally, until the vegetables are soft and golden, 8 to 10 minutes. Add the wine, and cook, scraping any browned bits off the bottom of the pot, until the wine has mostly cooked off. Pour in the stock and bring to a boil.

3. Return the meat to the pan and lower the heat so the mixture bubbles gently but steadily, and cover. Cook, stirring and turning the shanks every 30 minutes or so, until the meat is very tender and pulling away from the bone, 1½ to 2 hours.

4. When you are ready to serve, mix the remaining teaspoon garlic with the lemon zest and parsley and sprinkle with salt and pepper (this is the gremolata); taste and adjust the seasoning. Transfer the meat to a warm platter and turn the heat to high; let the sauce bubble rapidly, stirring frequently, until it becomes thick and glossy, 3 to 5 minutes. Serve the meat with the hot sauce spooned over, the gremolata sprinkled on top, and the polenta or rice on the side.

Mustardy
Mushroom and
Kale Stroganoff,
page 376

Stroganoff

The best throwbacks to 1960s family cooking—like the Americanized versions of this iconic Russian beef-and-sour-cream stew—should remain simple and hearty. Is the meatless Mustardy Mushroom and Kale Stroganoff the biggest break with retro tradition? Not with familiar mushrooms standing in for the meat and a deeply flavored gravy thickened by stirring in pureed beans. Water is all you need for One-Pot Stroganoff, which gets all the flavor it requires from seared ground beef. It's easy but don't walk away; you need to stir every couple of minutes. The twist in Beef Stroganoff with Fried Black Pepper Spaetzle is to use steak and cook it that way—still a little pink—instead of braising. That frees up time to start making the rich, German-style mini dumplings that will stand in for egg noodles.

● ONE-POT STROGANOFF

makes: 4 servings
time: 40 minutes

3 tablespoons unsalted butter

1 pound ground beef

1 onion, chopped

Salt and pepper

2 tablespoons flour

2 tablespoons tomato paste

2 teaspoons paprika

1 tablespoon Worcestershire sauce, or to taste

12 ounces dried egg noodles

½ cup sour cream

¼ cup chopped fresh dill

1. Put the butter in a large pot over medium heat. When it foams, add the beef, and sprinkle with salt and pepper. Cook, stirring frequently and breaking up any large pieces until it's no longer pink and browns in places, 5 to 10 minutes. Add the onion and cook, stirring occasionally, until soft and jammy, 5 to 10 minutes.

2. Add the flour and cook, stirring frequently, until the flour coats the meat mixture and turns golden, 2 or 3 minutes. Add the tomato paste and paprika and stir until fragrant. Pour in 4 cups water, add the Worcestershire sauce and a pinch of salt, and bring to a boil.

3. Add the noodles, and reduce the heat so the mixture bubbles gently. Cook, stirring occasionally, until the noodles are tender but not mushy, 6 to 10 minutes, depending on their thickness. Remove from the heat and stir in the sour cream; taste and adjust the seasoning, adding more Worcestershire if you like. Serve garnished with the dill.

● MUSTARDY MUSHROOM AND KALE STROGANOFF

makes: 4 servings
time: 30 minutes

Salt

4 tablespoons olive oil

1 pound cremini mushrooms, sliced

Pepper

1 large or 2 small leeks, trimmed, well rinsed, and chopped

4 garlic cloves, sliced

1½ pounds lacinato kale, rinsed and chopped (stems included)

1 teaspoon paprika

½ cup dry white wine or water

2 cups vegetable stock (see page 87), or water, or more as needed

2 tablespoons Dijon mustard

12 ounces wide, flat whole wheat pasta

1½ cups cooked cannellini beans (see page 82), with some of the cooking liquid

1. Bring a large pot of water to a boil and salt it. Put the oil in a large skillet over medium heat. When it's hot, add the mushrooms, sprinkle with salt and pepper, and raise the heat to medium-high. Cook, stirring occasionally, until they release their liquid and the pan begins to dry, 8 to 10 minutes.

2. Add the leek and garlic and sprinkle with salt and pepper. Cook, stirring often, until soft, 3 to 5 minutes. Add the kale and paprika, toss to coat, then pour in the wine and cook, scraping any browned bits off the bottom of the pan, until the wine has reduced by half, just a minute or 2.

3. Add the stock and the mustard and bring to a boil. Adjust the heat so the mixture bubbles gently, and cook, stirring occasionally, until the kale stems are soft and the leaves are silky, 10 to 15 minutes.

4. Meanwhile, add the pasta to the boiling water, and cook, stirring occasionally, for 5 minutes, then start tasting. When the pasta is tender but still has some bite, scoop out 1 cup of the cooking water, then drain.

5. Put the beans in a food processor with a spoonful or so of the cooking liquid from the pot; puree until smooth. When the kale is ready, stir in the beans. If the mixture is too thick, add more stock ¼ cup at a time, stirring after each addition. Cook, stirring frequently, until the sauce is warmed through. Taste and adjust the seasoning, and serve hot, spooned over the pasta.

● BEEF STROGANOFF
with fried black pepper spaetzle

makes: 4 servings
time: about 2 hours

Salt

2 cups flour

Pepper

3 eggs

1 cup milk, or as needed

8 tablespoons unsalted butter

1½ pounds beef sirloin

2 large onions, halved and sliced

1 tablespoon Dijon mustard

4 canned whole tomatoes, chopped

1 cup chicken stock (see page 43) or water

½ cup sour cream

3 tablespoons chopped fresh dill, for garnish

1. Bring a large pot of water to a boil and salt it. Combine the flour with 1 teaspoon pepper and a large pinch of salt in a bowl. Lightly beat the eggs and milk together in a separate bowl and then stir into the flour. If necessary, add a little more milk to make a batter about the consistency of pancake batter. Fill a large bowl with ice and water.

2. Scoop up 1 heaping tablespoon of the batter and drop it into the boiling water; small pieces may break off, but the bulk should remain largely intact and form a rough disk. Continue to scoop and drop the batter into the pot, using about one-fourth of the batter for each batch and stirring to make sure none of the dumplings stick to the bottom of the pot. When the spaetzle rise to the surface, about 1 minute later, cook for another minute or 2, then transfer with a slotted spoon or strainer into the bowl of ice water. Repeat until all the batter is used up. Drain the spaetzle. (At this point, you can toss with a bit of olive oil and refrigerate, tightly covered, for up to a day.)

3. Put 2 tablespoons butter in a large skillet and turn the heat to medium-high. Season the steak with salt and pepper. When the butter foams, add the steak and cook, undisturbed, until it browns on the bottom and releases easily from the pan but is still blood-rare in the middle, 3 to 5 minutes. Turn and sear the other side, no more than 3 minutes. You want it a couple steps rarer than your ultimate goal. Transfer the meat to a cutting board and let it rest.

4. Add the onions to the pan; lower the heat to medium, and cook, stirring occasionally and adjusting the heat as necessary to prevent burning, until caramelized and jammy, 30 to 40 minutes. Stir in the mustard, tomatoes, and stock. Bring to a boil, then adjust the heat so the mixture bubbles gently and cook, stirring once in a while, until it thickens a bit. Mix in the sour cream; taste, adjust the seasoning, and turn off the heat.

5. Meanwhile, put 2 tablespoons butter in another large skillet over medium-high heat. When the foaming subsides, add enough spaetzle to cover the bottom of the pan without crowding. (You will have to work in batches; add some of the remaining 4 tablespoons butter with each batch.) Adjust the heat so the dumplings sizzle without burning and cook, undisturbed, until the bottoms brown a little, 3 to 5 minutes. Toss with a spatula and cook until they're as golden and as crisp as you like, 3 to 5 minutes more.

6. Slice the meat thinly on the bias. If necessary, warm the onion mixture over medium heat until it's just beginning to bubble. Stir in the beef and any juices from the cutting board. Divide the spaetzle among 4 shallow bowls, and spoon the stroganoff on top. Garnish with the dill and serve right away.

Tagine

The name for this dish comes from the Moroccan cooking vessel used to make it, which allows steam to condense in the narrow top and trickle back down into the stew. It's a genius design, but other vessels and techniques can work the same way. When you bake Moroccan-Spiced Chicken with Carrots, and Olives—and resist the urge to open the oven—the result is remarkably like what comes out of a tagine, with the added bonus of crisp chicken skin. For a spectacular Vegan meal, don't skip through the slightly finicky process of making Chickpea-Almond Dumplings à la Tagine; a spoonful of preserved lemons (page 380) takes it over the moon. For the dramatic Whole Fish Tagine with Chermoula, choose the freshest, most sustainable fish you can find (see page 369), even if that means multiple smaller fish or even fillets or steaks.

● MOROCCAN-SPICED CHICKEN
with carrots and olives

makes: 4 servings
time: 40 minutes

1½ pounds carrots, peeled if you like

1 large onion, halved and sliced

¾ cup pitted green olives

1 tablespoon ground cumin

1 teaspoon ground cinnamon

½ teaspoon ground turmeric

Salt and pepper

8 bone-in, skin-on chicken thighs (about 1½ pounds)

2 lemons, halved

¼ cup chopped fresh cilantro, for garnish

1. Heat the oven to 425°F and position a rack near the top. Cut the carrots diagonally into 1-inch pieces. Put them in a 9 by 13-inch baking pan and scatter the onion and olives on top.

2. Combine the cumin, cinnamon, and turmeric in a small bowl with a generous sprinkle of salt and pepper; toss to combine. Sprinkle half the spice mixture over the vegetables. Put the chicken on top of the vegetables and rub all over with the remaining spices; turn them skin side up. Tuck the lemons here and there. Pour 3 cups water into the pan.

3. Transfer the pan to the oven and bake until the chicken skin is browned and crisp and the meat is no longer pink at the bone, 30 to 40 minutes. Garnish with the cilantro, and serve hot directly from the pan with a big spoon to get all the juices.

CHICKPEA-ALMOND DUMPLINGS À LA TAGINE

makes: 4 to 6 servings
time: 1½ hours, plus 24 hours for soaking

1¼ cups dried chickpeas

½ cup raw almonds

1 cup packed fresh cilantro, tough stems removed,
    plus more for garnish

6 garlic cloves

1 teaspoon ground coriander

2 teaspoons ground cumin

½ teaspoon cayenne, or to taste

½ teaspoon baking soda

Salt and pepper

2 tablespoons olive oil

1 large onion, chopped

1 tablespoon chopped fresh ginger

2 teaspoons ground turmeric

Two 3-inch cinnamon sticks

2 tablespoons Quick Preserved Lemons
    (recipe follows); or use good-quality
    store-bought

⅓ cup chopped dried apricots

1 pound ripe tomatoes, chopped (drained canned
    is fine)

12 ounces waxy potatoes, rinsed and cut into
    1-inch chunks

12 ounces eggplant, cut into 1-inch cubes

1 cup green olives, pitted if you like

2 cups vegetable stock (see page 87)

1. Put the chickpeas and almonds in a large bowl and cover with water by 3 or 4 inches—they will triple in volume as they soak. Soak for at least 18 or up to 24 hours, checking once or twice to see if you need to add more water to keep the chickpeas submerged.

2. Drain the chickpea mixture well. Pulse the 1 cup cilantro and 2 garlic cloves in a food processor to chop them and add chickpeas and almonds, ½ teaspoon coriander, 1 teaspoon cumin, the cayenne,

baking soda, 1 teaspoon salt, and ½ teaspoon pepper; pulse until pasty, stopping to scrape down the sides of the bowl as necessary. Add water 1 teaspoon at a time only if necessary for the machine to do its work; the idea is to keep the mixture as dry as possible. Taste and adjust the seasoning, adding more cayenne if you'd like. Cover and refrigerate the dumpling batter until you start the sauce. (You can make it up to a few hours in advance.)

3. Put the oil in a large pot over medium-high heat. Add the onion and cook, stirring occasionally, until it softens, 3 to 5 minutes. Slice the remaining 4 garlic cloves and add it with the ginger, ½ teaspoon coriander, 1 teaspoon cumin, the turmeric, and cinnamon sticks; cook, stirring often, until fragrant, about a minute.

4. Add the preserved lemons, apricots, tomatoes, potatoes, eggplant, olives, and stock. Sprinkle with a large pinch of salt and almost as much pepper; bring to a boil. Reduce the heat to a gentle simmer, cover, and cook until the eggplant and tomatoes break down and the potatoes are almost but not quite fork-tender, 25 to 30 minutes.

5. Drop ¼ cup-sized dollops of chickpea batter onto the stew, handling them as little as possible. Adjust the heat so the mixture bubbles gently, cover, and cook until the dumplings are cooked through, hold together, and are firm to the touch, 30 to 35 minutes. (Be careful: They go from tender to tough quickly.) Taste and adjust the seasoning. Serve hot, garnished with the cilantro.

QUICK PRESERVED LEMONS

Use 1½ teaspoons salt and 1 tablespoon sugar for every 2 unwaxed lemons. Chop the lemons—rinds and all—and discard the seeds. Toss with the salt and sugar, then transfer to a jar. Let it sit out at room temperature for 4 to 8 hours, shaking every hour or so. Refrigerate for up to 1 week. Makes as many lemons as you like in 8 hours.

● WHOLE FISH TAGINE with chermoula

makes: 4 servings
time: 3 hours

1 teaspoon cumin seeds

½ teaspoon coriander seeds

1½ cups fresh cilantro, tough stems removed

1½ cups fresh parsley, stems removed

2 garlic cloves, chopped

1 teaspoon paprika

½ teaspoon cayenne

½ cup olive oil, plus more for the sauce

¼ cup fresh lemon juice

3 to 4 pounds whole fish (like striped bass, arctic char, or rainbow trout), cleaned and gutted

Large pinch saffron

1 pound all-purpose potatoes (like Yukon Gold)

1 pound ripe Roma (plum) tomatoes, sliced crosswise

¼ cup Quick Preserved Lemons (opposite); or use good-quality store-bought

½ cup chopped raw pistachios

1. Put the cumin and coriander seeds in a small dry skillet over medium-low heat. Toast, shaking the pan occasionally, until fragrant and slightly browned, 3 to 5 minutes. Pulverize in a spice or coffee grinder.

2. Make the chermoula: put the cilantro, parsley, garlic, paprika, cayenne, oil, and lemon juice in a food processor or blender with the toasted spices. Pulse a few times, then run the machine until smooth, adding water 1 tablespoon at a time if necessary to help the machine do its work. Taste and adjust the seasoning. Reserve half the sauce, top with a thin layer of oil (without stirring), cover tightly, and refrigerate the reserved portion until you put the fish in the oven.

3. Cut 3 diagonal slashes through the skin on both sides of the fish. Rub the remaining chermoula all over the outside and inside of the fish. (Or just rub the seasoning all over whatever fish you have.) Put the fish on a rimmed baking sheet and refrigerate for at least 4 hours and up to 8.

4. Heat the oven to 350°F. Put the saffron in a heatproof bowl and pour 8 cups boiling water over it. Peel the potatoes and use a mandoline or very sharp knife to slice them as thin as possible. Layer them evenly on the bottom of a roasting pan or deep baking dish large enough to hold the fish; top with the tomatoes. Cover the baking dish tightly with foil and transfer to the oven. Bake, undisturbed, for 30 minutes, then check every 10 minutes after, until the potatoes are nearly done. Carefully remove the pan from the oven.

5. Spread a double layer of cheesecloth over the vegetables close to the edges of the pan. Put the fish on top of the cheesecloth and stuff with the lemon. (If using fillets or steaks, put the lemon under the cheesecloth.) Pour in enough of the saffron-steeped water to come one-third up the pan. Sprinkle the top with a little salt and pepper.

6. Tightly cover the pan again and cook until the fish is just opaque and flakes without looking dry, 40 to 60 minutes. Use the cheesecloth to lift the fish from the pan, transfer to a cutting board, and discard the cheesecloth. Taste the vegetables and juice and add a little salt and pepper if necessary.

7. Filet the fish: transfer to a cutting board and use a sharp knife to cut along the spine, through the top of the fillet. Make a deep vertical incision just below the gills, from the top of the fish to the bottom, keeping the spine and head attached. Carefully run the knife along the backbone and the ribs (parallel to the cutting board), through the belly flap so the fillets separate from the bones in one piece. Divide the vegetables and fish among shallow bowls, spoon some of the braising liquid over the top, and garnish with pistachios. Stir the reserved chermoula and pass it at the table with the pan juices.

Steak

The family of meat cuts—usually beef—have cooking methods as controversial as they are innovative. The idea that you must first sear meat over high heat to "seal in the juices" isn't always the best step. For thick cuts, try the reverse-sear method in the Bistro Rib-Eye and Frites with Creamed Watercress recipe. The most famous flat and flavorful cut of relatively lean beef from the cow's undercarriage is the flank, and you will save lots of time on the Skillet Flank Steak with Charred Onions by cooking it in big pieces. Calling an oversized mushroom "steak" is also likely to enflame. But it's common now to take a hefty vegetable—as in the Portobello au Poivre—and prepare it like steak.

● SKILLET FLANK STEAK
with charred onions

makes: 4 servings
time: 20 minutes

1½ pounds flank steak, about 1 inch thick

3 tablespoons unsalted butter

Salt

2 onions, sliced into rings

2 tablespoons fresh lemon juice

Pepper

1. Pat the steak dry and cut it against the grain into 2 or more pieces to fit in a large skillet. (You'll clearly see the long lines running down the meat; you want to slice perpendicular to those lines.)

2. Put 2 tablespoons butter in the skillet over low heat. When the butter melts, add the steak, sprinkle the top with salt, turn it, and salt the other side. Cook, undisturbed, until it begins to firm up and lose its pinkness on the edges, 5 to 10 minutes, depending on the thickness; turn and cook the other side until it's no longer pink on that side, but still quite red at the center, 1 to 5 minutes more, depending on the thickness.

3. Raise the heat to high and sear the steak until it's one step before your desired doneness, probably less than 1 minute on each side. Transfer the steak to a platter and add the onions and remaining tablespoon butter to the pan; sprinkle with salt. Cook, stirring a few times, until the onions soften and char in places without burning, 3 to 5 minutes.

4. Pour any accumulated juices from the steak into the pan with the onions along with the lemon juice, 2 tablespoons water, and lots of pepper. Scrape up any browned bits from the bottom of the pan and cook, stirring constantly, until the sauce is thick and glossy, just a minute or 2. Slice the steak against the grain as thin as you can, and serve it topped with the onions and pan juices or return the slices to the skillet to toss in the sauce and garnish with a sprinkle of salt and pepper.

PORTOBELLO AU POIVRE

makes: 4 servings
time: 30 minutes

SUBSTITUTION IDEA If you can't find green peppercorns, substitute lots of cracked black pepper and a
squeeze of lime juice.

1 tablespoon green peppercorns in brine, rinsed
   and drained

1 jalapeño, seeded and chopped, or to taste

1 large shallot, cut into chunks

3 garlic cloves

Salt and pepper

One 14-ounce can coconut milk

4 tablespoons coconut oil

4 large portobello mushroom caps, or 6 small
   (about 1½ pounds total)

¼ cup chopped fresh cilantro, for garnish

1. Crush the green peppercorns on a cutting board
with the side of your knife. Put the jalapeño, shallot,
and garlic into the food processor and sprinkle with
salt and pepper. Pulse until finely chopped but not
pureed. Add the coconut milk and green peppercorns and pulse once or twice just to combine; taste
and adjust the seasoning.

2. Put 2 tablespoons coconut oil in a large
skillet over medium-high heat. Rub the remaining
2 tablespoons coconut oil on the mushroom
caps, then sprinkle both sides with salt and lots of
pepper. When the oil is hot, put the mushrooms in
the pan, taking care not to crowd them (if they're
very large you might be able to fit only 2 at a time).
Cook, undisturbed, until browned and crisp on
the bottom, 6 to 8 minutes. Turn and repeat
on the other side. Transfer the mushrooms to a
serving platter.

3. Pour the peppercorn sauce into the pan and
cook, scraping up any browned bits, until slightly
thickened, 2 to 3 minutes. Pour the hot sauce over
the mushrooms, garnish with cilantro, and serve.

BISTRO RIB-EYE AND FRITES
with creamed watercress

makes: 4 servings
time: about 2 hours

1 large bone-in rib-eye steak, 2 to 3 inches thick (about 2½ pounds)

Salt and pepper

5 ounces fresh watercress, rinsed, dried, and trimmed

1 cup heavy cream

2 tablespoons unsalted butter, at room temperature

½ teaspoon grated lemon zest

Good-quality vegetable oil, for deep-frying

1½ pounds starchy potatoes (like russets), scrubbed

1. Rub the steak on all sides with salt and pepper, and let it come to room temperature.

2. Make the creamed watercress: Bring a large pot of water to a boil and salt it; fill a large bowl with ice and water. Put the watercress into the boiling water and cook until bright green, less than a minute; immediately transfer to the ice bath with a slotted spoon. As soon as it is cool enough to handle, drain well and squeeze with your hands to remove as much water as possible. Put the cream and watercress in a blender or food processor, and puree. Transfer the mixture to a medium saucepan over medium heat. Add the butter and sprinkle with salt and pepper. Cook, stirring occasionally, until the mixture gently bubbles and thickens. Keep warm (or refrigerate for up to several hours and reheat just before serving). Stir in the lemon zest, then taste and adjust the seasoning right before using.

3. Put 2 to 3 inches oil in a large pot over medium heat and bring to 300°F. Put a dry cast-iron skillet in the oven and heat to 325°F.

4. Cut the potatoes (peels and all) into shoestrings (a mandoline or food processor is helpful here) and dry thoroughly with paper towels. Working in batches, add them to the oil a handful at a time, adjusting the heat as needed to maintain the temperature. Fry the potatoes, stirring occasionally, until they float to the top but haven't started to color, about 5 minutes, depending on the size. Drain on paper towels. Repeat with the remaining potatoes. (You can make the fries to this point up to an hour or so ahead before proceeding.) Remove the pot from the heat but save the oil.

5. Put the steak in the hot pan and roast in the oven, undisturbed, until it releases easily and has an internal temperature of about 100°F, 5 to 15 minutes, depending on the thickness of the cut. Leaving the oven on, transfer the skillet to the stovetop, turn the steak, and cook, undisturbed, over medium-high heat until the second side sears and releases easily from the pan, 2 to 5 minutes. Put the pan back in the oven with the other side down, cooking it to one stage before your desired doneness. If you want rare, remove the steak when its interior measures 125°F, or even a little bit less; for medium-rare, 135°F. Transfer to a platter to rest for at least 5 minutes and up to 15.

6. Reheat the oil, this time bringing it to 375°F. Working in batches, fry the potatoes until crisp and deeply colored, just a few minutes. Transfer to a paper towel–lined plate and sprinkle with salt.

7. Slice the steak and pour the meat juices over the slices on a serving platter. Serve with the hot frites and pass the creamed watercress at the table.

Chop House

There's little difference between a steak and a chop. Generally, I say steaks come from cows or buffalo; chops are cut from pork or veal—or now for either, vegetables. Who really cares what you call 'em as long as they're good. The offbeat flavors in the Pork Chops with Riesling Sauce are definitely that, with a lovely pan sauce that cuts through the richness of the meat. Gorgeous, thick, big bone-in rib chops are best for Rye-Stuffed Pork Chops with Mustard Cream. (Serve it with a simple roasted or steamed vegetable.) Thick-Cut Pomegranate-Glazed Eggplant "chops" are a hefty, aromatic, center-of-the-plate Vegan option that's ideal for entertaining.

● PORK CHOPS
with riesling sauce

makes: 4 servings
time: 20 minutes

SUBSTITUTION IDEA If you don't have a sweet wine, use dry white and add a teaspoon of sugar.

2 tablespoons olive oil

4 center-cut pork chops, no more than 1 inch thick (about 1½ pounds)

Salt and pepper

2 shallots, or 1 red onion, halved and sliced

1 cup Riesling or other sweet, fruity white wine

2 tablespoons cold unsalted butter, cut into small pieces

1. Put the oil in a large skillet over high heat. Pat the chops dry and sprinkle with salt and pepper. When the oil is hot, add the meat and cook, undisturbed, until the bottoms are browned and the chops release easily, 1 to 3 minutes, then turn and repeat for the other side. They should still be pink inside. Transfer the pork chops to a plate and return the skillet to medium heat.

2. Add the shallots to the pan and cook, stirring occasionally, until they are softened and begin to brown in places, 3 to 5 minutes. Pour in the wine and bring to a boil, scraping up any browned bits from the bottom of the pan. Cook, stirring frequently, until the wine has reduced to a thin syrup, just a minute or 2. Add the butter and stir until it melts and the sauce thickens, another minute.

3. Return the chops to the pan and cook, turning at least once, until they're coated with the sauce but still a little pink at the center, about a minute. Taste and adjust the seasoning, adding lots more black pepper. Serve the chops hot, drizzled with the sauce.

Rye-Stuffed
Pork Chops with
Mustard Cream,
page 389

THICK-CUT POMEGRANATE-GLAZED EGGPLANT

makes: 4 servings
time: 1 hour

½ cup pomegranate molasses (or marmalade)

1 tablespoon chopped garlic

1 teaspoon ground cumin

3 tablespoons fresh lemon juice, or to taste

Salt and pepper

6 tablespoons olive oil

About 1½ pounds large eggplant, cut crosswise into 1-inch slices

1 pomegranate, seeded, or 2 peeled, chopped oranges

2 ripe tomatoes, chopped

2 tablespoons chopped fresh mint, or 2 teaspoons dried

½ teaspoon ground allspice

1. Whisk together the pomegranate molasses, garlic, cumin, 2 tablespoons lemon juice, and ¼ cup hot water. Season with salt and pepper, then add 4 tablespoons oil, whisking until incorporated. Taste and adjust the seasoning. Put the eggplant slices in a shallow dish in a single layer and pour the marinade over all. Let sit for 30 minutes, turning once or twice. Heat the oven to 400°F.

2. Grease a large rimmed baking sheet with 1 tablespoon oil. Lift the eggplant slices from the marinade, letting any excess drip off, then put them on the pan in a single layer. (It's okay if they're touching.) Bake, undisturbed, until they're sizzling, 5 to 10 minutes, then turn and spoon some leftover marinade onto each piece. Repeat twice more, turning, basting, and roasting the eggplant until it is caramelized and easily pierced with a fork, another 10 to 15 minutes total.

3. While the eggplant is roasting, put the pomegranate seeds in a medium bowl and add the tomatoes, mint, remaining tablespoon lemon juice, the allspice, and remaining tablespoon olive oil. Sprinkle with salt and pepper and toss to combine; taste and adjust the seasoning. Serve the eggplant chops hot or at room temperature, topped with a spoonful of the relish.

RYE-STUFFED PORK CHOPS
with mustard cream

makes: 4 servings
time: 45 minutes

6 ounces rye bread, torn into large pieces

4 bone-in pork rib loin chops (not center cut), 1 to 1½ inches thick, trimmed of excess fat (about 2 pounds)

Salt and pepper

1 teaspoon caraway seeds

1 tablespoon chopped garlic

2 tablespoons chopped fresh sage

¾ cup grated Emmental cheese (about 3 ounces)

3 tablespoons olive oil

¼ cup dry white wine

½ cup chicken stock (see page 43), or water

¼ cup heavy cream

2 tablespoons Dijon mustard

1. Heat the oven to 325°F. Put the bread in the food processor and pulse until it's ground to coarse crumbs. Trim the pork chop bones of any fat and bits of meat, scraping them as clean as possible (this is called "Frenching"). Chop the scraps into small bits and transfer them to a large ovenproof skillet over medium heat. Sprinkle with salt and pepper and cook, stirring occasionally and adjusting the heat so the mixture sizzles without burning, until the fat melts and the pieces brown and crisp, 10 to 15 minutes.

2. Carefully cut a slit into the meaty edge of each chop with a small, sharp knife; insert the tip and work it around inside the chop to create a pocket without cutting all the way through the edges.

3. When the pork bits are ready, remove all but 2 tablespoons of the fat from the pan and add the breadcrumbs, caraway seeds, garlic, and sage; cook, stirring frequently until the mixture is golden and fragrant, 3 to 5 minutes. Transfer to a bowl and sprinkle with salt and pepper. Add the cheese and stir to combine. Taste and adjust the seasoning.

4. Rinse and dry the skillet, add the oil, and swirl. Cut eight 6-inch pieces of kitchen twine. Stuff the chops with the breadcrumb mixture until they're full but not bursting. Secure each chop with 2 pieces of twine. Put all the chops in the skillet and transfer to the oven.

5. Roast until the meat is still pink inside but the stuffing is hot, 15 to 25 minutes, depending on its thickness; an instant thermometer in both the meat and the stuffing should read 140°F. Turn off the oven and put a heatproof platter inside to warm. Carefully transfer the skillet to the stove and cook on high heat until the bottoms are browned, 2 to 3 minutes, then carefully turn and sear on the other side. Snip the strings and remove them. Carefully take the platter from the oven, add the chops, and let rest on the counter while you make the sauce.

6. Return the skillet to medium-high heat. Pour in the wine and cook, scraping up any browned bits from the bottom of the pan, until the wine is reduced by about half, 1 to 3 minutes. Add the stock and cook, whisking constantly, until quite thick, 3 to 5 minutes more. Whisk in the cream and mustard and remove from the heat; taste and adjust the seasoning. Serve the pork chops with the sauce.

Sausage

From store-bought links to grinding and seasoning your own meat, it's all covered here. Hearty greens with garlic and sausage is one of my favorite Italian combinations, especially since it barely requires any effort to taste fantastic, any way you put the pieces together, but especially in the Easy recipe. Fat is critical for both texture and flavor in sausages, even when they're made from plants. So for the Merguez-style Vegan sausage patties, don't try to skimp on the oils. You don't need to go out and buy a stuffer for one Homemade Spicy Sausage, either. Just ask a butcher for caul fat—a similar free-form casing. The results are at least as good without the fuss.

● SAUSAGE AND ESCAROLE
with garlic bread

makes: 4 servings
time: 35 minutes

SUBSTITUTION IDEA Since smoked sausage is fully cooked, you're really only warming it up and crisping the escarole. To use fresh hot or sweet Italian sausage instead, slice each lengthwise with kitchen scissors, not quite all the way through, then spread the sausages over the greens, cut side down, and roast as directed.

About 1½ pounds escarole, rinsed, dried, and trimmed

½ cup grated Parmesan cheese (about 2 ounces)

1 tablespoon fresh lemon juice

Salt and pepper

4 smoked Italian sausage links (about 1 pound)

4 tablespoons olive oil

4 thick slices crusty bread

1 large garlic clove, peeled and cut in half

1. Heat the oven to 450°F. Chop the escarole into bite-sized pieces and pile it into a large, ovenproof skillet or baking dish; sprinkle with the Parmesan, lemon juice, and a little salt and pepper.

2. Put the sausages on top of the escarole and drizzle everything with 2 tablespoons oil. Transfer the pan to the oven and bake, undisturbed, until the escarole is tender and the sausage is cooked through and browned, 10 to 15 minutes.

3. After the gratin has been cooking about 10 minutes, put the bread on a baking sheet and drizzle with the remaining 2 tablespoons oil. Put in the oven and toast without turning until it's as golden as you like, 5 to 10 minutes. While the bread is still hot, rub each slice with the cut side of the garlic. Serve everything hot.

MERGUEZ TEMPEH SAUSAGE PATTIES
with roasted carrots

makes: 4 servings
time: about 1 hour

1 pound tempeh

4 teaspoons dark sesame oil

Salt and pepper

5 tablespoons olive oil, or more as needed for pan-frying

1 small onion, chopped

1 tablespoon chopped garlic

1 teaspoon ground cumin

½ teaspoon ground coriander

½ teaspoon fennel seeds

1 tablespoon harissa or other chile paste

1½ pounds carrots, roughly the same size

1 teaspoon paprika

½ teaspoon cayenne

½ cup tahini, with a tablespoon or so of its oil

2 tablespoons fresh lemon juice, or to taste

¼ cup chopped fresh parsley

1. Heat the oven to 425°F. Set up a steamer in a large pot over boiling water and crumble the tempeh into the basket. Cover the pot and steam the tempeh without stirring until it's soft and plump, 10 to 15 minutes. Reserve ¼ cup of the steaming water, and transfer the tempeh to a food processor. Add the sesame oil, sprinkle with salt and pepper, and pulse a few times, then transfer the tempeh to a large bowl.

2. Put 2 tablespoons olive oil in a large skillet over medium heat. When it's hot, add the onion and garlic and cook, stirring occasionally, until the vegetables are soft and golden, 5 to 8 minutes. Add the cumin, coriander, and fennel seeds, sprinkle with salt and pepper, and stir constantly until fragrant, about a minute. Add the mixture to the tempeh along with the harissa. Stir to fully incorporate; taste and adjust the seasoning.

3. Line a baking sheet with wax paper or parchment. Stir the reserved soaking water into the tempeh sausage 1 tablespoon at a time, until you can pinch a piece together between your fingers and it stays together. Form the mixture into 12 patties, transfer to the prepared pan, and refrigerate to set while you cook the carrots and make the sauce. (You can make the sausages up to 1 day in advance and refrigerate them, covered.) Wipe out the skillet.

4. Put the carrots on a rimmed baking sheet, drizzle with 1 tablespoon olive oil, and sprinkle with the paprika, cayenne, and some salt and pepper. Toss to combine and roast, shaking the pan a few times, until just tender and browned, 10 to 15 minutes.

5. Put the tahini and some of its oil in a small bowl; add ½ cup warm water and the lemon juice, and whisk until smooth. Sprinkle with the parsley and some salt and pepper. Taste, adjust the seasoning, and let sit.

6. Put the remaining 2 tablespoons olive oil in the skillet over medium heat. When it's hot, add a few of the sausage patties, being careful not to crowd the pan, and cook, undisturbed, until they brown and release easily from the pan, 2 to 3 minutes. Turn and cook the other side the same way. As they finish, transfer them to a plate and repeat with the remaining patties, adding more oil as needed. Serve the sausages with the carrots, passing the tahini sauce at the table.

● HOMEMADE SPICY SAUSAGE
over caramelized fennel

makes: 4 to 6 servings
time: at least 1 hour

2 pounds boneless pork shoulder, with its fat

8 to 12 ounces skinless pork belly

1 tablespoon minced garlic

2 teaspoons fennel seeds

1 tablespoon red chile flakes, or to taste

2 teaspoons salt, or more as needed

½ teaspoon pepper, or more as needed

¼ cup ice water

2 large white onions

3 medium or 2 large fennel bulbs

8 ounces caul fat or natural hog casings
    (about 1½ inches wide), for stuffing

2 tablespoons olive oil

½ cup dry white wine

1. Cut the pork shoulder and belly into 1-inch cubes. Put about 2 cups of the meat into a food processor and pulse in short spurts until it's minced. Take your time and be careful not to pulverize the meat. As you finish each batch, transfer it to a bowl.

2. Add the garlic, fennel seeds, red chile flakes, 2 teaspoons salt, and ½ teaspoon pepper to the ground meat and mix with your hands to incorporate; add a little ice water if the mixture seems very dry. Heat a skillet over medium-high heat and fry a pinch of the mixture for a couple minutes or until fully cooked. Taste and add more salt or spices to the sausage mixture as necessary. Cover and chill for at least 1 hour (up to 5 days in the fridge, or freeze for up to 3 months).

3. Trim off the tops of the onions and peel. Trim roots from the onions and remove any dirt, but leave the root ends intact. Cut the onions in half vertically, lay them cut side on the cutting board, and slice the onions as thin as you can manage from stem end to trimmed top. Trim the fronds from the fennel and cut the fennel the same way.

4. If using a stand mixer with sausage-stuffing attachment: Be sure to read the manufacturer's instructions. Soak the casings in water to cover until soft; flush them under running water. Slide the entire length of the casing on the stuffing attachment, leaving about 3 inches of casing on the end. Slowly feed the meat mixture, being careful not to overfill, and tie the sausage every 4 inches. (Store extra casings lightly salted in an airtight container in the freezer for up to 1 year.)

If shaping by hand: Spread the caul fat open on a work surface. Divide and shape the sausages into 8 links or patties. Put one at the edge of the sheet. Fold the top of the caul fat over the sausage, then the sides, and then roll the sausage until it's fully encased. Cut off the remaining caul fat. Repeat with the rest of the sausage.

5. Heat the oven to 400°F and put the racks in the top and bottom thirds of the oven. Put the onions and fennel in a large roasting pan with the oil and sprinkle with salt and pepper. Roast on the bottom rack, stirring a few times, until silky and caramelized, 25 to 30 minutes.

6. Put the sausage in a large skillet and roast, undisturbed, until the bottom is browned, 10 to 15 minutes, then turn. Continue roasting until the sausages are evenly browned all over and the juices run clear when poked with a thin knife, another 15 to 20 minutes.

7. Transfer the sausages to a cutting board and pour off all but 1 tablespoon of the fat. Heat the skillet over medium-high heat, and when the skillet is hot, add the wine and cook, scraping up any browned bits from the bottom of the pan, just a minute or 2. Pour the pan sauce into the roasting pan with the vegetables and toss to coat. Serve the sausages hot on a bed of the roasted vegetables.

Meatballs

When done right, they're tender and light. Bright red ingredients make Beetballs with Red Pepper Crema stand out among a sea of vegan burgers and balls. The trick is to cook the quinoa so long it will feel instinctively wrong. The Easy Free-Form Swedish Meatballs improve on the classic in two ways. First, since the most time-consuming part is shaping the balls, the shortcut is to let two spoons do the work. I've eliminated the gravy-making step by using a tomato sauce seasoned with spices found in Swedish cooking. Szechuan Beef Pearl Balls are almost like a wrapper-free steamed dumpling. Seek out (or order online) the few key ingredients and the rest is simple.

● FREE-FORM SWEDISH MEATBALLS

makes: 4 servings
time: 35 minutes

Two 28-ounce cans crushed tomatoes

2 tablespoons sugar

2 teaspoons ground allspice

2 teaspoons ground cinnamon

Salt and pepper

½ cup breadcrumbs (see page 173)

⅓ cup milk

3 tablespoons unsalted butter

1 small onion, chopped

1½ pounds ground beef, or 12 ounces pork
    and 12 ounces beef

1. Put the tomatoes, sugar, allspice, and cinnamon in a large pot over medium-high heat. Season with salt and pepper and bring to a boil, then reduce the heat so the mixture bubbles gently. Cook until the sauce thickens and the flavors start to come together, at least 15 minutes, while you make the meatballs.

2. Soak the breadcrumbs in the milk, stirring once or twice until the liquid is absorbed, 5 to 10 minutes. Put 1 tablespoon butter in a large skillet over medium-high heat. Add the onion, sprinkle with salt and pepper, and cook, stirring occasionally, until the onion softens, 3 to 5 minutes. Scrape the onion into a bowl and add the breadcrumbs and meat. Sprinkle with salt and pepper and stir just until combined. Cook a small amount in the skillet until no longer pink; taste and adjust the seasoning.

3. Wipe out the skillet and add the remaining 2 tablespoons butter. Melt over medium-high heat. Using 2 spoons, scoop and drop rounds of the meat mixture into the skillet. Cook in batches, turning occasionally, until the meatballs are browned all over, 8 to 10 minutes. Transfer them to a plate as they finish cooking and repeat with the remaining meat mixture.

4. When all the meatballs are browned, add them to the tomato sauce and toss gently to coat. Adjust the heat so the sauce bubbles steadily and cook, stirring once or twice until the meatballs are firm and the sauce thickens, about 5 minutes. Serve hot or warm, right from the pot if you like.

Beetballs with
Red Pepper
Crema,
page 396

● BEETBALLS
with red pepper crema

makes: 4 servings
time: 45 minutes

5 tablespoons olive oil

1½ cups red quinoa, rinsed

Salt

½ pound beets, peeled

2 cups cooked kidney beans (see page 82; or one 15-ounce can), drained

4 scallions, chopped

6 teaspoons chopped garlic

¼ cup fresh cilantro, tough stems removed

1 tablespoon chili powder

2 teaspoons ground cumin

½ teaspoon paprika

Pepper

2 roasted red peppers (see page 132), peeled and seeded

¼ cup almond milk

1. Heat the oven to 375°F. Use 2 tablespoons of the oil to grease a large rimmed baking sheet.

2. Put the quinoa in a medium saucepan along with 4 cups water and a large pinch of salt. Bring to a boil and adjust the heat so the water bubbles gently. Cook, stirring occasionally, until the quinoa is thick, like mashed potatoes, and the kernels are no longer distinct, 30 to 40 minutes. As it cooks, adjust the heat and add small amounts of water to keep the bottom from burning but keep the mixture dry. Cover, remove from the heat, and let it sit for at least 5 or up to 15 minutes, then transfer it to a large bowl.

3. Grate the beets with the shredding disk on your food processor or with a box grater. Transfer them to the bowl with the quinoa and fit the machine with the metal blade. Add the beans, scallions, 5 teaspoons garlic, the cilantro, chili powder, cumin, and paprika, then sprinkle with salt and pepper. Pulse until coarsely chopped but not pureed. Add to the quinoa mixture and stir to combine, then taste and adjust the seasoning.

4. Roll about 2 tablespoons of the mixture into a ball between your hands, and put it on the prepared baking sheet. Repeat with the remaining mixture. Brush the meatballs with 1 tablespoon oil. Bake the meatballs, shaking the pan halfway through, until they're browned all over, 25 to 30 minutes total.

5. Make the crema: Clean the food processor and fit it with the metal blade. Put the remaining teaspoon garlic in the food processor with the red peppers and almond milk and season with salt and pepper. With the machine running, slowly drizzle in the remaining 2 tablespoons oil. Stop to scrape down the sides, then let it run again until a smooth sauce forms. Taste and adjust the seasoning. Serve the beetballs hot, drizzled with the sauce.

● SZECHUAN BEEF PEARL BALLS

makes: 4 servings
time: about 10 hours, largely unattended

1½ cups glutinous or sticky rice

2 tablespoons sesame seeds

1 tablespoon Szechuan peppercorns

1 pound boneless beef chuck, cut into large
    chunks

4 scallions

1 cup fresh cilantro, tough stems removed

1 egg, lightly beaten

Salt

1 tablespoon good-quality vegetable oil

3 tablespoons Chinese black (Chinkiang) vinegar

2 tablespoons soy sauce

1½ teaspoons dark sesame oil

1. Cover the rice with cold water by at least 2 inches and soak overnight. Drain well.

2. Put the sesame seeds in a dry medium skillet over medium-low heat and toast, shaking the pan occasionally, until they are fragrant and toasted, 3 to 5 minutes. Transfer to a bowl. Repeat with the Szechuan peppercorns, toasting until they are fragrant and starting to brown, 3 to 5 minutes. Put them in a mortar and pestle or spice grinder and pulverize them.

3. Put the beef, scallions, and ½ cup cilantro in the food processor and pulse until well ground but not pureed. Add the egg, sprinkle with salt and the ground Szechuan pepper, and pulse a few more times to combine; transfer to a bowl.

4. Grease a rimmed baking sheet with the vegetable oil. Spread the drained rice on another rimmed baking sheet or a plate. Scoop up a tablespoon of the beef mixture, gently roll it into a ball, then roll the meatball in the rice. Transfer to the greased baking sheet and repeat until you have used up all the meat. Refrigerate until ready to cook.

5. Mix the toasted sesame seed mixture with the vinegar, soy sauce, and sesame oil. Whisk to combine, then taste and adjust the seasoning

6. Rig a steamer in a large pot so that the water will remain below the food, and line the basket with parchment. Add the meatballs and bring the water to a boil. Adjust the heat so the water bubbles enthusiastically, cover, and steam (checking the water level occasionally) until the rice is tender and sticky and the meat is cooked through, 10 to 15 minutes. Serve hot with the dipping sauce.

● Stuffed Meatloaf
with Red Gravy,
page 401

Meatloaf

Sorry, no ketchup-glazed version here. But the All Out is a huge meatball, with a molten cheese center. Bet you've never seen one of those before; it's possibly the most over-the-top recipe in the book. First and easiest is the Super-Crisp Mediterranean Meatloaf with Balsamic; you bake it in a square pan or skillet so there's as much crust as insides. Lentil Loaf with Mushroom Jus demonstrates that Vegan meatloaf can be moist, flavorful, and something on par—or better than—meaty meatloaves. Forget the mashed potatoes and serve noodles with this meatloaf. Try brown rice spaghetti tossed in sesame oil to soak up some of the rich mushroom sauce, and add a green salad.

● SUPER-CRISP MEDITERRANEAN MEATLOAF
with balsamic

makes: 4 to 6 servings
time: 30 minutes

1 tablespoon olive oil

1 egg

¾ cup chopped Kalamata olives

½ cup crumbled feta cheese

1 tablespoon minced garlic

1½ pounds ground beef (no more than 80% lean)

Salt and pepper

2 tablespoons balsamic vinegar

1 tablespoon honey

1 lemon, cut into wedges

1. Heat the oven to 450°F. Grease a 9-inch square baking dish or medium skillet with the oil.

2. Beat the egg in a large bowl. Add the olives, cheese, garlic, and beef and season with salt and pepper. Gently fold the ingredients together with your hands until they just come together and no more. Transfer the mixture to the prepared pan and pat it into a wide shallow loaf in the center no more than 2 inches thick (it won't go to the edges).

3. Whisk together the vinegar and honey in a small bowl and season with a little salt and lots of pepper. Brush the top of the loaf with the glaze. Bake, basting 2 times, until the top is caramelized and the loaf is 160°F at the center, 25 to 30 minutes. Let cool for a few minutes before slicing. Serve hot, warm, or at room temperature with the lemon wedges.

● **LENTIL LOAF** with mushroom jus

makes: 6 to 8 servings
time: 2 hours

¾ ounce dried porcini mushrooms

Salt

6 tablespoons olive oil

1 cup brown rice

1 cup green lentils, rinsed and picked over

½ cup walnut pieces

3 or 4 red Swiss chard leaves (about 8 ounces), stems and leaves chopped

2 tablespoons chopped garlic

2 tablespoons tomato paste

1 tablespoon smoked paprika

Pepper

1 pound cremini mushrooms, rinsed, dried, and chopped

1 small sweet onion (like Vidalia)

2 fresh thyme sprigs

1 cup port or red wine

1. Put the dried mushrooms in a medium bowl and cover with 2 cups hot tap water. Use a plate if necessary to keep them submerged and soak until pliable, 15 to 20 minutes. Lift the dried mushrooms out of the bowl with a slotted spoon, reserving them and the soaking liquid.

2. Bring a large pot of water to a boil and salt it. Grease a 9 by 5–inch loaf pan with 2 tablespoons oil. When the water comes to a boil, add the rice and lentils and cook, stirring occasionally, for 20 minutes. Drain, reserving about 1 cup of the liquid.

3. Put a large dry skillet over medium heat and add the walnuts, shaking the pan occasionally, until toasted and fragrant, 3 to 5 minutes. Transfer the walnuts to a food processor. Add 2 tablespoons oil to the skillet and turn the heat to medium-high. When it's hot, add the chard and garlic and cook, stirring occasionally, until the stems are tender,

3 to 5 minutes. Stir in the tomato paste and paprika and cook until the paste has darkened slightly, 1 to 2 minutes. Sprinkle with salt and pepper and add the mixture to the food processor.

4. Add half the lentils and rice to the food processor and pulse the machine several times until the mixture loosely comes together. Fold in the remaining rice and lentils; the mixture should be firm but wet enough to stick together when you squeeze a small amount in your palm. If not, add some of the reserved cooking liquid, 1 tablespoon at a time, until it does. Taste and adjust the seasoning. Put the mixture in the prepared pan and smooth the top. Cover the loaf to prevent it from drying out while you start the sauce, or refrigerate for up to a day (bring to room temperature before proceeding).

5. Rinse and dry the skillet. Put the remaining 2 tablespoons oil in the pan over high heat. When it's hot, add the cremini mushrooms and onion, sprinkle with salt and lots of pepper, and cook, stirring frequently until the mushrooms release their liquid; then let the mixture cook undisturbed until the pan becomes dry again and the vegetables sizzle, 10 to 15 minutes. Lower the heat to medium and cook, stirring once in a while, until the mushrooms and onions are quite tender and golden, another 5 to 10 minutes.

6. Heat the oven to 425°F, with the oven rack in the middle. While the vegetables are cooking, bake the loaf until it is firm and pulls away from the pan, 25 to 30 minutes. (An instant-read thermometer should register at least 160°F.) Let it sit a few minutes before slicing.

7. Add the rehydrated mushrooms to the skillet along with the thyme, port, and 1 cup of the soaking liquid and bring the mixture to a boil. Cook, stirring often, until the wine has reduced by half and the mushrooms are tender, 10 to 15 minutes. Remove the thyme, taste, and adjust the seasoning. Serve thick slices of the lentil loaf with the mushroom mixture spooned over.

● STUFFED MEATLOAF with red gravy

makes: 6 to 8 servings
time: 2 hours

5 tablespoons olive oil

4 ounces pancetta, chopped

1 large onion, chopped

2 tablespoons chopped garlic

2 tablespoons tomato paste

Two 28-ounce cans whole tomatoes

2 fresh oregano sprigs

2 bay leaves

1½ ounces Italian or French bread (stale is fine)

½ cup milk

2 pounds mixed ground meat, ideally equal parts
beef chuck, veal, and pork shoulder

1 egg, lightly beaten

½ cup grated Parmesan cheese (about 2 ounces),
plus more for serving

¼ cup plus 2 tablespoons chopped fresh parsley,
plus more for garnish

Salt and pepper

½ cup ricotta cheese

¼ cup chopped fresh basil

8 ounces fresh mozzarella, chopped

1. Heat the oven to 400°F. Put 2 tablespoons oil in a large pot over medium heat. Add the pancetta and cook, stirring once in a while until browned, 3 to 5 minutes. Add half the onion and half the garlic and cook, stirring again, until soft and golden, 5 to 8 minutes. Add the tomato paste and cook until slightly darkened, 1 to 2 minutes. Add the tomatoes and their juice, oregano, and bay leaves. Bring to a boil, then adjust the heat so the mixture bubbles gently. Partially cover and let the sauce simmer, stirring once in a while until the meatloaf is ready, or at least 1 hour. (You can make the sauce up to a few days ahead of time. Reheat before serving and remove the oregano and bay leaves.)

2. Use 1 tablespoon oil to grease a large roasting pan. Rip the bread into big pieces and pulse in the food processor until coarsely ground; put ½ cup breadcrumbs in a large bowl, reserve the rest (if any) for another use. Add the milk and let the mixture sit until the bread absorbs the liquid.

3. Put 2 tablespoons oil in a large skillet over medium heat. When it's hot, add the remaining onion and garlic and cook until soft and translucent, 3 to 5 minutes. Remove from the heat to cool. Add the onion mixture to a large bowl with the breadcrumbs and add the meat, egg, Parmesan, and ¼ cup parsley and season with plenty of salt and pepper. Mix by hand just enough to combine. (To taste and adjust the seasoning, cook a small pinch of the meat in a pan or microwave.)

4. Combine the ricotta, basil, and remaining 2 tablespoons parsley in a small bowl, and sprinkle with salt and pepper. Fold in the mozzarella. Taste and adjust the seasoning.

5. Transfer the meat mixture to the prepared roasting pan, shape it into a ball, and use your fist to make a well in the top. Fill with the cheese mixture and mold the meat back into one seamless ball, enclosing the filling completely. Bake until an instant-read thermometer inserted into the meat reads 160°F and the filling reads at least 145°F, 60 to 70 minutes. Let the meatloaf sit for 10 to 15 minutes before slicing. To serve, cut the meatloaf into wedges, ladle some sauce on top, garnish with parsley, and pass grated Parmesan at the table.

Pot Pie

The Holy Grail of projects—which is probably why frozen pot pies remain so popular. The Easy recipe for homemade Chicken-and-Biscuit Pot Pie busts that myth into flaky bits and puts homemade pot pie on the table in an hour with very little effort. At least once, everyone should try Moroccan Pastilla—my meatless spin on the classic North African sweet-and-savory chicken pie. Garlicky Chicken Pot Pie is basically the same filling as the French "Chicken in a Pot," only instead of an inedible crust, this is topped with a pastry so good there won't be a bite left.

● CHICKEN-AND-BISCUIT POT PIE

makes: 4 servings
time: about 1 hour

2½ cups milk, or more as needed

2½ cups and 2 tablespoons flour, or more as needed

2 teaspoons baking powder

1 teaspoon salt, or more as needed

⅓ cup olive oil

2 tablespoons unsalted butter

1½ pounds boneless, skinless chicken thighs

1 onion, chopped

2 carrots, chopped

1 celery stalk, chopped

Pepper

1 cup peas (frozen are fine)

1. Heat the oven to 450°F. Put the milk in a saucepan and warm over medium heat until just steaming (or heat in the microwave in 10-second intervals until just above body temperature).

2. Put the 2½ cups flour, the baking powder, and salt in a large bowl and stir to mix. Add the oil and 1 cup milk, and stir until the dough is just mixed; be careful not to overmix; lumps are fine. If it's

too dry and hasn't come together, add more milk 1 tablespoon at a time and stir. If the dough is too wet, add 1 tablespoon of flour and stir once. The dough should drop like biscuit batter from a spoon. Let the dough rest while you make the filling.

3. Put the butter in a large ovenproof skillet over medium heat. When it melts, add the chicken, onion, carrots, and celery; sprinkle with salt and pepper and cook, turning occasionally, until the chicken is just cooked through but not browned, 10 to 15 minutes. Transfer the chicken to a cutting board and cut into bite-sized pieces.

4. Return the chicken to the skillet and sprinkle with the remaining 2 tablespoons flour. Reduce the heat to medium-low and cook just until the flour turns golden. Slowly pour in the remaining 1½ cups milk and cook, stirring occasionally, until the sauce coats the back of a spoon. Stir in the peas and remove from the heat; taste and adjust the seasoning.

5. Drop the dough mixture onto the filling, 1 heaping tablespoon at a time, until you use it all up (space the mounds of dough as evenly as you can, but don't bother to spread them out). Bake until the mixture is bubbling and the crust is golden, 10 to 15 minutes. Sprinkle the top with salt and serve right away.

MOROCCAN PASTILLA

makes: 4 servings
time: 45 minutes

SUBSTITUTION IDEA Ras el hanout is a distinctive Moroccan spice mix that can contain up to 100 spices. If you don't have access to a good-quality blend, substitute garam masala, which has similar characteristics.

1 pound parsnips, peeled and cut into 1-inch chunks

1 red onion, quartered

4 garlic cloves, smashed

½ cup dried apricots

½ cup pitted dates

1 cup pitted green olives

½ cup raw almonds

3 tablespoons olive oil, plus more for brushing

Salt and pepper

1 tablespoon ras el hanout (see the note above)

1 cup fresh cilantro, tough stems removed, chopped

Grated zest of 1 lemon, plus lemon juice if needed

8 ounces phyllo dough sheets, thawed in the refrigerator overnight

1 tablespoon confectioners' sugar

1 teaspoon ground cinnamon

1. Heat the oven to 400°F. Put the parsnips, onion, garlic, apricots, dates, olives, and almonds in a food processor, working in batches if the bowl is too crowded, and pulse to chop, scraping down the sides now and then, until the pieces are about the size of peas.

2. Put the oil in a large skillet over medium-high heat. When it's hot, add the chopped mixture and 1 cup water and sprinkle with salt and pepper. Cook, stirring occasionally and adjusting the heat so the mixture sizzles without burning, until the parsnips soften and the pan is mostly dry, 10 to 15 minutes. Add the ras el hanout and cook until fragrant, about 1 minute. Turn off the heat and stir in the cilantro and lemon zest. Taste and adjust the seasoning, adding a little lemon juice if you like.

3. Grease a 9-inch pie pan with oil. Cut 8 sheets of phyllo into 9-inch squares (discard the scraps). Put 1 square in the bottom of the pie pan, allowing the corners to hang over the rim of the pan. Brush the top of the dough with oil. Set another phyllo sheet on top at a 45° angle and brush with oil. Repeat with another 2 sheets, fanning them out to evenly cover the sides of the pan.

4. Spread the vegetable mixture evenly in the phyllo-lined pan. Top with 4 more phyllo squares, again brushing each with a little olive oil and offsetting the corners. Fold the edges of the phyllo from the top and bottom layers under and into the sides of the pan to enclose the pie. Brush the top with oil and cut a few small slits into the top of the pie to allow hot air to escape while baking. Cover with foil.

5. Transfer the pastilla to the oven and bake for 15 minutes, then remove the foil. Bake until golden-brown and crisp, 5 to 10 minutes. Combine the sugar and cinnamon in a small sieve and shake over the top of the pie to lightly dust, cut into wedges, and serve hot or at room temperature.

GARLICKY CHICKEN POT PIE

makes: 6 to 8 servings
time: about 4 hours, largely unattended

1 whole chicken (3 to 4 pounds)

3 tablespoons olive oil

Salt and pepper

1 onion, unpeeled but quartered

4 carrots, cut into chunks

4 celery stalks, plus some leaves if possible, cut into chunks

1 small bunch fresh thyme

5 heads garlic, broken into cloves and peeled

1 cup dry white wine

1 cup plus 2 tablespoons flour, plus more for rolling

8 tablespoons (1 stick) cold unsalted butter, cut into chunks, plus more for greasing

4 tablespoons ice water

½ cup heavy cream

1 tablespoon chopped fresh tarragon

1 egg

1. Turn the oven to 400°F and put a large, dry oven-proof skillet on a rack in the lower third. Rub the outside of the chicken with the oil, and sprinkle with salt and pepper.

2. When the oven is scorching hot, 10 or 15 minutes later, carefully put the chicken in the skillet breast side up. Roast, undisturbed, until an instant-read thermometer inserted in the thickest part of the thigh reads at least 155°F or the juices run clear when you cut into a thigh down to the bone, 40 to 60 minutes, depending on the size. Carefully remove the pan from the oven and transfer the chicken to a platter to cool. Pour off the fat, but don't wipe out the skillet.

3. When the chicken is cool enough to handle, remove the meat from the bones in big pieces, and put the carcass, bones, skin, and any juices from the platter in a large pot. Cover and refrigerate the meat until ready to use.

4. Add the onion, carrots, celery, and thyme to the pot with the carcass and just barely cover with water (break the carcass up a bit if you need to so it's all submerged), and bring the liquid a boil. Reduce the heat so the liquid bubbles steadily and cook, stirring occasionally, until the liquid reduces by an inch or so and the stock is fragrant, about 1 hour. Strain, pressing on the solids to get as much liquid as possible, and return the stock to the pot, but leave off heat. Discard the solids.

5. Put the garlic in the skillet used to roast the chicken and cook over medium heat, stirring frequently, until the cloves brown in spots and begin to soften, 3 to 5 minutes. Add the garlic to the stock. Add the wine to the pan and return to the heat, cooking and scraping up any browned bits from the bottom of the pan until the pan is deglazed; pour the wine into the pot. Bring the stock mixture to a

boil, lower the heat so it bubbles steadily, and cook, stirring occasionally, until the stock reduces to about 1½ cups, 15 to 30 minutes, depending on how much you started with. (The sauce and chicken can be prepared ahead and refrigerated for up to 2 days.)

6. To make the crust, combine the flour and ½ teaspoon salt in a food processor and pulse once or twice. Add the butter and pulse until the butter and flour are blended and the mixture looks like cornmeal, about 10 seconds. With the machine running, add the ice water 1 tablespoon at a time, stopping as soon as the mixture holds together when pinched (you may not need all of it). Turn the dough onto a lightly floured work surface and form into a ball. Wrap in plastic and freeze for 10 minutes or refrigerate for at least 30 minutes. (You can refrigerate the dough for up to 3 days or freeze, tightly wrapped, for a few weeks.)

7. When you're ready to assemble the pie, heat the oven to 400°F. Grease a 2-quart baking dish with butter and put it on a rimmed baking sheet. Cut the chicken into bite-sized chunks and combine it with the garlic sauce, cream, and tarragon; taste and adjust the seasoning. Pour into the prepared baking dish.

8. Sprinkle your work surface with flour, turn out the dough, and sprinkle it with a little flour. If the dough is hard, let it rest for a few minutes. Roll, adding flour, rotating, and turning the dough as needed until the dough is about 2 inches larger than your baking dish. If the dough is sticky, add a little flour (if it remains sticky, and it's taking you more than a few minutes to roll it out, refrigerate or freeze again for 10 minutes).

9. Roll the dough onto the rolling pin, then carefully unroll so it falls over the baking dish. Trim all but ½ inch of the overhanging dough with a knife, then tuck it under itself around the edge. Crimp the dough firmly onto the rim of the baking dish. Beat the egg with 2 tablespoons water and brush onto the pastry. Use a sharp knife to cut 3- or 4-inch-long slits in the center of the crust. Bake until the top is golden and the filling is bubbling, 40 to 45 minutes. Break open the crust at the table and serve with a big spoon.

Pot Roast

My definition: a roast braised in a covered pot, with vegetables along for the ride. The biggest departure from tradition here is Pork Tenderloin Simmered in Peanut Sauce. Infamous for being bland and dry, this super-lean cut actually works perfectly in a quick, rich braise. The idea for Stuffed Cabbage Pot Roast is from the French dish known as *lou fassum*, where the filling is tucked between the leaves of a whole head and reassembled before poaching. And I'm counting Braised Pastrami as a pot roast—and an amazing accomplishment—with curing and smoking steps first, before the braising. Please take heed to the notes before the recipe. Nailing the details is part of brisket's charm.

● PORK TENDERLOIN
simmered in peanut sauce

makes: 4 servings
time: 30 minutes

2 tablespoons good-quality vegetable oil

One pork tenderloin (1 to 1¼ pounds)

Salt and pepper

2 tablespoons chopped fresh ginger

1 bunch scallions, white and green parts separated and sliced

½ cup peanut butter

1 teaspoon red chile flakes, or to taste

3 tablespoons Worcestershire sauce

2 tablespoons fresh lemon juice, or to taste

1. Put the oil in a large skillet over medium-high heat and cut the pork in 2 pieces to fit in the skillet if necessary. When the oil is hot, add the pork and sprinkle with salt and pepper. Cook, turning once, until browned on both sides, 8 to 10 minutes total. Transfer the meat to a plate.

2. Add the ginger and scallion whites, and cook until soft, stirring often, 2 to 3 minutes. Add the peanut butter and red chile flakes and mix, then add the Worcestershire sauce and 1 cup water. Stir to combine, scraping any browned bits off the bottom of the pot. If it's too thick, add water 1 tablespoon at a time; the sauce should just coat the back of a spoon.

3. Bring the sauce to a boil, turn the heat to very low so it just barely bubbles, nestle the pork in the sauce, and cover. Cook until an instant-read thermometer inserted into the thickest part reads 140°F, 10 to 15 minutes. Add the lemon juice, taste, and adjust the seasoning. Let the pork rest for 5 minutes, then slice crosswise into medallions. Serve hot, with the sauce spooned on top and garnished with scallion greens.

STUFFED CABBAGE POT ROAST

makes: 4 to 6 servings
time: 2 hours, largely unattended

1 head green or savoy cabbage (about 2 pounds),
   bottom trimmed and outer leaves discarded

Salt

3 tablespoons olive oil

1 large onion, chopped

2 carrots, chopped

1 celery stalk, chopped

2 tablespoons chopped garlic

Pepper

1 tablespoon celery seeds

One 28-ounce can crushed tomatoes

½ cup hazelnuts

1 cup steel-cut oats

1 cup fresh parsley, tough stems removed

2 tablespoons chopped fresh chives, for garnish

1. Put the cabbage stem end down in a large, deep pot; add a few large pinches of salt and enough water to cover it by 2 inches. Bring to a boil, then adjust the heat so it bubbles steadily. Cook, undisturbed, until a skewer meets only some resistance when inserted into the center and the outside leaves no longer feel "squeaky," 10 to 15 minutes. (If your pot isn't deep enough and the water doesn't cover the cabbage, let it sit off the heat, covered, until the exposed part is tender, 5 to 10 minutes more.) Carefully transfer the intact cabbage to a colander to drain, stem end up.

2. Clean the pot and add the oil; turn the heat to medium-high. When it's hot, add the onion, carrots, celery, and garlic and sprinkle with salt and pepper. Cook, stirring occasionally, until soft and starting to turn translucent, 3 to 5 minutes. Add the celery seeds and cook until fragrant, a minute or 2. Add the tomatoes and 1½ cups water and bring to a boil, then turn off the heat. (You can make the sauce to this point 1 or 2 days ahead of time, if you like, and refrigerate it. Let it come to room temperature before proceeding with the recipe.)

3. Put the hazelnuts in a medium skillet and toast over medium heat until golden and fragrant, 3 to 5 minutes. Transfer to a food processor.

4. Line a bowl large enough to hold the cabbage with 2 layers of cheesecloth, with the corners hanging over the edges. Put the cabbage in the bowl stem end up and cut around the core at an angle to remove it. Remove enough interior cabbage leaves to hollow out a pocket about 3 inches wide. Chop the trimmings roughly and add to the food processor with the nuts. Add the oats and parsley, and sprinkle with salt and pepper. Pulse until the oat mixture is coarsely chopped; taste, and adjust the seasoning.

5. Separate the cabbage leaves without breaking up the head and spoon the stuffing into the crevices. Gather the cheesecloth around the cabbage and tie the corners with string. Lower the cabbage into the tomato sauce, core end down. If necessary, add enough water to bring the liquid about halfway up the cabbage. Bring the sauce to a boil, then adjust the heat so the mixture bubbles gently. Cover and cook, checking once in a while to make sure the bottom isn't burning, until the cabbage is very tender (that skewer can now be easily inserted), 40 to 50 minutes. Cut into wedges and serve hot, garnished with chives.

● BRAISED PASTRAMI

makes: 6 to 8 servings
time: 8 days, largely unattended

PASTRAMI PERFECTION Curing salts are not interchangeable, nor is pink salt the same as Himalayan salt. It's also important you get the thicker, flat end of the brisket and not the tapered point. Test the meat often, as there is a window of tenderness in the cooking spectrum between tough and tough again.

3 tablespoons coriander seeds

3 tablespoons black peppercorns

4 to 10 small dried hot chiles (like Thai or pequin), to taste

3 tablespoons turbinado sugar

⅓ cup kosher salt

1½ teaspoons curing salt (also called pink salt or Prague Powder #1)

One 4- to 5-pound flat-end beef brisket

Wood chips (like hickory, apple, or cherry)

Sliced rye bread, coarse and smooth mustards, and pickles

1. Put the coriander seeds, peppercorns, and chiles in a medium skillet over medium heat. Cook, shaking the pan occasionally, until the spices are fragrant and toasted, 3 to 5 minutes. Transfer to a food processor and pulse a few times to start to break down. Add the sugar, salt, and curing salt, and process until everything is evenly ground.

2. Pat the brisket dry with paper towels and rub with the cure. Carefully transfer to a jumbo (2-gallon) freezer bag, adding any of the spice mixture that has fallen off. Seal the bag, pressing out as much air as possible. Refrigerate for 7 days, turning every 2 days.

3. After 7 days, bring the brisket to room temperature. Heat the oven to 250°F. Cover the bottom of a roasting pan with hickory chips and add just enough water to moisten them and prevent burning; do not submerge them. Put a rack over the chips and put the brisket on the rack, fatty side up. Cover the entire pan with foil, making a tent over the top so smoke can circulate around the meat and sealing it tightly so none can escape.

4. Put the pan in the oven and cook until an instant-read thermometer inserted into the thickest part of the pastrami reads 140°F, 1½ to 2½ hours.

5. Transfer the pastrami to a large pot and pour in enough boiling water to cover halfway, making sure you don't pour the water directly on the pastrami and wash away the crust. Bring the water back to a boil and adjust the heat so the water just barely bubbles. Cover and cook undisturbed for 90 minutes, then slice off a small piece from a corner and taste. If the meat is tender and slices easily, it's done. If not, sample every 15 minutes or so until the meat is tender but not yet falling apart, up to another 60 minutes.

6. Transfer the meat to a cutting board and let rest for at least 30 minutes. Slice against the grain and serve with rye bread, mustard, and pickles.

Pan Roast

Here's one of the most foolproof cooking methods: Brown the food in a pan, then stick it in the oven until everything is done on the inside too. Brown-Butter Salmon with Tomatoes and Capers literally takes minutes if you like the salmon a little underdone as I do; and if you don't, it only takes a couple minutes more. There's a big timesaver in the Vegan recipe too; just eat the crisp roasted skin in Smashed Acorn Squash with Cilantro Pesto. The divide-and-conquer approach in the not-so-traditional Porchetta Pan Roast is another cheater move—one that intensifies the impact of the Italian seasonings and maximizes the sear factor by forming four small "roasts."

● BROWN-BUTTER SALMON
with tomatoes and capers

makes: 4 servings
time: 15 minutes

4 tablespoons unsalted butter

Salt and pepper

4 thick salmon fillets or steaks (about 1½ pounds total), skin on

1 pint cherry or grape tomatoes, halved if you like

1 tablespoon drained capers

Lemon wedges

1. Heat the oven to 475°F. Put the butter and a sprinkle of salt and pepper in a large skillet over medium-high heat. When the foam subsides, add the salmon and sprinkle with salt and pepper.

2. Cook, undisturbed, until the salmon sizzles and the butter darkens, 2 to 3 minutes. Scatter the tomatoes and capers around the fish and transfer the pan to the oven.

3. Roast without turning until the salmon browns on top and the inside is as cooked as you like (you've got to peek between the flakes with a knife to check), 3 to 8 minutes. (If you'd rather they be opaque all the way through, then leave in the oven for up to 8 minutes. Just don't overcook them or they'll be dry.) Serve the salmon steaks with the tomato-caper sauce spooned on top, passing the lemon wedges at the table.

SMASHED ACORN SQUASH
with cilantro pesto

makes: 4 servings
time: 40 minutes

2 acorn squash (about 3 pounds total)

12 tablespoons olive oil, or more as needed

1 tablespoon coconut oil (or 1 additional tablespoon olive oil)

Salt and pepper

2 cups cooked black beans (see page 82; or one 15-ounce can), drained

1 cup corn kernels (thawed frozen is fine)

6 ounces tortilla chips, crumbled

¼ cup chopped chipotle chiles in adobo sauce, or to taste

2 cups loosely packed fresh cilantro sprigs, tough stems removed

¼ cup fresh lime juice, or as needed

2 scallions, cut into chunks

1 tablespoon chopped garlic

1. Heat the oven to 400°F. Halve the squash through the stem ends. Scoop out the seeds and fibers in the cavities, then halve again. Put the seeds in a small bowl and cover with water.

2. Heat 2 tablespoons olive oil and the coconut oil in a large skillet over medium-high heat; sprinkle the flesh side of the squash with salt and pepper. When the oil is hot, put the squash in the skillet skin side down and cook, undisturbed, until the squash sizzles and starts to smell fragrant, 5 to 10 minutes. Transfer the skillet to the oven and roast without turning until the squash is barely fork-tender and the skin is browned, 20 to 25 minutes.

3. While the squash is roasting, drain the seeds, remove any squash fibers, and dry thoroughly. Mix with 1 tablespoon olive oil and sprinkle with salt and pepper. Spread in an even layer on a baking sheet, and bake until golden and crunchy, 5 to 10 minutes, shaking the pan once or twice during cooking.

4. Mix the beans, corn, chips, 2 tablespoons olive oil, and chopped chipotle and adobo; sprinkle with salt and pepper, then taste and adjust the seasoning.

5. Put the cilantro in a food processor or blender with a large pinch of salt. Add the lime juice, scallions, garlic, toasted squash seeds, 4 tablespoons olive oil, and 4 tablespoons water. Puree, stopping to scrape down the sides of the container if necessary, and adding the remaining 4 tablespoons olive oil gradually. If the mixture is still too thick, add water 1 tablespoon at a time. Taste and adjust the seasoning, adding more lime juice if you like.

6. When the squash is ready, carefully remove the pan from the oven and flatten the pieces with a spatula or potato masher. Sprinkle with the tortilla mixture and return to the oven. Bake until the topping is browned in spots and the squash is tender, 5 to 10 minutes. Serve hot or warm, with cilantro pesto drizzled on top.

● PORCHETTA PAN ROAST

makes: 4 to 6 servings
time: at least 4 hours, largely unattended

2 tablespoons fennel seeds

2 tablespoons black peppercorns

¼ cup chopped fresh rosemary

¼ cup chopped garlic

2 tablespoons grated lemon zest

Salt

¼ cup olive oil

1 boneless pork shoulder roast, with skin
   (about 2 pounds)

Pepper

4 ounces skin-on pork belly, cut into 1-inch pieces

4 ounces pancetta, cut into 1-inch pieces

1 cup red wine

1. Put the fennel seeds in a small dry skillet over medium heat and cook until fragrant, 2 to 3 minutes. Transfer to a mortar or food processor. Add the peppercorns, rosemary, garlic, lemon zest, and a large pinch of salt. Grind or pulse until finely chopped, then, stirring or with the motor running, slowly drizzle in the oil.

2. Put the pork skin side down on a large cutting board and butterfly it: Using a long, sharp knife, cut the roast down the center with the grain to within 1 inch of the skin. Then, holding the knife parallel to the cutting board, cut through the meat horizontally from the center almost but not quite to the edge; repeat in the other direction, again cutting from the center out to the edge. Open the meat like a brochure; the roast should now be half as thick and twice as long.

3. Sprinkle with salt and pepper on both sides, then turn the meat cut side up, wide side facing you. Spread with the herb mixture. Roll tightly lengthwise to make a short, fat roll and secure with 4 pieces of string, evenly spaced. Refrigerate the roast, uncovered, for at least 2 hours or up to 24.

4. Heat the oven to 425°F. Cut the roast crosswise into 4 equal slices, then bring to room temperature, at least 30 minutes.

5. Put the belly and pancetta in a large skillet over medium-low heat and cook, stirring occasionally, until the pieces have browned in spots and some of the fat has rendered, 8 to 10 minutes. Remove with a slotted spoon and reserve. Turn the heat up to medium-high and put the porchetta slices in the skillet, cut side down. Cook, undisturbed, until the pork sizzles and smells amazing, 2 to 3 minutes. Carefully turn the slices and transfer the pan to the oven. Roast, without turning, until the pork is fork-tender and an instant-read thermometer inserted reads 150°F, 15 to 20 minutes. Carefully transfer the slices to a serving platter.

6. Pour off all but 3 tablespoons of the fat and put the pan over high heat. Add the wine and cook, stirring and scraping up any browned bits, until it's reduced by half, 5 to 10 minutes. Drizzle the wine sauce over the roast, scatter the crisp belly and pancetta on top, and serve hot or warm.

● Roast Chicken
for the Week,
page 416

Sunday Dinner

Many folks—busy ones especially—like to devote one day of the week to preparing and eating a hearty meal and then living off the leftovers. These three recipes are for those days. Or an actually relaxing Sunday. My idea of killing two birds with one stone is to throw a couple chickens in the same roasting pan and end up with Roast Chicken for the Week. Butternut Wellington is a vegetable showstopper based on the classic English crust-enclosed roast. And nothing has the power to gather people around the table like prime rib: fatty and crisp on the outside, tender and rare inside; marrow au jus and popovers ratchet up the experience to another level.

● ROAST CHICKEN FOR THE WEEK

makes: at least 8 servings
time: 1 hour, largely unattended

2 whole chickens (3 to 4 pounds each)

6 tablespoons olive oil

Salt and pepper

2 lemons

1 bunch fresh parsley, thyme, rosemary, or
   oregano

1. Heat the oven to 400°F, with a rack in the lower third. Put a large roasting pan on the rack. While the oven heats, trim the excess fat from the chickens, remove the neck and giblets, pat the chickens dry with a paper towel, rub the outsides with the oil, and sprinkle with salt and pepper. Cut the lemons in half. Put half the herbs in the cavity of one chicken and half in the other. Put 2 lemon halves in each chicken.

2. When the pan is scorching hot, 10 or 15 minutes longer, carefully put the chickens in the oven breast side up and not touching, if possible. Roast, undisturbed, until an instant-read thermometer inserted in the thickest part of the thigh reads at least 155°F or until the juices run clear when you cut into a thigh down to the bone, 40 to 60 minutes, depending on the size of the chickens. If one is ready before the other, remove it so it doesn't overcook. Carefully remove the pan from the oven.

3. One at a time, tip the birds to let the juices from the cavity flow into the pan, then transfer the chickens to a cutting board to rest for at least 5 minutes. Remove the lemon halves from the cavities. Add about ½ cup water to the roasting pan, scrape any browned bits off the bottom, and pour the juices into a small saucepan. Squeeze in the juice from one lemon half. Let the pan juices sit for a few minutes; use a spoon to skim off some of the fat that rises to the top, then bring the mixture to a boil and cook until slightly thickened and reduced, about 5 minutes. Taste and adjust the seasoning, adding more lemon if you like.

4. Carve one bird and serve it with the warm pan juices. Let the other bird cool completely before covering tightly and transferring to the fridge along with any leftover sauce. Use the meat for meals throughout the week, and save the carcasses in the freezer for up to 3 months to make chicken stock (see page 43).

BUTTERNUT WELLINGTON

makes: 6 to 8 servings
time: about 2 hours

1 ounce dried porcini or shiitake mushrooms

1 butternut squash (about 1½ pounds), cut into
    1-inch cubes (about 5 cups)

7 tablespoons olive oil, plus more for brushing

2 teaspoons paprika

1 teaspoon ground allspice

Salt and pepper

1 cup chopped walnuts

2 pounds cremini mushrooms, sliced

2 fresh thyme sprigs

¼ cup dry red wine

10 sheets phyllo dough, thawed and kept covered

1 pound shallots, peeled and sliced

3 tablespoons cider vinegar

1. Heat the oven to 350°F. Put the dried mush-rooms in a medium bowl and cover with 2 cups boiling water. Put the squash cubes in a large bowl with 2 tablespoons oil, the paprika, and allspice, and sprinkle with salt and pepper; toss to combine. Spread the squash on a baking sheet and bake until it releases easily from the pan, is browned in spots, and is just starting to get tender, 15 to 20 minutes.

2. Put the walnuts in a large dry skillet over medium heat and toast, shaking the pan occasionally, until browned and fragrant, 3 to 5 minutes. Mix the wal-nuts and roasted squash in a large bowl.

3. Put 3 tablespoons oil in the skillet over medium-high heat. When it's hot, add the fresh mushrooms and 1 thyme sprig and sprinkle with salt and pepper. Lift the porcini from their soaking liquid (save it for another use) and add them to the pan. Cook, stir-ring occasionally, until the mushrooms are browned and the pan is dry, 10 to 15 minutes. Add the wine and cook, scraping any browned bits off the bottom of the pan, until the wine has cooked off. Remove from the heat.

4. Add 1 cup cooked mushrooms to the squash and put the rest in a food processor. Carefully (there will be steam) process until finely chopped. Put the mixture back in the skillet over medium heat and cook, stirring frequently, until it's completely dry, 5 to 10 minutes.

5. Smear 1 tablespoon oil on a rimmed baking sheet. Lay 1 sheet of phyllo dough on the baking sheet, brush with oil, and sprinkle with salt and pepper. Repeat with 4 more sheets. Make an identical stack of 5 phyllo sheets on a cutting board with the longer edge closest to you.

6. Spread the chopped mushroom mixture in the center of the phyllo stack on the baking sheet, leaving a 2-inch border all around. Spoon the squash mixture on top of the mushrooms. Fold the phyllo up around the filling, then carefully drape the second stack of sheets on top, tucking the excess under the roast. Brush the entire package with oil. Bake until the squash is soft and the phyllo is golden brown, 20 to 25 minutes. Clean the skillet.

7. Put the shallots in the skillet over medium heat. Cover and cook, stirring every 5 minutes or so, until the shallots are dry and beginning to stick to the pan, 10 to 15 minutes. Add the remaining tablespoon oil, the remaining sprig of thyme, and a large pinch of salt, and turn the heat down to medium-low.

8. Cook uncovered, adjusting the heat as necessary to prevent burning, and stirring occasionally, until the shallots are soft, tender, and as dark and soft as you want them, another 5 to 20 minutes. Pour in the vinegar and sprinkle with salt and pepper. Cook, scraping any browned bits from the bottom of the pan, until the vinegar has mostly bubbled away, 2 to 3 minutes. Discard the thyme; taste and adjust the seasoning. Slice and serve hot, passing the shallot relish at the table.

● PRIME RIB
with popovers and marrow au jus

makes: 4 to 6 servings
time: about 4 hours, largely unattended

One 2- or 3-rib bone-in prime rib roast
    (about 5 pounds)
5 tablespoons unsalted butter, melted
Salt and pepper
6 marrow bones, each about 3 inches long
2 eggs
1 cup milk
1 teaspoon sugar
1 cup flour
1 tablespoon chopped fresh thyme
1 cup Cabernet Sauvignon
2 fresh rosemary sprigs

1. Take the roast out of the refrigerator an hour before you plan on cooking to bring it to room temperature. Evenly drizzle 4 tablespoons melted butter into the cups of a 12-cup muffin or popover pan.

2. Heat the oven to 200°F. Put a rack inside a large roasting pan and put the meat on the rack, fat cap up. Sprinkle with salt and pepper and rub the seasonings into the meat. (If you don't rub it in, your sauce might be too salty.) Put the marrow bones in the roasting pan around the meat.

3. Roast the prime rib until an instant-read thermometer registers about 110°F for rare or 115°F for medium-rare, 1½ to 2 hours. (You can cook it longer if you like your meat well done, but don't let it go above 140°F. To get the most accurate idea of how the roast is cooking, test the temperature in a couple different places, taking care not to hit the bone.) Remove the roast from the oven and let it sit. Scoop the marrow from the bones into a bowl and mash with a fork.

4. Raise the heat to 425°F, and adjust the oven racks so that there's room for both the roasting pan and the popover pan. Put the prepared popover pan in the oven to heat.

5. Make the popovers: Put the eggs, milk, the remaining 1 tablespoon melted butter, the sugar, and 1 teaspoon salt in a large bowl. Beat in the flour a little bit at a time and add the thyme; keep beating until the mixture is lump-free.

6. Carefully remove the muffin tin or popover pan from the oven and fill each cup halfway with the batter. Return both the popovers and the roasting pan with the meat into the oven. Cook until the ribs develop a crust and the meat is rare to medium (a thermometer should read between 120° and 130°F, 15 to 20 minutes; add another 5 to 10 minutes and take it out between 140° and 150°F for medium-well to well done), then remove the meat and reduce the heat to 350°F. Continue baking the popovers until they are puffed and browned, watching to make sure the sides don't burn, another 10 to 15 minutes. Cool on a rack until ready to serve.

7. Transfer the roast to a platter, bone side down, and remove the rack from the pan. Skim off all but 2 or 3 tablespoons of the fat and put the roasting pan on 2 burners over medium-high heat. Add the wine, 1 cup water, the marrow bones, reserved marrow, and rosemary and bring to a boil, stirring constantly to incorporate the marrow; taste and adjust the seasoning. Thickly slice the meat, carving it off the bones if you prefer or including them with some of the pieces, and serve, spooning a little of the sauce on top and passing the rest with the warm popovers at the table.

Thanksgiving

The biggest meal of the year doesn't have to include turkey, nor does it need to be a days-long, laborious project. But if that's what you want, the whole shebang is covered here too. Butter makes everything taste like Thanksgiving—even a simple turkey leg with cracker-meal and vegetable dressing. Many vegetarians and vegans associate Thanksgiving with an abundance of carbs, lots of brown foods, and Tofurky; you'll do a lot better than that with Autumn Galette with Brussels Sprouts and Chestnut Cream. If you expect nothing less from a traditional Thanksgiving turkey feast than bird, stuffing, and gravy, I've trimmed Dry-Brined Turkey with Oyster-Cornbread Stuffing and Gravy down to ten well-timed steps, spread out over the course of four days.

● ROAST TURKEY LEGS
with cracker stuffing and lemon-sage butter

makes: 4 to 6 servings
time: 45 minutes

½ cup pecans

2 sleeves saltine crackers (about 60 crackers)

2 turkey drumsticks (about 1½ pounds each)

Salt and pepper

8 tablespoons (1 stick) unsalted butter

1 onion, chopped

2 carrots, chopped

2 celery stalks, chopped

½ cup milk

10 to 12 fresh sage leaves

1 lemon, halved

1. Heat the oven to 400°F. Pulse the pecans in a food processor until the pieces are about ¼ inch, then transfer to a bowl. Repeat with the saltines and add to the bowl. Sprinkle the drumsticks with salt and pepper.

2. Heat 4 tablespoons unsalted butter in a large ovenproof skillet over medium heat. When it foams, add the onion, carrots, and celery, and sprinkle with pepper. Cook, stirring occasionally, until the vegetables soften and the onion is translucent, 5 to 8 minutes. Add the cracker-nut mixture and ¼ cup of the milk and stir to coat; taste and adjust the seasoning, adding more pepper if you'd like, though you probably won't need any salt.

3. Put the drumsticks on top of the dressing, facing opposite directions. Put the skillet in the oven and roast for 20 minutes. Carefully lift each turkey leg, stir the dressing underneath, and turn the drumstick. Add the remaining ¼ cup milk if the dressing looks dry. Continue roasting until the drumsticks read 165°F on an instant-read thermometer, another 10 to 20 minutes, depending on the size. (If the drumsticks vary greatly in size, you may need to remove one from the oven before the other.)

4. Put the remaining 4 tablespoons butter and the sage in a small skillet over medium heat. Squeeze in the lemon juice and cook, stirring, until fragrant and bubbling and the sage has darkened; taste, adjust the seasoning, and keep warm. Slice the turkey and serve with the stuffing and drizzled with the sauce.

Dry-Brined Turkey,
with Oyster-Cornbread
Stuffing and Gravy,
page 422

● AUTUMN GALETTE
with brussels sprouts and chestnut cream

makes: 4 to 6 servings
time: about 3 hours, largely unattended

1 cup plus 3 tablespoons all-purpose flour,
    plus more for rolling

½ cup chestnut or whole wheat flour

¾ teaspoon salt, or more as needed

10 tablespoons olive oil

⅓ cup ice water

8 ounces fresh chestnuts

Pepper

12 ounces Brussels sprouts

2 shallots, sliced

1 apple, cored and chopped

½ cup dry white wine

2 tablespoons chopped fresh sage

1. Combine the flours and ¾ teaspoon salt in a food processor and pulse once or twice. Add 6 table-spoons of the oil and turn on the machine; process until the oil and flour are blended and the mixture looks like cornmeal, about 10 seconds. With the machine running, slowly add the ice water, stopping as soon as the mixture stays together when pinched (you may not need all of it).

2. Turn the dough out onto a lightly floured work surface and form into a ball. Wrap in plastic and refrigerate for at least 30 minutes. (You can refrig-erate the dough for up to a couple of days or freeze, tightly wrapped, for up to a couple of weeks.)

3. Make a shallow cut on the flat side of each chest-nut and put them in a large pot with enough water to cover. Add a pinch of salt and bring to a boil. Cook, stirring once or twice, until the shells soften, about 10 minutes, then turn off the heat. When they're cool enough to handle, remove a few chest-nuts at a time and peel off the outer and inner

skins. Transfer the meat to a food processor, sprinkle with salt and pepper, and puree, adding water 1 tablespoon at a time, until it is the consistency of cream cheese; taste and adjust the seasoning. Transfer to a bowl and refrigerate. Rinse out the food processor and use the slicing blade to shred the Brussels sprouts.

4. Put 3 tablespoons oil in a large skillet over medium heat. When it's hot, add the shallots and cook until golden and soft, 15 to 20 minutes. Add the sprouts, the apple, and wine and sprinkle with salt and pepper; cook, stirring occasionally, until the wine has cooked off and the mixture is quite soft, 15 to 25 minutes. Stir in the chestnut puree and the sage, taste, and adjust the seasoning.

5. Heat the oven to 350°F. Line a large baking sheet with parchment paper. Sprinkle a clean countertop with flour, unwrap the dough, and sprinkle the top with flour. If the dough is hard, let it rest for a few minutes. Use a rolling pin to roll with light pressure from the center out to ¼-inch thickness, rotating the dough slightly after each roll and adding flour only if the dough is sticking. Loosely roll the dough onto the rolling pin and transfer it to the prepared baking sheet.

6. Spread the vegetable mixture on the dough, leaving a 3-inch border all around. Lightly smooth the filling so it is the same thickness all over. Fold the sides up around the filling (you should have a big open circle at the top). Refrigerate the galette for 30 minutes.

7. Brush the top of the dough with the remaining tablespoon oil. Bake the galette until the crust is browned and the filling is steaming hot, 40 to 50 minutes. Cool a bit before slicing and serve hot or at room temperature.

● DRY-BRINED TURKEY
with oyster-cornbread stuffing and gravy

makes: At least 12 servings
time: 4 days, largely unattended

1 turkey (13 to 15 pounds), thawed if frozen

3 tablespoons salt, or more as needed

2 tablespoons smoked paprika

2 tablespoons grated orange zest

1 tablespoon pepper, or more as needed

1 cup plus 4 tablespoons (2½ sticks) unsalted butter, plus more for greasing

4 eggs

1 recipe Skillet Cornbread (opposite)

1 pound sweet Italian sausage, casings removed

2 large leeks, trimmed, well rinsed, and chopped

4 carrots, chopped

8 to 10 tender celery stalks from the heart, plus their leaves

1 dozen fresh oysters, shucked, with their liquid reserved

8½ cups chicken stock (see page 43), or more as needed

¼ cup chopped fresh chives

½ cup chopped fresh parsley

1 cup flour

2 tablespoons chopped fresh thyme

1 cup dry white wine

1. Four days before you want to serve the turkey, remove the neck and giblets from the cavity and cut off the wing tips; refrigerate these parts for the gravy. Rinse the carcass well inside and out, and pat it dry. Mix 3 tablespoons salt with the paprika and orange zest and 1 tablespoon ground pepper. Sprinkle the inside and outside of the turkey with the seasoning mixture as evenly as you can; rub it into the skin, exposed flesh, and the cavity. Put the turkey in an extra-large sealable bag, press out the air between the skin and plastic, and seal. (Or wrap it tightly in several layers of plastic.) Refrigerate on a rimmed baking sheet, breast side up, for 2 days.

2. After 2 days in the refrigerator, turn the turkey breast side down and return it to the refrigerator for 1 day. (Make the cornbread on Day 3 too. Let cool completely, then wrap it in foil or wax paper and refrigerate it until you're ready to make the stuffing. And if you haven't already, now's a good time to make the stock too.)

3. On the evening before you will serve the turkey, remove the bird from the bag. You will not see any salt, and the skin should be glistening but not dripping. If it is dripping, blot it dry with paper towels. Put the turkey breast side up on a rimmed baking sheet fitted with a rack and refrigerate, uncovered, for at least 8 hours or up to overnight.

4. On the day you plan to cook, remove the turkey from the refrigerator and let it sit at room temperature for at least 1 hour or up to 2. Heat the oven to 500°F and position the racks so you have room for both the turkey and stuffing. Put the turkey on a rack set in a large roasting pan with the breast facing up. Pour 1 cup water into the bottom of the pan and add the turkey giblets, neck, and the wing tips. Put the turkey in the oven, legs facing toward the back.

5. Roast until the top of the turkey begins to brown, 20 to 30 minutes, then lower the oven heat to 325°F. Continue to roast, brushing the bird with the pan juices every 30 minutes or so. If the pan gets dry, add more water ½ cup at a time so that there's always a little liquid in the bottom of the pan. The turkey is done when an instant-read thermometer inserted into the thickest part of a thigh measures 155–165°F. Figure at least 2½ hours and up to 5 hours, depending on the size of the bird.

6. While the turkey roasts, make the stuffing: Grease a 9 by 13-inch baking dish or pan with some butter. Beat the eggs in a large bowl and crumble in the cornbread, but don't stir yet. Crumble the sausage into a large skillet over medium heat. Cook until the meat is cooked through and crisped, 5 to 10 minutes. Transfer to the bowl with the cornbread along with any fat. Put 4 tablespoons butter in the skillet over medium heat. When it foams, add the leeks, carrots, celery, and celery leaves and sprinkle with salt and pepper. Cook, stirring occasionally, until the vegetables soften, 10 to 15 minutes. Add the vegetables to the bowl with the cornbread. Add the oysters and their juice, ½ cup stock, the chives, and parsley. Stir with a large spoon and fork to combine and break up the oysters a little.

7. Transfer the stuffing to the prepared baking dish. When the turkey registers about 140°F on an instant-read thermometer, put the stuffing in the oven and bake until the top is golden and crisp and the stuffing is hot throughout, 45 to 60 minutes. If the stuffing is browning too fast, or looks like it's drying out, drizzle with ½ cup stock and cover with foil. When the stuffing is ready, cover the baking dish with foil and lower the oven to 200°F. Keep warm for up to 2 hours.

8. Make the gravy: Bring the remaining 8 cups stock to a boil and keep warm. Put the remaining 1 cup (2 sticks) butter in a large pot over medium-low heat. When it melts, add the flour, sprinkle with salt and pepper, and whisk until smooth. Cook, stirring frequently and adjusting the heat as necessary so the roux sizzles but doesn't burn, until it's the color of caramel, 45 to 60 minutes. Slowly whisk in the hot stock and add the thyme, bring to a boil and cook, whisking often, until thick and velvety, about 20 minutes. Keep warm.

9. When the turkey is done, transfer the bird to a platter to rest for at least 20 minutes or up to an hour. Put the roasting pan over 2 burners on medium-high heat and add the wine. Cook, stirring to scrape up any browned bits and deglaze the pan until bubbling. Remove and discard the giblets, wing tips, and neck. Carefully pour the pan juices into the gravy and reheat as needed.

10. To carve the bird, start by cutting off the drumsticks, thighs, and wings; cut slices from the bones and put them on a platter. Remove the breast from the carcass by cutting down and outward away from the center bone; transfer the breast to a cutting board in one piece, slice crosswise as thick as you like, and transfer to the platter. Serve the turkey with the hot stuffing and gravy.

SKILLET CORNBREAD

Heat the oven to 375°F. Combine 1½ cups cornmeal, ½ cup flour, 1 teaspoon baking soda, and 1 teaspoon salt in a large bowl. Make a well in the center and add 1 egg and 1¼ cups yogurt. Whisk with a fork and gradually incorporate the dry ingredients without overmixing; there should still be lumps. Put 4 tablespoons unsalted butter in a 10-inch skillet over medium heat. When it melts, carefully pour most of the butter into the bowl, leaving behind enough to generously coat the skillet; swirl it or use a brush to distribute it evenly. Fold the butter into the batter; if it's dry and doesn't come together easily, add more yogurt, 1 tablespoon at a time, until it does. Carefully spread the batter into the prepared pan. Cook the cornbread over medium-high heat until it steams around the edges, 2 to 3 minutes, then transfer to the oven and bake until the sides have pulled away from the pan, the top is lightly browned, and a toothpick inserted into the center comes out clean, 20 to 25 minutes. Cut into wedges and serve hot or warm. Makes 6 to 8 servings in 35 minutes.

Acknowledgments

The combination of Easy, Vegan, and All Out recipes made this project a little like developing, writing, and photographing three cookbooks. I'm grateful for the help of many creative and diligent individuals who kept their heads on straight even while they worked their tails off.

On my team, as usual, Kerri Conan was indispensable. Emily Stephenson, who joined us here, approached producing this book with a keen, fresh eye for detail. Kate Bittman and Daniel Meyer contributed mightily to the idea machine. Grace Rosanova spent a year testing recipes, and did an awesome job (as you'll see).

We were with an incredible photo crew in Berkeley for the better part of a month to create these gorgeous images. I wanted Aya Brackett for this project from the start, and was happy to get her. Thanks to food stylist Lillian Kang, props to prop stylist Claire Mack and her husband, Dave Gantz, and gratitude for help from Julia Middleton, Naomi Gassel, Mike Byrne, Hannah Hughes, and Soraya Matos. Carrie Kartman, Matt Dorst, Julia, and Aya get awards for hospitality.

The evolution of this project began with Pam Krauss; we appreciate your vision, wit, and love. So many people at Clarkson Potter were generous and supportive: Aaron Wehner, Doris Cooper, Jenn Sit, Nina Caldas, Mark McCauslin, Derek Gullino, Alexandria Martinez, Kate Tyler, Natasha Martin, Carly Gorga, and the art and design team of Stephanie Huntwork, Ian Dingman, and Jan Derevjanik worked wonders.

Personally: Angela, none of this would have happened without you. And to my brilliant daughters, Kate and Emma, my new and fabulous sons, Nick and Jeffrey, my new playmate Holden, and my astonishing partner, Kathleen . . . all the love in the world and all the dinners I can possibly cook.

Index